W9-BEY-297

Applying Counseling Theories

An Online Case-Based Approach

Aaron B. Rochlen
University of Texas at Austin

PEARSON

Merrill
Prentice Hall

Upper Saddle River, New Jersey
Columbus, Ohio

Library of Congress Cataloging-in-Publication Data

Applying counseling theories / [compiled by] Aaron B. Rochlen.
    p. cm.
Includes bibliographical references and index.
ISBN 0-13-170082-0
  1. Psychoanalysis—Case studies—Computer-assisted instruction. I. Rochlen, Aaron B.

RC509.7.A67 2007
616.89'17—dc22

2006041552

Vice President and Executive Publisher: Jeffery W. Johnston
Publisher: Kevin M. Davis
Editorial Assistant: Sarah N. Kenoyer
Production Editor: Mary Harlan
Production Coordinator: Lisa Garboski, bookworks
Design Coordinator: Diane C. Lorenzo
Text Design: RoseDesigns
Cover Design: Diane Lorenzo/Candace Rowley
Cover Image: SuperStock
Production Manager: Laura Messerly
Director of Marketing: David Gesell
Marketing Manager: Autumn Purdy
Marketing Coordinator: Brian Mounts

This book was set in Berkeley Book by Techbooks/GTS Companies/York, PA. It was printed and bound by R. R. Donnelley & Sons Company. The cover was printed by R. R. Donnelley & Sons Company.

Copyright © 2007 by Pearson Education, Inc., Upper Saddle River, New Jersey 07458.
Pearson Prentice Hall. All rights reserved. Printed in the United States of America. This publication is protected by Copyright and permission should be obtained from the publisher prior to any prohibited reproduction, storage in a retrieval system, or transmission in any form or by any means, electronic, mechanical, photocopying, recording, or likewise. For information regarding permission(s), write to: Rights and Permissions Department.

Pearson Prentice Hall™ is a trademark of Pearson Education, Inc.
Pearson® is a registered trademark of Pearson plc
Prentice Hall® is a registered trademark of Pearson Education, Inc.
Merrill® is a registered trademark of Pearson Education, Inc.

Pearson Education Ltd.
Pearson Education Singapore Pte. Ltd.
Pearson Education Canada, Ltd.
Pearson Education–Japan

Pearson Education Australia Pty. Limited
Pearson Education North Asia Ltd.
Pearson Educación de Mexico, S.A. de C.V.
Pearson Education Malaysia Pte. Ltd.

10 9 8 7 6 5 4 3 2 1
ISBN   0-13-170082-0

CLOSER TO THEORIES

True Innovation

This product offers the power of the Web and the promise of a true understanding of counseling theories. Unique in product design and intellectual approach, it combines a book, interactive cases, and Web-based learning into one innovative product. Flexible enough to support any core theories text, it is also simple enough for all course delivery modes. Using this multisensory approach, readers learn what therapists do, why they do it, and how basic theories can be applied in clinical settings.

●●● applying counseling
THEORIES

closer to theories. **closer to clients.** closer to practice.

To begin, select a theory to apply:

Psychoanalytic	Behavioral
Analytical/Jungian	Cognitive
Adlerian	REBT
Self-Psychology	Reality
Time-Limited Dynamic	Family Systems
Client-Centered	Feminist
Existential	Constructivist
Gestalt	Solution Focused

message from developer
(download quicktime)

home | about project | merrill/prentice hall theory texts

Chapter 2

Analytical (Jungian) Psychology

Jeffrey Raff

Chapter Outline
Bridging the Theory-to-Practice Gap
Principles in Practice
Keys to Conceptualization
Interventions and Therapeutic Process
Using the Relationship
Adapting the Approach
Finding Your Niche
Process and Case Suggestions
Summary and Suggested Readings

21

Theory in Practice

A central goal of this product is to help readers grasp the fundamental principles that govern the application of 16 counseling theories. From Freud to feminism, the authors distill each theory into core principles to apply each theory. Each chapter translates the formal concepts, assumptions, and techniques of the theory into user-friendly guidelines for working with clients. Reading the book, one learns the essence of applying each theory and can delve into the original theorist's work, comprehensive theory books, or eclectic counseling approaches with clarity and understanding.

Practicing Perspective

Each chapter offers a practitioner's point of view and is written by an educator or therapist counseling from that perspective. Using a consistent structure, topics include:

- Bridging the Theory-to-Practice Gap
- Principles in Practice
- Keys to Conceptualization
- Interventions and Therapeutic Process
- Short- and Long-Term Goals
- Using the Relationship
- Adapting the Approach
- Finding Your Niche
- Process and Case Suggestions
- Summary and Suggested Readings

CLOSER TO CLIENTS

Diverse Cases

Three compelling cases capture the lives of Elena, Jane, and Theo and their unique presenting problems and concerns. Ranging in age from 17 to 54, these individuals are from diverse ethnic backgrounds, have been referred to counseling from various sources, and present with a range of issues. Using the innovative Website, readers learn firsthand about these individuals' lives, thoughts, and emotions and about how to approach counseling these clients using the framework of specific counseling theories.

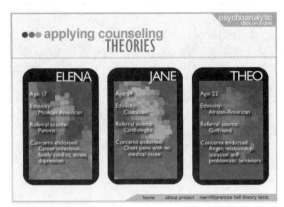

Clinical Interviews

As a central piece of this powerful product, Web-based videos capture central aspects of the client and therapist intake interview. More than a demonstration, these segments provide the raw data needed to analyze cases and apply counseling theories to clinical practice. Each video is 12 minutes long and covers presenting concerns, family background, interpersonal history, and coping strategies. Watching these videos brings one closer to the client and to the counseling process.

Written Intakes

Supporting the clinical video, written intake material appears on the Website and provide additional information about each client. These intakes help readers conceptualize the case and include the following sections:

- Reason for Referral
- Behavioral Observations
- Presenting Concerns
- Family Background
- Relational and Interpersonal History
- Coping Strategies
- Career Progress

CLOSER TO PRACTICE

Case Analysis

Adding an integrative, realistic dimension to the experience, case analysis sections offer an opportunity to engage in practice-based learning.

Six conceptualization questions ask users to recall what they have learned about a specific theory and how the theory's core concepts apply to a client's case. Users can examine each case from any of the 16 different theories. As users attempt to conceptualize cases from a particular theoretical perspective, they begin to understand what it means to practice from that particular perspective. Engaging in this process, they explore the differences in basic theoretical approaches, the therapeutic relationship, short- and long-term client goals, multicultural considerations, and specific limitations of each theory.

Ideal for practice and participation, this flexible design enables readers to examine each case from multiple theoretical perspectives and email their analysis directly to the instructor or fellow students.

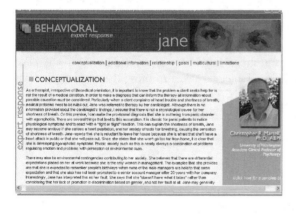

Expert Response

To support this practice-based exercise, each case analysis is accompanied by an expert response. Available after users have completed and submitted their own analysis, these sections contain the written comments from an expert who has analyzed the same case, using the same theory. Offering perspective and insight only years of practice can bring, these sections give readers a true understanding of a theory's clinical application and moves them closer to establishing their own counseling practice.

www.prenhall.com/rochlen

The Power of the Web. The Promise of True Understanding.

ACKNOWLEDGMENTS

I'll take some credit for the basic idea. Other than that, this entire project was a complete team effort. First, I have to thank the exceptionally skilled authors and therapists who contributed the chapters and expert responses. By participating in this project, each accepted the challenge of producing something truly different, a practical and clear description of how their selected approaches are actually conducted. Everyone came through in a big way, and I thank them for their effort and enthusiasm. Second, I appreciate and am indebted to the many technical people who lent their expertise to this project. Most notably, I thank Alicia Cho, who is responsible for the design and interface of the website. Alicia not only is incredibly skilled but also was patient and kind with the many requests for revisions over a two-year period (even when she was in Europe). I also thank Mike Bell for his exceptional video and editing skills and Ken Tothero for his technical support and expertise through several phases of the project. I thank the entire staff of the Learning Technology Center at the University of Texas, who supported this project from the beginning in providing financial, technical, and occasionally emotional support.

In consideration of the many hours spent in developing the characters/clients and serving as therapists, I express my appreciation to Kalina Brabeck, Scott Hosford, K. P. Prince, and Kristie Kirkpatrick (who also served as an actress in her own case). Richard Harris and Audrey Ynigez also deserve credit for playing the skilled roles of Theo and Elena in the video vignettes.

I would also like to thank several key players from Merrill/Prentice Hall whose support and expertise with the many stages of this project proved critical to my own mental health and ensured a quality final project. In particular, I thank Publisher Kevin Davis, who since walking into my office one day to "see what I was up to" until the end believed in the power and promise of this idea. I also appreciate Karen Balkin's many hours of editorial development and the work of Mary Harlan, who coordinated the production process. I also thank the many reviewers of the chapters who provided critical feedback to the project: Tim Davidson, University of Oklahoma; John Laux, University of Toledo; Linda L. Leech, University of South Carolina; Steven I. Pfeiffer, Florida State University; and Julia Y. Porter, Mississippi State University.

Finally, I would like to thank the many supervisors, professors, and advisors who have enabled me to truly appreciate the skill and talent it takes to bring theory into my own work with clients.

Aaron B. Rochlen, Ph.D.

Aaron B. Rochlen, Ph.D., is an Associate Professor in Counseling Psychology at the University of Texas at Austin. He teaches counseling theories courses at the undergraduate and doctoral level. Dr. Rochlen developed these materials based on observing that students wanted to better understand theories learned in the classroom and apply them in different contexts and situations. In addition, Dr. Rochlen sought to develop a set of learning materials that could utilize advancements in technology (e.g., websites and digital video) to better simulate counseling cases. Dr. Rochlen is also a licensed psychologist in Austin, Texas.

Ricardo Ainslie, Ph.D., ABBP, is a professor in the Department of Educational Psychology at the University of Texas at Austin and a Fellow in the Charles H. Spence Centennial Professorship in Education. He is also Adjunct Faculty at the Houston–Galveston Psychoanalytic Institute, a member of the San Antonio–Austin Psychoanalytic Society, and founding member and past president of the Austin Society for Psychoanalytic Psychology. He is a member of the editorial board for the journals *Psychoanalytic Psychology* and *Psychoanalysis, Culture, and Society* and also serves as an ad hoc reviewer for a variety of journals including *International Journal of Psychoanalysis,* and *Cultural Anthropology.* In books, articles, and films his work ranges from clinical topics to the application of psychoanalytic ideas to sociocultural issues. He has presented his work widely, including the annual meetings of the American Psychological Association's Division of Psychoanalysis, the American Psychoanalytic Association, and at numerous psychoanalytic institutes and societies. In 1998 he was selected to be one of the keynote speakers at the 20th Annual Margaret Mahler Symposium sponsored by the Philadelphia Psychoanalytic Institute, for his work on the psychology of twins. In 2002 he received the Texas Psychological Association's "Outstanding Contribution to Science Award." And in 2004 he was one of the recipients of the American Psychoanalytic Association's "Outstanding contribution to psychoanalytic education" award.

Judith R. Brown, Ph.D., is a psychotherapist in private practice, trainer of therapists, lecturer, and writer. She received her Ph.D. from the University of California in 1977 and has been licensed in Marriage and Family Therapy since 1976. She was a student of Fritz Perls in 1967 when he invited her to be a cotherapist with him in a 4-week Gestalt Therapy Workshop at Esalen Institute. In 1970 she began teaching the Gestalt approach in Europe, the United States, and Canada with her husband, George I. Brown. She is the author of books on couples' relationships and family dynamics as well as a number of articles. Her most recent articles are "Researcher and Instrument: An Exploration of the Relationship Between Gestalt and Qualitative Methodology," *Gestalt Review.* Vol. 1, No.1, 1997, "Relationship and Subjectivity in Supervision," in *Practical Applications in Supervision, Manual of California Association of Marriage and Family Therapists,* 1998, and "Working with Couples in the Current Environment," *Journal of Couples Therapy,* Vol. 8, 1999. Her most recent book is *The I in Science: Training to Utilize Subjectivity in Research,* published in 1996 by The Scandinavian University Press. A second edition of her first book, *Back to the Beanstalk: Enchantment and Reality for Couples,* was published by the Gestalt Institute of Cleveland Press in 1998.

Lucia A. Gilbert, Ph.D., is Vice Provost for Undergraduate Studies, Professor of Educational Psychology, and Frank C. Erwin, Jr. Centennial Honors Professor at the University of Texas at Austin. She studies two-earner families, women's career development, and gender processes in adolescence. She is the author of four books and numerous articles, including chapters on feminist therapy, and is the recipient of awards for teaching and research excellence.

Alan Kindler, MBBS, FRCP, is Director of the Institute for the Advancement of Self Psychology in Toronto and a founding member of the International Council for Psychoanalytic Self Psychology. He is an Assistant Professor of Psychiatry at the University of Toronto and a staff psychiatrist at St. Michael's Hospital. He is a Training and Supervising analyst with the Toronto Institute of Psychoanalysis and past president of the Toronto Psychoanalytic Society. He is on the faculties of the Toronto Institute of Contemporary Psychoanalysis, the Toronto Child Psychotherapy Program, and the Advanced Training Program in Psychoanalytic Psychotherapy in Toronto. He is also on the faculties of the Institute of Psychoanalytic Studies in Subjectivity in New York and the Institute of Contemporary Psychoanalysis in Washington, D.C. He is in private psychoanalytic practice in Toronto with a special interest in contemporary Self Psychology and supervision by telephone or video cam.

Hanna Levenson, Ph.D., has been specializing in the area of brief psychotherapy as a clinician, teacher, and researcher for over 25 years. She is Professor of Psychology at the Wright Institute, Berkeley, and Director of the Brief Psychotherapy Program at California Medical Center, San Francisco. Dr. Levenson is the author of over 75 papers and two books, the *Concise Guide to Brief Dynamic and Interpersonal Psychotherapy* and *Time-Limited Dynamic Psychotherapy (TLDP): A Guide to Clinical Practice.* Her professional videotape illustrating TLDP formulation and technique has recently been released. Dr. Levenson founded the Levenson Institute for Training, a center where mental health practitioners can receive in-depth training and certification in integrative, focused therapy. She also maintains a private practice in San Francisco and Oakland.

Rebecca J. Macy, Ph.D., ACSW, LCSW, is a licensed clinical social worker and an associate professor at the School of Social Work at the University of North Carolina at Chapel Hill. She joined the UNC faculty in 2002, after receiving her doctoral degree in social welfare from the University of Washington in Seattle. In 1993, she received her MSW from Tulane University in New Orleans, Louisiana, where she trained in clinical social work and focused on cognitive and narrative therapies. Following the completion of her MSW and before her doctoral studies, she worked in outpatient community mental health for four years in Indianapolis, Indiana. Her social work practice experience led her to be interested in the impact that violent victimization has on mental health. During her doctoral studies, she was a National Institute of Mental Health-funded Prevention Research Trainee. Her dissertation focused on sexual assault prevention and used cognitive theory to investigate the phenomenon of sexual revictimization. Her research applies social psychological and social cognitive theories toward better understanding the mental health consequences of violent victimization. Her current research activities include investigations of the physical and mental health consequences of violent victimization; processes for coping with traumatic events; best practice guidelines for community-based interventions with violence survivors; and the investigation of cognitive interventions for violence survivors and violence prevention. She is a second-generation social worker and cognitive practitioner. Both her parents are social workers, and her mother—who is a clinical social worker—first introduced her to the ideas of cognitive therapy.

Christopher R. Martell, Ph.D., ABPP, maintains an independent practice in Seattle and is an Associate Clinical Professor of Psychology at the University of Washington. Dr. Martell is a diplomat in both clinical psychology and behavioral psychology through the American Board of Professional Psychology. He is a Fellow of the American Psychological Association and past president of the Washington State Psychological Association. He has coauthored three books and many book chapters and articles on the topics of behavioral activation therapy for depression, behavioral couples therapy, and the application of cognitive-behavioral therapies with gay, lesbian, and bisexual clients. Dr. Martell was the 2004 recipient of the Washington State Psychological Association's Distinguished Psychologist Award.

Nancy L. Murdock, Ph.D., is Professor and Chair of the Division of Counseling and Educational Psychology at the University of Missouri–Kansas City. She is the author of *Theories of Counseling and Psychotherapy: A Case Approach* (Merrill/Prentice Hall). Dr. Murdock is an active researcher of Bowen Family Systems Theory. She teaches graduate courses in Family Systems Theory and Couples and Family Practicum and maintains a practice working with individuals, couples, and families.

Thorana S. Nelson, Ph.D., is currently a professor of marriage and family therapy at Utah State University. She is a licensed marriage and family therapist and is active in the American Association for Marriage and Family Therapy and the American Family Therapy Academy, and is one of the founders of the Solution Focused Brief Therapy Association. She has training in Solution Focused Brief Therapy and also is a trainer. She has coedited several books and numerous articles on various aspects of family therapy.

Jeffrey Raff, Ph.D., has been in private practice as a Jungian analyst in the Denver area since 1976. He graduated from the C.G. Jung Institute in Zurich in that year and received his Ph.D. from The Union Institute in 1978. He was the President and founding member of the C.G. Jung Institute of Colorado and is a member of the Interregional Society of Jungian Analysts and the International Association of Analytical Psychology. Aside from his private practice he has taught across the United States and in Europe on Jungian-related topics. He is the author of numerous articles and three books. His fourth book is due out in April of 2006.

J. Michael Russell, Ph.D., is Emeritus Professor of Philosophy and Emeritus Professor of Human Services at California State University, Fullerton. He is a Research Psychoanalyst and Training and Supervising Analyst for the Newport Psychoanalytic Institute. Michael teaches a wide range of courses in philosophy, human services, and psychoanalysis, many of which emphasize integrating these different perspectives within an experiential group format. Academic and research interests include existential psychoanalysis, philosophical assumptions of psychotherapy, existential group, and philosophical counseling. He has been the chair of each of his academic departments, chair of the training committee at the Newport Institute, and the recipient of awards as an Outstanding Teacher in the College of Human Development and Community Service, Outstanding Honors Faculty, and Distinguished Faculty Member in the College of Humanities, CSUF. With his wife

Valerie (also a therapist), several dogs, rabbits, and cats, he lives and practices in Brea, California.

Mary F. Schneider, Ph.D., has focused her professional work on the developmental and treatment needs of children and families. Prior to joining the faculty of the Adler School of Professional Psychology, she was a full professor in the Foster G. McGaw Graduate School at National-Louis University in Evanston, Illinois. She first developed her interest in Adlerian Psychology under the mentorship of Dr. Manford Sonstegard, a pioneer in the development of family education centers, and deepened her Adlerian training under the brilliant practice and scholarship of Dr. Harold Mosak. She married a generative Adlerian, Seymour Schneider. Sy and Mary Frances proceeded to debate Adlerian ideas day and night, enjoying the world through this shared lens and growing two fine sons under the umbrella of Adlerian philosophy. Mary Frances broadened her training in family therapy at the Family Institute at Northwestern, integrating Adlerian family therapy with modern and postmodern forms of family therapy. She currently teaches courses on Adlerian individual and family therapy at the Adler School of Professional Psychology. Her research interests focus on family violence and the use of the journal in the process of change.

Alissa Sherry, Ph.D., is currently an assistant professor in the Counseling Psychology Program at the University of Texas at Austin. She is active in constructivist training and research, having been mentored by William J. Lyddon at the University of Southern Mississippi. She completed an internship at the University of Oregon and a postdoctoral fellowship at Emory University School of Medicine. Her current research addresses issues related to attachment as well as sexual orientation.

Margaret S. Warner, Ph.D., is a full professor in the doctoral program in clinical psychology at the Illinois School of Professional Psychology/Chicago campus (a campus of Argosy University), and a cochair of the minor in client-centered and experiential psychology at that school. She is currently involved in the development of a certificate program in client-centered and experiential psychotherapy. Dr. Warner has a doctorate from the University of Chicago in Behavioral Sciences with additional clinical training at the Chicago Counseling and Psychotherapy Center, an offshoot of the original Counseling Center founded by Carl Rogers at the University of Chicago. Dr. Warner was formally a member of the provisional board that founded the World Association of Person-Centered and Experiential Psychotherapy and Counseling and the convener of Chicago 2000. The Fifth International Conference of Client-Centered and Experiential Psychotherapy where the world association bylaws were approved.

Janet L. Wolfe, Ph.D., received her doctorate in clinical psychology from New York University, where she is currently Adjunct Professor of Applied Psychology. She has a private consulting and therapy practice in New York City. She served for over 20 years as Executive Director of the Albert Ellis Institute, supervising interns and fellows and conducting individual and group therapy. Dr. Wolfe is the coeditor of the *REBT Resource Book for Practitioners,* author of *What to Do When He Has a Headache,* and coauthor (with Albert Ellis) of *How to Raise an Emotionally Healthy, Happy Child.* She has published over 100 chapters and articles and conducted hundreds of workshops in REBT/CBT and its applications to addictions treatment, anger management, and gender and relationship issues throughout

Europe, Latin America, Japan, Taiwan, and India. She has helped start numerous programs in clinics, schools, and agencies based on REBT/CBT principles.

Robert E. Wubbolding, Ed.D., received his doctorate from the University of Cincinnati in 1971. He was a high school teacher and counselor, elementary school counselor, and counselor at a halfway house for female ex-offenders. He is professor emeritus at Xavier University, director of training for the William Glasser Institute, and director of the Center for Reality Therapy. A psychologist and counselor, he has written 10 books on reality therapy including the comprehensive text *Reality Therapy for the 21st Century* and over 120 articles and essays about reality therapy and other topics. He has adapted reality therapy to the stages of recovery from addictions and to multicultural counseling. As an international instructor, he has taught reality therapy in Asia, Europe and the Middle East, as well as North America.

BRIEF CONTENTS

INTRODUCTION 1

CHAPTER 1   Psychoanalytic Psychotherapy   5

CHAPTER 2   Analytical (Jungian) Psychology   21

CHAPTER 3   Adlerian Psychology   37

CHAPTER 4   Self Psychology   53

CHAPTER 5   Time-Limited Dynamic Psychotherapy   75

CHAPTER 6   Client-Centered/Rogerian Therapy   91

CHAPTER 7   Existential Psychotherapy   107

CHAPTER 8   Gestalt Therapy   127

CHAPTER 9   Behavioral Therapy   143

CHAPTER 10   Cognitive Therapy   157

CHAPTER 11   Rational Emotive Behavior Therapy (REBT)   177

CHAPTER 12   Reality Therapy   193

CHAPTER 13   Family Systems Theory   209

CHAPTER 14   Feminist Counseling   225

CHAPTER 15   Constructivist Counseling   239

CHAPTER 16   Solution-Focused Brief Therapy   255

INDEX 271

CONTENTS

INTRODUCTION   1

CHAPTER 1   Psychoanalytic Psychotherapy   5
RICARDO AINSLIE
  Bridging the Theory-to-Practice Gap   6
  Principles in Practice   7
  Keys to Conceptualization   10
  Interventions and Therapeutic Process   11
  Short- and Long-Term Goals   14
  Using the Relationship   15
  Adapting the Approach   17
  Finding Your Niche   18
  Process and Case Suggestions   18
  Summary and Suggested Readings   19

CHAPTER 2   Analytical (Jungian) Psychology   21
JEFFREY RAFF
  Bridging the Theory-to-Practice Gap   22
  Principles in Practice   24
  Keys to Conceptualization   28
  Interventions and Therapeutic Process   29
  Short- and Long-Term Goals   31
  Using the Relationship   31
  Adapting the Approach   32
  Finding Your Niche   33
  Process and Case Suggestions   34
  Summary and Suggested Readings   35

CHAPTER 3   Adlerian Psychology   37
MARY FRANCES SCHNEIDER
  Bridging the Theory-to-Practice Gap   38
  Principles in Practice   39
  Keys to Conceptualization   42
  Interventions and Therapeutic Process   44
  Short- and Long-Term Goals   45
  Using the Relationship   46
  Adapting the Approach   47
  Finding Your Niche   48
  Process and Case Suggestions   49
  Summary and Suggested Readings   50
  References   51

CHAPTER 4   Self Psychology   53
ALAN KINDLER
*Bridging the Theory-to-Practice
   Gap   54
Principles in Practice   56
Keys to Conceptualization   62
Interventions and Therapeutic Process   65
Short- and Long-Term Goals   67
Using the Relationship   68
Adapting the Approach   69
Finding Your Niche   70
Process and Case Suggestions   71
Summary and Suggested Readings   73*

CHAPTER 5   Time-Limited Dynamic Psychotherapy   75
HANNA LEVENSON
*Bridging the Theory-to-Practice
   Gap   76
Principles in Practice   77
Keys to Conceptualization   79
Interventions and Therapeutic Process   82
Short- and Long-Term Goals   85
Using the Relationship   86
Adapting the Approach   86
Finding Your Niche   88
Process and Case Suggestions   89
Summary and Suggested Readings   90
References   90*

CHAPTER 6   Client-Centered/Rogerian Therapy   91
MARGARET S. WARNER
*Bridging the Theory-to-Practice
   Gap   92
Principles in Practice   93
Keys to Conceptualization   95
Interventions and Therapeutic Process   97
Short- and Long-Term Goals   99
Using the Relationship   100
Adapting the Approach   101
Finding Your Niche   103
Process and Case Suggestions   103
Summary and Suggested Readings   104
References   105*

CHAPTER 7   Existential Psychotherapy   107
J. MICHAEL RUSSELL
*Bridging the Theory-to-Practice
   Gap   108
Principles in Practice   110*

Keys to Conceptualization   *114*
Interventions and Therapeutic Process   *116*
Short- and Long-Term Goals   *120*
Using the Relationship   *120*
Adapting the Approach   *122*
Finding Your Niche   *123*
Process and Case Suggestions   *123*
Summary and Suggested Readings   *124*

CHAPTER 8   Gestalt Therapy   127
                 JUDITH R. BROWN
                 Bridging the Theory-to-Practice
                 Gap   128
                 Principles in Practice   129
                 Keys to Conceptualization   133
                 Interventions and Therapeutic Process   134
                 Short- and Long-Term Goals   136
                 Using the Relationship   136
                 Adapting the Approach   138
                 Finding Your Niche   139
                 Process and Case Suggestions   139
                 Summary and Suggested Readings   140

CHAPTER 9   Behavioral Therapy   143
                 CHRISTOPHER R. MARTELL
                 Bridging the Theory-to-Practice
                 Gap   144
                 Principles in Practice   145
                 Keys to Conceptualization   148
                 Interventions and Therapeutic Process   150
                 Short- and Long-Term Goals   151
                 Using the Relationship   152
                 Adapting the Approach   153
                 Finding Your Niche   153
                 Process and Case Suggestions   154
                 Summary and Suggested Readings   155
                 References   156

CHAPTER 10   Cognitive Therapy   157
                 REBECCA J. MACY
                 Bridging the Theory-to-Practice
                 Gap   158
                 Principles in Practice   159
                 Keys to Conceptualization   164
                 Interventions and Therapeutic
                 Process   166
                 Short- and Long-Term Goals   169
                 Using the Relationship   170
                 Adapting the Approach   171

Finding Your Niche 172
Process and Case Suggestions 174
Summary and Suggested Readings 174
References 175

CHAPTER 11   Rational Emotive Behavior Therapy (REBT)   177
                  JANET L. WOLFE
                  Bridging the Theory-to-Practice
                  * Gap 178*
                  Principles in Practice 179
                  Keys to Conceptualization 182
                  Interventions and Therapeutic Practice 183
                  Short- and Long-Term Goals 184
                  Using the Relationship 186
                  Adapting the Approach 187
                  Finding Your Niche 188
                  Process and Case Suggestions 188
                  Summary and Suggested Readings 189

CHAPTER 12   Reality Therapy   193
                  ROBERT E. WUBBOLDING
                  Bridging the Theory-to-Practice
                  * Gap 194*
                  Principles in Practice 195
                  Keys to Conceptualization 197
                  Interventions and Therapeutic Practice 199
                  Short- and Long-Term Goals 200
                  Using the Relationship 201
                  Adapting the Approach 202
                  Finding Your Niche 203
                  Process and Case Suggestions 204
                  Summary and Suggested Readings 204
                  References 206

CHAPTER 13   Family Systems Theory   209
                  NANCY L. MURDOCK
                  Bridging the Theory-to-Practice
                  * Gap 210*
                  Principles in Practice 212
                  Keys to Conceptualization 214
                  Interventions and Therapeutic Practice 216
                  Short- and Long-Term Goals 219
                  Using the Relationship 219
                  Adapting the Approach 220
                  Finding Your Niche 221
                  Process and Case Suggestions 221
                  Summary and Suggested Readings 222
                  References 223

CHAPTER 14   Feminist Counseling   225
              LUCIA A. GILBERT AND JILL RADER
                  Bridging the Theory-to-Practice
                      Gap 226
                  Principles in Practice 227
                  Keys to Conceptualization 231
                  Interventions and Therapeutic Practice 233
                  Short- and Long-Term Goals 234
                  Using the Relationship 234
                  Adapting the Approach 235
                  Finding Your Niche 236
                  Process and Case Suggestions 236
                  Summary and Suggested Readings 237

CHAPTER 15   Constructivist Counseling   239
              ALISSA SHERRY
                  Bridging the Theory-to-Practice
                      Gap 240
                  Principles in Practice 241
                  Keys to Conceptualization 245
                  Interventions and Therapeutic Practice 246
                  Short- and Long-Term Goals 248
                  Using the Relationship 249
                  Adapting the Approach 250
                  Finding Your Niche 250
                  Process and Case Suggestions 251
                  Summary and Suggested Readings 253
                  References 253

CHAPTER 16   Solution-Focused Brief Therapy   255
              THORANA S. NELSON
                  Bridging the Theory-to-Practice
                      Gap 256
                  Principles in Practice 257
                  Keys to Conceptualization 261
                  Interventions and Therapeutic Practice 262
                  Short- and Long-Term Goals 265
                  Using the Relationship 265
                  Adapting the Approach 266
                  Finding Your Niche 266
                  Process and Case Suggestions 267
                  Summary and Suggested Readings 268
                  References 269

INDEX   271

Note: Every effort has been made to provide accurate and current Internet information in this book. However, the Internet and information posted on it are constantly changing, so it is inevitable that some of the Internet addresses listed in this textbook will change.

Introduction

Aaron B. Rochlen

Like most of you, I gained an *academic* understanding of counseling theories in my coursework. From Freud to feminism, I thoroughly enjoyed learning about the origin, assumptions, and critical principles of all the classic theories that were intended to guide my clinical work and shape my theoretical orientation. However, when beginning to see clients as a graduate student, I struggled with how to apply these approaches in practice. I was aware of the major theoretical principles and assumptions, but was missing an understanding of how to actually use these approaches when sitting with a client.

This substantial gap between learning about theories and applying them with clients is the main reason I created these materials. In essence, my goal was to create a set of materials that would help students like you have a greater comfort in knowing how to apply the interesting, but occasionally abstract theories, in a meaningful way.

To meet this goal, I have invited 16 expert authors and therapists representing different theoretical approaches to write chapters translating the formal principles, assumptions, and techniques of their theories into user-friendly guidelines for working with clients. As you are reading these guidelines, keep in mind that the chapters are not intended to describe the theories in their entirety—there are some great theories books on the market that meet this objective. In addition, I always recommend that students read at least some of the original work representing the theorists.

Why did I choose 16 theoretical approaches? Sixteen is not a magic number—there are many more theories that therapists subscribe to in their work. In addition, many therapists practice from an integrative or eclectic perspective. Murdock, 2004, reported on six different studies addressing counselors' primary theoretical orientations, and eclectic was by far the top choice among reported counselors. Yet, more than 50 percent of therapists adhere to one specific theoretical orientation in working with their clients. Moreover, Murdock emphasized that even counselors who do identify themselves as eclectic or integrative report having a second theoretical orientation that provides a central influence to their work.

The point is simply that while many therapists do work from several different theoretical perspectives, it really is important for students to grasp the key features of the more "pure" theoretical approaches. Also, exploring many theoretical approaches will help you find those that are most consistent with your own personality and beliefs about people's problems and how clients change.

In addition to creating a text with the unique focus on the application of theories, I also wanted to create a learning tool that would allow students the opportunity to practice applying different theories before seeing clients. To meet this goal, we have developed an innovative web-based application that allows you to review cases and practice applying the theories. With the recent advances in technology, it seems like an ideal time to provide you with a fun, realistic, and engaging web-based application that gives you a chance to practice your case conceptualization skills.

There are two components to this project:

1. The text explains the application of the various theoretical approaches. Each chapter in the text presents a different theory and includes sections on Bridging the Theory-to-Practice Gap; Principles in Practice; Keys to Conceptualization; Interventions and Therapeutic Process; Short- and Long-Term Goals; Using the Relationship; Adapting the Approach; and Finding Your Niche. All these sections were created to communicate a real-world understanding of how clinicians use and apply key theoretical principles with their clients. The chapters conclude with a brief commentary on the process of conceptualizing the three cases (on the website) and include helpful suggestions. This commentary should serve as a springboard for you to begin reviewing the case material and practicing your own conceptualizations.

2. The website at www.prenhall.com/rochlen provides the training ground for conceptualizing the cases from the different theoretical perspectives presented in the text. In navigating the site, I recommend the following sequence:

From the homepage, you should first choose the theory that you would like to apply. This will then take you to a page where you can choose one of the three cases to practice (i.e., Elena, Jane, or Theo). Next, you will then have access to further details about the case, provided through a written intake and a video to download. The 12-minute edited video segments show presenting interviews with each of the three clients. These cases were carefully constructed to represent a diverse set of clients (in regard to age, gender, ethnicity, etc.). We also created cases that would involve presenting problems that are both realistic and had potential to be addressed by a range of different theoretical approaches. The video segments are in no way intended to represent a complete clinical interview (This could not possibly be done in 12 minutes!). However, they should provide you with some great material to use in answering the conceptualization questions as well as imagining yourself in the role of therapist with each of the respective clients. After carefully reviewing this material, you can then click the "submit analysis" button and begin your responses to the various conceptualization questions. You may want to discuss with your instructor which of the questions would be most helpful to respond to for various assignments. The submit analysis section also allows you to send your responses electronically via email (simply type the email address in the appropriate box).

Finally, after submitting your responses, you can then choose to review the conceptualization responses to the same set of questions submitted by the expert therapist representing your selected theoretical approach. For me, this is one of the most exciting features of the project. Keep in mind that the best procedure is to review these expert responses *after* completing your own responses. Also consider that with case conceptualization, there isn't necessarily a "right" answer. Most likely, you will see similarities and differences in the responses. This should provide important validation of your own responses while extending your knowledge and understanding of the approach.

Remember, these materials are intended to be used together. I suggest that you start by reading the chapter on a particular theory, then watch the video presentation of the cases. As you view each case, look for the key concepts of the theory that were discussed in the text. The text should provide the perspective through which you view the cases. For example, if you are trying to apply the theories discussed in the chapter on analytical psychology, you will first focus on deciphering primary and secondary complexes as you watch the videos.

Used together, these unique materials will provide you with an opportunity to learn about different theoretical approaches and how they play out in a clinical setting. You'll also have a chance to apply your knowledge and compare your responses with some of the experts in the counseling field as you work toward becoming a capable, compassionate therapist. It has been a lot of fun developing this project—and I hope that you will also enjoy using these materials and that they will be helpful toward your own professional development and in meeting your goals as a developing therapist.

REFERENCE

Murdock, N. L. (2004) *Theories of counseling and psychotherapy: A case approach.* Upper Saddle River, NJ: Pearson Education, Inc.

Chapter 1

Psychoanalytic Psychotherapy

Ricardo Ainslie

Chapter Outline

Bridging the Theory-to-Practice Gap
Principles in Practice
Keys to Conceptualization
Interventions and Therapeutic Process
Short- and Long-Term Goals
Using the Relationship
Adapting the Approach
Finding Your Niche
Process and Case Suggestions
Summary and Suggested Readings

BRIDGING THE THEORY-TO-PRACTICE GAP

Psychoanalysis has long been one of the most influential psychotherapy theories. Many contemporary counseling approaches have either incorporated psychoanalytic assumptions or been developed as a reaction to these assumptions. As you explore this theory, you will not only become aware of just how foundational its concepts are to our current thinking about psychotherapy, but you will also become aware of just how much this theory has become part of modern culture itself. For example, we might readily speak about a person being "in denial," or intuitively understand the value of self-understanding as a vehicle for restoring emotional equilibrium.

While psychoanalytic theory has undergone a variety of reformulations over the last century, these schools share a variety of ideas that lie at the core of the theory. Foremost among these is the view that, notwithstanding our genetic makeup, as human beings we are profoundly affected by experiences with others that take place over the course of our development. When we suffer from conflicts and psychological symptoms, these formative experiences are often implicated.

Bridging the gap between theory and practice may be more difficult with psychoanalytic theory than with other theories. This is due to the fact that psychoanalytic theory is quite complex and its concepts range from the highly abstract, such as "internalized object relations," to more the familiar, such as "repression." Furthermore, psychoanalytic theory is three theories at once: developmental, personality, and intervention. This means that an understanding of all three of these domains is optimal in order to understand how to implement psychoanalytic ideas within a therapeutic situation. This is the case because the rationale for a particular intervention may be drawing from the therapist's understanding of psychoanalytic developmental theory, for example, or from psychoanalytic assumptions about psychopathology. In addition, you may find that your initial explorations of psychoanalytic theory feel daunting given that in some respects this therapeutic approach is relatively unstructured. That is, there are general guidelines for a therapist's (and the client's) participation in the therapeutic process, but the choice of what to say and when to say it relies almost entirely on the therapist's empathic engagement with the client, with the therapist's understanding of the material that is being presented and its implications, and the therapist's understanding of the client's ability to engage particular topics or feelings. This is sometimes unsettling to beginning therapists who are comforted by more specific guidelines or instructions for what they are expected to do with their clients. However, if you can tolerate this ambiguity, you will soon discover that clinical work can be enormously gratifying both intellectually (because people's feelings and motivations are a fascinating puzzle) and personally (because it is rewarding to see people change as they come to better understand themselves).

A full understanding of psychoanalytic theory requires familiarity with the different psychoanalytic schools of thought. In many instances these have evolved as corrective responses to limitations within Freud's original theory, or as a response to evolving conceptualizations within related fields, such as cognitive development or child development more generally. However, it is possible to distill a set of core assumptions that psychoanalytic therapists tend to share when engaged in therapeutic work. As you consider exploring this theoretical approach, imagine yourself to be in the privileged role of one who gets to sit in a room with another person and listen to that person's life history; that is, imagine yourself as a clinician whose main interest is attempting to grasp what clients are really like and how they came to be this way. This is the most important feature of the psychoanalytically oriented therapists' mindset, the most important sensibility that they bring to the consulting room. The formulations and propositions that form psychoanalytic theory are ultimately a collection of ways of understanding the vital experiences that make us who we are or, alternatively, ways for understanding how best to explore the interior life of the clients who come seeking our assistance. But the essential commitment as a psychoanalytic psychotherapist is to understand the lives of those who seek treatment as fully as possible.

PRINCIPLES IN PRACTICE

1. *The dynamic unconscious.* Probably the most central, foundational concept within psychoanalysis is the notion of the *dynamic unconscious.* This postulate—that there are thoughts, feelings, and experiences that form part of our psychic reality and about which we may be unaware or only partly aware—is at the heart of a psychoanalytic perspective. But the key term here is "dynamic"; that is, the assumption that not only are we not aware of many of our thoughts and feelings, but also that these unconscious contents actively influence and shape the way that we think and feel, as well as what we do. The concept of the dynamic unconscious makes the understanding of your clients' unconscious thoughts and feelings central to solving the puzzle of why they do what they do and why they are so often unaware of *why* they are doing it (which makes it difficult for them to change). Psychoanalysis assumes that unconscious processes play a powerful role in our motivations and in how we understand ourselves and other people. For example, a successful medical researcher was surprised to discover while in therapy the extent to which his childhood feelings about his mother's multiple life-threatening illnesses had played a role in his later choice of professional careers. Such unconscious processes also play an important role in the formation of symptoms and other problematic thoughts, feelings, and behaviors, given that these are often produced by unconscious conflicts. While psychoanalysis is a complex theory comprised of a variety of schools and at times conflicting camps and perspectives, the notion of the dynamic unconscious is one of the shared and defining constructs of the theory that cuts across these camps.

2. *Defenses.* Another foundational psychoanalytic construct is the idea that unconscious *defenses* are part of how human beings engage the world. Specifically, they are part of how we manage anxiety and other conflictual feelings about what we have experienced, especially when those experiences have been emotionally charged and overwhelming. In psychoanalytic theory, defenses are considered both normal processes that all of us use as we adapt to the world around us and, when they become rigid and institutionalized, pathological, desperate attempts to isolate and contain thoughts, memories, and feelings, such as sexual feelings, anxiety, depression,

and anger. For example, the survivors of a natural disaster might use denial to ward off understanding the full implications of what has just transpired in order not to be overwhelmed. This normal use of defenses might make it possible for them to do what they need to do in order to mobilize themselves in the face of the immediate crisis. On the other hand, if the use of denial became so pervasive that it interfered with their ability to engage their world long after the crisis had subsided, this would be a pathological or symptomatic use of a defense. The latter produces conflicts and symptom formations that often require therapeutic intervention because they create problems with how we live our lives. The view of defenses as central to our psychological makeup and to our strategies for managing emotionally difficult feelings and experiences is a cornerstone of psychoanalytic theorizing. As a therapist you would try to be as aware as possible of how and when your clients mobilized defensive strategies and what issues invited such mobilization for this would give you vital clues to understanding your client's concerns.

3. *The developmental perspective.* The developmental perspective is another central frame of reference within psychoanalytic theory with respect to understanding psychopathology and personality theory more generally. The developmental perspective is reflected in the view that, for each of us, our psychology is a product of a unique developmental trajectory, influenced both by the characteristics of the family within which we grew up and by innate, genetic attributes, such as temperament, that are in constant interaction with a person's milieu. Over the course of a child's development, needs are organized around specific issues that are linked to those developmental circumstances, given that what a child needs from others changes over time. Children's capacity for understanding themselves and those around them is filtered through these developmental moments. For example, a child's experience of parental divorce is likely to vary depending on the age at which this familial disruption takes place. A child who is, say, five years old will find it more difficult to understand that the conflicts that led to the divorce have little to do with him, or that the fact that parents no longer love each other does not mean that they do not love him. On the other hand, a ten-year old child might readily understand that her parents love her notwithstanding their problems with each other. This is due, in part, to the fact that the older child is cognitively mature enough to understand relationships in a more complex and less egocentric manner. Thus, the same experience— parental divorce—might have a very different impact upon a child depending on the age at which it occurs and the circumstances surrounding it.

The developmental perspective requires us to consider the impact of emotionally charged events in the context of the juncture in a child's life in which they occur. It also includes the idea that the younger the child, the more vulnerable the child is to distorting intrusions from the environment, and the fewer resources the child will have to manage such experiences and how they influence his sense of self and of others. The developmental perspective builds into psychoanalytic theorizing a sensitivity to the psychological resources (or lack thereof) that were available to people when their lives were impinged upon by disruptive experiences. This means that psychoanalytically oriented clinicians are often asking the question, What childhood experiences are playing a part in these present-day difficulties? And, given their age at the time, what psychological resources were available to them at the time to help absorb these? This does not mean that we ignore real stressors and conflicts that may be at work in a person's current life. However, current stressors, and the way in which a person attempts to manage them, are assumed to be informed by personal history in important (and often unconscious) ways, and it is assumed that understanding those connections often leads to more competent engagements in our present-day lives.

4. *The structural perspective.* Another important lens through which psychoanalysis views personality is the *structural perspective.* That is, psychoanalysis assumes that experience becomes part of an *internal* process. Like the Piagetian concept of schemas or the attachment theory concept of internal working models, psychoanalysis assumes that meaningful experience becomes internalized. Psychoanalytic theorists use this term to denote the idea that these meaningful experiences, and the feelings attached to them, have become part of an internal psychic structure that has a profound role in shaping our engagement with the world and in filtering our understanding of ourselves and others within it. This is an important construct because it primes us to look for patterns, themes, and continuities in a client's life, all of which shed light on the client's internalized world. Such patterns are often unconscious and they may be reflected in activities that seem, on the face of it, disparate. For example, problems with an authoritarian parent may later be reflected in problems with a boss or supervisor, in a relationship to a partner, or in how the affected individuals are parenting their own children—links that may not be at all clear to the person in question. In other words, clients are often not aware of these patterns, or may only "encounter" them via others' reactions to their behavior and not grasp the broader implications of what is going on. This is one way in which a psychoanalytic therapist intervenes, by pointing out and interpreting the meaning of discerned patterns that the client cannot see clearly. But the concept of psychic structure alerts the therapist to the importance of remembering the client's material across sessions and to look for such patterns in the events the client describes from his current and past experiences.

Both the developmental perspective and the structural perspective have implications for a more general approach to therapy, what we might term the psychoanalytic interest in *narrative*. The importance and therapeutic value of putting one's experiences, one's life story, into words has long been one of the central tenets of psychoanalytic assumptions about how therapy cures. This began with Freud's famous dictum that hysterics "suffer from their reminiscences" and his discovery of "the talking cure." Within a psychoanalytic approach, the therapeutic situation is viewed, in part, as a narrative space: a setting within which clients are safe to tell their life stories. This is a profoundly important insight into the power of words and of narrative processes, yet, in my years of supervising master's and doctoral students, as well as practicing therapists, I have often been surprised at how difficult it is for therapists, especially when they lack clinical experience, to trust in this narrative process. They often feel that if they are not "doing" something they must not be acting as good therapists. They are not comfortable simply letting their clients talk and permitting their clients to use their therapy appointments as a vehicle for putting their concerns and their life stories into words. While there is more to therapy than simply listening to clients, providing a safe environment for clients to tell their story to a therapist who is genuinely interested, who desires to understand their life, and who is willing to allow them to explore their feelings about important events that have impinged on them and that have shaped their views about who they are, is considered essential and fundamental to a psychoanalytic approach to treatment. These elements are valued as indispensable to the therapeutic process.

KEYS TO CONCEPTUALIZATION

The central elements of a psychoanalytic conceptualization revolve around the effort to understand the unconscious conflicts and motives that may be at work in a client's life, including how these come into play within the client-therapist relationship. The question of how these elements contribute to the clients' experience of self, experience of others, and how these may shape the clients' behaviors and engagements with the world in which they live is the bread and butter of psychoanalytic conceptualizations. In *The Interpretation of Dreams,* his classic work on the topic, Freud argues that the dream cannot be understood without the dreamer. This same principle might be applied to all the interpretive moments within the therapeutic situation; the therapist is not omnipotent when it comes to understanding the client's unconscious world. Quite the contrary, the client's associations to the thoughts, feelings, or behaviors (including dreams) in question are indispensable to arriving at a meaningful understanding of them. This is why psychoanalytic therapists consider the *working alliance* to be so essential, for it is part of what permits the two people in the consulting room to collaborate in the service of better understanding the client's life experience. The therapist's reliable, engaged, and nonjudgmental approach to the therapy, as well as the understanding that the therapeutic conversations are confidential, help to create a backdrop of safety for the client to work on problems and risk explorations of material that is difficult to discuss. Such an endeavor is always complicated because when we say that there are unconscious feelings at work, what that implies is that the client does not fully understand these issues and, indeed, may be ambivalent about exposing these to the light. One part of the client wants to see, wants to understand, and wants to make sense of these deeper aspects of experience. Yet while another part of the client defends against this very prospect because it may mobilize anxiety, embarrassment, vulnerability, shame, anger, or other feelings which have a great deal to do with why the experiences in question have been maintained in the unconscious in the first place.

Another important framework for conceptualizing clinical material centers on the notion of *regression*. Psychoanalytic clinicians understand that when a person's emotional resources are taxed by life events (say the loss of a relationship, the death of a loved one, the loss of a job) such losses create enormous stress on an individual's psychological equilibrium. For example, a woman found herself increasingly depressed after an employment-related move to a new city. It was difficult for her to go to work or to socialize with people she met. This regression in her level of functioning was related to the stresses of the move, for she'd left behind a community and people she was close to. Regression to less optimal modes of functioning is often the result of stressful or emotionally taxing circumstances, which means that when a new client comes for therapy, one of the key questions might be how this crisis has affected this person's overall level of functioning? Are we seeing a fairly chronic set of symptoms or are we seeing this individual at her worst because of the immediate stressors that have brought her to therapy? Such questions help put the client's overall functioning in perspective and may give the clinician a clearer picture for the available psychological resources with which this client can work.

Psychoanalytically oriented clinicians tend to be very interested in fully exploring the *precipitating events* that bring the client into treatment at this particular time. It is assumed that these may reveal a great deal about the kinds of issues with which a client is struggling, as well as the ways in which the client copes with conflicts. For example, it turned out that, as a child, the client just described had lost her mother. That loss had been devastating to her. As an adult, when things were stable in her world, she functioned well. But when she was faced with losses, as was the case with her move to a new city, her earlier experiences rendered her quite vulnerable to regression. Exploring her current feelings of dislocation led her to explore her feelings about her mother's death, an exploration that eventually helped her mourn that loss and strengthened her ability to manage ordinary losses and dislocations in her present life. In other words, precipitating events are often not random; rather, they tend to be linked, if unconsciously so, with longer-standing conflicts, which is what makes them so disruptive.

INTERVENTIONS AND THERAPEUTIC PROCESS

Psychoanalysis has a unique way of structuring the therapeutic process. Though not always specifically delineated in psychoanalytic writings on therapeutic technique, the view that a therapist should approach each session with an attitude that is open-ended, exploratory, and uncovering in spirit is paramount. In other words, the therapist's key job is to be curious about the clients' lives and therefore to allow clients to bring into the therapy any aspect of their life that they feel is important to them at the moment, whether or not it is specifically linked to the presenting problem that brought them into therapy in the first place. There are psychoanalytic theorists, for example, who advocate that the therapist should approach each session "without memory or desire." Obviously this is impossible, but the axiom is intended to underscore the ideal that the clinician should allow *clients* to shape the direction of the therapy by talking about what feels important to them at the moment rather than forcing them to respond to the therapist's preconceived notions about what should be discussed. This readily distinguishes a psychodynamic approach to treatment from a therapeutic approach that targets specific behaviors or symptoms, for example, since the latter often requires that therapeutic engagements remain focused on those specific issues.

Psychoanalytically informed clinicians pay close attention to the *frame* of the therapeutic situation. That is, everything that might relate to the boundaries that define the client-therapist relationship is monitored closely. This begins with a careful adherence to the organization of the appointments themselves. For example, it is assumed that regularly scheduled appointments (typically not fewer than once a week and, in the case of psychoanalysis proper, as many as three to five appointments a week) occur at set times and that the clinician endeavors to be punctual when it comes to the beginning and closing of each session. This structure helps create a stable, consistent environment, features that optimize a client's sense that this is a reliable and "usable" therapeutic relationship. When appointments are too infrequent, the therapist at best has an opportunity to obtain a sketch of what has been going on in the client's life. While such summaries may touch on important issues, they tend to lack depth and specificity. Similarly, when a therapist frequently changes appointment times, this introduces a feeling of unreliability to the process and it is likely to lead clients to feel less comfortable sharing aspects of their lives that are emotionally charged or about which they feel quite vulnerable. Consistency not only helps clients develop a sense of safety and reliability in relationship to therapeutic work, it also permits useful exploration of departures from the structure. For example, a client may develop a pattern of showing up late for appointments following emotionally charged sessions in which new ground was explored. By interpreting this pattern to the client, the therapist can help the client begin to understand that a part of them is "resistant" to exploring feelings more deeply. For example, a therapist might say (being careful not to make the clients feel that they are being judged or that the therapist sees them as "bad") "I'm wondering if you've noticed that every time there's a session in which you have lots of feelings, you somehow manage to come late to the next appointment, like you did today. Maybe you are trying to show us how unsettling it is for you when your feelings get stirred up." Other common frame-related issues might involve phone contacts, the need for extra appointments, and client-therapist contact that occurs outside of the therapy hours, such as when a client and therapist cross paths at a social event, any of which might warrant discussion and exploration depending on the circumstances.

Through such exploration, clients may also begin to understand that they use similar defensive strategies of avoidance and distancing to manage painful feelings outside of their therapy appointments and that these have long been a staple of how they manage emotionally laden issues. The therapist's job of creating a therapeutic context that is stable and structured is very important, and it both helps the client to feel that the therapy is a safe environment and makes it easier to identify meaningful patterns that emerge as "disturbances" in the therapeutic frame. In a psychoanalytically informed treatment, the emphasis is on creating a therapeutic space within which such possibilities can be explored and used productively in the effort to understand the clients' lives and how their psychology works.

Another concept with which psychoanalytic clinicians often work is the so-called *blank screen*—that is, the therapist's relative anonymity. Within the different psychoanalytic schools, there is considerable variation with regard to the extent to which this is viewed as central to the work. There is also a great deal of variation between therapists in terms of how comfortable they feel adopting such an ideal as a guideline for how to interact with their clients in the course of therapy. What psychoanalytic clinicians mean by *blank screen* is that as part of the therapist's aim of creating a therapeutic space within which the work can optimally progress, and which clients experience as their own, the therapist attempts to interfere as little as possible when it comes to introducing the therapist's own life experiences within the therapeutic process. The focus should remain on the client and the client's concerns. To some psychoanalytic clinicians this might mean not answering personal questions ("Where are you going on vacation?" "Are you divorced?" "Do you have children?"). The premise here is not that it is "wrong" for clients to be curious about these or other aspects of the therapist's life, but, rather, that these questions are rarely without meaning and importance in relation to the client's concerns (see discussion of transference and countertransference, below). In order to explore them, it is necessary to create a therapeutic atmosphere within which it is understood that everything is "grist for the mill," at least in principle. After such questions are explored, the therapist may or may not feel comfortable answering them, but if the climate of the work is such that these kinds of questions are readily answered, then all too often there is a missed opportunity for a deeper understanding of the client's emotional life. Thus, the posture of neutrality or relative incognito that is often subsumed under the term blank screen is meant to foster a therapeutic climate in which the focus of attention is on the client's life and the client's feelings. Secondly, this approach is intended to facilitate a climate in which a more reflexive, less conventionally social relationship develops and within which everything is understood as worthy of exploration, from the most mundane question to the most disturbing childhood memory.

Free association is another important construct in psychoanalytic therapy and one that has also undergone an evolution from the early years of psychoanalysis. The essential element of free association is that it invites clients to allow their thoughts and feelings to go in whatever direction occurs to them, rather than feeling that they must pursue a focused line of conversation. Psychoanalytic theory assumes that such associations are often meaningful and fruitful. At the same time, the principle of free association requires a degree of discipline on the part of the therapist in order to be able to follow these associative lines. The therapist has to keep track of what the client is saying and has to listen for connections in the client's material, connections that may or may not be obvious. This construct is at the heart of the underlying spirit of open-ended dialogue that permits clients to bring a wide range of material into their therapy hours. In effect, free association instructs the therapist to be open-minded, to be inclusive, to think of the therapeutic process as one into which a client is encouraged to introduce a broad range of ideas, feelings, and experiences so that these may be explored and understood.

Repetition compulsion and enactment are key constructs of psychoanalytic theory. It is assumed, for example, that we all have a tendency to repeat traumatic or otherwise defining experiences that have occurred over the course of our lives. The reasons are twofold: we are driven either by a need to gain mastery over conflicts that may have been overwhelming or by the hope that they will turn out differently. Psychoanalytic clinicians try to be sensitive to the possibility that such repetitions may be at the core of current conflicts and symptoms. If clients keep repeating destructive patterns in relationships, this pattern may indicate that they are attempting to work out something that, if understood, might no longer require such self-defeating processes. For example, a client who was abused as a child repeatedly found himself, as an adult, entering into relationships in which he initially idealized the other person, but he always ended up being severely mistreated by his various partners. Similar dynamics may also become enacted within the therapy, creating interactions in which both client and therapist may unwittingly participate. Such enactments may be a form of unconscious "remembering" of something from the client's past or a communication of something that clients are feeling in relation to the therapy or to the therapist that they may not be able to put into words.

How does therapy cure? What is it that makes therapy helpful for the client and facilitates the resolution of the conflicts, symptoms, and concerns that brought them into treatment? Most psychoanalytic practitioners view insight as an important part of the change process. Insight refers, in part, to the process of bringing unconscious memories, thoughts, and feelings to consciousness, thereby helping clients gain an understanding about their life, and the range of experiences that have been formative for them. Freud emphasized that insight was *always* an affectively engaged experience. That is, mere intellectual understanding, devoid of the emotional context defining the experience was, in Freud's view, of little value in helping clients resolve their problems. However, genuine engagement with the experiences that have played a formative role in clients' development, especially as the experiences emerge within the context of experiencing or reexperiencing the feelings they have about them within the therapeutic situation, has long been the hallmark of the psychoanalytic path to cure or to personal change.

While insight is a vital construct in the psychoanalytic understanding of the ingredients that foster change, in recent decades the importance of the *therapeutic relationship* as a curative agent has become increasingly recognized in psychoanalytic theorizing. The client's relationship to the therapist is always important. For example, for individuals whose early development was characterized by mistrustful relationships with parental figures who were incapable of empathic attunement with the client's developmental needs, the experience of a therapeutic relationship with a therapist who is caring, reliable, and engaged can itself be powerful, changing the client's life in profound ways and leading to a new experience of human relationships that was heretofore not possible. The working alliance allows the client to tolerate the anxiety and discomfort of bringing difficult issues into the therapy, but it is often through the therapeutic relationship that a client comes to experience new ways of relating. As a therapist it is vital that you be genuinely attentive and involved; clients know when you are just going through the motions. In contemporary psychoanalytic theory, then, both insight and the therapeutic relationship itself are viewed as important vehicles for change and mechanisms through which clients are able to find new modes of functioning that are no longer encumbered by the neurotic conflicts that once interfered with their lives. The relative weight given to insight versus the relationship varies within different psychoanalytic schools and also as a function of the different proclivities for one over the other among therapists themselves.

SHORT- AND LONG-TERM GOALS

Psychoanalytic approaches to treatment are traditionally considered to be long-term and it is not unusual for a psychoanalytic therapy case to last one or two years, or, in the case of psychoanalysis, five to seven years. However, these concepts are useful even if you are only seeing clients for a few sessions, in groups, or in the context of crisis interventions. The association with longer-term work is partly a function of the open-ended character of this approach to therapy, and also a function of the understanding that specific symptoms or conflicts are often related to other issues. For example, clients may present with relationship concerns, but in the course of exploring these it may become evident that they suffer from underlying depression due to experiences of a loss during childhood. From a psychoanalytic perspective, it is not useful to focus on a specific symptom at the expense of a broader understanding of its sources. In this case, it might be that exploring clients' childhood losses can play an important role in changing the way in which the client relates to people in the present and thus have a significant impact on the problems that brought them into treatment in the first place (perhaps, for example, they've been too dependent, or too guarded as a function of these earlier, unresolved feelings). However, this is not necessarily a linear process and it might be that for a period of time exploring the client's depression actually takes precedence over exploring relationship issues. In other words, an overly rigid adherence to the original presenting symptoms might arbitrarily shut off the exploration of important experiences that form part of the client's emotional world, experiences that play a role in these symptoms, or that may be related to other concerns that only become evident after the therapist and client have been working together for a while.

The assessment of progress in psychoanalytic therapy can be complex. For example, in the scenario just described, the client might experience a period in therapy when, as she begins to discover that something important has been missing from her life since childhood, she actually feels more depressed, not less. This would be likely if the client is someone who has long been using defenses to protect herself against her sad feelings. In other words, as therapy succeeded in cutting through those defenses, in putting her in touch with her feelings about the losses from childhood, the depression would be felt more directly. This would be an example of a paradoxical process in which, for this person, becoming more symptomatic might reflect progress in the therapy. However, over time one would be looking for improvements in clients' overall functioning, in their movement toward the goal that Freud long ago outlined as the signpost of healthy functioning, namely, the capacity to love and to work without undue intrusions from one's neurotic conflicts.

Short-term goals, assuming a client is able to engage in a long-term therapy, typically revolve around establishing a working alliance with clients, in enlisting them as collaborators in the rich and complex process of exploring their lives, including aspects of their thoughts and feelings about which they may not be comfortable, or about which they may not be aware. However, this does not mean that psychoanalytic therapists attempt to force every therapy case into a long-term treatment paradigm.

USING THE RELATIONSHIP

The notion of the blank screen has given us the caricature of the psychoanalyst who says nothing during an entire session, for example. Most contemporary psychoanalytic practitioners would tend to view such a posture as extreme and anomalous. Indeed, today psychoanalytic practitioners tend to be much more aware of the fact that therapists bring a great deal to the treatment situation and that part of the work revolves around clients' responses to their therapists and vice versa. This makes therapy a complex interaction between two people rather than a one-dimensional process in which a client projects thoughts and feelings onto a "neutral" therapist who "reads" those projections and interprets them to the client. The psychoanalytic constructs of *transference* and *countertransference* are two key ideas for anyone attempting to understand a psychoanalytic approach to therapy. I have described above the idea that psychoanalytic theory emphasizes the notion of psychic structure in which important experiences and relationships become internalized and operate as powerful forces in our engagement with the world and in our experience of ourselves and others. Freud coined the term "transference" to describe the way in which we all impose those unconscious internalized processes on the world around us via our perceptions and via our interactions with others. Transference refers to the many ways in which clients "see" their therapists, perceptions that are assumed to be infused with the client's needs, fears, or conflicts, but also simply their unreflexive assumptions about the social world and their participation in it. For example, a client may fear that the therapist does not like him because the client feels that he is "bad" for the things he's done, because he is afraid that the therapist feels that he needs too much, or for some other reason. When the therapeutic situation feels safe to the client, he is able to voice these concerns directly, and that becomes a means for further understanding important concerns and their sources. However, it is also common for a therapist to see that the client is struggling with conscious and unconscious feelings about the therapist that are interfering with the work but which the client finds it difficult to put into words. In this context, a sensitive obser-vation, such as, "You seem worried that I am feeling critical of you because of the things you've been talking about," may help the client discuss transferential feelings and foster a deeper exploration of these concerns. Thus, by being attuned to how the therapist is being experienced by the client, the therapist is in a position to learn a great deal about how the client experienced significant others in childhood and the impact that these individuals had on them. Depending on the intensity of the transference feelings, the therapist and client may be in a position to experience, in vivo, what it was like for the client when he was young and vulnerable. Such experiences become powerful tools in the effort to under-stand the experiences that were so formative to the client.

Similarly, the term *countertransference* refers to the therapist's emotional response to the client's material. The term once had a pejorative implication, suggesting that the therapist's feelings indicated unresolved conflicts in the therapist's personality that were likely to have a destructive impact on the client. While such intrusions of a therapist's personal struggles and conflicts are always something to monitor closely, today the construct of counter-transference is much broader and includes the normal, human reactions that a therapist might have to a client's material, reactions that are understood to often be quite useful rather than being viewed as threats to the therapeutic process. Let's say, for example, that a therapist is working with a client who has a great deal of difficulty connecting with her emotions. As she listens to the client's flat description of a budding relationship that has not worked out, the therapist might find herself remembering an experienced loss of her own about which there is a feeling of sadness. In other words, in her private associations to the client's material she has encountered an emotional resonance that seems to speak to what the client is discussing but discussing in an emotionally detached manner. In this context, the therapist might say, "You're talking about this relationship quiet matter-of-factly, but I wonder if you aren't also feeling sad about things not working out between you." In this illustration, the therapist's countertransference feelings alerted her to a feeling that the client was having difficulty acknowledging and engaging. By paying attention to her own countertransferential feelings, the therapist is able to use this information to guide the interpretation she makes to her client, an interpretation that simultaneously helps the client understand her own feelings and also points out a defense that the client uses to keep herself emotionally disconnected (e.g., "I think we're seeing another example of how hard it is for you to let yourself feel things and how you try to disconnect yourself from your emotions when you feel sad or depressed.").

Thus, the therapist's countertransference feelings may still be a source of interference within the treatment situation, creating blind spots or leading the therapist to say or do things that are not productive to the progress of the therapy. However, contemporary understanding of the term has broadened significantly to include a range of feelings, reactions, and responses to the client's material that are not seen as problematic but, on the contrary, are viewed as vital tools to understanding the client's experience. What is key here is that clinicians develop the discipline to monitor their feelings during sessions, viewing these responses as a rich source of information for understanding clients and helping clients understand themselves. Just as importantly, the constructs of transference and countertransference are foundational to a broader understanding of the therapeutic situation as a complex relationship, a relationship that is viewed as an essential part of the curative process within a psychoanalytic approach to treatment.

ADAPTING THE APPROACH

While psychoanalytic therapy is typically associated with long-term work, the concepts that form the basis for this approach—the dynamic unconscious, the structuralization of personality variables, the use of defenses, or the management of interpersonal variables such as transference and countertransference, to name a few—are readily applicable to a broad range of settings and contexts. These include group work, crisis intervention work, telephone hotlines, consultation, assessment, and short-term therapeutic interventions. This is because these concepts help a clinician understand what is going on with a client regardless of the specific context in which they are being used. You need not subscribe to psychoanalytic theory more broadly or be doing long-term psychotherapy to find utility in these constructs. Similarly, clinicians with a psychoanalytic orientation may find themselves working in a variety of settings that have specific requirements and guidelines that make it difficult to work in a standard psychoanalytic format. A clinic or an insurance carrier, for example, may only permit the client to be seen for a limited number of sessions. In such circumstances, the clinician's understanding of what is going on with the client is still a powerful and valuable resource, notwithstanding the fact that the therapist's contact with the client will be restricted by these parameters. Indeed, therapists' enhanced understanding of the client might make clearer what issues or conflicts should be the focus of their work under these specific circumstances. Similarly, psychoanalytic approaches are often critiqued as being more tailored to upper-class, educated, verbal clients and less appropriate for work with low-income or ethnically diverse populations. Notwithstanding these historical trends, psychoanalytic concepts and treatment modalities have always been used with a wide range of populations. In Freud's time, for example, psychoanalysts operated clinics for low-income clients, and psychoanalysts have run well-known psychoanalytically informed treatment programs for indigent mothers and their infants and toddlers. Similar efforts can be found in many parts of the country today. In fact, there are many present-day psychoanalytic writers theorizing about the psychological experience of race and class and how such sociocultural variables play a part in the formation of individual psychologies as well as how they come to reside within the therapeutic situation.

FINDING YOUR NICHE

There are a variety of interesting contemporary psychoanalytic theories and it is difficult to summarize these succinctly. However, most share a great many assumptions and their particular versions of psychoanalytic theory have almost without exception emerged out of debates within psychoanalysis as new ideas and concepts have entered the field. As you think about developing your own therapeutic style, it might be useful to review some of the psychoanalytic assumptions about personality theory and development, including how people's psychologies work and what motivates them to do what they do, and see how comfortable you are with them. You might also find it useful to think about the ways that psychoanalytic therapists approach their work. For example, are you comfortable thinking in terms of unconscious motivations and unconscious conflicts? Can you see yourself being a little less interactive and social with your clients? Do you find people's life stories inherently interesting such that you would find it gratifying to listen to clients describe their experiences? Or are you, instead, more inclined to want to make suggestions and be more directive in your interventions? These are some of the questions that might help you decide whether this is a treatment approach that fits with your personal style.

Because many beginning therapists have little real exposure to psychoanalytic ideas except for the highly abstracted summations found in textbooks, it may be difficult for you to grasp the deeply humanistic and creative aspects that many psychoanalytic practitioners find meaningful about their clinical work. However, this approach should be of great interest to therapists who enjoy the process of listening to others' stories, who find it intellectually rewarding to grapple with the complex puzzle of human emotions and human motives, who feel frustrated by highly manualized treatment approaches, and who find the process of being empathically engaged with individuals who are struggling with painful life concerns rewarding.

PROCESS AND CASE SUGGESTIONS

As you approach each of the three cases that are included in this book, try to think about a few of the psychoanalytic ideas that have been described. For example, ask yourself what the core conflicts are for that person and how they are managing them, including what defensive strategies appear to be at work. In thinking about transference and counter-transference, you might also wonder about how the client's conflicts might be entering the relationship with the therapist and how they might make you feel if that person were working with you. Finally, as you make inferences about each of these clients' current relationships, you should try to speculate about ways in which these might be related to their childhood relationships to key people in their development.

1. *Elena.* Elena is experiencing an acute crisis that is making her feel anxious, angry, and depressed. Several clear-cut, precipitating events are creating a great deal of anxiety for Elena. Can you identify them? To what extent are aspects of these feelings

unconscious? Why might she not be fully aware of these issues or what conflicting feelings might be interfering with her being able to understand these issues clearly? How would you go about trying to help her understand these struggles and what are the relative contributions of cultural issues, developmental issues, and other emotional conflicts? Although Elena has lots of people making suggestions as to how she should manage her situation, she appears to be in a deep quandary as to what to do. This might help you see how hard it can be for clients to resolve their concerns even when they are receiving well-intentioned advice.

2. *Jane.* Jane is encountering significant difficulties responding to a variety of issues that are affecting her, in large measure because she is quite disconnected from her emotional life. She is an excellent illustration of the relationship between psychosomatic symptoms and unconscious feelings. How might you go about helping her understand the source of these bodily symptoms that appear to have no medical basis? In her clinical interview, she notes numerous issues about which you would expect her to have strong feelings but which she doesn't seem to be able to really engage. What hypotheses do you have as to the origins of this need to disconnect herself from her emotions? Clients who use somatization as a means of managing their feelings are often frustrating for therapists and may elicit strong countertransference feelings. This is due to the fact that the closer the therapist gets to the client's emotional life, the more resistant the client may become. Can you recognize such countertransference feelings as you listen to Jane talk about her concerns? What other countertransference feelings do you experience and how might they be helpful to you in understanding her concerns and how you might respond to them?

3. *Theo.* Theo appears to be struggling with a great deal of unconscious anger. As you think about his description of his family as he was growing up, what clues does he give as to why he is so angry? He also appears to feel a great deal of tension and conflict regarding his sexual feelings. To what extent do you feel that shame and guilt are taxing his resources and interfering with his relationship with his girlfriend? Theo also does not find it easy to trust people. He presents material from his relationship with his girlfriend, his friends, and via his dreams that underscores his concern that people may not really be there for him or that they may not really be interested in understanding his feelings. Do you feel that you can empathize with what this must feel like? How might you use this to help him understand this mistrust and how might you expect to engage these issues in the context of the working alliance and the therapeutic relationship?

SUMMARY AND SUGGESTED READINGS

Psychoanalysis has long been one of the most influential theories and its assumptions have been incorporated into many other contemporary counseling approaches. Psychoanalytic theory has undergone a variety of reformulations in the years since its inception and today it is actually comprised of a variety of schools, including the classical perspective, object relations theory, self psychology, and the interpersonal and relational schools. The various psychoanalytic schools share certain assumptions that lie at the core of the theory. Foremost among these is the view that, notwithstanding our genetic makeup, as human beings we are profoundly affected by experiences with others that take place over the course of development, and the assumption that emotional conflicts and psychological symptoms often have a great deal to do with these experiences. In addition, there are a variety of key concepts, such as the dynamic unconscious, defenses, and the idea of intrapsychic structure that are shared by these varying psychoanalytic schools. These schools also work with related therapeutic concepts such as transference, countertransference, and the working alliance. While each has its own view of how therapy helps people get better, all subscribe, to greater or lesser degrees, to some combination of insight and the use of the therapeutic relationship.

Bridging the gap between theory and practice may be more difficult with psychoanalytic theory than it is with other theories in part because psychoanalytic theory is at once a developmental theory, a personality theory, and a theory of intervention. This means that an understanding of all three of these domains is optimal in order to understand how to implement psychoanalytic ideas within a therapeutic situation. The following list of references is not exhaustive, but those interested in learning more about psychoanalytic ideas and how they relate to clinical work will find them useful.

Ellman, S. (2002). *Freud's technique papers: A contemporary perspective*. New York: Other Press.

Greenberg, J., & Mitchell, G. (1983). *Object relations in psychoanalytic theory*. Cambridge, MA: Harvard University Press.

Levy, S. (1984). *Principles of interpretation*. New York: Jason Aronson.

McWilliams, N. (1994). *Psychoanalytic diagnosis: Understanding personality structure in the clinical process*. New York: Guilford Press.

McWilliams, N. (2004). *Psychoanalytic psychotherapy: A practitioner's guide*. New York: Guilford Press.

Pine, F. (1985). *Developmental theory and clinical process*. New Haven: Yale University Press.

Pine, F. (1990). *Drive, ego, object, and self*. New York: Basic Books.

Chapter 2

Analytical (Jungian) Psychology

Jeffrey Raff

Chapter Outline

Bridging the Theory-to-Practice Gap

Principles in Practice

Keys to Conceptualization

Interventions and Therapeutic Process

Short- and Long-Term Goals

Using the Relationship

Adapting the Approach

Finding Your Niche

Process and Case Suggestions

Summary and Suggested Readings

BRIDGING THE THEORY-TO-PRACTICE GAP

I have been a Jungian analyst for 30 years and enjoy the work today as much as I did when I began. There is no greater work than helping people understand who they are and learn how to become their authentic selves. Whether it is interpreting dreams or discussing complexes, there is rarely a dull moment. This is not to say that the work of the Jungian-oriented counselor is easy, because it can be difficult to understand Jung's theories and sometimes hard to know how to apply them. But despite the challenge, working with individuals is a privilege. If you do the work well you gain from each session just as the client does.

C. G. Jung developed analytical psychology over a period of 60 years, during which time he revised and reworked his ideas many times. Beginning as a student of Freud, Jung broke with the Freudian school over what he considered its overemphasis on sexuality. Over the next six decades he wrote on every imaginable topic that concerns the human soul and developed a rich and intricate system.

Today, analytical psychology has broken into several camps, each with a certain perspective and emphasis. This chapter presents the model as originally conceived by Jung and his early collaborators. This classical model is still one used by most Jungian analysts and recognized as the kernel of Jungian practice by a vast majority of practitioners.

Many people in the therapy business find themselves attracted to Jung, but perplexed by the difficulty of his theory. In particular, some come to believe that Jungian theory is good as theory, but not useful in practice. In fact, it is not always apparent how Jungian concepts such as synchronicity or his work on medieval alchemy have anything to do with the practice of the counselor. However, I have found that all his ideas, from that of the archetype to that of synchronicity, appear, sooner or later, in depth analysis. In this chapter I cannot show the relevance of all his ideas for practical work, but instead will show how to use the theory of complexes in counseling. However, to give you an idea of how the rest of his theory comes into play, the complex is rooted in the archetype, so that if you penetrate deeply into the complex you discover the archetype, which comes to be as important as the complex in understanding your process and dreams. As you study yourself or your client you discover that chance events occur that open new ways of understanding, and so it becomes useful for you to study the theory of synchronicity. Eventually, if you work with the personal unconscious you will encounter the collective unconscious, and having the capacity to make sense of the experience changes its quality and keeps you from being overwhelmed by touching such a deep inner place. It turns out that all of Jung's theories are interwoven and you cannot experience one without touching on the rest. So if you work with the complex in the ways discussed in this chapter you will discover for yourself the relevance of the rest of Jung's ideas. When you do, you will discover realms of inner life that are meaningful and which can enrich the rest of your life.

Jung's leading idea, and one to which I shall refer many times in this chapter, is that of individuation. He believed that each person is unique and driven by an instinctual urge to be his or her unique self. A person is psychologically healthy only so long as he or she follows the path to uniqueness, but if that path is blocked by inner complex or external interference, a person develops a neurosis or even psychosis. The goal of analysis is, therefore, to help each client unearth his or her individual self and then to find ways in which that self may be lived in the world. Jung embodied his belief in this idea by treating each case as new and different and declaring that he needed to discover a new psychology for each person with whom he worked.

With this emphasis on uniqueness, analytical psychology discounts the possibility of finding one treatment or technique that works for everyone. Instead, the practitioner faces the challenge of finding answers and methods that work for each individual. The emphasis is on listening to the answers that arise within the client. Some Jungian analysts and therapists also reject diagnosis and treatment plans, because the former is a nonspecific and nonindividual concept and the latter ignores the psyche of the client. In order to ascertain the client's own solutions, Jungians focus on dreams. Jungians believe that dreams contain important information that can guide the client to individuation and therefore to psychic health.

The use of dreams and the insistence on following the client's inner guidance makes working with individuals stimulating. However, there is much more to working with clients than analyzing dreams. In fact, many clients do not remember their dreams at all, and so you must find a different way to discover their inner voice and the situation of the unconscious.

From the earliest period of his work to the last, Jung was fascinated by what he termed "complexes." In the theory of the complex we discover the key to the therapeutic practice of analytical psychology. Jung put so much emphasis on the complex that analytical psychology was first known as complex psychology. Jung defined the complex as a grouping of psychic elements—parts of the psyche, such as feelings, memories, and images—centered on a nuclear element. The complex thus consists of a center formed of an image that gives the complex its meaning, and a large number of associated elements. For example, the mother complex has as its center the image of mother. Each person has a different picture of mother formed by experience and innate disposition. The image might be of a devouring witch or a loving, nourishing woman. The image at the center acts as a magnet, attracting other psychic material. For instance, if I have a witch at the core of the complex, I may perceive all women as witches, and each memory or bad experience I have of women attaches to the complex. Complexes are therefore dynamic, constantly growing by pulling new psychic contents into their sphere of influence. I shall discuss the theory of the complex at length in the next section. For now it is important to situate the complex within the individuation process.

Complexes, if too large and intrusive, prevent a person from becoming herself, since the complex blocks a more natural expression of the self. It is the task of the counselor to uncover the complexes and remove any obstructions they might be creating, thereby allowing the individuation process to flow naturally. On the other hand, complexes, if kept to normal size, open the door to the unconscious. If a particular complex becomes active, it challenges the client to deal with the issue around which a complex formed. If the client is brave and willing to face the issue she often experiences insight and transformation. In such a case, the complex actually spurs a person into taking actions that lead to growth. The positive side of the complex, then, is that it challenges you to grow and to deal with specific issues. Significantly, complexes contain not only repressed material but material from the unconscious that has never before been conscious. By attending to this material, the client is brought into closer relationship with the unconscious, allowing her to discover aspects of her inner self. Alternatively, the complex is destructive if it grows too large and therefore inhibits the client's ability to live fully and freely. In either case, analysis consists of dealing with complexes. How that might be done is the subject of the next section.

PRINCIPLES IN PRACTICE

Keeping in mind that our goal is to free the client to become her authentic self, our first objective is to discover what blocks exist that keep her from reaching this goal. There are frequently external blocks, as when other people make demands on her that keep her from attending to her own needs and desires. Elena's case illustrates this nicely. The parental demands on Elena to stay at home and care for her mother are creating tremendous pressure on her, because they conflict with what she wishes for herself. She must either act in what seems a selfish way or give up her dreams and stay at home. Both solutions are uncomfortable and she thus finds herself unable to follow her own natural path of development.

Often, of course, the blocks are within the person. In such cases it is the pressure of a complex that prevents the client from following an instinctual process. There may be no outward sign of blockage or the discomfort it creates, but symptoms ultimately may appear. Jane's case is a good example. On the face of it her life is fine, but she has psychosomatic heart problems. Such symptoms usually indicate the existence of a complex that has not been faced. Symptoms are often like dreams in that they are symbolic expressions of the complex and its contents. If Jane were to imagine what was hurting her heart so much, she might come up with an image that accurately reflects the complex. For this reason, I frequently ask clients to imagine their symptoms in order to gain more information about the nature of the complex that is connected to the problems.

In order to understand the practical application of complex theory it is necessary to offer some of its main features. I can only deal with the essentials here, and I recommend that the interested student pursue the study of complex theory and its therapeutic applications.

1. *Complexes are feeling-toned.* Initially, keep in mind that complexes are feeling-toned; that is, they create powerful emotions and emotional responses. When a complex is activated within your psyche, you feel disturbed and upset. Often you experience anxiety or compulsive behavior and find yourself acting in strange ways that are very disturbing but hard to avoid. To say a person is "in a complex" means that his normal ego has been taken over by the complex. In such a psychological state, he says and does things he later regrets. Theo's case demonstrates this aspect of complexes. He finds himself angry with people and especially with his girlfriend, or flooded with jealous thoughts that he cannot control and about which he subsequently feels regret. Without identifying the complex as yet, I can certainly say that he is in a complex at those moments. We have all experienced such states when, flooded with powerful feelings, we act out of control and say things we do not mean. At other times, depending on the complex, we might find ourselves unable to speak at all, and shy away from all contact without knowing why. The behavior associated with complexes is wide-ranging but typically involves uncontrollable feelings and

perceptions. Complexes, if large enough, even cause the strange ways of acting found in psychoses.

Complexes, however, are not only negative. They open the door to the unconscious and therefore to the possibility of accessing inner wisdom and guidance. Normally, complexes operate in the negative way, but in counseling they can begin to operate more positively. A person who has the courage to face the complex and work with it diligently often learns that, after a difficult period of dealing with old issues and conflicts, the complex begins to produce dreams or insights that are new and no longer related to personal history or childhood. In such a case we say that the client has touched the collective unconscious and the archetype. The feelings produced now are no longer disruptive or compulsive, but range from feelings of awe to those of inspiration and resolve. Such positive influences of the complex only come after sustained effort and can require a long therapeutic process that can sometimes last for years.

2. *Complexes are autonomous.* In addition to being feeling-toned, complexes are autonomous. To understand this concept you must remember that Jungians take the unconscious very seriously. The ego, or the center of consciousness, does not control everything that happens in the psyche. In fact, the ego probably controls very little. Therefore, when a complex is activated, it functions as something working outside conscious control. A person neither wills to be in nor wills not to be in a complex. Equally, a person cannot control his behavior while in the complex. It is as if the complex takes over the mental programming and programs exactly how it wants the person to behave and, without insight, the person behaves that way. Looking at our own behavior and the behavior of others, people we know and people in history, we discover that much of what we do comes from complexes. When working with clients it is important to keep this in mind. Good advice, common-sense solutions, or stern admonitions have no effect whatsoever on complexes and will not help your client cope with them.

3. *Mother and father complexes.* Analysts debate the question of how many complexes exist, but in my experience, there are a small number that you see repeatedly in working with people. The two most prevalent complexes are the father and mother. Complexes form around essential issues in life, and what could be more essential to a child than father and mother? Every human being has these complexes, though their nature differs widely. Complexes can be either positive or negative. Positive does not mean good but rather points to a positive relationship between the ego and the central image of the complex—that is, either father or mother figures. The quality of the complex derives not only from the parents, but from interactions with other people and situations. The father complex governs external world situations, in which you deal with authority figures, power issues, and the great challenge of finding your place in the world. Complexes are slightly different in men and women although, for the most part, their effects are the same. A negative father complex in a man makes him doubt his own power and authority, and may make him either hostile or too subordinate to authority figures. Whenever the man deals with job issues or people he finds intimidating, the complex will move into action and prevent the man from seeing clearly or acting as he normally would. Positive father complexes are very rare in a man. I worked with one such person in 30 years. He felt inspired

by his father, who was an artist, and sought to emulate him by also being an artist. When he realized that wasn't right he changed directions with little difficulty, feeling the support of the inner and outer father. But a positive complex is not all good. It often makes the man so content that he feels no urge to grow. He is content to do as his father did and to let things slide. Though more difficult, negative complexes help people grow more than positive ones.

A woman with a negative father complex has the same issues with authority and power, feeling inadequate and intimidated, or hostile and overbearing. She has trouble feeling she can be herself in the world and she also usually has trouble in relationships with men. She often treats a man as if he were her father, and she may oscillate between giving herself away to the man or trying to dominate him completely. Women with positive father complexes are not as rare and are confident and assured in the world and in relationships. In many cases, however, they create problems in relationships with men by seeking a man as perfect as they found their father, and finding that most men do not measure up. They may also assume a subordinate role to a man to make him into a father figure whom they can serve.

The mother complex governs the inner world, self-love, and relationships. A man with a negative mother complex has trouble with intimacy and may be overly critical. He desires the love of women, at the same time fearing that they will dominate or even devour him. He protects himself by shutting off feelings or being private and secretive. With a positive mother complex, a man is comfortable with women and enjoys their company and also feels content with himself and his feelings. He may ruin relationships by comparing every woman with his mother. Sometimes he lacks any real ambition and is happy to drift or even live off others. A woman with a negative mother complex finds it hard to like herself for she is afraid she is just like her mother. She may unconsciously adapt every attitude and behavior to resist or horrify mother, and she avoids anything mother wants. If the complex is severe she will reject her own femininity completely and despise anything she finds feminine. In this complex, women also find it difficult to support their own feelings or to trust them at all. With a positive mother complex a woman is happy with her self and her femininity and enjoys being like and with mother. However, she may live in mother's orbit so totally that she never learns about her own nature.

There are other complexes that are important, such as the money complex, sex complex, and complexes around food and body issues. I shall, however, use only the father and mother complex in the discussions that follow, as well as my analysis of the cases, for the sake of simplicity. These two complexes may appear in a variety of ways in different clients, but they should be recognizable despite the differences.

4. *Size of the complex.* Complexes also vary in the size and manner in which they disrupt someone's life. I will present several different possibilities that were first described by one of Jung's original followers, Jolanda Jacobi.[1]

In the first situation, the complex remains unconscious to the client and is not strongly activated. In this case it remains somewhat dormant but still blocks normal

---

[1] *Complex, Archetype, and Symbol in the Psychology of C. G. Jung*, 15–16

flow of life. For example, a man with a father complex finds himself uncomfortable with his boss and cannot find the courage to put forth his own ideas. Outside the situation with his employer, however, he is rarely disturbed by the complex.

In the second state, the complex has become swollen with psychic energy and competes with the ego for control of the personality. Such a person is neurotic and at war with herself and may experience compulsive behavior or other patterns related to borderline personality types. A major complex like the mother complex controls much of the person's behavior and attitudes. The size of a complex indicates how much of the psyche it controls. The counselor can usually determine this by observing the client's responses, but it may take time to uncover the true extent of the complex.

If the complex continues to grow, it reaches the third state and actually functions as an alternative ego. This duality of egos yields behavior associated with multiple personality disorder.

If the complex grows still further it may engulf the ego completely, resulting in temporary or permanent psychosis.

5. *Healing the complex.* Alternatively, the person may discover the nature of the complex and the ways in which it makes him behave. The counselor must provide this information. In this model the counselor takes an active role in explaining the complex and the ways in which it works. Although the client initially has only an intellectual awareness of the complex, it usually provides a degree of relief because he feels that he has uncovered a truth about himself that explains his behavior. The worst part of living in a complex is feeling crazy or not understanding your behavior. Having an explanation is a great relief. The client must, however, move beyond simple cognitive understanding to experience in a felt way the manner in which the complex operates in his life. With help from the counselor, most clients become adept in recognizing the complex and its patterns. The next step is to take action and resist the complex. Once you have recognized the pattern the complex produces, you must violate that pattern as often as possible. If, for example, a woman rejected her own femininity as a result of the mother complex, she must discover ways to accept that side of herself. At first this seems impossible, but, often with the help of the counselor and her own dreams, she discovers part of her feminine nature that she can relate to and slowly begins to build bridges to it and heal old wounds. This is slow work, requiring patience on the part of the counselor and client, and it forms the nitty-gritty of analytical work.

Keeping in mind our goal of helping the client become herself, it is necessary to recognize the dominating complex, the strength it has, and the behavior associated with it. Once this is known, the counselor helps the client recognize the patterns associated with it and, eventually, to break free of those patterns. Once the client manages to break free and, normally, when she is feeling well, the next complex arises. The whole process must be done over in exactly the same way. Usually the complex that appears second is far more difficult than the first because a person normally represses the most difficult issues. However, since the counselor and client have successfully dealt with the first complex, they usually feel confident about tackling the second.

Such therapeutic work requires that the counselor be familiar with complexes and the ways in which they operate. In addition, she must know ways in which they may be resisted. Listening well is the best method for discovering and fighting the complex, as we shall see in the next section.

KEYS TO CONCEPTUALIZATION

When a client comes through the door for the first time, the counselor takes a history and asks for the presenting concerns. As the counselor listens, she seeks to comprehend the patterns that the personal background reveals. I will illustrate the way this is done by using an example from my practice.

The client was a woman of 40 who had recently divorced. She was raising a nine-year-old girl and was happy with having divorced. She herself was a therapist but had not practiced for five years, and she was having trouble finding the motivation to begin again, though she needed the money. She had periods of depression, excessive drinking, and an acute sense that she would never succeed. In her history she explained that both parents were depressed as she grew up, but that she identified with her father most. He had committed suicide when she was 14, which was a terrible blow and caused her to feel responsible for his death. Shortly thereafter she began to act out sexually and was at odds with her mother. She was a creative and talented person but every time she began to excel in any way, she gave up the effort or sabotaged it. She had difficulty dealing with the world or feeling that she could charge people for her work since she wondered if she could ever actually help anyone. When the need arose to deal with worldly issues she avoided them and fell into a depression.

In listening to her story, I asked myself two questions: what type of person was she and what was the dominating complex? I felt that she was a creative woman who needed to find ways to safely express her creativity, and that she was most likely a good therapist who needed to make an effort to start her practice. Looking at her history, which complex would you identify as the one needing work first? Which is the most severe complex? Remembering that the father complex governs outer world situations we see that she has a negative father complex that blocks her efforts to deal with the world. It is fairly easy to recognize the patterns associated with this complex—her avoidance of worldly problems, her conviction that she cannot succeed—but to understand how to help her break free of the complex you must learn more about her experience with her father, her experiences in her profession, and her relationship to men. The more severe complex is actually the mother complex, though she said very little about mother. This is typical of the deeper, more repressed complex, because clients are often unaware that it exists as a problem for them. The primary complex, though less severe, is more conscious and is the one the client presents because she is more aware of how it affects her life.

In taking the client's history I always listen for the dominant complex and, when that is identified, the more damaging but less obvious complex also emerges. That is, if the father complex presents itself, the mother complex is more extreme and more unconscious and the opposite is true as well. The next concern is to determine the extent of the complex and in what areas it is affecting the client's life. The client's presentation reveals this information in a number of ways. Eliciting the history allows the client to discuss those problems of which she is aware. She may speak of relationship issues and problems at work. I generally allow the client to speak about whatever she wishes without interruption. I pay attention to what she says, how she says it, and how her body reacts as she is speaking. Complexes influence the choice of words as well as the body's posture and reactions. For example, the client may fidget when speaking of her husband, or begin to noticeably tremble or sweat when discussing food. Such reactions are termed complex indicators and there are a number to look for. Does the client stutter or perseverate—that is, does she repeat the same word or phrase? Does the client blush or suddenly stop talking? Pay attention to anything that seems out of the ordinary or unusual. I recall a client who laughed each time she touched on her pain. These signs all reveal that a complex has been activated. If you observe a complex indicator note the topic that elicited it and you will have a hint as to where the complex resides. Even if you have determined the dominant complex, you must next discover what other parts of the client's psyche are controlled by it. A large complex controls most of the psychic life of an individual and the counselor can map it by tracking the complex indicators. Notice, as one example, how Jane reacted when the counselor asked her about her sexual relationship with her husband. Clearly the question activated a complex.

It is equally important to pay attention to what the client has not said because this often reveals the hidden complex. Once the client finishes, I begin to ask questions about the things she failed to mention. I doubt, for example, that Jane would have brought up sexuality without being asked. With practice and attention to what the client says, how she says it, and her whole demeanor as she says it, the counselor can learn to spot complexes and some of their patterns within the first session or two. With this information the counselor is ready to face the question of how to work with this particular person.

INTERVENTIONS AND THERAPEUTIC PROCESS

From the Jungian perspective, the goal is to facilitate the individuation process through which a client becomes a whole person able to manifest in the world. The closer clients come to wholeness the more they exhibit healthy behavior both internally and externally. The work with the complexes, then, does not require that they be removed, but rather explored and made conscious so that their intrusive behavior is eliminated.

I would divide the work with complexes into three main stages. In the first, the client struggles to recognize the complexes and their influence on him. This is mostly a cognitive process in which the client learns the nature of the complex and the ways in which they determine his behavior and disrupt his life. During this phase, the counselor intervenes by explaining the complex and pointing out ways in which he notices its role in the client's life. The client speaks of his issues and problems as well as life events that occurred during the time right before the session, and the counselor not only listens but, at the appropriate time, points out what complex behavior took place. For example, a client discusses a fight with his wife over money (an all-time favorite!) and reveals that he grew so frustrated and angry he had to leave or get violent. The fact that he feels this anger in a relationship situation points to the mother complex and the counselor asks about his relationship to his mother. He replies that he got along with his mother, but the counselor asks him to give an example of getting on well and perhaps an example of when he did not get on so well with her. In my experience the greatest asset the counselor has is a good question. Many schools frown on asking questions but I find that it not only uncovers information but puts some pressure on the client to feel feelings and think deeply about his situation. It may be uncomfortable, but is a great way to bring up material from the unconscious.

If a client's responses belie the existence of a complex, ask questions. Do not judge or demand, but in a neutral way ask questions that seem relevant. In the above situation, with enough questions, it turns out that the client, in fact, feared his mother, who could be cutting and critical. His defense against her was to behave as she wished but inside he felt rage that he could not express. This anger comes out at his wife with whom he feels safe enough to express it, though here too he must leave after a short time. Of course, if we wanted to complicate the situation, we would address his money complex, which was also activated, and we would have to consider the complexes of the wife as well.

The counselor goes on to explain the complex and the behavior derived from it. After a few sessions, the client grasps the nature of the complex but is unable to control his behavior. This brings up the next phase of complex work, which moves from purely cognitive understanding to a felt sense. The counselor helps the client move to a deeper realization of the complex by discussing situations in which it occurs. The counselor probes the client's feeling-state and asks him to keep a record of the times he is in the complex and how it feels. Usually within a few months, the client experiences a deepening familiarity with the complex feelings and how to recognize them. When the client recognizes that he is entering a complex, he must "hold the tension," which means he must resist the complex pattern by refusing to follow it or by substituting some new behavior for it. The longer the client can resist the complex pattern, the freer he becomes of it, though this is by no means easy. If he begins to free himself from the pattern, however, new, healthier ways of behaving in the situation will become possible. Once he experiences choice instead of compulsion in a complex situation, the client has reduced the power of the complex to acceptable limits.

The most important part of complex work is holding the tension with the complex. Even if the client has no idea of how to escape the complex pattern, holding the tension stimulates what Jung called the transcendent function, which is a psychological mechanism that creates a new state of consciousness. If the client holds the tension with the complex, the transcendent function eventually comes into play, creating a new way of perceiving. Having experienced transformation, the client will often automatically deal with the complex situation in a new way. Thus, the most important intervention the counselor makes is helping the client recognize the complex pattern and then encouraging him to hold the tension. Holding the tension simply means refusing to act as he always acted. Being aware of the complex and its patterns provides the insight the client needs to break free, which permits real transformation to occur. After this transformation the power of the complex is greatly reduced.

Complex work is not a quick or easy form of therapy. It requires time and dedication on the part of the counselor as well as the client.

SHORT- AND LONG-TERM GOALS

The short- and long-term goals of Jungian work blend together. The long-term goal is to enable the client to discover her authentic nature and to express it in the world. In order to accomplish this task, the client must deal with her complexes. Dealing with complexes consists of first making them conscious and then holding the tension by resisting their patterns. If the client succeeds in accomplishing these tasks, the transcendent function comes into play, transforming her state of consciousness. As her consciousness alters, her sense of self does so as well. Whenever the transcendent function occurs, the individual experiences a transformation that brings her closer to her inner self. Thus the short-term goal of dealing with the complexes sets the stage for the long-term goal of becoming herself.

At the practical level, this makes working with the complexes of the greatest significance. Only by dealing with the complexes and helping the client develop the courage to hold the tension with them does the counselor move the client closer to the inner self. Therefore, the counselor pays the strictest attention to discovering the complex patterns, making them conscious to the client, and supporting the client as she struggles to fight their compulsive influence. The whole process may repeat itself with each complex and, depending on the client, each complex might take considerable time to master. Patience is required, as is a good understanding of the nature of complexes and the way they work. In addition, and perhaps most importantly, the counselor must trust the natural process of the psyche. No solution is anywhere near as good as the one created by the transcendent function, and while this function may seem mysterious, once the counselor witnesses its power he will trust it completely.

Because of the power of the complexes and the need to understand them, Jungians always undergo their own counseling before working on other people. There are many reasons for this, not the least of which is that experiencing the complexes and the transcendent function in yourself is the greatest training for working with other people.

USING THE RELATIONSHIP

The relationship between the therapist and the client is special. It is not like any other relationship. Analytical psychology terms this special relationship transference and countertransference. I am not addressing the theoretical nature of this relationship here, but the practical aspects of it. As I do so it is a good idea to keep in mind how significant this relationship is for both parties in creating a transformative environment.

In my experience it is very important to like your clients. This may seem obvious but it is not always so. In certain situations the counselor has no choice but to work with whomever walks through the door. Inevitably, you deal with people you don't always like, but it is important to have some positive feeling toward them. At the very least you should respect them as individuals. I have known counselors who talked about their clients with great scorn or with a condescending attitude. Such an attitude actually poisons the counseling environment. The feeling a counselor has toward a client is termed countertransference and it is wise to be aware of countertransference issues, because they influence how you treat your clients. If, for example, a counselor has not worked on his mother complex and a client triggers that complex, it is very difficult for him to do good work with that individual. If he has had his own counseling and recognizes what is happening, the situation is tenable. However, if he is unaware that he is in a complex with the client, his reactions will not be in the client's best interest. One of the requirements for having a good relationship with clients is to know yourself and to know where your personality ends and that of the client begins. Having proper boundaries is essential as a counselor.

If the counselor likes the client and enjoys working with her, the client senses it. The client feels met and *seen* and this helps create the transference. In transference, the client *transfers* a powerful part of her psyche onto the counselor. A man with a negative father complex may transfer the positive father image onto the counselor, seeing in him the father he never had. He hangs on every word, takes every suggestion, and feels criticized or approved of depending on how the counselor responds. The power in this relationship is great and it must be used with care. If the counselor treats the client with respect, explaining complexes and their effect, offering suggestions about how to deal with them and how to recognize them, the client responds. The transference gives the client courage, a positive sense of self, and a willingness to endure the therapeutic process.

Every client is different and the counselor must adapt his approach to fit a particular individual's needs. He can be honest and confront one, while having to be gentle and supportive with another. In one case he can openly discuss the complex and in another he cannot. Paying attention to the needs of a client, and working with that client in a way that meets her needs, proves not only more effective therapeutically but creates trust and a solid relationship between client and counselor. Instead of forcing all clients to fit one mold, the effective counselor allows them to find their own style of working. The client's working style must also fit the counselor, and if it does not, then the counselor should not work with that client. If both people are comfortable with the therapeutic style and relationship there is a strong chance of transformation.

Even in short-term work, transference is a major tool in creating a successful therapeutic outcome. It is important to recognize the positive value of the therapeutic relationship but, at the same time, to treat it with great respect. In the eyes of the client the counselor is never just an ordinary person, but one endowed with special qualities and value. Used well, the transference supports the client in his endeavors to free himself from the unwanted effects of the complex, but, used carelessly, it can cause great harm. One must always be mindful of the relationship in counseling and take care that it suits the needs of the client. One part of tending the relationship is to adapt the particular approach that is required.

ADAPTING THE APPROACH

Paying attention to the client allows you to adapt your approach to fit the situation. Some clients have more insight than others into their psychological situation; some are more intelligent while some have a greater capacity for feeling. Working with feelings with a person who is out of touch with them requires great care. I learned this when trying to get a man I worked with to attend to how a particular complex felt to him. He simply did not know what I was talking about. I tried to be helpful by saying, "Tell me how you feel right now." He could not because he had no idea how to feel his feelings and got frustrated and angry with me. I had to change course completely and work with more intellectual concepts. Then he relaxed again. As mentioned, every client is different. If you have one agenda for all, you will fail with many. I remember it was fashionable at one time for counselors to help all their male clients feel and get in touch with their feminine side. While a good idea, such sweeping generalizations work poorly in counseling. Pushing a client in a direction he is not ready to take always creates problems. One discovers the psychic state of the client and how he functions, and then one works with his strengths rather than his weaknesses. Because of the power of the therapeutic relationship most clients try very hard to please the counselor and if the counselor expects changes the client cannot experience, the client suffers a great deal. In dream work, you learn that each client has his own dream vocabulary and you cannot interpret the dream correctly without taking that into consideration. It is the same with every aspect of the client's personality for each client is unique. Since the goal of this approach is to encourage that uniqueness, it is the task of the counselor to honor that as much as possible.

Every client has a different way of perceiving and functioning and each has a different cultural and ethnic background. Naturally these differences require the counselor to find a way to communicate well with the client. I have worked with individuals of different ethnic groups, different ages, and different religious orientations, and I have discovered that each of these variables makes a significant impact on how the client perceives what I am saying. To cite an obvious example, you do not normally criticize a parent to someone from China as the parent culturally is supposed to be held in great respect. To speak about the father complex, therefore, I had to find a different vocabulary than the one I normally used. While doing the initial interview the counselor should begin to formulate ideas about the language of the client and recognize any need to change her normal way of speaking. The key to such flexibility is finding a comfortable way to work as a counselor.

FINDING YOUR NICHE

There is nothing so important in counseling as finding a comfort zone for performing therapy. No one can do all kinds of counseling or work comfortably with every client. One discovers that one has a liking for a particular form of counseling and for some types of clients. I have friends who enjoy working with psychotics, while I do not. Others specialize in working with anorexics or the obese, and so on. When first beginning work with people, it is advisable to work with as many types of clients as possible to gain experience and to discover the work for which you are most suited. It is also a good idea to experiment with different approaches as well.

Analytical psychology normally works best for longer-term counseling and, while the concept of complexes certainly applies in short-term work, to actually transform the complex may take considerable time. If you prefer short-term work this is probably not the approach for you. In addition, since this approach emphasizes the client's uniqueness and frowns on a formulaic approach, there is considerable ambiguity in how to work with individuals. I have known counselors who could not tolerate such ambiguity and preferred approaches that explained what to do and how to do it in every case. If you do not think you would like following the client's process without always knowing where you are headed, this is not a good approach for you. This approach also involves a good amount of intervention as well as discussion about the nature of complexes and how to work with them, so those who prefer less intervention and less discussion might not want to adopt it.

There are other dimensions to this approach that I do not cover in this chapter. Dream work adds a fascinating dimension to working with individuals, though it requires a good deal of study as well. The exploration of the collective unconscious and archetypes allows you to study not only the nature of human life as it applies to clients but also to understanding the world. However one embraces Jungian work, it demands study, the exploration of your own psyche, and a commitment that should not be undertaken lightly.

On the other hand, if you have the time to invest in your clients and have as your goal their transformation into the person they could be, this approach is very rewarding. There is nothing more satisfying than watching clients change, become less conflicted and more able to express themselves, and find the confidence they need to live successfully in the world. To understand fully the nature of complexes requires a good deal of study and a willingness to work on your own issues. Following this approach requires constant self-examination and a commitment to do your own work, but in the end, often to your surprise, you discover that you have changed at least as much as your client.

PROCESS AND CASE SUGGESTIONS

Applying this theory to the three cases on the website is both interesting and fun. Having only one interview, the task is more difficult but manageable. The questions that I ask while looking at the video are: Which complex is easiest to observe? What might the hidden complex be? How severe do the complexes appear? Does the client offer any hints on how to work with the complexes? How do I imagine working with this client? And, finally, would I like to work with this individual?

1. *Jane*. Jane's case illustrates how a complex may produce physiological consequences. In many cases, illnesses both physical and psychosomatic derive from complexes, especially repressed ones. Jane's case as well reflects the situation of a person who has little insight into her own psychological situation and issues. This lack of attention to her feelings has led to psychosomatic issues. In dealing with her case, it is thought-provoking to imagine how you might work with her, since she is very guarded and wishes to present herself as someone who is happy with no real problems.

2. *Elena*. Elena's case illustrates several issues young people have in breaking away from home, but it is complicated by cultural issues. This is a case in which understanding cultural factors is essential because it is important not to judge either her or her family. You cannot simply put pressure on her to break away from her family without alienating her. Her case also illustrates the way a positive complex works, for she loves her mother and her family very much but risks losing her freedom to them. Positive complexes grow out of situations in which the individual and the parent love each other, which, on the face of it, is a good thing. However, often the

love acts as a force preventing the child from emancipating appropriately. It is tempting to identify with the parents and make the same choices they do. Elena resists this pull, which is to her credit, but clearly she is conflicted and her ultimate choice remains in doubt. Counseling in this situation could be instrumental in helping her individuate while remaining comfortable in her family and culture.

3. *Theo.* Theo's issues grow out of his dysfunctional family and the way in which his parents modeled violent, angry behavior. Unlike Elena, he is not comfortable in his family, though he remains close to his brothers. The violence that erupts uncontrollably in him illustrates the way in which a strong complex can take over the personality and create feelings and behaviors that later are rejected. At the time, however, they are compelling and difficult to resist. As an outsider who feels alienated and alone, Theo has trouble finding other models of behavior that would depotentiate the complex. However, his willingness to enter counseling, even though motivated by his girlfriend, is a good sign. Counseling could help him a great deal by showing him the nature of his complex and alternative ways to act.

There are certain questions that one might ask while listening to the interviews. What complex did you notice during the presentation? Are both complexes present or only one? Does the person offer any solutions to them? I also always ask myself if I like the person and the way she presents herself. Ask yourself if you like Jane? Why or why not? Would you enjoy working with her? What about Theo and Elena? Your reactions to the person during the initial interview are often just as important as observing their reactions. Finally, what patterns do you observe in the presentations? Patterns often tell you where the complex lies. For instance, Theo says several times that his girlfriend is a "good girl." What might this mean to him and does it point to a complex? Elena repeatedly states that no one listens to her—does this motif reflect a complex and how would it impact the way you worked with her? Learning to recognize patterns is the key to discovering complexes as well as possible solutions to them.

SUMMARY AND SUGGESTED READINGS

The theme of this chapter has been the complex. Analytical psychology seeks to help an individual uncover the complex, bring it to awareness, and reduce its debilitating effects. Once this is accomplished, the client becomes the person she was born to be and gets in touch with her inner values and directions. I have emphasized the complex because it forms the center of the counseling process. Though dream work is a central part of Jungian analysis, the focus on the complex applies even when dream work is used. If you apply the theory of the complex to the three cases, you will get a feel for how analytical psychology functions in the counseling context. However, skill in recognizing complexes and working with them takes time and effort. It is important to have supervision as you learn these skills. It is also highly recommended that you have your own therapeutic process. Knowing your own complexes is by far the best preparation for working with other people. If you do not recognize your own complex, how will you recognize the complex of the client?

Applying the complex model to the three cases will help you to ground the material presented in this chapter in an actual situation. It is also informative to observe the complexes of people around you and how they influence behavior. A good counselor observes well and pays attention to everything about the person observed, especially repeated phrases, patterns, and unusual behavior.

Continued study is also very important. Combining observation with theoretical study provides a good combination. Unfortunately, there is no way to make Jungian work easy. I always recommend that people read Jung himself but, as his work is difficult, this is not always possible. The best book of his to begin with is *The Structure and Dynamics of the Psyche,* in which he outlines all the essentials of his theory, from dream work to complex theory. Jolanda Jacobi's book, *Complex, Archetype, and Symbol,* is a wonderful introduction to the theory of the complex and its importance. June Singer's work, *Boundaries of the Soul,* introduces the reader to analysis and the way in which it is conducted.

These are but a few of the many books written on analytical psychology. Jung himself wrote over 20 books, and other students of his work have added many more. Exploring the world of the complex and the unconscious is fascinating and enriches your work with people immeasurably. I encourage any who find this approach compelling to continue to study it. At the same time I repeat that experience is the best teacher and makes the theory your own.

Jung said that the doorway to the unconscious was the complex. It might equally be said that the royal road to understanding clients, the behavior of people in general, and the nature of history lies in the complex. In this chapter I have only been able to touch on the way in which complexes determine behavior and the powerful struggle to escape from them. Even more important than the ways in which the complex determines behavior is the way in which consciousness and selfhood are born from the struggle against them. To whatever degree you help a person find freedom from the complex, you help her become a whole, strong person, and there can be no greater goal than that in the profession you have chosen to follow. I have listed below the three books mentioned as well as three others for further reading.

Von Franz, Marie Louise. (1991). *Dreams.* Boston, Mass: Shambhala. Distributed in the U.S. by Random House.

Von Franz, Marie Louise. (1996). *The interpretation of fairy tales.* Boston: Shambhala.

Jacobi, Jolanda. (1971). *Complex, archetype, and symbol in the psychology of C. G. Jung.* Bollingen Series. Princeton, NJ: Princeton University Press.

Jung, C. G. (1969). *The structure and dynamics of the psyche.* Bollingen Series. Princeton: Princeton University Press.

Jung, C. G., & Jaffe, Aniela. (1989). *Memories, dreams, reflections.* Aniela Jaffe, Ed. New York: Vintage.

Singer, June. (1972). *Boundaries of the soul.* Garden City: Doubleday.

Chapter 3

Adlerian Psychology

Mary Frances Schneider

Chapter Outline

Bridging the Theory-to-Practice Gap

Principles in Practice

Keys to Conceptualization

Interventions and Therapeutic Process

Short- and Long-Term Goals

Using the Relationship

Adapting the Approach

Finding Your Niche

Process and Case Suggestions

Summary and Suggested Readings

References

BRIDGING THE THEORY-TO-PRACTICE GAP

Adlerian psychology, also known as individual psychology, is as much a philosophy of life as it is a school of psychology. Based on the work of Alfred Adler, individual psychology appeals to me because of Adler's optimistic stance regarding the individual's creative role in addressing the challenges of life as well as Adler's focus on the role of social interest in living a satisfying life.

Adler's commonsense perspective looked at mental health as a set of life task challenges that face each of us. Healthy individuals create a place and a way of belonging that is satisfying to the self and collaborative with others in each life task area: work, social community, and love/sex.

So take a moment and ask yourself, has it been your life experience that you are challenged to develop meaningful work? Challenged to develop friendships and social relationships? Challenged to define your sexuality and create a collaborative life with a partner? Do you also feel challenged to learn your own operating instructions and making meaning of this life?

According to Adler, mental health involves responding to each life task challenge in creative and personally satisfying ways while taking into account what is also good for others. Unhealthy movement is viewed as egocentric in nature—self-involved and inconsiderate of the needs of others. Unhealthy behavior is devised by the individual to reduce feelings of inferiority, to seek superiority over others, and to dodge the challenges presented by the life tasks.

Adler stressed the creativity of the individual as the author of his or her own life. Rejecting the determinism of Freud, Adler held that our movement was much less determined by our past and much more influenced by our pull toward future goals. This teleological or goal-oriented perspective means that individuals experience life as an attraction toward or pull toward creating the future in each life task area. Now ask yourself, don't you experience life this way? Aren't you constantly pulled toward actively creating your visions and dreams in each life task area?

How do each of us learn how to respond to the life task challenges? We respond through patterns of behavior that Adlerians call the lifestyle (LS). The lifestyle patterns are the individual's conscious and unconscious ways of operating in each life task area—patterns that we learn and create in our family constellation.

It is in our first social context, the family constellation, that each individual creates a blueprint for how to find a place with others. We create this blueprint using our private logic from observing the patterns and values modeled by our parents; our birth order and our struggles with our siblings; and the influences of extended family and culture. This blueprint or lifestyle holds conscious and unconscious ideas about how we find our place with others (belong); about the life goals we form and our modes of operation in achieving these goals (purpose); as well as our core beliefs about ourselves and others. We use these life style patterns to address the life tasks. Some patterns work beautifully while others get us into trouble.

Therapeutic change for Adlerians involves a process of awakening to the patterns of the lifestyle that surface though our unsatisfactory attempts to address life task challenges. The client is helped to create reflective space to consider old patterns of reacting and is invited to actively create new patterns of choice—patterns that honor the individual's gifts, talents, and desired goals as well as promote the good of the whole group involved in the specific life task area. Social interest suggests that in each life task area we make a contribution that is unique to our gifts and talents while at the same time contributing to the welfare of the entire group. Adler understood that we were a global society—insight that is both prophetic and filled with social idealism. Adler understood that every person, regardless of gender, race, or socioeconomic level, desires to achieve personal mastery through the actualization of his or her gifts. The rise of the women's movement and the push for racial inclusion bear out this principle. For Adlerians, social interest encompasses a type of socialistic humanism that looks to human behavior and choice as a part of the evolutionary process.

It is a paradox that while Alfred Adler's name is not well known, many of his ideas form the foundational scaffold of current psychological thought. Besides the concepts of lifestyle, social interest, and goal orientation, Adler gave us ideas like birth order, compensation, overcompensation, masculine protest, aggressive drive, and the inferiority complex. Adler advocated for the prevention of mental health problems through group peer support. He developed family education centers where individuals and families could share life's challenges learning reflective practices that optimized social interest as well as individual development.

PRINCIPLES IN PRACTICE

Adlerians view therapy as a learning process—a process of moving from the state of "felt minus" to the state of "felt plus" in addressing challenges brought by the life tasks. The practice of Adlerian therapy has four stages: (1) establishing the client-therapist relationship; (2) collaborating to understand the client's lifestyle and patterns of movement; (3) generating insight into useful and less useful lifestyle patterns; and (4) anchoring a reorientation of lifestyle choices to the client's current life task challenges. During these stages the Adlerian therapist will help the client cultivate changes that focus on these key principles:

- The ways the client belongs with others (the client's social roles) in the life tasks of work, community, sex/love; as well as the degree of social interest the client exhibits towards others in these life task areas
- The purpose of the client's behavior—the goals of the client's behavior and the modes of operation employed by the client to achieve these goals
- The lifestyle beliefs and the private logic of the client regarding beliefs about the self (self-concept); beliefs regarding how we should function in each life task area (self-ideals); beliefs about how others "should be" and how life "should operate" (worldview); and beliefs about the nature of right and wrong (ethical convictions)

During the initial session, I expect that everything clients do or do not do, say or do not say, including their attitude, appearance, movements, and conversation, will offer clues to their private logic: their way of belonging (finding a place), their movement toward goals, and their beliefs about how the self and others "should" operate. I know the client has come to therapy because he or she is feeling inferior to the life challenge that faces him or her. I know that this "felt sense" of inferiority drives the fear, worry, and anxiety that the client is experiencing.

Adlerians believe we are challenged in life because our beliefs about "who we are" clash with beliefs about "who we should be" or "how life should operate" and thus we experience a felt sense of inferiority—not being up to the task of solving the problem. Therefore, I begin to wonder what beliefs clients might hold that are generating this sense of inferiority? I also wonder how clients are compensating for feelings of inferiority? Is it through denial, distancing, excuses (which are usually offered with the phrase "yes, but"), or through overcompensation, postures of superiority, forcing their way, or even useful problem-solving that has been dismissed too quickly. I am curious about the stories clients can tell me regarding the way they have addressed this same life task challenge in the past. I am interested in their methods, goals, degree of satisfaction, and amount of social interest displayed in these memories.

Listening to the client's presenting stories with the Adlerian principles in mind deepens my understanding of the client's current challenge and weaves a bond of rapport with the client. Rapport rests on my ability to understand the client's challenge as well as recognize my own skill level in supporting this type of client with this specific set of challenges. As a therapist, knowing what I do well helps me establish goodness of fit with the client as well as signals when consultation, supervision, or referral are of value.

In this initial phase, I come to understand the client's dilemma and coping style (from the client's point of view) as well as seek to establish the client's preferred line of movement. I ask the Adlerian question—"If I had a magic wand and could make this problem go away with a wave of that wand, what would be different?" This type of preference question helps establish the client's line of preferred movement—the general direction of the "felt plus" (which will be discussed shortly).

The second component of therapy is to investigate and come to agreement on the client's lifestyle patterns and the relationship between these patterns and the presenting problem. During this phase of therapy, the therapist and client collaborate to develop an understanding of the dynamic movement of the client. It is during this phase of therapy that many therapists employ the formal process of the lifestyle inventory (LSI). The lifestyle inventory process is an in-depth social history. Like autobiography, the LSI asks the client to recall early life stories and generates information regarding the client's beliefs about themselves (self-concept); beliefs about what they "should be" (self-ideal); meanings and values regarding aspects of the world in general (worldview); and values regarding moral behavior (ethical convictions).

During the LSI process, clients share information and stories that paint a picture of the dynamics of their early years. Clients are asked in-depth questions regarding siblings' identifying traits; the composition and values in the family constellation; the dynamics of birth order; their childhood physical development and early school experiences; their socialization with peers; their awakening to sexual information and gender identity; their observations regarding parental values and behavior (guidelines); the nature of the family atmosphere; the qualities present in the parental relationship; the spiritual values and practices; as well as socioeconomic and cultural influences.

The myriad of stories generated by the client on these topics are organized by the therapist into a working summary called the *family constellation*. This family constellation summary describes the first society in which the client found a place: the family atmosphere and values, the parental guidelines, and the interactions; sibling roles, type of roles, the client cultivated, the challenges of these roles, the client's goals and modes of operation—ways of getting these needs met.

The second aspect of the lifestyle inventory involves collecting the client's early recollections. Early recollections (ERs) are vivid memories generated before the age of eight or nine that the client can recall as if they were a mental videotape or DVD. These memories generate a set of early convictions that include both basic mistakes and basic assets. The cognitive distortions of these early generalizations involve such things as "overgeneralization," "false or impossible goals of security," "misperceptions of life and life's demands," "minimization or denial of one's worth," "faulty values" (Mosak 2005, p. 70) as well as sets of basic abilities, aptitudes, and gifts.

The LSI is an extremely bonding experience between therapist and client. It is, in essence, the sharing of the early years. This information highlights the client's private logic, roles, goals, patterns, and preferred modes of operation. Often the summary generates a character profile—a personality pattern that we term a typology. This pattern helps the therapist understand the rigid roles the client uses to find a place in this world, how the client operates with others, how the client moves through life, scene by scene, with certain purposes and expectations. No typology or pattern is right or wrong—it is all in the use of the typology and the degree of social interest demonstrated by the user. Examples of common typologies include: getting, controlling, pleasing, fixing, rescuing, driving/pushing, and excitement seeking.

It has been my experience that the lifestyle process fosters awakening as clients assume an observer perspective toward their life. Identifying and observing old reactive patterns helps clients suspend the desire to "react" and encourages them to stop all action and reflect. Often doing nothing (certainly not doing the old familiar patterns) is the first step in the process of active change. During this phase, we are helping clients step back and look at their life stories with the intent of making personal meaning of these stories. We are helping clients watch themselves as well as others—watch and evaluate what it means to be this way. As clients awaken to the reflective task of observing their own life story, they begin to "see" their role in the challenge of the presenting problem. They begin to awaken to their part in life's drama—the way inferiority feelings generate methods of coping.

The third aspect of therapy involves harvesting clients' gifts, creativity, and preferences and encouraging clients to use their new insights as they begin to experiment with preferred modes of action—most especially in the face of the presenting problem. Clients are ready to move away from old automatic reactive patterns because they are becoming aware that these patterns result in a "felt minus" and contribute only to feelings of inferiority. During this stage of therapy clients have decreased "reactive" patterns and with the encouragement of the therapist begin to create a plan of action that enhances their preferences and gifts. Once they have planned options and considered possible consequences, clients are encouraged to experiment in real life by taking action. Often these first attempts at personalized solutions feel awkward because they are actively facing feelings of inferiority. After taking action, clients are encouraged to reflect on the results and meaning of these new actions. At this point in the process, the therapist beings to actively encourage clients to cultivate practices of self-reflection. Meditation, prayer, journaling, and peer support are all practices that open reflective space for the client to continue the work of living a meaningful life.

During this phase of therapy the most important new choices and "as if" experimentations involve cultivation and development of the client's most authentic values, gifts, and abilities. Therapy focuses on experimentation with these assets in ways that allow the clients to experience the beauty of their true self within the frame of social interest. This focus on the "felt plus" side helps clients claim and actualize aspects of the self that might have only been vague dreams.

The fourth aspect of therapy is the process of "reorientation." During this phase, client and therapist collaborate to help the client solidify, integrate, and normalize the emerging lifestyle choices. This is also a period in which client and therapist consider the ways that the old lifestyle patterns might creep back into the client's thoughts and actions. This phase involves anchoring new choices and becoming aware of how mistaken beliefs continue to inform us all about the need for ongoing reflective space for preferred choice. At the reorientation phase, clients understand the value of inspecting life choices and patterns. They are working with a new set of tools—tools that foster reflection as well as exercise new beliefs. Reflection and choice make life more challenging, but also more satisfying. Every life task area seems to offer more options, more creative choice, and more challenge. During this phase, the client begins to own the value of self-reflection as a process that helps catch old reactive patterns and offers space to consider and plan value-based preferences. Life as experienced in each life task area is more creative, enriching, and filled with responsibility, choice, and satisfaction.

During this phase of therapy, I am interested in helping the client develop steady and reliable patterns of self-reflection; deepen the paths of self-discovery and creativity; own methods for attending to self-care; and commit to principles and practices that foster self-management. During this phase many clients commit to communities of concern (i.e., Alcoholics Anonymous, Al-Anon; mindfulness groups, gender-based groups, spiritual communities) that help deepen practices of self-care and self-development. These practices cultivate methods of self-coaching that anchor personal transformation.

KEYS TO CONCEPTUALIZATION

When I begin to conceptualize a case, I focus on three basic principles of individual psychology: *socialization (the way the client seeks to belong), goal orientation (the line of movement or purpose chosen by the client), and cognitive beliefs (the meanings and values demonstrated by the client)*. During and between sessions, I ask myself strategic questions regarding these three constructs. I feel that clients select particular stories (events) from their lives to discuss in therapy because these stories demonstrate both the struggles they are experiencing, and also the beliefs, attitudes, roles, and goals they are using to create a life. These stories have plot lines that involve the participation of other characters, the challenges of other points of view, and the possibility of choices that foster either a sense of positive movement (creative unfolding—in Adlerian terms, the *felt plus*) or a sense of negative movement (failure, stagnation, or what Adlerians term the *felt minus*). In these stories clients experience feelings of inferiority—dissatisfaction regarding their ability to address the problem. These stories open a window for the therapist to view the client's private logic regarding belonging, personal goals, and beliefs.

Focusing on the *client's socialization (way of belonging)* is an essential element of Adlerian theory. Alderians hold that all of us—in our own unique ways—are socially embedded. We each find meaning as a part of a social network. Adlerians believe that the family constellation is the individual's first and primary socialization experience. Often, the roles clients construct in the family of origin (such as hero, victim, placater, entitled one, mediator) are the same roles they continue to seek throughout life in other social settings. These automatic ways of belonging are the ways they "find a place" with others. Only over time do they come to realize that these roles cause life task challenges.

The family is the individual's first society. Adlerians view neurosis as a distortion in a person's social view, so I ask myself how clients choose to belong in social settings. What place do they seek and find with others in the life tasks of work, social relationships, love/sex? Under what conditions do they feel that they do or do not belong? With what kind of people do they identify? What roles did they play in their childhood, with siblings, peers, and authority figures and how do these roles surface in their current social interactions? What modes of operation guide their sense of belonging? Are they sick and tired of any specific role? Attracted to some other way of being? And most important of all, how does social interest (the good of the whole group) figure into the way they have exercised interpersonal roles? How do they express social interest in their modes of belonging or is self-interest paramount?

Focusing on the concept of *goal orientation (teleological or goal-oriented movement),* Adlerians believe that people are choosers. Each individual is a creative problem-solver and problem-solving involves movement toward particular goals. Each person is much more driven by goals (unconscious or conscious goals) than determined by physical or environmental variables. Individuals create their current experiences because they are pulled toward some personal fiction, goal, or desire. They hold out ideals and create their lives as they move toward those ideals.

I am constantly asking myself what the client's "line of movement" is in this specific story. Toward what value are clients moving and for what purpose? Are they avoiding a life task? What is the purpose of their behavior and symptoms? How does purpose relate to the presenting problem? How is their purpose useful as well as not useful (what effects does it have on both the self and on others)? What is their striving all about? Does it have anything to do with past roles? What fictions might they be holding about themselves that keeps this line of movement activated? Has this line of movement been a rewarding way of striving in the past? What are the values behind this line of movement? What is their response when I ask their lines of preferred movement? Have they been able to make pre-ferred choices that develop their gifts and talents?

The *cognitive (meaning-making and lifestyle)* aspect of the theory holds that individuals create their own subjective interpretation of life events based on their own private logic. Toward that end, as a therapist I am interested in gathering the clients' cognitive map—the set of self-defeating and self-enhancing beliefs that they have been using to face current life challenges. Clashes in beliefs generate "inferiority feelings"—that is, a sense of not being "up to" handling the general life task challenge. The lifestyle assessment helps generate their beliefs regarding the self, the self-ideal, their "picture of the world," and their ethical beliefs. These beliefs are then discussed in terms of the presenting problem.

The symptoms of the presenting problem serve to stop authentic movement or to sidestep authentic movement in the life task areas of work, social relationships, and sex/love. Clients bring the presenting problem to therapy for purposes of reflection—to create space before the next chosen action. Thus, they come to therapy usually at the crisis point in a personal plot line—in their own line of movement. They seek therapy because they already sense a need for reflective time so that the next set of choices will result in a more satisfying experience in any or all of the life task areas.

INTERVENTIONS AND THERAPEUTIC PROCESS

The majority of tactics that Adlerians advocate are insight and action-oriented interventions. Mosak and Maniacci (1998) offer the beginning therapist a bountiful menu of basic Adlerian tactics. Three key interventions include the lifestyle inventory process, the use of early recollections, and the use of dreams.

The lifestyle inventory (Mosak and Shulman) is the central technique used in most individual and couples work. It is a detailed early autobiography, which asks the client to recall stories and descriptions of childhood experiences during the first eight years of life. This information investigates and gathers information regarding siblings childhood physical development; traumatic experiences; school experiences; childhood fantasies and the meaning given to life; childhood gender and sexual information; social relationships; the guidelines, attitudes, and preferences of the parents; the nature of the parental relationship; religious and cultural family values; and the presence of any additional parental figures.

The outcome is a story of the client's life in order to make sense of it. This history is bonding and generative for both therapist and client.

The lifestyle information is assembled into a summary of the family constellation. This summary details the way clients found their place in the family of origin and highlights family values and the general methods of operation (ways of moving) that the client and others in the family used to move toward their goals.

Early recollections—detailed memories of events before the age of eight—are collected in the second phase of the LSI process. These form the core of the client's current self-concept, self-ideal, mode of operations, and ethical beliefs. They are summarized and organized into two sets: interfering convictions and assets.

The early recollections are a rich source of therapeutic material. Their images and metaphors are powerful visual tools to remind clients of values and choices they desire to move toward or away from. Adlerians use a wide variety of techniques to mine the ERs in therapy. They are investigated using reframing methods, journaling, role playing, improvisational techniques, art therapy, and dance therapy.

Adlerians view dreams as a powerful, metaphorical form of communication with the self. Dreams raise issues that are of current interest or challenge to the dreamer. They are rich with symbols and metaphors regarding current challenges in the client's life. Reoccurring dreams often point to lifestyle issues. Adlerians encourage the client to become aware of dreams—to learn methods of capturing and reflecting on the content through journaling, art, or shared conversations.

While many of the techniques foster insight, Adlerian therapy is also action-oriented. Thinking through new options and planning for change is important, but all that cognitive work is meaningless without the courage to act. Doing something different—that is, taking action—is the ultimate test of therapy. Adlerians acknowledge that there is no greater courage than the courage to be willing to fail. Action involves facing those fears that generate feelings of inferiority. It is "doing" that produces our greatest lessons, our finest victories, and our most magnificent learning.

SHORT- AND LONG-TERM GOALS

Understanding the presenting problem and gathering a clear idea of the client's therapeutic expectations helps us establish short-term and long-term goals. The short-term goal is usually a solution-focused intervention with the intent of addressing the presenting problem. Long-term goals address lifestyle beliefs and patterns of interaction that interfere with life task satisfaction as well as social interest.

Short-term goals address issues of safety and case conceptualization. During this initial session, I am screening for any sign that safety issues need to be addressed. If the client's behavior or ideation makes the client unsafe for the self or for others, then a containment practice is in order (i.e., safety contract, hospitalization, psychiatric referral, child abuse intervention, partner abuse intervention, police contact).

I also wonder about the set of best practices that are associated with the nature of the client's presenting problem. Is a consultation or a referral warranted? At the same time, I begin to speculate regarding my best path to achieving rapport with the client. Are we on a path to an easy collaboration? Is there a friendly joining attitude? An openness as the client shares the current lifestyle challenge? Is there a good fit between us?

The short-term goals of therapy involve solving or "patching" the initial problem that brought the client into therapy. The short-term solution work might involve four to six sessions and terminates when the client resolves the conflict that propelled therapy. While long-term goals may not evolve for all clients, long-term therapeutic goals often emerge from the therapeutic material generated from clients' perceptions of the ways that their lifestyle has impacted each of the life task areas. Clients may come into therapy with a relationship problem and upon resolving that problem discover patterns that require or would benefit from therapeutic intervention over time. Perhaps the client awakens to substance abuse issues; struggles with OCD; or has a realization of an unacknowledged gift, talent, or dream. These realizations offer challenges that are best addressed through more long-term goals.

It has been my experience that satisfied clients may come to therapy when faced with a life task challenge, address that challenge, leave therapy, and return again when faced with another major challenge. While major long-term issues surfaced in the initial sessions, clients may need more life experiences to anchor these awakenings. They may leave therapy and come back again ready to face the next aspect of the awakening. In the area of addictions this type of awakening—seeing the issue clearly and then going back into "not seeing"—is a common pattern and one that can go on for a period of years.

In addition to receiving therapy, clients are encouraged to continue self-coaching processes through group support. Self-coaching processes are continued and deepened when a client joins a self-help group. These groups foster continued growth through self-reflection as well as through service to others with similar needs. Men's or women's groups, substance abuse or eating disorders groups, Adult Children of Alcoholics or Al-Anon, Artist's Way groups, cancer or wellness groups, incest survivor groups, meditation groups, and church or spiritual groups are just a few examples. These peer support communities foster social interest as well as personal development.

USING THE RELATIONSHIP

Adlerian therapy is viewed as a learning process with the therapist to establish a working relationship characterized by mutual respect and equality. Adlerians sit face to face with the client (not behind a desk or using the analytic couch). The general style of therapy is insight-oriented, which involves asking questions, carefully reflecting on clients' responses, and working to help clients discover, revise, challenge, and create meaning in their own lives—meaning that honors the self while at the same time displays social interest in each of the life task areas. Adlerian therapists emphasize the active role of the client in this process of therapy—a role that highlights creativity, optimism, and responsibility. Adlerians work closely with the client to align goals and to generate a type of collaborative movement that compels the client forward.

The issue of lifestyle patterns and the typologies generated by these patterns does provide a challenge for the therapist. Each typology holds expectations for the roles that others "should" play in the client's life. The therapist will not be exempt from these roles and expectations. Clients are lifelong experts at casting these expectations and believing deeply in them as their due from others. Clients can be extremely convinced and convincing, so the therapist needs to be aware and reflective about the roles each typology offers the therapist. Getters will want to "get more"; controllers will attempt to control the agenda—especially to avoid topics that generate an out-of-control feeling; dependent individuals will often avoid making decisions or work to get the therapist to make them; pleasers will want to do what pleases the therapist. Adlerians watch for these typology challenges. "Ah, remember that pleasing pattern? Are you, by any chance, imagining that you are pleasing me (or someone else) by picking this option?"

It is important for therapists to like the client—that is, to feel rapport, concern, empathy, and an easy ability to encourage the client. When rapport is not easily achieved, it is best for therapists to refer the client to a therapist who is likely to be able to achieve rapport.

Adlerian therapy can be solution-focused in nature and thus short-term therapy or it can be a longer process of deep change. The length of therapy depends on the nature of the presenting problem, the depth of support that the client needs to address the problem, and the nature of the client's mental health issues.

ADAPTING THE APPROACH

Adlerian therapy can take many forms: individual therapy, couples therapy, group therapy, family therapy, art therapy, drama therapy, and cotherapy. Certainly the individual and highly personal needs of the client dictate the both the general approach to the presenting problem as well as the type of intervention. Individuals come to the therapeutic process influenced not only by their unique family and life events, but by sets of unique cultural, religious, and socioeconomic forces.

It is important to me as a therapist to open space for the consideration of these influences and their impact on both the client and our working relationship. I have worked with individuals from a variety of cultures, religions, and socioeconomic levels. It has always been important for me to open a line of communication regarding our cultural match or cultural differences. It has also been of major importance to discuss religious preferences and process. I routinely ask clients to share and employ their most valuable spiritual tools. It has also been routine for me to ask about cultural practices as the client and I codesign specific therapeutic rituals. I am always concerned that the client's values, beliefs, tools, and rituals are honored. Every single therapeutic ritual of forgiveness that I can recall was a collaboration built on the client's cultural and spiritual values.

If a client expresses concerns about a lack of cultural or religious match, I work to secure a referral for a better match. It has not been my experience that any client rejected therapy with me due to cultural or religious issues, but it has been my experience that I have sought out a better cultural match when issues of culture and religion were intricately woven into the presenting problem. For example, a young Islamic woman presented for therapy in despair over her father's decision that she marry a man he had "matched" her with. By the end of the initial session, she revealed that she was a lesbian, concerned about the rage that she would face if she revealed this fact to her family. I found an Islamic cleric who offered the client protection, understanding, and support in the process of handling her family.

It is important to open space in therapy for dialog regarding cultural, religious, gender, and socioeconomic differences. With space, these issues surface within the context of problems and life task challenges and become a part of the context of the problem.

Gender is one major issue that requires adaptation for client and therapist. I have found that gender matching (client and therapist of the same sex) is often a good idea for a foundational experiences in therapy, but secondary experiences with the opposite gender opens space for new challenges and understandings.

Gender challenges are an important topic in Adlerian therapy. One of the central ideas in Adlerian therapy—one that caused a major rift between Adler and Freud—was Adler's idea of the masculine protest. Adler felt that women wanted the privileges and powers granted to men in society so that they might have the same opportunities for choice and self-development that were afforded to men. While it is important to note that men also suffer from issues of power and control, suffice it to say that Alder did not believe in the Freudian ideas of penis envy; he felt women had power and choice envy. The women's movement is evidence of Adler's prophetic position on this issue.

Regardless of the degree of cultural change in terms of women's rights as evidenced in Western society, fierce debate continues regarding the nature of a "real woman" and the nature of a "real man." This debate surfaces everywhere in our global culture—in our family experiences, in advertisements, in schools and universities, and inside our selves. Cultural and religious influences spice the debate. Our notions of gender form one of the largest issues that we are forced to confront as we define who we are as a man or a woman. Not to mention that with time, experience, and personal development, these ideas continue to change.

FINDING YOUR NICHE

Adlerians, who are an extremely democratic and welcoming group, practice in clinical settings serving individuals, couples, and families. They are best known for conducting pioneer work in the development of family education centers as well as establishing a broad tradition of parenting literature. They have founded schools, day care centers, substance abuse centers, and domestic violence centers. They are classroom teachers, university professors, researchers, parents, parent educators, court advocates, police officers, politicians, businesspeople, coaches, counselors, and therapists.

If you are attracted to Adler's ideas, there is a place for you in the Adlerian community. Do some basic reading (www.adlerbiblio.com); contact the North American Society of Adlerian Psychology regarding student membership in your area of interest; join NASAP and become active nationally and with other Adlerians in your area; consider taking a course at the Adler School of Professional Psychology or spend a summer vacation with other Adlerians at the International Congress of Adlerian Summer Schools and Institutes (ICASSI). This week-long program and group vacation is offered every summer in a different country. At ICASSI, seasoned Adlerians, young professionals, parents, children, and graduate students debate new ideas and enjoy the unique atmosphere of this international Adlerian community. Student scholarships are available.

Adlerian theory and practices thrive through NASAP—the North American Society of Adlerian Psychology (www.info@alfredadler.org)—with its annual spring convention. Consider applying for a student scholarship for NASAP and attend this exciting yearly event. If you have finished your dissertation or are working on a research project consider a presentation at NASAP. Take a look at Adlerian writing and research to consider the wide array of interests addressed by Adlerians. Current theory and research in Adlerian psychology is centered in the quarterly *Journal of Individual Psychology* (University of Texas Press). Check into the many lines of professional training offered at the Adler School of Professional Psychology in Chicago. In additional to traditional degrees, the Adler School offers certificates in Marriage and Family Therapy, Hypnosis, Gerontology, Substance Abuse and Sexual Addiction, Police Advocacy, and Organizational Development. The Adler School of Professional Psychology is the international center of Adlerian theory, graduate training, research, and practice (www.adler.edu).

PROCESS AND CASE SUGGESTIONS

1. *Elena.* Elena comes to therapy stating that she is not her usual self. Everyone who loves her agrees that her troubled state makes her seem changed. She is altered. Her energy is different—she appears to have pulled out of her regular life. Pulled in several directions, she is literally stuck.

   Watch Elena's session and pay attention to her body language. Can you find the section of the video where the "real" Elena shows up? Replay the session and pay close attention to the story that goes with her energetic body language. What does this energy mean?

   Is there a gender challenge in Elena's story? Is Elena caught up in confusing ideas about what a "real woman" should be and even what a "real man" should be? How might cultural ideas and family examples interface with these gender ideas?

   Developmentally, what is normal about the challenge that Elena faces with her parents and her life? What factors complicate this normal challenge?

   Is there a chance that other members of the family might own components of this presenting problem? What would that mean about treatment?

2. *Jane.* It took extreme physical symptoms to bring Jane to therapy. Where did Jane think the medical problem was located? What would be the psychological significance of pain in this area? What would be the psychological significance of awakening in this area?

   Watch Jane's session and pay attention to her body language. Can you find the section of the video where the "real" Jane shows up? Replay the session and pay close attention to the story that goes with Jane's happier body language. What does this energy change mean?

   Is there a gender challenge in Jane's story? Did Jane grow up with set ideas about what a "real woman" should be and what a "real man" should be? How might parental, religious, and cultural ideas lend themselves to conclusions about the value of men versus the value of women?

   Have you heard of the idea of a midlife crisis? Developmentally, why does a midlife crisis happen? What aspects of the interview might buttress this idea?

   What other members of this family might also need therapy? What ideas do you have about their possible struggles?

3. *Theo.* Theo came to therapy indirectly. What type of pressure brought him into therapy? Does he own any aspects of this problem? What aspects?

   What type of family atmosphere did Theo experience during his early years? Did he grow up with ideas about what "real woman" should be and what "real men" should be? How do these experiences affect him now?

   As a therapist who would take this case, what issues of containment are present that you need to address?

   As you listen to Theo's story, where did he find support? What are the implications of this type of support for his recovery?

SUMMARY AND SUGGESTED READINGS

While this chapter offers you a basic orientation to how an Adlerian therapist conceptualizes casework and views therapeutic intervention, this section offers you some suggestion on what you might read to begin to deepen these Adlerian ideas.

The most prolific Adlerian writer who is still teaching and writing today is Dr. Harold Mosak. His current work offers easy-to-digest formulations of Adlerian theory and practice. I advocate that newcomers to these ideas read *A Primer of Adlerian Psychology* (Mosak and Maniacci, 1999) and the "Adlerian Psychotherapy" chapter in *Current Psychotherapies* (Mosak, 2005). These readings offer an overview of theory as well as provide examples of the use of lifestyle assessment in the process of therapy. *Adlerian Therapy: Theory and Practice* (Carlson, Watts, and Maniacci, 2006) lays out the theory with the clarity, enthusiasm, and depth of understanding that comes from gifted practitioners.

The most beautifully written biography of Alfred Adler is *The Drive for Self: Alfred Adler and the Founding of Individual Psychology* (Hoffmann, 1994). This work reads like a novel and captures the flavor of Adler's times. Hoffmann offers the reader a front-row seat at the birth of our discipline, tracing the emergence of Adler's perspective and contrasting it with Freud's perspective. Ellenberger's work, *The Discovery of the Unconscious* (1970), is a wonderful blend of theory and history.

If you are a clinician who desires an Adlerian discussion of DSM-IV, you will want to pick up the highly readable and student-friendly *Psychopathology and Psychotherapy* (Sperry and Carlson, 1996). This work offers an Adlerian perspective on DSM-IV disorders and discusses treatment options for each disorder. *Tactics in Counseling and Psychotherapy* (Mosak and Maniacci, 1998) offers both clinician and student-therapist a host of Adlerian interventions. This book is a joyful read, expands the scope of interventions, and is an extremely useful resource when the therapist feels challenged by a "stuck" client. For individuals who run any kind of group process—therapeutic or work-related—*Adlerian Group Counseling and Therapy: Step-by-Step* (Sonstegard and Bitter, 2004) is a little treasure as is *Adlerian Family Counseling: A Manual for Counselor, Educator, and Psychotherapist* (Christensen, 1993).

If you find yourself hooked on Adlerian principles after reading one of the introductory books mentioned above, then go directly to two classic works that are a "must read" for the budding Adlerian: *On Purpose* (Mosak, 1977), which is a collection of Harold Mosak's published papers, and *Contributions to Individual Psychology* (Shulman, 1973), a collection of the published papers of Bernard Shulman. Mosak and Shulman founded the Adler Institute of Chicago, which is currently the Adler School of Professional Psychology. These papers reflect decades of clinical work and teaching devoted to Adlerian ideas. If your conscience begins to bother you and you wonder if you have social interest, read Mosak's delightful article entitled, "'I don't have social interest': Social Interest as Construct" (1991) and bring social interest into your life.

Adler took his ideas directly to parents and teacher because he believed that many lifestyle problems and challenges could be prevented through better parenting techniques and child-centered, psychologically informed educational methods (Adler, 1970). Adler's preventive focus for both parents and teachers is echoed in a solid tradition of parent guidance materials. Dreikurs' ideas on parenting, first voiced in *Children: the Challenge* (Dreikurs and Soltz 1964), and on teaching, in *Maintaining Sanity in the Classroom* (Dreikurs, Grunwald, and Pepper 1982), have been refined and modernized in the collection of materials called STEP: Systematic Training for Effective Parenting and STET: Systematic Training for Effective Teaching. These materials, published by American Guidance Service, Inc., are listed below. The STEP materials are extremely popular as a base for parent study groups in Family Education Centers throughout the United States.

REFERENCES

Adler, A. (1929). *The science of living*. New York: Greenberg.

Adler, A. (1957). *Understanding human nature* (W. B. Wolfe, Trans.). Greenwich, CT: Premier Books. (Original work published 1927.)

Adler, A. (1958). *What life should mean to you* (A. Porter, Ed.). New York: Prestige. (Original work published 1931.)

Adler, A. (1964). *Social interest: A challenge to mankind* (J. Linton & R. Vaughan, Trans.). New York: Capricorn. (Original work published 1933.)

Adler, A. (1970). *The education of children* (E. Jensen & F. Jensen, Trans.). South Bend, IN: Gateway Editions. (Original work published 1930.)

Adler, A. (1983). *The neurotic constitution* (B. Glueck & J. E. Lind, Trans.). Salem, NH: Ayer. (Original work published 1912.)

Adler, A. (1983). *The pattern of life*. Chicago: Alfred Adler Institute. (Original work published 1930.)

Adler, A. (1983). *The practice and theory of individual psychology* (P. Radin, Trans.). Totowa, NJ: Littlefield, Adams. (Original work published 1920.)

Beecher, W., & Beecher, M. (1955). *Parents on the run*. Marina Del Ray, CA: Devorss.

Boldt, R. (1994). *Lifestyle types and therapeutic resistance: An Adlerian model for prediction and intervention of characterological resistance in therapy*. Unpublished doctoral dissertation, Adler School of Professional Psychology, Chicago.

Cameron, J. (1992). *The artist's way*. New York: Jeremy P. Tarcher/Putnam.

Carlson, J., Watts, R. E., & Maniacci, M. (2006). *Adlerian therapy: Theory and practice*. Washington, DC: American Psychological Association.

Christensen, O. (1996). *Adlerian family counseling: A manual for counselor, educator, and psychotherapist*. Tucson, AZ: University of Arizona.

Dinkmeyer, D., & McKay, G. D. (1973). *Raising a responsible child*. New York: Simon & Schuster.

Dinkmeyer, D., Sr., McKay, G. D., & Dinkmeyer, D., Jr. (1997). *The parent's handbook: Systematic training for effective parenting (STEP)*. Circle Pines, MN: American Guidance Service.

Dinkmeyer, D., Sr., McKay, G. D., & Dinkmeyer, D., Jr. (1980). *STET: Systematic training for effective teaching*. Circle Pines, MN: American Guidance Service.

Dreikurs, R., Grunwald, B. B. & Pepper, F. C. (1982). *Maintaining sanity in the classroom* (2nd ed.). New York: Harper & Row.

Dreikurs, R., & Soltz, V. (1964). *Children: the challenge.* New York: Duell, Sloan, Pearce.

Ellenberger, H. F. (1970). *The discovery of the unconscious.* New York: Basic Books.

Freud, S. (1965). *The interpretation of dreams* (J. Strachey, Trans.). New York: Avon Books. (Original work published 1900).

Hoffman, E. (1994). *The drive for self: Alfred Adler and the founding of Individual Psychology.* Reading, MA: Addison-Wesley.

Manaster, G. J., & Corsini, R. J. (1982). *Individual psychology: Theory and practice.* Itasca, IL: F. E. Peacock.

Mosak, H. H. (1977). *On purpose.* Chicago: Alfred Adler Institute.

Mosak, H. H. (1991). "I don't have social interest": Social interest as construct. *Individual Psychology 47,* 309–320.

Mosak, H. H. (2005). *Adlerian psychotherapy.* In R. J. Corsini & D. Wedding (Eds.), *Current psychotherapies* (7th ed., pp. 53–95). Florence, KY: Thomson/Brooks/Cole.

Mosak, H. H., & Maniacci, M. P. (1998). *Tactics in counseling and psychotherapy.* Itasca, IL: F. E. Peacock.

Mosak, H. H., & Maniacci, M. P. (1999). *A primer of Adlerian psycholgy.* London: Brunner/Mazel.

Mosak, H. H., & Schneider, S. (1977). Masculine protest, penis envy, women's liberation, and sexual equality. *Journal of Individual Psychology 33,* 193–201.

Mosak, H. H. & Shulman, B. (1988). *Life style inventory.* Bristol, PA: Accelerated Development.

Popkin, M. (1987). *Active parenting: teaching cooperation, courage and responsibility.* San Francisco: Harper & Row.

Shulman, B. H. (1973). *Contributions to individual psychology.* Chicago: Alfred Adler Institute.

Sonstegard, M. A., & Bitter, J. R. (2004). *Adlerian group counseling and therapy: step-by-step.* New York: Brunner-Routledge.

Sperry, L., & Carlson, J. (1996). *Psychopathology and psychotherapy.* Bristol, PA: Accelerated Development.

Vaihinger, H. (1965). *The philosophy of "as if."* (C. K. Ogden, trans.). London: Routledge & Kegan Paul. (Original work published 1911.)

Chapter 4

Self Psychology

Alan Kindler

Chapter Outline

Bridging the Theory-to-Practice Gap

Principles in Practice

Keys to Conceptualization

Interventions and Therapeutic Process

Short- and Long-Term Goals

Using the Relationship

Adapting the Approach

Finding Your Niche

Process and Case Suggestions

Summary and Suggested Readings

BRIDGING THE THEORY-TO-PRACTICE GAP

When Heinz Kohut first described his approach to the psychoanalytic treatment of narcissistic personality disorders almost 40 years ago, he initiated a new therapeutic model that has been found useful in the treatment of most forms of psychological disturbance. The self psychological approach emphasizes, but does not restrict itself to, "empathic understanding." Using empathic understanding, counselors strive to understand the client from the client's perspective. They try to grasp the client's world as the client experiences it. Because the subjective world of the client is such a focus of attention and understanding, you will obviously need suitable ways to organize and conceptualize it. The "self" is one such construct that has been found to be very useful. It is a way of summarizing the whole range of a person's experiences of themselves in the world over time and includes feelings, memories, fantasies, and familiar inclinations to action (or nonaction). The self is the overall subjective world of the person. "Selfobject experiences" are those that contribute positively to a person's sense of self. Praise for a job well done usually provides a selfobject experience in that the recipient feels better about himself, more energetic, and more confident. Criticism, on the other hand, may trigger loss of energy, shame, or hurt feelings. You will find, as we go along, that the detailed appreciation of the self of the client, influenced always by the presence or absence of selfobject experiences, contributes usefully to your understanding of her.

As you begin to practice this approach, you will learn how full of interesting surprises this undertaking can be, and how important it is to be constantly open to corrections, modifications, and fine-tuning of your understanding of the client's experience. This openness to the client's point of view is particularly true of the client's experience of you, the therapist, even at those moments when the therapy seems to be going well. Clients may perceive therapists in ways that may diverge quite significantly from the therapists' view of themselves. The acceptance and exploration of these disparities often leads to deeper understanding of the emerging relationship but can be quite a challenge until you get the hang of it.

Kohut's early model provided a way of formulating the subjective worlds of clients who are easily wounded emotionally and therefore habitually protect themselves against the inevitable injuries of relational life. His empathic listening led him to an understanding of his clients' pressing needs for very specific responses from others to enable them to continue participating in a calm, organized, and lively manner. When the counselor fails to provide the needed response to such sensitive clients there is a change in the client's participation in the dialog, sometimes sudden and/or severe, sometimes gradual and/or subtle. To make the counselor's life even more difficult, even the counselor having a different opinion or belief than the client may injure such clients. In more confident clients who are less vulnerable, you may detect slight shifts in energy levels and fluidity of speech that may cue you in to the client's comfort or discomfort with your responses. The importance of the self-sustaining, or selfobject, dimension of these moments will be discussed later when we look more closely at the selfobject concept. It is important to stress here that appreciating that such clients need precise responses so that they won't feel injured does not demand that the counselor always provide them. That would be an impossible requirement. Your awareness of these needs merely helps you to be alert to the frequent occurrence of "empathic failures" in the counseling relationship.

Understanding the subjective world in this way will orient your listening to all clients, whatever their clinical diagnosis. You will begin to appreciate, for example, the pressing need of some of your clients for certain kinds of selfobject experiences, which protect, sustain, and/or enliven their sense of self. Clients who need to be at the center of attention, the life of the party, and who strive to entertain you, might be demonstrating a pressing need for continuous affirmation and applause. Without it they don't feel acceptable to those around them. You will also begin to consider certain symptom patterns and syndromes as manifestations of actual or threatened self-disorganization or urgent attempts to bolster a fragmented or depleted sense of self. In the case of Elena discussed later, for example, we see the devastating impact on her self-confidence when her career ambitions are responded to as a betrayal of her family rather than Elena's healthy ambition deserving of their affirmation.

On the other side of the relationship, you might also understand more fully your own participation in the counseling relationship by considering your own self-experiences and selfobject needs as you interact with your clients. Compare, for example, the impact of a grateful, admiring client on your self-confidence and enthusiasm with that of a critical, dissatisfied, and resentful client. Recognizing such subjective responses in yourself in response to your client's dissatisfaction might help you calm yourself and remain more reflective. From this calmer state you may be able to attend more accurately to the source of your clients' unhappiness with you, from their point of view. This may make it more possible for you to appreciate more accurately your client's needs, fears, and self-defensive strategies and thereby influence constructively your own participation in the therapeutic relationship.

You can see from the foregoing that the clients' sense of self and their need for, or defensive avoidance of, selfobject experiences, provides a very basic framework for the counselor's empathic listening and understanding. Character traits, symptomatic acts and experiences, relational inclinations, even psychosis, are all considered from within the client's subjective world. Using the framework of clients' vulnerable sense of self, their specific selfobject needs, and defenses against the frustration of such needs, you can begin to understand and help your clients. It is worth noting that, from the self psychological perspective, defensiveness is understood to be in the service of protecting the vulnerable self from further injury and disruption. Previous lived experience leaves such clients acutely aware of their proneness to injury and a sense of their emotional fragility. For such a person, repetitions of emotional injuries sustained in earlier development seem to be inevitable and are to be avoided at all costs. Such individuals harbor a sense of dread that such experiences will be repeated in any future relationship and they protect themselves in various ways. These self-defensive actions often contribute to their problems in living and their presenting symptoms. The counseling relationship is no exception for them and is fraught with the usual dangers that need to be defended against.

Let me give you some examples to illustrate these ideas. Haughty, arrogant behavior may be understood as clients' well-established efforts to protect themselves from anticipated hurtful responses of others. These expectations may be conscious and part of their irritable attitude to the world. Or they may be unconscious and only gradually appreciated as counselors sense their way into the sense of danger in the subjective world of the client. An "in your face" attitude of defiance and contempt may serve to fend off exposure of their "futile" need for a smiling response, if not enthusiastic approval. The presumption of futility emerged from their earlier lived experience of the repeated frustration of these crucial needs for approval (selfobject needs). Repetitive experiences of this kind establish the expectation that the open expression of such needs will only expose the client to further hurt and humiliation. In the self psychological approach, defensive behavior such as haughty arrogance is understood as protecting the vulnerable self by a preemptive strike against the needed, and therefore dangerous, other. As an objective observer, we may be struck by the relational ineptness of such interpersonal behavior. On the other hand, from the empathic perspective of the self psychological observer, we are able to appreciate its self-protective purpose and "survival" value to the client.

We could explore many familiar symptoms and character traits from this point of view. If you read further in the self psychology literature you will find many clinical examples illustrated and formulated along these lines. But for now, let us look in more detail at some of the theoretical principles of the self psychological approach and its application to clinical practice.

PRINCIPLES IN PRACTICE

When you study the theory of self psychology in more detail, you will come across many theoretical concepts and principles of practice to assist you in your counseling work. I will introduce you here to four key principles that may guide you in your learning and your efforts to think about the cases provided. The first is the "listening perspective" by which our clinical data is obtained during the initial assessment and subsequently during counseling. Then we will consider the sense of self and the need for selfobject experiences as frameworks upon which we can begin to organize our clinical understanding, Finally we will consider the important counseling function of putting our understanding of the client into words. In this way we provide words for experiences that previously could not be described and therefore could not be easily reflected upon. The enhancement of your clients' capacity to reflect upon self based on your communicated understanding is a central curative goal of this approach. There is a lot to master and I will try to keep the language familiar and nontechnical so that you can get the feel of this approach and begin to apply it clinically.

1. *Listening perspective.* If there is one feature that characterizes the self psychological approach to counseling, it is the empathic listening perspective. The counselor strives to listen to clients from within their own subjective world and to appreciate their unique experience in as much detail as possible. This sounds easy because we do it all the time in many of our relationships, both professional and personal. But it's not always easy, and with some clients, it can be extremely difficult and require painstaking trial and error. But here is a useful hint. Affects (feelings, or emotions) are the essential guides to empathic listening. They can be like a magic thread that we follow towards an accurate understanding of our client's experiences. The specific affects we identify as we listen to the client tell us most about their subjective experience. How do they feel about the loss of their partner, their dog, their hair?

They could be sad, relieved, or angry or a mixture of all three. How do they experience their outbursts of rage? They might be ashamed, fearful, or proud. Of course, as clinicians, we don't ignore objective data such as the client's physique and posture, personal hygiene or mode of dress, or manifestations of disturbed thinking or perceiving. But, when we inquire empathically, we are particularly interested in how these physical or cognitive manifestations are experienced by clients and what they tell us about the clients' experience of themselves in the world. Is our client's unusually tall stature a source of pride and confidence that strengthens their self or is it a source of self-conscious shame which weakens their self? Does that person's ethnic features contribute to his sense of belonging, or do they estrange him from others? We recognize that the client's feelings may change in different contexts rather than remaining constant. The tall man may be shy and withdrawn at a social event, but confident and assertive at basketball practice. Note the central importance of affects in all these examples.

This latter example of the tall man illustrates how our empathic listening perspective includes an appreciation of the context of our client's subjective experiences. We attend to the triggering events and the background setting associated with whatever experience is being explored. Often, in the course of counseling, it is our own participation that provides the triggers for our client's experience. It can be enormously helpful when we accept this reality in the service of greater empathic understanding. A simple example might help illustrate this latter point. Your client tells you she is hurt by your "obvious" anger towards her. You have no awareness of this in yourself. To make matters even more confusing, you might even have been feeling warmly towards her at that moment. Rather than deny her perceptions and risk offending her by contradicting her experience, you might try exploring with her how she senses the anger in you. What are the cues that tell her that you feel that way towards her? This inquiring approach may allow deeper understanding of her experience than your challenge to its accuracy. I have learned surprising things about myself by encouraging my clients to describe their experiences of me.

The counselor's openness to correction by the client is an essential part of the empathic listening perspective. This openness to correction is supported by the counselor's recognition that our theories of human behavior, while useful in guiding our understanding, may at times lead us astray. Hence we hold our theories lightly and try to stay flexible in our approach to understanding of our clients' unique worlds of experience.

The empathic or "subject-centered" listening perspective is privileged in the self psychological approach and is the source of essential clinical information, as I have pointed out above. But it can also be helpful to listen to the client from the point of view of someone in a relationship with her. This is referred to as the "other-centered" listening perspective. In this way, we take note of our own subjective responses as we interact with the client to help us understand the kinds of relationships she is likely to establish with others through her impact on them. We attend to the feelings we notice in ourselves, and consider how these feelings are evoked and how they might play a role in the client's other relationships, especially if these relationships are problematic. Are we drawn to the client or do we feel pushed away? Do we look forward to the appointment or are we filled with dread? Are we excited and interested, or bored and sleepy? Do we feel valued or diminished? Any or all of these responses may be useful information in our efforts to more fully understand our client's relational world.

2. *The state of the self.* The self, as it is used in self psychology, is difficult to define without lapsing into concrete "reifications" that defeat the purpose of being flexibly open to the unique details and patterns of subjective experience. The self is used to refer to the overall subjective world of the person, its familiarity and continuity over time, its uniformity and complexity, its affective tone, and its responsiveness to the personal and impersonal environment. It is close to what we mean when we use the word "self" colloquially as in "I feel good about myself, today" or "I was not myself when you saw me last night." You can see how we tend to objectify our own subjectivity in our day-to-day usage. Think about the "I" and the "me" in these communications and how they differ in meaning from "self."

As you listen to clients' symptoms and life story, try to listen to the narrative themes, their coherence, richness of detail, and their affective qualities and variations. Consider how "together" clients experience themselves to be in general and at specific moments in time. If their story emerges in a fragmented manner, or clients describe episodes where they clearly felt scattered, "not themselves," disorganized, or driven to certain specific "unwanted" or "unfamiliar" behaviors, they may be experiencing a "fragmented" self. If the client feels drained of energy or motivation consider this a "depleted self." If they feel excited, overactive, and out of control, you might think of them as describing an "overstimulated" self. Next, consider your clients' responsiveness and vulnerabilities to environmental or relational events. Listen for negative affects such as depression, shame, or anxiety often associated with a sense of disorganization and loss of function. If the client describes such feelings, try to elicit the events triggering them. In this way you will begin to understand the contexts in which your client's subjective world is disrupted. As you do this, try to sense other experiences that they might have needed to modify or prevent such self states from emerging. Would a word of praise or an enthusiastic smile have prevented the state of self-depletion from overwhelming them? Can you recognize any strategies they utilize in the service of self-protection or restoration? Do they try to hide from rather than expose themselves to potentially hurtful and disappointing or, on the other hand, overstimulating and arousing situations? Later, you will be considering the case of Theo, who describes a loss of control of his self in the form of rage when he is hurt or disappointed. This is a very common response to hurt and humiliation.

Another way of thinking about this is to consider what kinds of emotional environment your client tends to seek out, or avoid, in order to protect, maintain, or restore their functional competence, vitality, and emotional stability. In more theoretical terms we would ask the question: "What are their selfobject needs?" If, for example, a client seeks out men in a relentless, driven, even dangerous, manner, she may be expressing her needs for recognition and affirmation at the expense of other needs such as safety, intimacy, or self-respect. Another approach would be to ask what kinds of events seem to trigger disruptions to the client's sense of inner cohesion and vitality; in theoretical terms, what are the typical selfobject failures in their life? Through your understanding of their repetitive failures to obtain the needed responses, you will learn more about your clients' selfobject needs. You will also understand, from these repetitive events, more about their unique vulnerabilities, strengths, and self-regulatory strategies. How do their symptomatic behaviors protect them from further disorganization and loss of vitality, and how do they fail? It can be clinically useful to bear in mind that the most pathological and maladaptive behavior, from *your* perspective as the counselor, may have significant self-protecting or self-regulating value, from the *client's* perspective. The recklessly promiscuous client described above might be an example. Self psychologists refer to this striving for stability, enlivenment, or toward competence and new growth as the "leading edge" of personal development. The client's repetitive symptomatic and relational behaviors, which we are more likely to notice and attend to clinically, are called the "trailing edge." The client referred to above may be regulating her profound emptiness and depression through her dangerous sexual involvements and it may help her if you, as her counselor, are able to recognize this aspect of her behavior rather than focus only on the self-destructive qualities. In other words, it is often useful for the counselor to identify the client's continuing attempts at forward developmental movement even when it is hidden within the most relentlessly repetitive dysfunctional behavior. This understanding can distinguish the counselor's responses from those of many others in the clients' community who are naturally focused on their self-destructive or harmful behavior.

3. *The need for selfobject experiences.* Clinical experience, supported by modern studies of child development, reveals that certain kinds of experience are needed for healthy development and ongoing functioning reflected in a well-regulated and lively sense of self. The pervasive absence of these needed experiences during development may lead to lifelong difficulties attributable to a fragile and rigidly defended sense of self. It may manifest in later life as an intense hunger or need associated with driven efforts to acquire them (for example, the praise-hungry person) or devitalized states of despair and hopelessness about ever having such needs met (for example, the pessimist, "glass half empty" person) or both. Kohut discovered three main categories of such developmental experiences essential to healthy self-development in his psychoanalytic treatment of narcissistically vulnerable clients: mirroring selfobject experiences, idealizing selfobject experiences, and twinship or alter-ego selfobject experiences. While these specific kinds of selfobject needs may dominate the therapeutic relationship, either in the foreground or background, many other kinds of selfobject experiences may be delineated, depending on the nature of the triggering event. Adversarial selfobject experiences, for example, are triggered by the invigorating struggles between adversaries who are enlivened by the struggle, physical or mental. Whenever we have any of our needs met we are likely to feel an increase in pleasure or relief of distress, both of which may be associated with an increased sense of vitality and cohesion of the self. Hence, there are, in fact, limitless triggering events that may give rise to selfobject experiences.

    Mirroring selfobject experiences amplify positive affective tone, such as a sense of pride or competence. For children, "the gleam in the mother's eye" (as Kohut said) in response to their very existence is the quintessential mirroring experience of normal development. The approval of others, recognition of one's achievements, the audience's applause, and the diploma at the end of a course are familiar examples of this ubiquitous realm of experience continuing through life. The person for whom such recognition has been adequately provided during development is likely to feel confident, ambitious, energetic, and playful within the normal affirming ambience of everyday life. Affirmation can be sought and received appropriately and its absence can be tolerated. When deprived of needed affirmation, such individuals can right themselves with minimal short-lived distress. In theoretical terms, they have a strong, resilient self.

Idealized selfobject experiences are those that calm, soothe, and strengthen the self by relieving negative affects such as fear, shame, or anger. Their availability during development provides the opportunities for the acquisition of self-soothing competence. A child's experience of being securely held in a calm parent's arms after some distressing event is the prototypical developmental moment. The sense of belonging to a respected family, club, peer group, religious or national group may be a source of this kind of calming and strengthening experience throughout life. The counselor's reliable availability and calm attention to the client's painful experiences may evoke these same experiences in the therapeutic relationship. The developmental outcome of these experiences is the establishment of a capacity to self-soothe under duress. Such a client might be an unruffable person who experiences distress appropriately but who does not spin out of control and suffer from anxiety attacks or debilitating shame. Such a person is likely to have comfortable relationships with idealized groups and institutions such as religious, political, or professional organizations expressive of sustaining values and ideals.

Twinship or alter-ego selfobject experiences are derived from a sense of sameness, like-mindedness, often, but not only, established with the same sex parent. The son working side by side with his father and the daughter with her mother are normal healthy manifestations of twinship experiences. The acquisition of skills and abilities seems to emerge from these experiences, along with the strong sense of belonging to the human race, and a sense of affiliation with other like-minded and like-bodied people. These needs are met throughout life by being one of the adolescent peer group, or the family or clan or religious congregation, or ethnic group.

Other kinds of selfobject experiences have been described through the sustained use of empathic observation. Adversarial interactions may possess a quality of vitalizing enjoyment that contributes to a strong assertive self, comfortable with an argument or dispute. The four-year-old boy wrestling with his father, or racing him to the tree, or outwitting him some way is enjoying the adversarial struggle with a stronger rival who welcomes his efforts as part of his healthy development. Such positive experiences facilitate the integration of assertiveness and aggression into healthy attachments. Their absence may render clients less competent to deal with controversy because they are vulnerable to loss of control of their emotions. They may be limited by their dread of confrontation or shame over their assertive needs, which they fear may lead to destructive aggression.

Your knowledge of these categories of selfobject experience will assist you in recognizing your client's attempts to obtain them or avoid them and this will, in turn, contribute significantly to your depth of empathic understanding. I have tried to provide you with a basic outline and you may want to study them in more detail. If so, you can read about them in some of the references provided at the end of this chapter. But for now, it is worth thinking about clinical material with these in mind as you try to formulate the client's subjective life. I think they will become a bit easier to use as you think about the clinical material in the exercises ahead.

4. *The articulation of the client's subjective experience.* Having listened empathically in order to understand your client's experience as accurately as you can, what should you do with this understanding? From the very beginning of your first encounter, you should attempt to communicate to your client how you understand what he or she has told you. In this way, you will engage the client by demonstrating how carefully you listen and how you make sense of what you hear. You thus demonstrate your understanding as well as your way of thinking about it as you put into your own words the details of your client's experience. At the outset, this may be as simple and straightforward as responding with: "I can see how sad that is for you" or "What a frustrating experience that must have been." Notice the centrality of affects in these responses. As things move along and your understanding becomes more complex then you might say something like the following. "So what you are telling me is that your partner always stays silent when you are upset. When that happens, you know he is judging you, and that makes you feel embarrassed and that leads to you feeling angry. Do I have that right?" In this example, you would be demonstrating not only your careful identification of the affects that organize the client's experience but also your understanding of their relational context and the specific cues that trigger her feelings—for example, her partner's silence. Your intention here would be, first and foremost, to confirm the accuracy of your understanding or to have it modified by the client. Secondly, your intention would be to further the process of inquiry into the experience by setting an example through your close attention to the details. And thirdly, inquiry is also fostered by the safety created by your commitment to understanding your client accurately and nonjudgmentally. Through your understanding you may be adding a further level of understanding, sometimes referred to as an *interpretation*. In the example above, you are adding the possibility that the client's anger was consequent to feeling judged and humiliated and that these feelings were triggered by the partner's silent response to her distress. You can see, by this example, how counselor and client together construct a verbal version of a complex set of experiences, which can lead to further understanding of its origins and meanings in the "here and now" as well as in the "there and then." In the above example, the appreciation of the humiliating impact of the partner's silence might open up further understanding of this particular moment. It might bring to mind earlier experiences that facilitate further understanding of the current interaction. "I remember my mother's stony face when I was upset with her" might be an example. The emergence of such a memory of a parent who withdrew when the client became distressed or, alternatively, resorted to shaming strategies to control her, might shed further light on the development of this pattern of response to her current partner's silence and serve to deepen her understanding of herself.

5. *The disruption-repair sequence.* I have described above the impact on the client's self of selfobject experience (cohesion, vitality, functional competence) and of self-object failure (disorganization, distress, loss of energy, loss of function). Appreciating these categories of experience will make you more sensitive to the inevitable self-disruptions that occur in the counseling dialog. Minor lapses in your empathic understanding or your maintenance of the frame (for example, coming late for an appointment or canceling due to illness) might trigger aversive reactions. Such aversive reactions may be of an aggressive or avoidant kind. The client might become angry and critical, or, alternatively, lose energy and withdraw emotionally from the dialog. The subjective sense of self-cohesion may be lost and symptomatic behavior may emerge. The client may, for example, resume alcohol abuse, become depressed or anxious, or not turn up for the next session. When this happens, counselors will begin the process of exploring the disruption in order to restore the empathic link through empathic understanding. They will enlist the client's assistance in understanding the details of the "selfobject failure" and how they contributed to it. When this is attended to successfully, the therapeutic relationship is deepened because both client and counselor have a deeper appreciation of what they mean to each other. In particular, they might reach a deeper understanding of the nature of the selfobject dimensions of their relationship. Now they might know, for example, that the counselor's punctuality has meant more than either had realized because it conveyed the counselor's respect for the client. The accepting understanding of such feelings of injury may restore the selfobject bond and deepen the exploration of such vulnerabilities, not only to the counselor but to all relationships.

   One of my clients would fall completely silent whenever I moved in my chair while he was talking. Once I realized that the trigger was my sudden, even if (for me) slight, movement, we were able to explore its significance to him. It meant that I was no longer listening with the complete attention that he had come to rely upon to feel safe to express his innermost thoughts. My mirroring selfobject provision had been lost, with devastating impact on his sense of self. At that moment he lost track of his thoughts and was engulfed with a sense of shame, which paralyzed him so that he could not talk.

KEYS TO CONCEPTUALIZATION

I have emphasized the self psychological emphasis on the client's subjectivity to encourage you to attempt to understand your clients' presenting concerns from within their point of view. Now you might be wondering how we make the details of the clients' subjective life clinically relevant. So let us now consider some of the ways to organize this clinical material using some key self psychological concepts.

1. *Self states and patterns.* Our sense of self (or our self experience) might be thought of as the familiar patterns of subjective experience we derive from our sense of feeling competent to influence the world we live in, our sense of how the world will respond to us, and our overall organization of these expectations and responses to them.

Hence, our sense of self is very much born of, sustained by, disrupted by, our interactions with others as we proceed through life. Our main guide to our own or another's sense of self is through the feelings that are experienced at any moment in time and over time. Feelings tell us what we are experiencing, whether it is good or bad for us, what we need to do about it, and what we might need, or need to avoid, for ourselves. They are essential guideposts to the state of the subjective world as we try to understand the state of the self and the various motivations in our clients and in ourselves.

As you take in the details of your client's presentation, consider some of the following possibilities. Try to evaluate their sense of themselves as being competent and in charge of their life versus feeling burdened, overwhelmed, and helpless. Try to ascertain the qualities of the experiences of significant people in their life and the expectations that have evolved from these experiences. Do they report disappointments, injuries, hurts, and humiliation? Are they shocked by these experiences or do they fulfill their expectations? Are relationships a source of vitality and hope, or does debilitating deprivation and despair predominate? Do your clients have easy access to their feelings and do they trust them as guides to understanding their self and their relationships with others? Or, instead, do they find their own feelings to be unpredictable, hard to read, and distracting rather than clarifying of their needs and motivations. Do some persistent self-states dominate the client's self-organization, causing uncontrollable recurring difficulties as in the case of states of despair, euphoria, rage, or fear? You will have some chance to think about this question in the case of Theo.

2. *Selfobject experiences: successes and failures.* As you listen to your clients' self-narratives as they tell you why they have come to see you and what has taken place in their lives in the recent and distant past, you will attend particularly to their experiences of relationships and the qualities of responsiveness reported. Do they tend to describe relationships as gratifying or frustrating their mirroring, idealizing, or twinship needs? Just to remind you how these might be recognized, consider the following: Do your clients seem to feel recognized, affirmed, understood in the important relationships they describe? Or do they feel belittled, ignored, and humiliated? These considerations point towards mirroring needs being met or frustrated. Are those upon whom they rely for security and strength reliable and calming or painfully disappointing and rejecting? Have they felt part of a family, community, peer, or ethnic group that stabilizes their sense of who they are and provides them with a sense of belonging? The answers to these questions may point you towards the presence or absence of idealizable selfobject experiences in each client's world. Do your clients describe a lifelong deprivation of selfobject experience to which they have become accepting and passively accommodating? Or do they describe that absence with a tone of frustration and with a sense of entitlement to something better? Feelings of helplessness and emptiness suggest the former while irritability, anger, or indignation suggest the latter. I think that it will be obvious to you by now what a significant role affects play in your empathic understanding of these themes.

Evaluating mirroring needs may require particularly close attention to the details of relationships and the way they are experienced. Sometimes it is obvious, as when clients describe shaming judgment instead of the needed affirmation or recognition in response to their achievements. A parent's critical comment: "you could have done better" in response to a proudly presented school report is easy to recognize, especially if it is delivered with irritation or derisive withdrawal. But the more subtle lack of appropriate attunement in responses in which the words are affirming but the "music" (the affective tone and intensity) is flat may not be so easily appreciated. Even more subtle in their damaging impact might be the parent's affirming responses, which are mechanically delivered when the client do not feel good about what they have produced. Such unattuned responses may indicate how little is required or expected and that the parent is not really in touch with the child's sense of accomplishment or feelings of failure. Repetitive experiences of this nature may lead some clients to the profound sense that no one really cares about their strivings for competence, leading to shame-filled retreats from the challenges of life in which they are called upon to display their abilities. In others, this may be defended against through unreasonable demands for approval at all times, the so-called "mirror-hungry" person.

3. *Self-enhancing and self-protective strategies.* Earlier, I gave you an example of how aggressive, in-your-face, demanding behavior, experienced by others as haughty arrogance, might be understood as a self-protective strategy. Such an interpersonal strategy might emerge in the course of development when responses to attachment needs have been persistently inadequate, even traumatizing. While some children will tend to retreat in fear or shame, leading to self-preservation through distance and solitude, others may utilize their aggressive skills effectively in self-defense. You can see from these examples how strategies may evolve that are useful for the developing children at the time, given the nature of their attachment relationships, but remain fixed and inflexible as they proceed through life, even when the possibility of different relationships may occur. Their difficulties in relationships persist because the experience of closeness is associated with a sense of danger to the self and is fended off in these and a myriad of other ways.

On the other hand, it can be useful to consider the possibility, from the empathic perspective, that some behaviors are self-enhancing or self-strengthening in that they strengthen, energize, and improve the organization of the self. Many healthy and valued behaviors can provide this function, activities such as exercise, reading literature or poetry, artistic expression, humanitarian activities, and community involvement. But, from the empathic perspective, many pathological behaviors serve a similar function. Addictions, including drugs and gambling, sexual promiscuity, obsessional thoughts, and compulsive behaviors, even psychoses may be understood as serving a self-strengthening function. Clients' driven need to repeat their symptoms may be understood as a manifestation of their need to strengthen a fragile self.

These are ways you can usefully consider the problems your clients bring you. I think you will find that, in doing so, your empathic capacities will be enhanced. You will be less likely to be experienced by your client as judgmental and critical, and thus more likely to facilitate the therapeutic process.

4. *Model scene construction.* One of the ways you can deepen your understanding of your clients is through utilizing the developmental perspective. This allows you to consider the developmental precursors and traumatic events of earlier life that may

have contributed to the clients' problems of today. Much has been written of this and our understanding of human development has expanded enormously in the last three decades. I have found the use of model scene construction to be a helpful tool in this pursuit of a developmental perspective on current clinical experiences. I will give you a very brief introduction here but you will need to read further to grasp the richness of this approach.

Model scenes are interactions that may be taken from the clients' history, from their memories or dreams, from interactions with you in the treatment, or from interactions with others in their life. These interactions seem to capture some important aspects of the client's development. The counselor and the client may look together at the details of the interaction, including the subjective elements, the behavioral sequences, and departures from the "normal" for such a developmental event. The earliest memory of one of my clients was waking up in a crib in the hospital after his tonsillectomy at age 3. He saw his father standing close by and remembers repeating: "It's all right, Daddy. It's all right." These words would come out of his mouth even now, 40 years later, when he was upset and felt hurt or needy. Instead of expressing his distress he would still say: "It's all right" over and over again. We see from this example that the child's appropriate expectation of the father's comforting response had already been replaced by an automatic attempt to comfort him. This scene allowed my client and me to look closely at the attachment scenarios that shaped his inhibitions about complaining or expressing discomfort. In this way, he became able to reflect upon behavior that had been quite automatic and had not been experienced as problematic or dysfunctional. It did, however, interfere with his capacity for intimate relationships where the capacity to express distress is an essential component.

Several examples of model scenes will be available for you to consider when you look at the case examples later. Theo elaborates one of his as the comic strip character, the Incredible Hulk.

INTERVENTIONS AND THERAPEUTIC PROCESS

The most important rule governing the self psychological approach to the therapeutic process is that *understanding always precedes explanation*. We can only try to explain what we have first understood accurately through our empathic immersion in our client's subjective life. Thus, our attempts to interpret meanings always follow our arrival at a comfortable understanding. In the words of Heinz Kohut: "Psychoanalysis interprets what has first been understood." In this case, understanding emerges from our ongoing inquiry into the subjective world of the client and its full elaboration. As I have already described, in "Principles in Practice," your early interventions will focus on the detailed elaboration of your clients' subjectivity. This understanding will include the contextual nature of their experience. For example, what evokes anxious preoccupation, or what are the triggers for an overexcited state?

The disruption-repair sequence is a cornerstone of the self psychological therapeutic process. The initial attention to the details of subjective life fosters the emergence of selfobject experiences in the therapeutic relationship. These are considered selfobject transferences and are often quite conscious and acknowledged by the client: "I feel really supported by your attention." But they might also be present in the background and remain unconscious until something goes awry. The counselor might misunderstand something important or sensitive in the clients' account of their life. The counselor might be late for an appointment, or even forget an appointment. (Yes, we all do it.) A holiday or illness may interrupt the therapeutic rhythm. Any of the above, or something quite unexpected, might trigger a loss of self-cohesion, an eruption of negative affects such as anxiety, depression, or shame along with a loss of function such as effectiveness at work. This may be obvious immediately in the course of a session, or not until the next session. It might be communicated by a phone call before the next session. When this happens, the counselor considers the possibility that a "disruption" has occurred and that the client has been affected by something the counselor has done, or failed to do.

When this happens it is very important to try to explore the nature of the selfobject failure that has led to the client's disrupted self and the associated aversiveness. This task can be quite a challenge, especially when a client is upset and you, the counselor, have no idea what has upset them. By asking the client about how they began to feel upset and/or thinking about it yourself, you might gain some understanding of the onset and your contribution to it, always from the client's point of view. I can't stress enough the importance of the efforts to see the disruption through the clients' eyes, even though their perspective may put you as the counselor in a less than perfect light. Clients will attribute certain intentions or motives to you as they explain their experience of the disruption. These may be accurate, completely false, or, most commonly, a mixture of both. For the purposes of empathic inquiry, it can be very constructive to "wear these attributions" provided by the client ("you hold me in contempt," or "you don't care about me," or "you think I'm stupid") in order to further the exploration of his role in the disruption. It might seem natural to directly challenge such experiences: "you see your own anger in me rather than accepting it in yourself," or to gently indirectly challenge the veracity of her perceptions of you: "It feels *as if* I am angry at you." For many vulnerable clients these interventions only add to the disruption rather than conveying understanding of it. If you are able to "wear the attribution" you might ask: "How did I express my anger towards you?" This invites clients to add more information about their experience of you and to further explain precisely how you hurt their feelings. The goal is to find a way to articulate the client's experience of the counselor that has triggered this disrupted state. When this is successfully done, an empathic bond is reestablished (the client feels understood by the counselor) and the selfobject dimension of the therapeutic relationship is restored. (The client once again experiences the counselor as affirming, strong, calm, and reliable, or like-minded and familiar, or possessing some other self-strengthening quality.) The client's self is revitalized and restabilized with a return of functional and emotional equilibrium. In addition to the above, a deeper understanding of the selfobject dimension of the transference may be reached by client and counselor, thereby deepening the therapeutic relationship.

The coconstruction of model scenes is an extremely useful component of the therapeutic process, allowing the understanding of the past to contribute to our understanding of the present. A particular story from the past such as an early memory, a dream, or a fantasy, or an actual interaction between the client and counselor may serve as a prototypical interaction capturing an important relational pattern with significant consequences for future psychological events. The playful exploration of the event may assist in deepening the understanding of patterns of experience and behavior. I gave you an example above of my client who recalled, as his earliest memory, comforting his father on awakening from his tonsillectomy. As we construct such model scenes with our clients, we also have in our minds some version of what should have happened and how this diverges from the normal developmental prototype. In the example of the early memory, we would expect a very different interaction between a scared post-operative child and a parent with the reassurance going in the opposite direction. Using this as a model of this client's attachment relationships allowed further understanding of his relational expectations and his typical self-protective strategies. He expected his unhappiness and distress to be an unwelcome burden that would estrange him for anyone he needed and he protected himself from such estrangement by automatically assuring the other person that he did not need them to comfort him.

SHORT- AND LONG-TERM GOALS

Your *short-term goals* should include the establishment of a friendly and safe atmosphere through your careful attention to the client's comfort, and your provision of a reliable frame with regular appointments, a clear and sensitive financial arrangement, and explanations of what to expect in terms of schedules, length of sessions, vacations, and cancellations. Within this framework of safety you will demonstrate, by your responses to your clients, how much importance you place on your understanding of their experiences. In this way you foster a shared interest in their subjective experience rather than problem labeling and solving from the perspective of an outside observer.

Your success in achieving these short-term goals would be indicated by your clients' increasing comfort in elaborating their subjective world, even when it is uncomfortable and unfamiliar. Sometimes you will receive assurances in the form of your client saying: "I can't believe I told you that" or some other version of surprise at their openness and the welcome but unfamiliar sense of safety in their relationship with you.

Your *long-term goals* might include greater access to your clients' subjective experiences, their specific needs for responsiveness, increasing self-reflective competence, and more resilience in the experience of selfobject failure (self-righting capacity). You might find yourself acting more like a coach assisting the client to think about a particular experience in more detail. When clients describe inexplicable shifts in affects or moods, perhaps characteristic of their presenting difficulties, you might encourage them to return to the precise moment of change and think about it in greater detail. "Take me back to that moment when you found yourself losing energy and confidence as you spoke to your supervisor. Let's run that back in slow motion and look at it together and try to see exactly how it happened." When this is possible and clients respond to your encouragement with greater detail about their affective life, you can be assured that things are going well.

The increased openness and the expanded access to your clients' subjective world may lead to shifts in your initial understanding of their problems. Minor difficulties may reveal themselves to be part of more substantial problems in your clients' ability to live in the world. The trust you help establish may allow them to reveal quite severe vulnerabilities that restrict their range of functioning more than was initially apparent. A presenting problem with a particular relationship may be only a surface manifestation of a profound difficulty in self-esteem regulation leading to various dysfunctional behaviors needed to bolster a very fragile self.

USING THE RELATIONSHIP

Although the therapeutic, relationship in the self psychological approach emphasizes the counselor's interest in accurately understanding the client's subjective world, it does not ignore the ongoing impact each of the participants have on each other as they communicate verbally and nonverbally during the times they spend together. Sometimes the details of the relationship have to be included in the empathic inquiry rather than ignored as if they are not important. These details may include the ages, sexes, ethnic, cultural, and educational and professional details and the inevitable influences these may have on each other. An older male counselor with a young female client will create quite a different atmosphere than the opposite arrangement. Two men or women of the same age might experience the relationship very differently again.

The ease with which this safe therapeutic relationship can be established and maintained will vary enormously, depending on who the client and counselor are to each other. When you find yourself responding to the client strongly, either positively or negatively, this is inevitably going to affect how you listen, what you hear, and how you respond to it.

As we listen empathically, we are quite actively involved in organizing how we understand what we hear. We may not like to think of it, but as we do this, we are conveying both verbally and nonverbally much information about our own responsiveness to our clients. For this reason, we try to stay aware of our own "inner conversations," our own reflections on what our client is telling us and what it means to us. We appreciate that the subjectivities of both participants are constantly affecting each other in terms of how they each experience themselves, how they each experience the other, and how they interact with each other. In this sense, the empathic listening perspective is very interactive and involves both participants. It is well to keep in mind that counselors' personal assumptions about the world will significantly influence how they understand, and respond to their client's behavior and experiences at any moment. If you think very differently about relationships, for example, you may be critical of a client's infidelity, or, by contrast, painfully submissive fidelity. On the other hand, if you think the same way the client does, we may be less likely to inquire into the personal meanings that certain behaviors hold for that client. You automatically accept the client's point of view as correct. Each of these tendencies can interfere with the role of the counselor as empathic inquirer. For example, a male counselor, listening to a male client describe his anger at his wife's rejecting behavior may find himself responding and understanding quite differently then would a female counselor. If he is dealing with some conflicts in his own life with a female partner, this may deeply affect his responses to the client and his empathic understanding may be shaped accordingly. Each may focus on different details. In each case, a different empathic understanding may emerge. With the male counselor, for example, the man's need for mirroring responsiveness may capture the counselor's attention and understanding. With the female counselor, the man's unreasonable expectations and his partner's vulnerability may be the focus of her empathy. In yet another case, perhaps with either male or female counselors, the man's self-denial and long-suffering persistence in an impossible relationship might come to the fore of their attention.

So far, I have emphasized the empathic listening perspective and the articulation of the client's subjective experience as the counselor's main functions. There are times in the therapeutic process when counselors are required to respond in a more "authentic" manner, and to say something from within their own experiential world. These moments may be very useful therapeutically but they are restricted in range by therapeutic considerations and the ethical boundaries of a professional relationship. Within these limits, however, there are many moments when counselors will choose to express their own responses to the client in order to further the inquiry into the client's subjective experience. They might tell a client how wonderful she looks today when she appears well turned out for a special event, or how much they admire the progress she is making in areas of self-regulation such as abstinence from drugs. They might, on the other hand, tell her that they can't abide her treatment of her child, or partner, and insist that she cease her self-destructive or destructive-to-others behavior. Enactments might include the offering of supportive contact by telephone or email between sessions, a warm handshake at the end of a session, or even an encouraging arm around the shoulder of someone floundering under the impact of despair and aloneness due to bereavement or abandonment. When you do find yourself participating in this manner, it is vital that you stay attentive to the sequences that lead up to, and follow, such events. As a counselor you must be ready to deal with the possible negative fallout of your spontaneous and authentic participation. You must also be interested in understanding the benefits to your client when they go well.

ADAPTING THE APPROACH

Empathic accuracy is very much affected by the similarities and differences between the counselor and client; the empathizer and empathized-with. When cultural, ethnic, life stage, sexual orientation, spiritual values, and even affective vitality are significantly different, the speed and accuracy of empathy is reduced. When the client differs significantly from you in any or all of these ways, it is important that you pay attention and be prepared to slow down, ask for help from the client or from a colleague or consultant, and above all, remain open to correction of your assumptions. If you are able to remain open to correction, you might find that you learn a great deal about other cultures, lifestyles, and orientations to the world. But most of all, you may learn a great deal about yourself.

The self psychological approach tends to view aggression as a reaction to injury to the self. As with all affective states, it is understood in context rather than as an internally generated drive. Usually the precursor to an outburst of anger or aggressive behavior is some hurt, rejection, embarrassment, or loss. The appreciation of this sequence will usually bring great relief and assist your clients' in their efforts to regulate themselves because it provides them with an ability to reflect more competently. However, some aggressive and impulsively angry clients are not relieved by the counselor's efforts to understand their rage in this way. Instead, they feel increased humiliation when their anger and aggressive behavior are viewed as reactions. It further reduces their sense of competence and effectiveness and further humiliates them. Their rage feels like a fundamental part of them and to see it as a reaction to something else feels diminishing and may even provoke further rage. It may be important, when dealing with such clients, to try to assess the meaning of their rage to them before proceeding to understand it on this basis.

Some cultures and family traditions see counseling in terms of advice giving and are frustrated confused or humiliated by the counselor's efforts to understand their experience. The counselor role is valued as a source of wisdom, guidance, and rules to live by. It may be necessary to acknowledge this and to provide it where possible, delaying or even avoiding the empathic stance. It may be perceived as weakness or disinterest, even blaming, rather than a welcome attempt by another to understand the client's problem.

In those clients who reveal early in the assessment that they are exquisitely sensitive to any disagreement, confrontation, or even to the counselor's unique perspective, the empathic approach so emphasized by the self psychological approach might be integrated into other approaches in order to establish a working therapeutic relationship.

The self psychological approach has been well described in work with children using play therapy. The metaphors of play lend themselves well to the appreciation of self-states and selfobject needs and their regulation. One feature of this modality is the importance of staying within the play metaphor rather than converting it into the "adult" language of the counselor.

FINDING YOUR NICHE

While the application of the empathic listening stance advocated by self psychology may be of universal value, it may provide difficulties for beginning counselors who naturally require a paradigm with which they can organize their thoughts. The constructs of self psychology may be too vague and nonspecific for the beginner. If this is a concern you might start with a more specific model that deals with the objective data of the therapeutic process. Later, when you feel more comfortable, you might try to experiment more with empathic listening. It is not for everybody because it does expose the listener to new and, at times, strange worlds of experience. It is comforting to have a map when we are in a strange place and theory often helps us deal with the unfamiliar worlds we visit with our clients.

Those of you who are comfortable with the empathic method of gaining access to your clients but still need more theory to guide you through the inevitable complexities will find some of the more contemporary branches of self psychology very rewarding. Motivational systems theory is rich with concepts that integrate modern clinical theory with developmental theory and neuropsychological thought. Guided by an overriding "spirit of inquiry," it integrates a wide range of contemporary theories with the self psychological emphasis on the subjective experiences of client and counselor and the exploration of the selfobject dimensions of all relational experiences. Contemporary attachment theory and nonlinear dynamic systems theory have also been integrated with self psychology.

Those who are more inclined to use their own experience as a guide and stay closely in touch with their own subjectivity might find the intersubjective approach a useful elaboration of self psychology and more suited to their own sensibilities. In this approach, the clinical phenomena are always understood as emerging at the interface between the two interacting subjectivities of client and counselor. This approach offers a critique of psychoanalytic models that fall prey to the "myth of the isolated mind" in which the mind is conceived of as a container with contents, having an inside and an outside, and capable of independent existence unaffected by other subjectivities. This model stresses both the subjective and the relational elements of the therapeutic process and of the significant events in clients' development that may help you understand their present-day interactions and experiences.

Should you become more interested in developing your skills in applying this approach to more intensive and long-term treatments, you will need to experience some personal therapy yourself to assist you in your ongoing self-reflection as you immerse yourself more deeply in the complex life of your clients. You will learn more about normal and pathological development, the work with dreams as a further source of understanding of subjective life, and the different approaches found useful in specific conditions such as psychosis, addictions, victims of trauma, and those suffering from somatizing disorders, to name a few.

PROCESS AND CASE SUGGESTIONS

Let us now turn to the three cases available for you to apply some of these ideas I have been describing. Elena, Jane, and Theo are three clients with clinical problems that you will likely find very relevant to your future practice. Hence, they offer very appropriate challenges to budding counseling skills. I found the case descriptions to be full of relevant and well-organized information. They are complemented by video clips that show us who the clients are, how they expressed themselves, and how they related to the consultant-interviewer. I have provided you with some of my thoughts about each client. I have applied the self psychological approach outlined above so that you can compare your own efforts to immerse yourself empathically in each of their subjective worlds as well as your attempts to formulate these worlds in terms of the clients' self-organization and their needs for, and fears of, selfobject experience.

1. *Elena.* The case description of Elena will provide you with an opportunity to think about a high school student dealing with some common and painful issues that threaten her emerging sense of adolescent self. Elena forces us to ponder the choices faced by a teenager caught between the conflicting values of her family culture and her peer group. As you attend to the case of Elena you might keep these questions in mind. How did her unique personal development prepare her for such a dilemma and how might it have undermined her competence to negotiate this phase of her life? How does she make use of her abilities to calm herself and hold her self together, while all around her are failing to meet her needs? When we meet

her in the video, how do you experience her inclination to relinquish her own career ambitions to meet the needs of her mother? How might your response influence your exploration of that issue with her?

2. *Jane.* Jane is a very different, but—I think you will find—an equally compelling and relevant clinical challenge. Jane is a middle-aged, highly competent, professional woman who experiences her difficulties through bodily distress rather than through an awareness of emotional pain. Try to think about the challenges involved for her counselor to whom she has been sent by her physicians for help. I would suggest some further questions to keep in mind as you approach the case of Jane. What are the challenges to the self-cohesion and vitality of a woman at this phase of life, caught between the demands of career, motherhood, and her sense of her responsibilities as a dutiful wife and daughter? What inner and external resources does she muster to assist her in righting her injured and burdened sense of self? How does a woman with built-in "old-fashioned" values and ideals strengthen her self in this modern era when contemporary roles and expectations of women have changed dramatically? How might you assist her to attend to her emotional cues of distress when she is so clearly committed to a somatic explanation?

3. *Theo.* Theo will take you to yet another challenging realm as a budding counselor. Here you will encounter a bright young African American man in college who is struggling with problematic relationships and explosive anger. As you learn about Theo, you will enter the world of a young man struggling with self-regulation, particularly the control of his anger. Your task as a self psychologically informed counselor is to try to understand the subjective world of a man who, despite feeling himself to be in constant danger of losing control, longs for a successful career and to preserve his relationship with his girlfriend. It is likely unfamiliar to you and therefore likely to be quite a challenge to understand Theo's fragile sense of self-control, his transformation into states of uncontrolled rage, and his limited understanding of his needs of others. Hold on to these important questions as you acquaint yourself with Theo. What life experiences may have left him with such a fragile self, so vulnerable to injuries? What self-strengthening experiences have been helpful in the past and what has been tried unsuccessfully? How might a counseling relationship contribute to Theo's capacity to find selfobject experiences in his relational milieu? How does he try to regulate himself and how might you assist him in his quest to establish more successful strategies?

As you approach these clinical presentations, it might help to keep these organizing questions in mind. *What is the dominant state of the client's sense of self?* Be guided by affects (feelings) reported by the client. How does the client tend to experience himself or herself in the world? To what extent does he or she feel calm and "together," lively, and energetic or focused and confident about her (his) goals, aspirations, and abilities. To what extent do they feel anxious or fearful, depleted of energy and hope, disorganized and scattered, or unable to function as in the past. You will arrive at different conclusions about the state of the self in the three cases.

What triggers are you able to identify that contribute to each client's disrupted self-states? Do particular people, or specific responses trigger the disrupted self-states reported? Is there a pattern of unmet selfobject needs contributing to a chronically devitalized or disorganized self?

Are there recognizable patterns of unmet selfobject needs in the client's story of relationship difficulties? Are there, for example, many experiences in which feelings of competence are not responded to in an affirming way and achievements not acknowledged? Such events would indicate a deficit in mirroring selfobject experience. Have valued leaders or teacher or parental figures disappointed or rejected the client, indicating a lack of idealizing selfobject experience?

What self-strengthening and self-vitalizing strategies has the client been able to use in the past, and what are they currently attempting? Does the client avoid situations to protect him- or herself? How successful are these strategies in the short and long term? Meditation and music, or fitness training with a social group, might be very adaptive and self-strengthening. They open up new possibilities for self-organizing and self-strengthening experiences. Addictive behaviors such as alcohol or drug use, gambling, or sexual promiscuity may all be self-calming or energizing in the short term, but they are anything but useful for personal growth and future maintenance of self-esteem. Instead of opening up new possibilities, they are more likely to become repetitive, compulsive, and destructive behaviors.

Are there interactions described that seem to represent prototypical events that capture the lived past as it has impacted the client's development, shaped expectations for future encounters, and therefore contributed to present-day experiences and relationships? These events may be memories, fantasies, dreams, or interactions with the counselor during sessions. Not being picked up at nursery school followed by the indifference of attachment figures to ensuing distress or protest, being chided for not eating, or for eating too much, may all be valuable representations of developmental themes that shape the future sense of insecurity in attachments to others in the former example, and of a sense of competence in the regulation of nutrition in the latter. What are the normal interactions that should have taken place instead of the ones reported?

SUMMARY AND SUGGESTED READINGS

You have now been introduced to self psychology and have had an opportunity to practice its application to case material. In your formulations of the three cases, you will have utilized the essentials of this approach. You should now have a sense of how the empathic perspective is applied clinically. This will allow you to try it whenever you need to augment whatever approach you are using with clients, particularly when you sense some difficulties emerging in your work. It is always helpful to have the empathic listening perspective available, even if it is not your primary mode of evaluating clinical material and responding to your clients. You will inevitably find yourself confronted with unexpected problems at some time in your working life. Such problems may include pronounced or prolonged negativism and/or aversiveness, impasses in which nothing you try seems to help, or difficulties understanding the client's needs or dissatisfactions. The empathic listening stance in which you try to understand the clients' experience, especially their experiences of you the counselor, is a valuable strategy to bring to bear on impasses of this nature.

This introduction to the self psychological approach has only touched on the basic principles of self psychology theory and practice. To more deeply and flexibly apply this approach, you will benefit from a more detailed knowledge of the concepts and their elaborations and modifications. I have suggested further reading below.

No amount of reading, however, can replace the use of expert supervision of your cases by an experienced clinician who understands this approach. The supervision of clinical work must include a "microscopic" attention to process as it unfolds between client and counselor. Only by this detailed examination of clinical material is it possible to have your efforts at empathic immersion monitored and evaluated. Only by the close reading of "She (client) said:, I (counselor) said:" can you, assisted by a supervisor, follow the process of the clinical exchange to learn if you are on track with your client or if you have gone astray. It is amazing how much there is to learn by observing "what happens next" after any therapeutic intervention.

For a more in-depth coverage of Kohutian self psychology, the following references would do nicely:

Bacal, H. (1998). *Optimal responsiveness: How therapists heal their patients*. Howard Bacal. (Ed.), Northvale, NJ: Aronson.

Basch, M. (1983). Empathic understanding: A review of the concept and some theoretical considerations. *J. Amer. Psychoanal. Assn., 31*: 101–126.

Buirski, P., & Haglund, P. (2001). *Making sense together: The intersubjective approach to psychotherapy*. Northvale, NJ: Aronson.

Kohut, H. (1959). Introspection, empathy and psychoanalysis. *J. Amer. Psychoanal. Assn., 7*: 459–483. Also in *The search for the self,* Vol. 1. P. Ornstein (Ed.), New York: I.U.P.

Kohut, H. (1982). Introspection, empathy and the semi-circle of mental health. *Inter. J. of Psychoanal, 63*: 395–407. Also in *The search for the self,* Vol. 4, 537–567. P. Ornstein (Ed.), New York: I.U.P.

Lee, Ronald R., & Colby, Martin, J. (1991). *Psychotherapy after Kohut: A textbook of self psychology*. Hillsdale, NJ: Analytic Press.

Lichtenberg, J. (1991). What is a selfobject? *Psychoanal. Dialogues 1*(1): 455–479.

Lichtenberg, J. D., & Kindler, A. R. (1994). A motivational systems approach to the clinical experience. *J. Amer. Psychoanal. Assoc. 42*(2): 405–420.

Lichtenberg, J., Lachmann, F., & Fosshage, J. (1992). *Self and motivational sytems*. Hillsdale, NJ: Analytic Press.

Siegel, Allen M. (1996). *Heinz Kohut and the psycholgy of the self*. New York: Routledge.

Stolorow, R. D., Brandschaft, B., & Atwood, G. E. (1987). *Psychoanalytic treatment: An intersubjective approach*. Hillsdale, NJ: Analytic Press.

Wolf, Ernest S. (1988). *Treating the self: Elements of clinical self psychology*. New York: Guilford Press.

Chapter 5

Time-Limited Dynamic Psychotherapy

Hanna Levenson

Chapter Outline

Bridging the Theory-to-Practice Gap

Principles in Practice

Keys to Conceptualization

Interventions and Therapeutic Process

Short- and Long-Term Goals

Using the Relationship

Adapting the Approach

Finding Your Niche

Process and Case Suggestions

Summary and Suggested Readings

References

Some material in this chapter is from *Time-Limited Dynamic Psychotherapy: A Guide to Clinical Practice* (©1995 by Hanna Levenson, reprinted by permission of Basic Books, a division of Perseus Books).

BRIDGING THE THEORY-TO-PRACTICE GAP

Think of the last time you met someone who immediately rubbed you the wrong way. For no apparent reason, this person approached you in an off-putting manner—perhaps being intrusive, boisterous, or even intimidating. What was your response? You probably had some reaction—obvious or subtle—to such provocative behavior. You may have glared at the person with your heart beating rapidly and your palms clenched into fists. Or you may have lowered your head and looked away. Your reactions probably affected this person's further behavior. Over time, such interactions come to shape how we think and feel about others and ourselves. They help determine the way we interact in the world, which further affects the way others respond to us. This cycle continues in an endless loop, strengthening our view of ourselves and others. Eventually, the nature of these interactions forms templates in our minds of what we can expect to get from others and give to others. These templates of how our social lives work have far-reaching implications for our hopes, joys, and problems. Such working models built up over past experiences in combination with our present interactions form the basis of the interpersonal approach to psychotherapy.

So, too, in therapy, the manner in which clients approach their therapists and the manner in which therapists respond to their clients have much to do with the nature of the ensuing therapeutic process and progress. As stated succinctly and accurately by a trainee learning to apply interpersonal dynamic psychotherapy, "This approach assumes that a client has unwittingly developed over time a self-perpetuating, maladaptive pattern of relating to others, and that this pattern underlies the client's presenting issues. The therapist's job is to use the clinical relationship to facilitate for the client a new experience of relating, allowing the client to break the old pattern and thereby resolve the presenting issues."

Over 25 years ago, Hans Strupp and Jeffrey Binder developed time-limited dynamic psychotherapy (TLDP), an interpersonal, time-sensitive approach. Previously, brief treatments (20 sessions or less) were used only with high-functioning clients (for example, above average intelligence, psychologically minded, introspective). But TLDP was designed to be applicable to a broad range of clients, even those who had difficulties forming good working relationships (therapeutic alliances) with their therapists. The goal of TLDP is not the reduction of symptoms as such (for instance, anxiety, depression), although improvements in symptoms are expected to occur; rather, the focus is on changing ingrained patterns of interpersonal relatedness or personality style. TLDP uses the relationship that develops between therapist and client to kindle fundamental changes in the way a person interacts with others.

The interpersonal view of TLDP focuses on transactional patterns where the therapist is embedded in the therapeutic relationship as a participant observer or observing participant. A wonderful *New Yorker* cartoon captures the essence of this viewpoint. It shows a woman from the audience walking onto a theater stage where an Elizabethan drama is taking place. One actor, seeing her approach, says to his fellow actor, "But wait. Ellen doth approach." Ellen had been observing the play, but now she was going to enter the spotlight and join the action on stage. She at once becomes a part of the drama, but at the same time is an audience member observing the drama. So, too, in an interpersonal therapy, the clinician participates fully in trying to form a relationship with the client, and in so doing gets caught up in the client's "drama," acting out a complementary role. However, the therapist also has the ability (hopefully) and responsibility to step outside the immediate unfolding scenario and perceive the action from a more objective vantage point.

PRINCIPLES IN PRACTICE

1. *People are innately motivated to search for and maintain human relatedness.* In attachment theory terms, the infant's orientation to stay connected to early caregivers is based on survival needs. We are hardwired to gravitate toward others (newborns, for instance, are more likely to gaze at designs in the shape and structure of a face than at more abstract patterns). The more we are able to establish a secure interpersonal base, the more likely we are to develop into independent, mature, and effective individuals. I think of how so many people in the Twin Towers of 9-11, when faced with an impending horrific death, reached for their cell phones for the sole purpose of making contact with a loved one.

   By recognizing this basic drive for relatedness in your clients, you have a powerful lever to promote growth. For example, a client of mine was more than reluctant to give up his daily marijuana use, but when he understood how it was creating a serious wedge between him and his wife that might cost him her love and companionship, be became motivated to quit.

2. *Maladaptive relationship patterns are acquired early in life, become schematized, and underlie many presenting complaints.* How one relates as an adult typically stems from relationships with early caregivers in the following manner. If these caregivers (usually parents) are attuned to the needs of the child and are accessible, the child feels secure and is able to explore the environment feeling safe and loved. If the caregivers are inconsistent, rejecting, and/or unresponsive, the child will feel insecure and could become anxious or avoidant. Early experiences with parental figures result in mental representations of these relationships or working models of one's interpersonal world. These experiences form the building blocks of what will become organized, encoded experiential, affective, and cognitive data (i.e., interpersonal schemas) informing the child about the nature of human relatedness, and what is generally necessary to sustain and maintain emotional connectedness to others. Children then filter the world through the lenses of these schemata, which allow them to interpret the present, understand the past, and anticipate the future. Unfortunately, these schema can become a dysfunctional, self-fulfilling prophecy if early interpersonal experiences are faulty. For example, a client of mine had parents who treated him in an authoritarian and harsh manner. Consequently he became overly placating and deferential because it was a way he could survive and still stay connected to them. His experiences led him to expect that others would treat him badly if he were not compliant. He entered therapy because he was living a life filled with anxiety and a sense of dread.

   While early childhood experiences are usually the major contributor to the development of lifelong patterns, there are some situations where life-altering adult experiences have overwhelmed previous templates. Several years ago, I treated many Vietnam combat veterans at a Veterans Administration hospital. These veterans had, for the most part, nurturing childhoods but were now anxious, hypervigilant, suspicious, and sometimes combative. Their horrible war experiences had so dramatically changed their previously benign models of how their social worlds worked that they were now seeking and needing help.

3. *Such patterns persist because they are maintained in current relationships (circular causality).* From a TLDP framework, individuals' social expectations are not seen as fixed at a certain point, but rather as continually changing as they interact with others. Although one's dysfunctional interactive style might be learned early in life, this style must be supported in the person's present adult life for the interpersonal difficulties to continue. However, what often happens is that people act in ways that provoke in others the very behavior they are so afraid of getting. Let's go back to the client, I mentioned. His placating and deferential behavior became well practiced into adulthood. As an adult, his meekness allowed others to take advantage of him at best and treat him harshly at worst. In other words, his submissiveness invited the very behavior he was most afraid of (dominance by others). Furthermore, since his template was derived and perpetuated outside of his awareness, he continued to be at its mercy. I am reminded of the saying that a fish has no idea of water. So it is with working models. They have an enormous impact on our lives, but we just take them for granted as the way life is.

      On the other hand, if my client could have the experience of being assertive and being treated with respect instead of harshness, this would run counter to his internalized working model. From a TLDP perspective, with more and more of these experiences he would be expected to shift (over time) to a more robust and enlivened view of himself and his relational world.

4. *Therefore, in TLDP, clients are viewed as stuck, not sick.* Clients are seen as trapped in a rut which they helped dig, not as deficient. The goal of therapy is to help them get out of that rut.

5. *Maladaptive relationship patterns are reenacted in the therapeutic relationship.* Clients interact with the therapist in the same dysfunctional way that characterizes their interactions with significant others (i.e., transference), and try to enlist the therapist into playing a complementary role (i.e., countertransference). From an interpersonal therapy perspective the therapist is pulled to join the clients in acting out their lifelong dysfunctional style. As an interpersonal therapist, I see this as an ideal opportunity, because it provides me with the very situation that gets the client into difficulties in the outside world. I have a chance to *observe* the playing out of the client's maladaptive interactional pattern, and to *experience* what it is like to try to relate to that individual. I become the *participant observer* mentioned earlier. The interactionist position of TLDP holds that the therapist cannot help but react to the client—that is, the therapist inevitably will be pushed and pulled by the client's dysfunctional style and will respond accordingly. The therapist inevitably becomes "hooked" into acting out the corresponding response to the client's inflexible, maladaptive pattern. I think of it as the therapist's unwittingly becoming the client's dance partner in a well-rehearsed two-step.

To go back to my subservient, placating, anxious client, in the initial sessions I found myself becoming more reassuring, more confident, and more directive in my manner than usual—more "the expert." I was being hooked into a complementary style that fit with his lead in the dance.

It is critical that the therapist eventually get unhooked. To do this, therapists must realize how they are fostering a replication of the dysfunctional pattern. Then they can use this information to attempt to change the nature of the interaction in a more positive way, thereby engaging the client in a healthier mode of relating. In addition, therapists can invite the client to look collaboratively at what is happening between them (i.e., metacommunicate), either highlighting the dysfunctional reenactment while it is occurring or guiding the client to a healthier, more functionally adaptive way of relating through a series of new experiences.

Since dysfunctional interactions are sustained in the present, the therapist can concentrate on the present to alter the client's dysfunctional interactive style. Working in the present allows change to happen more quickly because there is no assumption about having to work through childhood conflicts and discover historical truths. This emphasis on the present has tremendous implications for treating interpersonal difficulties in a brief time frame.

6. *TLDP focuses on one chief problematic relationship pattern.* While clients may have a repertoire of different interpersonal patterns depending upon their states of mind and the particulars of the situation, the emphasis in TLDP is on discerning what is a client's most pervasive and problematic style of relating. In opera, when characters walk onto the stage, the orchestra plays their theme music. In TLDP, I think of looking for the client's predominant melody. Figuring out what is the chief pattern is a matter of logic (what gets subsumed under what) and clinical attunement.

7. *The change process will continue after the therapy is terminated.* The goal in TLDP is to interrupt the client's ingrained, repetitive, dysfunctional cycle. In so doing, the intention is to promote forays into healthier behavior, which theoretically would be responded to differently (more positively) by others, thereby increasing the probability that the person will again engage in a more satisfying manner. At the end of a brief therapy, such changes have only begun to take hold. It is expected that over time as the individual has more opportunity to practice such functional behaviors, the interactions with others and the resulting more positive internalized schemas would become strengthened. As I like to say, the therapy sessions end, but the therapy continues in the real world.

KEYS TO CONCEPTUALIZATION

In the past, psychodynamic brief therapists used their intuition, insight, and clinical savvy to devise formulations of cases. While these methods may work wonderfully for the gifted or experienced therapist, they are impossible to teach explicitly. One remedy for this situation was the development of a procedure for deriving a dynamic, interpersonal focus—the cyclical maladaptive pattern (CMP). Briefly, the CMP outlines the idiosyncratic vicious cycle of maladaptive interactions that a particular client manifests with others. These cycles or patterns involve inflexible, self-defeating expectations and behaviors, and negative self-appraisals, that lead to dysfunctional and maladaptive interactions with others.

The role of the CMP is critical in TLDP. Specifically, it plays a key role in guiding the clinician in formulating a treatment plan. I use the CMP as an organizational framework that makes a large mass of data comprehensible and leads me to think of ways of intervening that could be helpful. A CMP should not be seen as an encapsulated version of "the truth," but rather as a plausible narrative, incorporating major components of a person's current and historical interactive world. A successful TLDP formulation should provide a *blueprint* for the therapy. It helps me describe the nature of the problem, leads me to figure out the goals for treatment, serves as a guide for the types of interventions I might choose, enables me to anticipate reenactments within the context of the therapeutic interaction, and provides a way to assess whether the therapy is on the right track—in terms of outcome at termination as well as in-session mini-outcomes. The focus provided by the CMP permits the therapist to intervene in ways that have the greatest likelihood of being therapeutic. Thus there are possibilities for the therapy to be brief and effective. As you can see, the CMP is invaluable for the interpersonal therapist.

To derive a TLDP formulation, the therapist lets clients tell their own story in the initial sessions rather than relying on the traditional psychiatric interview that structures the client's responses into categories of information (for example, developmental history, education). By listening to *how* clients tell their story (such as deferentially, cautiously, dramatically) as well as to the content, the therapist can learn much about the client's interpersonal style. The therapist also explores the interpersonal context of the client's symptoms or problems. When did the problems begin? What else was going on in the client's life at that time, especially of an interpersonal nature?

Then the clinician obtains data that will be used to construct a CMP. As I listen to clients in the opening session(s), I pay attention to and seek out information by using four categories:

1. *Acts of the self.* These acts include the thoughts, feelings, motives, perceptions, and behaviors of the client of an interpersonal nature. For example, "When I meet strangers, I think they wouldn't want to have anything to do with me" (thought). "I am afraid to go to the dance" (feeling). "I wish I were the life of the party" (motive). Sometimes these acts are conscious as those above, and sometimes they are outside awareness, as in the case of a woman who does not realize how jealous she is of her sister's accomplishments.

2. *Expectations of others' reactions.* This category pertains to all the statements having to do with how clients imagine others will react to them in response to some interpersonal behavior (act of the self). "My boss will fire me if I make a mistake." "If I go to the party, no one will ask me to dance."

3. *Acts of others toward the self.* This third grouping consists of the actual behaviors of other people, as observed (or assumed) and interpreted by the client. "When I made a mistake at work, my boss shunned me for the rest of the day." "When I went to the party, guys asked me to dance, but only because they felt sorry for me."

4. *Acts of the self toward the self (introject).* In this section belong all the clients' behaviors or attitudes toward themselves—when the self is the object of the interpersonal

pattern. How do clients treat themselves? "When I made the mistake, I berated myself so much I had difficulty sleeping that night." "When no one asked me to dance, I told myself it's because I'm fat, ugly, and unlovable."

5. *Interactive countertransference.* In addition to the four patient categories, an important fifth category pertains to the therapist. When I am with a client, I ask myself what it is like to try to relate to this person. Am I pushed or pulled to respond in a certain way? For example, am I anxious, solicitous, or withdrawn? Remember how earlier I described how I became directive in talking with my client?

The therapist's feelings and behaviors as they pertain to the client are just as important to recognize and track in an interpersonal treatment as those of the client. This complementary way of responding is called the interactive (i.e., interpersonal) countertransference (i.e., responding to the client's transference to the therapist). You have probably heard of countertransference as referring to the therapist's unconscious conflicts and unique responses to the patient because of these unresolved conflicts. Here I am using countertransference in a different sense—to refer to how the therapist gets pushed and pulled by the client, regardless of the therapist's own unique personality makeup. I would expect *any therapist* to get pulled in similar ways in interacting with certain clients. If you were working with my placating client, you would probably be more assertive and directive with him, because he is so submissive. Of course, each therapist has a unique personality that contributes to the particular shading of the reaction which is elicited by the client (for instance, when *you* are directive, it might look different from my version), but the TLDP perspective is that the therapist's behavior is *chiefly* shaped by the client's evoking patterns.

After gathering information on the five categories, the therapist listens for themes in the emerging material by being sensitive to commonalities and redundancies in the client's transactional patterns over person, time, and place. The therapist's reactions to the client should make sense given the client's interpersonal pattern.

All this information is used to develop a CMP narrative—a narrative that tells a story of the client's predominant dysfunctional interactive pattern. For example, a short-hand narrative for my client might sound something like: this is a man who is anxious and deferential (acts of the self), and expects others to be forceful and decisive (expectations). Other people in his life take advantage of his submissiveness, and his therapist became directive and assured with him (acts of others). These responses from others confirm for him that the world is unsafe and leaves him feeling vulnerable and inadequate (introject). Feeling this way about himself leads to his being anxious and deferential, and we come full circle.

The CMP can be used to foresee likely transference-countertransference reenactments that might inhibit treatment progress. By anticipating client resistances, ruptures in the therapeutic alliance, and so on, the therapist is able to plan and improvise appropriately. Thus when therapeutic impasses occur (for example, the client is a passive and not an active participant in his treatment), the therapist is not caught off guard, but rather understands the situation and is ready to act appropriately—a necessity when time is of the essence. From the CMP formulation, the therapist then discerns the goals for treatment. For specifics on this process, see the section "Short- and Long-Term Goals."

The last step in the formulation process involves the continuous refinement of the CMP throughout the therapy. In a brief therapy, the therapist cannot wait to have all the "facts" before formulating the case and intervening. As the therapy proceeds, new content and interactional data become available that might strengthen, modify, or negate the working formulation.

INTERVENTIONS AND THERAPEUTIC PROCESS

Implementation of TLDP does not rely on a set of techniques. Rather, it depends on therapeutic *strategies* that are useful only to the extent that they are *embedded in a larger interpersonal relationship*. These strategies should not be thought of as separate techniques applied in a linear, rigid fashion, but rather as guidelines for the therapist to be used in a fluid and interactive manner. Table 5.1 contains a list of commonly used TLDP intervention strategies.

In TLDP, the therapist specifically addresses what is going on between the therapist and client as they try to form a working relationship (Strategy 1). This focus on the here-and-now transactions provides the building blocks for understanding how the interaction may be a microcosm of the client's interpersonal difficulties in general. The therapist actively encourages the client to explore thoughts and feelings about the therapist (Strategy 2) and

TABLE 5.1

Vanderbilt Therapeutic Strategies Scale*

TLDP Specific Strategies

1. Therapist specifically addresses transactions in the client-therapist relationship.
2. Therapist encourages the client to explore feelings and thoughts about the therapist or the therapeutic relationship.
3. Therapist encourages the client to discuss how the therapist might feel or think about the client.
4. Therapist discusses own reactions to some aspect of the client's behavior in relation to the therapist.
5. Therapist attempts to explore patterns that might constitute a cyclical maladaptive pattern in the client's interpersonal relationships.
6. Therapist asks about the client's introject (how the client feels about and treats him- or herself).
7. Therapist links a recurrent pattern of behavior or interpersonal conflict to transactions between the client and therapist.
8. Therapist addresses obstacles (e.g., silences, coming late, avoidance of meaningful topics) that might influence the therapeutic process.
†9. Therapist provides the opportunity for the client to have a new experience of self and/or the therapist relevant to the client's particular cyclical maladaptive pattern.
10. Therapist discusses an aspect of the time-limited nature of TLDP or termination.

*Butler, S. F., & the Center for Psychotherapy Research Team (1995). Manual for the Vanderbilt Therapeutic Strategies Scale. In H. Levenson, *Time-limited dynamic psychotherapy: A guide to clinical practice.* Basic Books, New York, pp. 243–254.
† Item written by H. Levenson

conversely to discuss how the client imagines the therapist might think or feel about the client (Strategy 3). In this way the therapist can begin to get a sense of the way client puts together his or her interpersonal world. It can sometimes be helpful for the therapist actually to self-disclose his or her countertransferential pull to the client's specific behaviors (Strategy 4). In this way the therapist can guide exploration of possible distortions in the clients' perceptions of others or help the client appreciate his or her impact on others. For example, with my timid client, I said to him that I noticed I was treating him like a child at times and I found this curious since I usually did not interact with clients in this way.

Throughout the therapy, the therapist attempts to discover and discuss with the client any themes emerging in the content and process of the client's relationships (Strategy 5). These explorations enable the client to become more aware of problematic patterns of behavior (CMP). Asking about how the client treats him- or herself (Strategy 6) can further be used to understand how interpersonal processes between others influence the person's view of self and vice versa.

The therapist can help depathologize the clients' CMP by guiding him or her in understanding its historical development. From the TLDP point of view, symptoms and dysfunctional behaviors arise when individuals attempt to adapt to situations that threaten their interpersonal relatedness. For example, in therapy my client began to understand that as a child he had to be subservient and hypervigilant in order to avoid beatings. This realization enabled him to view his present passive style less negatively and allowed him to have some compassion for his childhood plight.

In TLDP a potent intervention capable of providing a new understanding is thought to be the therapist's linking the client's recurrent patterns of behavior to transactions between the therapist and client (Strategy 7). While most of the therapy will be devoted to examining the client's problems in relationships *outside the therapy,* it is through the therapist's observations and interpretations about the reenactment of the cyclical maladaptive pattern *in the sessions* that clients begin to have an in vivo understanding of their behaviors and stimulus value. By ascertaining how an interpersonal pattern has emerged in the therapeutic relationship, the client has perhaps for the first time the opportunity to examine the nature of such behaviors in a safe environment.

A very common error in technique is for the therapist, who is alert to discerning relationship themes, to point out such patterns to the client long before the client has had the opportunity to experience such redundancies in interacting with the therapist. These types of premature interpretations are usually met with surprise, hostility, and/or confusion on the part of the client and can lead to serious ruptures in the working alliance. If the therapist has decided it is the apt time to link a recurrent pattern of behavior with others to transactions between the client and him or herself, he or she should make them as detailed and concrete and possible. Such specificity helps the client experientially recognize himself or herself in the situation.

In Strategy 8 the therapist addresses obstacles (such as coming late, silence) that might influence the therapeutic process. In TLDP these obstacles often are the meat surrounding the CMP skeletal structure. That is, such defensive maneuvers help the therapist discover the manner in which the client tries to maintain a familiar, albeit, dysfunctional pattern. Resistance from the perspective of TLDP is viewed within the interpersonal sphere—as one of a number of transactions between therapist and client. The assumption is that the client is attempting to retain personal integrity and ingrained perceptions of himself or herself and others. The client's perceptions support his or her understanding of what is required to maintain interpersonal connectedness. Resistance in this light is the client's attempt to do the best he or she can with how he or she construes the world.

Therefore, the manner in which the client "resists" will be informative regarding the client's interactive style. The therapist often has the experience of hitting a wall when confronted with the client's resistance. This wall often demarcates the boundaries of the client's CMP. Rather than continue to hit the wall in an attempt to break through it, the TLDP therapist can stand back, appreciate the wall, and invite the client to look at the wall also (i.e., metacommunication). Such an approach often avoids power plays with hostile clients and helps to promote empathy and collaboration. Because the focus in TLDP is on the interpersonal interaction, the therapist always has the process (between therapist and client) to talk about when a therapeutic impasse has occurred. It is this focus on the interactive process that is absolutely essential to this interpersonal approach.

One of the most important treatment strategies is providing the opportunity for the client to have a new experience of him- or herself and/or the therapist that helps undermine the client's CMP (Strategy 9). The following examples of how to intervene with two clients with seemingly similar behaviors but differing experiential goals illustrate the strategy. Marjorie's maladaptive interpersonal pattern suggested she had deeply ingrained beliefs that she could not be appreciated unless she were the charming, effervescent ingénue. When she attempted to joke throughout most of the fifth session, her therapist directed her attention to the contrast between her joking and her anxiously twisting her handkerchief. (New experience: The therapist invites the possibility that he can be interested in her even if she were anxious and not entertaining.)

Susan's lifelong dysfunctional pattern, on the other hand, revealed a meek stance fostered by repeated ridicule from her alcoholic father. She also attempted to joke in the fifth session, nervously twisting her handkerchief. Susan's therapist listened with engaged interest to the jokes and did not interrupt. (New experience: The therapist can appreciate her taking center stage and not humiliate her when she is so vulnerable.) In both cases the therapist's interventions (observing nonverbal behavior; listening) were well within the psychodynamic therapist's acceptable repertoire. There was no need to do anything feigned (for example, laugh uproariously at Susan's joke), nor was there a demand to respond with a similar therapeutic stance to both presentations.

In these cases the therapists' behavior gave the clients a new interpersonal experience—an opportunity to disconfirm their own interpersonal schemata. With sufficient quality and/or quantity of these experiences, clients can develop different internalized working models of relationships. In this way TLDP is thought to promote change by altering the basic infrastructure of the client's transactional world, which then influences the concept of self. My experiential goal for my timid client was to help him experience himself as being assertive and in charge, and correspondingly to experience me as less directive and controlling. I deferred to him whenever possible and followed his direction. At first, this made him uncomfortable, since it was so out of keeping with his experience. Over time, however, he took more and more the lead and we developed a collaborative relationship rather than a hierarchical one.

The last strategy is designed to support exploration of the client's reactions to the time-limited nature of TLDP. Issues of loss are interwoven throughout the therapy and do not appear just in the termination phase. Toward the end of therapy, the best advice for the TLDP therapist is to stay with the dynamic focus and the goals for treatment, while examining how these patterns are evidenced when loss and separation issues are most salient.

How does the TLDP therapist know when the client has had "enough" therapy? In doing TLDP, I use five sets of questions to help me judge when termination is appropriate. First and foremost, has the client evidenced interactional changes with significant others in his or her life? Does the client report more rewarding transactions? Second, has the client had a new experience (or a series of new experiences) of himself or herself and the therapist within the therapy? Third, has there been a change in the level on which the therapist and client are relating (from parent-child to adult-adult)? Fourth, has the therapist's countertransferential reaction to the client shifted (usually from negative to positive)? And fifth, does the client manifest some understanding about his or her dynamics and the role he or she was playing to maintain them?

If the answer is "no" to more than one of these questions, then the therapist should seriously consider whether the client has had an adequate course of therapy. The therapist should reflect why this has been the case and weigh the possible benefits of alternative therapies, another course of TLDP, a different therapist, nonpsychological alternatives, and so on.

As with most brief therapies, one course of TLDP is not considered to be the final or definitive intervention. At some point in the future, the client may feel the need to obtain more therapy for similar or different issues. Such additional therapy would not be viewed as evidence of a TLDP treatment failure. In fact it is hoped that clients will view their TLDP therapies as helpful and as a resource to which they could return over time. This view of the availability of multiple, short-term therapies over the individual's life span is consistent with the position of the therapist as family practitioner.

SHORT- AND LONG-TERM GOALS

The TLDP therapist seeks to provide a *new experience* and a *new understanding* for the client. The first and major goal in conducting TLDP is for the client to have a new relational experience. "New" is meant in the sense of being different and more functional (i.e., healthier) than the maladaptive pattern to which the person has become accustomed. And "experience" emphasizes behaving differently and emotionally appreciating behaving differently. From a TLDP perspective, behaviors are encouraged that signify a new manner of interacting (for instance, more flexibly, more independently) rather than specific, content-based behaviors (such as going to a movie alone). The new experience is actually composed of a set of focused experiences throughout the therapy in which the client has a different appreciation of self, of therapist, and of their interaction. These new experiences provide the client with experiential learning so that old patterns may be relinquished and new patterns may evolve.

The focus of these new experiences centers on those that are particularly helpful to a client based on the therapist's formulation of the case. The therapist identifies what he or she could say or do (within the therapeutic role) that would most likely alter or interrupt the client's maladaptive interactive style. The therapist's behavior gives the client the opportunity to disconfirm his or her interpersonal schemata. The client can actively try out (consciously or unconsciously) new behaviors in the therapy, see how they feel, and notice how the therapist responds. This information then informs the client's internal representations of what can be expected from self and others. This in vivo learning is a critical component in the practice of TLDP.

A tension is created when the familiar (though detrimental) responses to the client's presentation are not provided. Out of this tension new learning takes place. Such an emotionally intense, here-and-now process is thought to "heat up" the therapeutic process and permit progress to be made more quickly than in therapies that depend solely upon more abstract learning (usually through interpretation and clarification). I believe this experiential learning is important for doing brief therapy, and becomes critical when working with a client who has difficulty establishing a therapeutic alliance or exploring relational issues in the here and now. As Frieda Fromm-Reichmann is credited with saying, what the client needs is an experience, not an explanation.

The second goal of providing a new understanding focuses more specifically on cognitive changes. The client's new understanding usually involves an identification and comprehension of dysfunctional patterns. To facilitate such a new understanding, the TLDP therapist can point out repetitive patterns (i.e., metacommunicate) that have originated in experiences with past significant others, with present significant others, and in the here and now with the therapist. Therapists' disclosing their own reactions to the clients' behaviors can also be beneficial. In this way clients begin to recognize how they have similar relationship patterns with different people in their lives, and this new perspective enables them to examine their active role in perpetuating dysfunctional interactions.

The therapist (in conjunction with the client) aims to generate new experiences and new understandings. In reality, the therapist is pleased with any movement possible toward these goals, with the understanding that even slight shifts might result in major changes down the road. The short-term goals are to give the client repeated tastes of what it is like to interact more fully and flexibly within the therapy and to some extent to experiment with what is being learned in his or her outside social world. The long-term goals, which the brief therapist understands will be achieved after the therapy is concluded, include the person's having a richer set of interactions with others stemming from and reinforcing his or her more satisfying sense of self.

USING THE RELATIONSHIP

In TLDP, the therapy is all about using the relationship. As has been previously described, the TLDP therapist uses the relationship to help figure out the problematic pattern (formulation) and to provide corrective transactional experiences (intervention).

ADAPTING THE APPROACH

TLDP was developed to help therapists deal with clients who have trouble forming working alliances due to their lifelong dysfunctional interpersonal difficulties. However, it could be applicable for any individuals who are having difficulties (such as depression, anxiety, emptiness) that affect their relatedness to self and other. Strupp and Binder (1984) outlined five major selection criteria for determining a client's appropriateness for TLDP: First, clients must be in *emotional discomfort* so they are motivated to endure the often challenging and painful change process, and to make sacrifices of time, effort, and money as required by therapy. Second, clients must *come for appointments and engage with the therapist*—or at least talk. Initially such an attitude may be fostered by hope or faith in a positive outcome. Later it might stem from actual experiences of the therapist as a helpful partner.

Third, clients must be *willing to consider how their relationships have contributed* to distressing symptoms, negative attitudes, and/or behavioral difficulties. The operative word here is willing. Suitable clients do not actually have to walk in the door indicating that they have made this connection. Rather, in the give-and-take of the therapeutic encounters, they evidence signs of being willing to entertain the possibility. It should be noted that they do not have to understand the nature of interpersonal difficulties or admit responsibility for them to meet this selection criterion.

Fourth, clients need to be *willing to examine feelings* that may hinder more successful relationships and may foster more dysfunctional ones. The person must also be capable of distancing from these feelings in order to collaborate with the therapist in examining them.

And fifth, clients should be capable of having a *meaningful relationship* with the therapist. Again, it is not expected that the client initially relates in a collaborative manner. But the potential for establishing such a relationship should exist. Clients cannot be out of touch with reality or so impaired that they have difficulty appreciating that their therapists are separate people. Previously, I endorsed the Strupp and Binder selection criteria. My present thinking, however, is that TLDP may be helpful to clients even when they do not quite meet these criteria as long as the therapist can discern a CMP. This hypothesis needs to be empirically tested.

Development and use of the CMP in treatment is essential to TLDP. It is not necessarily shared with the client but may well be, depending on the client's abilities to deal with the material. For some clients with minimal introspection and abstraction ability, the problematic interpersonal scenario may never be stated as such. Rather, the content may stay very close to the presenting problems and concerns of the client. Other clients enter therapy with a fairly good understanding of their own self-perpetuating interpersonal patterns. In these cases, the therapist and client can jointly articulate the parameters that foster such behavior, generalize to other situations where applicable, and readily recognize their occurrence in the therapy.

Since TLDP acknowledges that both therapist and client bring their own personal qualities, history, and values to the therapeutic encounter, this theory has the potential to be especially sensitive to the factors involved in treating clients from different races, cultures, sexual orientations, and so on. However, as pointed out by LaRoche (1999), proponents of the interpersonal-relational approach could do a much better job of explicitly considering the larger context in which any therapy takes place. "It seems crucial to extend...[the notion] of transference to include the organizing principles and imagery crystallized out of the values, roles, beliefs, and history of the *cultural* environment" (p. 391, emphasis added). Thus, it is of paramount importance that the therapist be aware of and understand how cultural factors (in the inclusive sense of the word) may be playing a role in the client's lifelong patterns and in interpersonal difficulties including those that might manifest between therapist and client. From a relational point of view, the client's interpersonal style outside of the therapy office is an amalgamation of specific problems, attachment history, sociocultural context, strengths, life stage, familial factors, and values, just to mention a few. All these contribute to the client's assumptive world, or working model. If a therapist did not consider these factors, important interactive dimensions could be missed or misunderstood, thereby endangering the entire therapeutic process and outcome.

As part of this understanding, the therapist should have some comprehension (based on the available clinical and empirical data in the literature) of the normative interpersonal behavior and expectations for people with similar backgrounds (cultural data). And this should be distinguished (to the extent possible) from the individual's CMP (idiosyncratic data). For example, in one of the cases presented on the website, the client is a 22-year-old, African American man. I, a white woman, am old enough to be his mother. He complains of fears of being controlled, ignored, and vulnerable. Is this to be understood as part of his idiosyncratic CMP, or as part of a set of experiences he shares with other black men in our society? And if it is shared by others with a similar cultural background, is his manifestation of it more extreme? To the extent that this client is having these issues with people in his life who are of the same gender and race, the hypothesis that these experiences have an idiosyncratic component is strengthened.

In addition, within the therapy office, the therapist must also consider how cultural factors take on an active role. Perhaps this client is saying he feels ignored and vulnerable because his therapist is someone from the dominant, white culture (a cultural transference-countertransference reenactment). If this is the case, his therapist could make a seriously erroneous error by inferring that this is a more global problem for him. From a TLDP perspective, it is important to be aware of the dangers of making assumptions based solely on transference-countertransference enactments. This again highlights the importance of a comprehensive and evolving formulation using the CMP categories.

The best way to judge if a CMP is more an artifact of differences between therapist and client, is to gauge the therapist-patient interactions in the here and now of the therapy sessions in light of what the patient says about expectations of and behavior from other people (especially to the extent that they are of the same race, gender, age, or other relevant parameters). Having said this, however, the therapist must always be vigilant for cultural ignorance and bias having an untoward effect on the therapy. Ridley (2006), writing on multicultural considerations in case formulation, points out that models that rely on the scientist-practitioner model and use hypothesis testing allow an examination of cultural elements in a relatively seamless way. He particularly notes that "TLDP incorporates continual evaluation and refinement of working hypotheses."

FINDING YOUR NICHE

The dynamic interpersonal approach runs the gamut from those who emphasize the internalized representations of the client's world to those who focus on the impact of the larger society and everything in between (such as TLDP). What they have in common is that they do not see "pathology" as emanating from inside the person in a biologically predestined way, but rather as located in the transactional world in which that individual resides.

Furthermore, there is more of an emphasis on the real life experiences of people. There are several different therapeutic approaches within this model. (See Levenson, Butler, Powers, and Beitman, 2002 and Messer and Warren, 1995 for more information on various brief, dynamic-interpersonal models.)

If your temperament is more introverted and you detest being focused, then the make-every-session-count emphasis of TLDP is not going to be easy for you. Similarly, if you can only bear to see yourself as a neutral, always benign professional who is trying to help an impaired individual, the two-person framework implicit in the interpersonal approach would not be for you. The interpersonal therapist has to be prepared to get into the trans-actional game as a participant-observer and should not be content to sit on the safer, more distant sidelines offering wise comments as a healer. In the role of participant-observer we often learn some things about our own attitudes and behaviors that challenge our concepts of who we think we need to be as helpers.

PROCESS AND CASE SUGGESTIONS

As you approach each of the three cases on the website, give yourself some time to really imagine sitting across from the person depicted. See yourself attempting to have an inter-personal relationship with each one—a professional relationship—but a relationship nonetheless.

1. *Elena.* Elena, a 17-year-old Mexican-American female, is not making good eye contact with you. She is clearly anxious, tense, and frustrated. Picture yourself there with her. Let her tell her own story. As she does, be aware of what you are feeling and thinking. As Elena begins to talk about her past and present, begin to see how her life is filled with people important to her. How does she react toward these people? How do they react toward her? Do you begin to hear some similar themes? Try to hear the melody of the interaction (the process), not just the lyrics (although the content of what she is saying may also be of importance.) As the session goes forward, are there ways you feel yourself pushed or pulled to inter-act with her? For example, do you find yourself ready to propose solutions to her dilemmas. She is so young and so needs some sound advice, or does she? Perhaps you know what it is like to be the good child.

2. *Jane.* Let yourself also be fully in the room when you turn to the case of Jane, a Caucasian woman in her 50s. She was referred by her cardiologist and you can see that she is frustrated just being there. She shares some of her difficulties, but also reassures you that "everything is good" in her life. She so steadfastly maintains that she is fine except for a heart problem that you wonder what to do next. But as you listen to her story, definite themes emerge. The conflicts Jane is experiencing might seem clear to you, but she is definitely in the dark. What an awkward position to be in as a therapist. Will she let you in? Could your perceptions be wrong? What if she really does have a heart condition that could cause her to die if it's not discovered soon? Perhaps you start thinking about going into another profession.

3. *Theo.* Now do the same kind of immersion with Theo. He is a 22-year-old, African American senior in college. People are of extreme importance to him. In fact, his main impetus for entering therapy is that his girlfriend told him that she would end their relationship if he did not seek help. Theo is a bit of a puzzle. He says he often feels as though he is "going to explode," but in the session he seems quite calm and even-tempered. He keeps good eye contact with you. As you listen to him, themes begin to emerge. He is so lonely and people in his life seem to have treated him badly. Will you experience him as intimidating or will he see you as experiencing him in this way and if so, how can you maintain an alliance with him?

SUMMARY AND SUGGESTED READINGS

To learn more about TLDP, there are three major texts (Binder, 2004; Levenson, 1995; Strupp and Binder, 1984). There are also several helpful videos that demonstrate the actual practice of TLDP with clients.[1] Workshops and in-depth training in various models of dynamic interpersonal therapy are given nationally and internationally. Ongoing clinical supervision, preferably with videotape or audiotape, is the best way to increase your competence in learning how to apply theoretical concepts and clinical strategies in real case situations. I personally have found this way of working to be a very rewarding and involving way to help people.

REFERENCES

Binder J. L. (2004). *Key competencies in brief dynamic psychotherapy: Clinical practice beyond the manual.* New York: Guilford.

LaRoche, M. J. (1999). Culture, transference, and countertransference among Latinos. *Psychotherapy, 36,* 389–397.

Levenson, H. (1998). *Time-limited dynamic psychotherapy: Making every session count.* Video and viewer's manual. San Francisco: LIFT.

Levenson, H. (1995). *Time-limited dynamic psychotherapy: A guide to clinical practice.* New York: Basic Books.

Levenson, H., Butler, S. F., Powers, T. A., & Beltman, B. (2002). *Concise guide to brief dynamic and interpersonal therapy.* Washington, DC: American Psychiatric Press.

Messer, S. B., & Warren, C. S. (1995). *Models of brief psychodynamic therapy: A comparative approach.* New York: Guilford.

Ridley, C. R. (in press). Multicultural considerations in case formulation. In T. D. Eells (Ed.), *Handbook of Psychotherapy Case Formulation.* New York: Guilford.

Strupp, H. H., & Binder, J. L. (1984). *Psychotherapy in a new key.* New York: Basic Books.

---

[1]For instructional TLDP videotapes contact: Levenson Institute for Training (LIFT), 2323 Sacramento Street, Second Floor, San Francisco, CA 94115 (Liftcenter@aol.com); American Psychological Association, 750 First Street NE, Washington, DC 20002; Psychological and Educational Films, 3334 E. Coast Highway #252, Corona del Mar, CA 92625.

Chapter 6

Person-Centered Therapy

Margaret S. Warner

Chapter Outline

Bridging the Theory-to-Practice Gap

Principles in Practice

Keys to Conceptualization

Interventions and Therapeutic Process

Short- and Long-Term Goals

Using the Relationship

Adapting the Approach

Finding Your Niche

Process and Case Suggestions

Summary and Suggested Readings

References

BRIDGING THE THEORY-TO-PRACTICE GAP

A few years back, a professor on an accreditation visit to the Illinois School of Professional Psychology commented, "We teach empathy in a two-hour session at my school. I can't imagine why you need a twelve-week required course at your school!" "Two hours!" I thought. "Students barely get a grasp on sensitive, empathic responding in twelve weeks! I'm still working on it after twenty years!" Clearly, I feel strongly about this. Empathy and genuineness are two of the most strongly documented qualities associated with psychotherapeutic success (Bozarth, Zimring, and Tausch, 2001). Yet, research also shows that therapists tend to be blissfully ignorant about how little their clients feel they are really understood by their therapists (Rogers, 1980).

Client-centered therapists spend years listening to audiotapes of client sessions noticing whether their moment-to-moment responses are accurate and attuned, and paying attention to whether they were feeling genuinely connected to their clients in that moment. In the end, I want to be able to say to my clients, "Just about anyplace your experience takes you—whether it is tortured or mundane, noble or shocking, coherent or psychotic I will be there with you in an empathic, genuine, prizing way." Just about every week my psychotherapy takes me to all those sorts of places. I am still riveted and moved and in awe of my clients' process. And, I am still learning about it.

Basing their work in the theories of Carl Rogers (1957, 1959), person-centered therapists believe that positive, growthful tendencies are inherent in human nature. And they have a strong ethical commitment to supporting the uniqueness and existential freedom of human beings. These two beliefs together make person-centered therapists very passionate about their approach to therapy. Person-centered therapists believe that if people really know who they are, they are likely to be better than experts at designing their own right next steps in life than any expert is likely to be.

Some people find that belief in such positive, "actualizing" tendencies in human nature makes intuitive sense, while others feel this is counterintuitive. How can you expect people to change if you don't point out where they are stuck or tell them what to do to change? Person-centered practitioners were among the first in the field of psychology to engage in rigorous process and outcome research. Findings from more than 50 years of research have continued to back Rogers' original claim. When clients engage in therapeutic relationships that are genuine, empathic, and prizing,[1] they tend to find their own deeply personal ways of making sense of their experience and improve by all sorts of psychological measures (Bozarth, Zimring, and Tausch, 2001). Person-centered therapy can be considered to be an "empirically supported treatment" with results that compare well with those of other more directive psychotherapeutic approaches—in both short-term and long-term psychotherapy, with both mildly disturbed and severely disturbed clients (Elliott, Greenberg, and Lietaer, 2004).

This raises two large questions for person-centered theorists. How is human nature organized so that it has these potentials toward spontaneous, self-directed change? And

---

[1]Rogers uses a number of words interchangeably. "Congruence" is equivalent to "genuineness" and "unconditional positive regard" is equivalent to "prizing."

what is the role of relationships with other human beings in developing and in fostering these positive self-directed potentials?

Person-centered theorists suggest that people may feel "incongruence," or a lack of personal wholeness for a number of reasons. Rogers (1957, 1959) proposes that they may experience "conditions of worth" from childhood that make it difficult to contemplate feelings or ways of being that differ from those valued by their parents. As a result, experiences held within the total organism don't get integrated into the self. Later theorists have suggested that clients may experience contradictions that come from a variety of sources and possess multiple views of themselves that just haven't been worked out yet (Cooper et al., 2004). Warner (2000, 2002) notes that people may have difficulties with their fundamental abilities to process experience, making such processing feel difficult for them and/or for their therapists. Frequently, "difficult process" results from neglect or trauma in early childhood, which alters the natural development of processing capacities. Also, whatever their childhood experience, clients often feel some sort of difficult process at newer, more unfamiliar edges of their experience.

Whatever the source of incongruence, person-centered theorists suggest that when people feel safe, personally valued, and empathically understood they tend to look at aspects of their experience that would otherwise be quite threatening (Rogers, 1957, 1959; Warner, 1997). And when they attend to their experience, it is likely to change, which relieves psychological symptoms, and to move in positive and prosocial directions.

PRINCIPLES IN PRACTICE

The following are some of the things that I would typically do as I try to maintain relationships characterized by Rogers' "core conditions" of empathy, genuineness, and prizing.

1. *Believe in the client's potential for self-directed change.* For beginning therapists this may be just a hypothesis that they hold while trying on this approach to therapeutic work. But as therapists get more experience and skill at person-centered work, this belief in client's potential for self-directed change tends to become deeply ingrained. This experience-based belief in the client tends to support person-centered therapists during times when progress isn't so obvious. Sometimes clients seem to be going headlong in unpromising directions—maybe growing more defensive or depressed. But, typically, when they follow their process to its very worst it turns around and comes back in a more positive direction. And the positive directions that clients find tend to be deeply personally grounded and uniquely and surprisingly their own. Sometimes clients don't seem to be personally present or talking about the sorts of things that are likely to engender change. But then, before the therapist's eyes they will express an emotionally grounded understanding of their own life situations. Some clients don't even seem to be coherent, but when therapists stay closely attuned to their seemingly psychotic or nonsensical expressions, they start to be personally connected and to make sense—often with a feeling of delight and pleasure in the relationship with the therapist.

2. *Work on abilities to convey empathic understanding in sensitive, accurate ways.* Empathic understanding sounds easy, but it isn't. Research shows that half-baked efforts at expressing empathy can actually flatten clients' emotions and stop them from exploring sensitive issues (Sachse, 1990). Lots of therapeutic approaches talk about empathy, but person-centered theorists have been doing serious thinking and research about moment-to-moment empathic responding for more than 50 years (Bozarth et al., 2001, Hendricks, 2001). There's a lot to learn here that takes serious work listening to audiotapes of client sessions over and over again with experienced consultants.

3. *Realize how easily the therapist's own small, well-intentioned comments and questions can covertly take over and dominate the client's process.* Clients often have had a lifetime of being told to feel and think the way authority figures want them to feel and think. It takes a lot of courage for them to start paying attention to the still small voice of their own experience. Most person-centered therapists are *very* careful about the questions and comments they make. They watch carefully for the blank, puzzled look that clients get on their faces just before they are about to give up on paying attention to their own experience. I have found that when I paraphrase even one word incorrectly with a schizophrenic client of mine, he is likely to comment, "I don't know, doctor, you know more about these things than I do."

4. *Stay real.* Person-centered therapists try to notice when they are saying empathic words, but are feeling disconnected or irritated or controlling inside themselves. Often, these sorts of feelings are a sign that there is something that isn't worked out in their own life experiences. Usually the first step is to process their own reactions with a third person, asking questions such as, "Why is it that I feel the need to rescue the client in this situation, when I usually trust clients' own decisions?" "What is it about this client's process that leaves me feeling irritated, when I usually feel compassionate toward client dilemmas?" Carl Rogers (1957) suggests that if complicated feelings remain, it is better to be honest with clients than to pretend that you are a better person than you are. This is especially true if clients ask direct questions. Clients typically have a whole lifetime of dealing with people who haven't been quite honest, and they are likely to sense it pretty quickly if therapists try to fudge.

5. *Stay differentiated.* All people have their own experience and way of looking at the world with a whole lifetime of history behind it. Person-centered therapists try very hard to avoid reading their own ideas and interpretations into experiences that clients haven't yet clarified for themselves. And they strongly object to making clients responsible for therapist experiences. I may feel irritated with a client, but the client doesn't *make* me feel irritated. I may respond to a client in certain complicated ways, but clients don't have any mysterious capacity to project their feelings inside of me. I may feel the need to intervene if clients seems likely to hurt themselves, but this doesn't mean that the client "unconsciously" wanted me to intervene. Inferring these kinds of client powers tends to separate the therapist from the very real and immediate experiences of the client. And it stops therapists from taking a serious look at why they react to clients in the exact ways that they do.

6. *Stay aware that each person is culturally situated.* Therapists see life through unique personal lenses that are grounded in their own cultures of origin. Therapists can

easily distort client experiences to fit their own preconceptions, or miss the level of vulnerability that often goes with being an outsider to the cultural mainstream.

7. *Avoid language that implies that experts have access to a single right truth.* Psychology sometimes tries to imitate the natural sciences by speaking as if key concepts that have an a priori validity outside of anyone's particular worldview (Warner, 1999). So, for example, a therapist might respond to a client request by saying that honoring the request would not be "appropriate" or that it would "cause regression" or that it would be "enabling." When therapists use this kind of language with clients, they create a sense of mystification that denies that any particular person or agency has responsibility for positions being taken. Using that sort of language the therapist sidesteps addressing *who* would have an objection to granting the request, or what *beliefs or reasons* they have for finding it problematic, and on what sorts of *personal or institutional experience* that assessment is based. In doing this they undermine the genuineness of the therapist-client relationship. And even when therapists use this sort of language as a shorthand in their own thinking and communication with each other, they run a serious risk that they will start thinking about the world in this sort of depersonified way.

8. *Intervene, if at all, in ways that are as transparent, collaborative, and differentiated as possible.* Sometimes extratherapeutic issues come up that require the therapist to take over the process for some period of time. Perhaps clients are in immediate danger of doing serious harm to themselves or others. Perhaps the therapist is required to fill out reports about clients for some government agency. Person-centered therapists do as much as they can to keep clients empowered in these situations, and to give them back full control over the therapeutic process as quickly as possible. For example, one person-centered therapist who worked at an agency that required her to fill out reports about each client's progress toward goals let the client know right away that this was a requirement at her agency. She suggested that they take the last ten minutes or so of each session to do this. The therapist then would ask, "What do you think about our session today? Is there anything that we talked about that was relevant or helpful in relation to the goals you've set?" If she felt any disagreement with the client's own assessment she would then tell the person what her concerns or disagreements were and what they were based on. She was *transparent* in letting the client know that the requirement for reports existed, *collaborative* in engaging the client in the process and *differentiated* in her clear and honest communication about who wanted the reports and why.

KEYS TO CONCEPTUALIZATION

Person-centered therapy relies on the same universal human capacities for self-healing and personal growth regardless of the nature and the degree of psychological distress presented by the client. These human capacities continue to operate whether the initial source of the person's difficulty is psychological, biological, or social. The main questions, therefore, focus on how to manifest empathy, genuineness, and prizing in particular sorts of client situations. Several questions commonly emerge:

1. How do you negotiate a mutually agreeable way of organizing a therapeutic relationship, one that honors the real experience of both the client and the therapist?
2. Is the client experiencing forms of "difficult" process or extremes of mistrust of experience and relationship that require special therapist sensitivity and attunement?
3. Is the client experiencing culturally based ways of looking at the world that may need special therapist sensitivity or attunement?
4. When do you intervene in ways that have not been asked for by the client?

In terms of personal negotiation, a very important initial question is whether this particular client wants to engage in therapy and has any expectations or wishes as to how the therapy might be structured. For the therapists, there are important questions as to what sorts of therapy relationship they feel comfortable and competent to engage in. If, for example, a client wants to engage in hypnotic retrieval of memories, a therapist may not feel qualified to do that, but would feel comfortable with various forms of guided imagery. Similarly, questions may arise as to whether the client prefers to engage in individual, family, or group sessions.

A second question is whether clients seem capable of and oriented toward a self-directed exploration of their issues. This is not about whether the client has real and perhaps anguishing problems. But some clients are able to offer a beginning articulation of what is wrong. And they are able to some significant degree to touch on aspects of their issues that are felt but not yet clear to them. Under these circumstances therapy sessions are likely to feel at least somewhat rewarding almost right away. Clients are likely to experience some felt relief from speaking and being understood, and to at least feel less alone in their situation. They may well notice that their feelings shift as they talk and find that they have new insights into their issues. This sort of well-developed capacity for processing issues isn't at all a requirement for person-centered therapy, but it does tend to make the initial therapeutic connection easier to negotiate for both therapist and client.

A number of issues may require particular awareness and sensitivity from the therapist. Some clients experience what I think of as "difficult process." I have found three kinds of difficult process most common within person-centered therapy. Clients who are experiencing "fragile process" (Warner, 1997, 2000, 2002) have difficulty holding particular experiences in attention at moderate levels of intensity. As a result they tend to have difficulty starting and stopping these experiences, and often feel discomfort or shame in the process. Given this difficulty holding onto their own experience, they often have difficulty taking in the point of view of another person without feeling that their own experience has been annihilated.

Clients who experience "dissociated process" quite convincingly experience themselves as having selves that are not integrated with each other for periods of time (Warner, 1998, 2000; Coffeng, 1996, Roy, 1991). They may experience a disunity, alternating between different autonomous experiences of self that feels "crazy" to themselves and to others. Clients who have a psychotic style of processing have difficulty forming narratives about their experience that make sense within the culture, or which offer a predictive validity in relation to their environment. Prouty (1994, 2001) describes clients experiencing psychotic process as having impaired contact with "self," "world," and "other." Often, such clients experience voices, hallucinations, or delusions that are neither culturally accepted nor easy to process (Prouty, 1994).

Some clients, whether or not they experience difficult process, simply seem to have a strong disinclination to pay attention to their own experience (Sachse, 1998). This may be based on very strong childhood socialization that suggests that it is selfish or counterproductive to make too much of one's own feelings. At its extreme, such clients may experience physiological symptoms and bodily sensations without having any sense that these are connected to their lived experience.

In addition to difficult process, some clients experience extremes of overall mistrust of experience and of relationships (Warner, 2001). Early traumatic relationships are particularly likely to leave clients with a deep learning that bodily felt experience can be a torture and that other adults often make these experiences worse. This can set up certain kinds of paradox within the therapeutic relationship, as the client may simultaneously have deep wishes to engage and deep wishes to avoid direct attention to personal experience. Likewise they may have deep longings for human connection and simultaneously have deep wishes to avoid such connections. These sorts of difficult process or distrust of experience and relationship require particular sorts of sensitivity and attunement on the part of the therapist.

Issues related to culture and lifestyle also can make special demands on the empathic capacities of the therapist and may need special attention. Therapists who come from a dominant culture can easily read their own way of looking at the world into the experience of clients. The experience of trying to explain oneself to people of another culture or lifestyle group is difficult at best. Clients are likely to experience added levels of vulnerability if they feel any sense of stigma or discrimination.

A final question for a person-centered therapist is whether there are reasons for introducing interventions or suggestions that have not been asked for by the client. This issue may occur if there is some reason for thinking that there is medical, legal, financial, educational, or psychiatric information that is not available to clients that is highly relevant to the client's well-being. It may arise if client communications indicate serious risks of harm to the client or to others. And, it may arise if there are legal, institutional, or professional requirements with which the therapist is obligated to conform.

INTERVENTIONS AND THERAPEUTIC PROCESS

The person-centered approach does not endorse content-oriented interpretations or directives, which it would see as undermining the client's own capacities for change. Rather, it tries to create a climate that encourages and fosters clients' own natural tendencies to process experience and to delineate their own right next action steps. Many person-centered therapists avoid any systematic interventions at all; others offer process suggestions or teaching when clients seem to be at an impasse.

The relational capacities that allow therapists to maintain high levels of genuine and prizing personal contact with clients without the need to take control over the client's process are central to the success of person-centered therapy. These qualities develop over a therapist's lifetime of personal reflection and consultation, without preset rules for training.

The empathic understanding response process is more susceptible to direct learning and practice. At its simplest level, the therapist is trying to convey empathic understanding in such a way that the client feels understood, that the therapist is "walking in the client's shoes." The therapist is trying to hear what is central to the clients right now in the moment of their speaking. Even asking probing questions is generally seen as likely to throw the client off from an inward attending to what is important in this moment.

The therapist is trying to get the point of what the client is conveying with exactness. This involves not only the client's feelings, but what exactly the client makes of the situation. Beginning therapists often believe that they have heard exactly what the client has conveyed, but are astounded when they actually listen to tapes that they have missed a great deal while trying to formulate their next probing response.

A second key aspect of empathic responding involves making space for client attempts to express aspects of their experience that are not yet clear (Gendlin, 1990). Remembering the continuum of client clearness of experiencing based on Gendlin's theory may help with this.

Bodily processes (heart rate, blood pressure, and the like)	Physical sensations (pain in neck, tightness in chest)	Felt but unclear —felt sense —images —gestures	Partially articulated ("Something about George gets to me")	Fully articulated (I feel x about y for z reasons)

When clients feel new to therapy or unsafe in a relationship, they are more likely to speak from their preconceived views of their situations, and speak more like the fully articulated end of the continuum.

A male client may initially say, "They're all against me. Nobody will give me a chance!" But as he feels more safe with the therapist he may venture something like "From the beginning, I have had a queasy feeling about this whole situation. Like I could never be good enough somehow no matter what I did. I can just picture the look on my father's face when he lost his job." These partially articulated senses of the client's situation have enormous richness to them. They tend to convey the totality of the person's lived experience of the situation, as it is felt in the body. And when clients hold these experiences in attention, they are particularly likely to open to experiential changes and to new insights. Beginning therapists often push clients away from this felt richness by making the client's experience more clear than it is ("You feel that you are never going to succeed in this situation.") or by being stimulated to make connections or ask probing questions at that point. ("Why do you feel that your life will be like your father's?")

Person-centered therapists suggest that the client is most likely to find the unique personal meaning of these felt experiences if the therapist can stay with the immediate bodily felt experience without making it any more clear than it is ("Something about that whole job situation has given you a queasy feeling, right there in your stomach?") And likewise, clients are more likely to sense new edges of their experience if the therapist can stay with the vividness of scenes that the client touches on. Saying "You can just picture that look on your father's face when he lost his job" will often connect with the immediacy of client experience in ways that accurate, but more abstract responses such as "Your father was quite upset about being unemployed" do not.

Person-centered therapists are much less likely to rely on directed questions or interpretive comments than therapists in other orientations. Responses from the therapist's frame of reference are most common under a number of circumstances:

1. If the client asks a direct question or makes a direct request that the therapist is able to respond to while maintaining a therapeutic relationship that is genuine, empathic, and prizing
2. If the client seems to be making a clear point, but the therapist is confused as to what the client is trying to say
3. If some major risk to the client or others takes precedence over the client's self-directed work—such as serious threats of suicide or homicide, or some situation that the therapist is legally required to report to authorities
4. If the client is describing high-risk personal circumstances that might be illuminated by knowledge that the therapist has or that could be offered by other professionals—such as psychiatrists, medical doctors, or lawyers. For example, a client might be describing psychological symptoms that could, if the client chose to pursue that course, be alleviated by medications
5. If the client is experiencing considerable frustration in handling situations for which process education—such as training in communication skills, experiential focusing, or progressive relaxation—is available. Under these circumstance, therapists may note that they (or others) could undertake training or coaching of these skills with the client if the client would like this

SHORT- AND LONG-TERM GOALS

Rogers proposes that a variety of goals that other orientations structure into therapy occur spontaneously within client-centered therapy. These include clients' becoming more open to experience and less defensive, more realistic and objective, more effective in problem-solving, better adjusted, having higher positive self-regard, having an internal locus of control, having fewer psychological symptoms, perceiving others more realistically, and behaving in more creative ways (Rogers, 1959).

In moment-to-moment practice, however, person-centered therapy has a primary focus on trying to understand the client's own goals, rather than on goals determined by experts in the field of psychology. If the client's goals aren't clear, the therapist aims to stay with the client through a process in which goals and motivations become more clear. The process itself is very powerful in helping clients to find their own voice, when they may often have felt confused or divided or powerless in the past. Often in a first session the therapist can hear the client's implicit wishes for the therapy relationship or ideas as to how the therapy relationship should go.

This formation of the therapy relationship is a two-person negotiation in person-centered therapy. Therapists are not trying to decide what would be good for clients from a position of authority. Rather, therapists are trying to understand what the client wants and to see if they can do this while remaining genuine and prizing. If the client is unfamiliar with the therapeutic process in general or with self-directed modes of exploring personal issues, therapists may want to explain their view of how this might be beneficial to the client.

USING THE RELATIONSHIP

Given the low reliance on techniques and interpretations, the relationship gains particular importance in person-centered therapy. The genuineness of connection between the therapist and the client tends to allow therapists and clients to find mutually valuable styles of working together. Many clients have had terrible relationships with authority figures in their past, and will sidestep or resist attempts by outside authorities to control them. The very freedom to sense what issues are important and to have control over the speed and manner with which they approach them often lets clients take risks that they haven't taken in the past. Notably, person-centered therapists don't assume that it is a "defense" or "resistance" if clients step away from emotionally loaded issues for some period of time. Rather, they are likely to see this as the clients' finding their own right rhythm of emotional work.

Understanding the place that the therapist has in the client's life is one very important kind of empathy. Genuineness, empathy, and prizing are relational qualities that clients have typically wanted all their lives, and they have often been frustrated and disappointed in their wish for these qualities in early caregiving adults. As a result, being in a therapeutic relationship in which they are receiving these qualities often brings about wishes and fears grounded in earlier relationships. The therapist may well be writ large in the client's life as a result. If a therapist is ten minutes late to a session, that may be more distressing than if a friend were hours late. If a therapist misses just a few words that relate to a vulnerable aspect of the clients' experience that they have struggled to express, this may shut down the levels of closeness that had developed previously in the relationship.

Person-centered therapists work very hard to be empathically attuned to these sorts of issues and to understand even awkwardly or partially expressed client concerns. However, they don't typically feel the need to point out relationship patterns. They find that all too often these sorts of relationship observations pull clients away from their own very immediate processing, and they tend to put the therapist in the role of a controlling or critical authority. Client-centered therapists have found that the lived experience of having a genuine, personal-valuing, and empathic therapeutic relationship tends to be healing in itself, whether or not these relationship qualities are ever discussed explicitly. And when relationship issues are relevant to clients they tend to bring them up and discuss them on their own.

Many clients have difficulty saying what they feel to authority figures directly. So they may communicate feelings about the therapist in a few words while leaving the session, or they may embed questions about the therapist in some larger story. For example, one client who was worried about whether I felt genuinely engaged in her issues commented on the way out of a session, "I admire your work so much. It must be really hard to concentrate all day on such difficult, troubled people." A client who was afraid that I would no longer accept her if she talked about lesbian feelings asked, "So, is it true that homosexuality is an incurable disease? I have a cousin who might be gay. I suppose that she needs a lot of psychiatric help." Person-centered therapists aren't trying to develop experience-distant theories about the client. But they do try to be sensitized to what the client is conveying about the relationship in such a way that clients do not have to work hard to get across relationship issues that are on their minds. This can be delicate, since the therapist may have to read between the lines to get what the client really wants to say.

The fact that person-centered therapists view clients as the best authorities over their own lives greatly influences the way that person-centered therapists think about relationships. Rather than spending consultation sessions thinking about what would be "good for" the client, therapists try to understand what the client is asking for and decide whether they can offer that while remaining genuine, empathic, and prizing. For example, suppose that a female client wanted to know if she could call the therapist at home when she was having flashbacks. The therapist would not be asking, "Is this good for a client in this particular diagnostic category or this particular developmental phase?" since the therapist believes that clients are capable of sensing for themselves what is likely to be helpful. The therapist also would not be asking, "Is this an appropriate thing for clients to ask of therapists?" since the very word "appropriate" implies that there is a single depersonified right way to do things. There is no such thing as an inappropriate question or request in person-centered therapy.

Rather, the therapist would be asking, "Given the unique person that I am, can I comply with this request while remaining empathic, genuine, and prizing?" This places a great deal of responsibility on the therapist to remain genuine and self-aware. If I have some freedom in my living situation, I may well be comfortable with client phone calls. On the other hand, if I need my private time and will end up resenting intrusions, the whole genuineness of the relationship will be imperiled if I agree to the client's request. Similar issues arise in relation to client questions about the therapist's life. Person-centered therapists don't make a rule that "it isn't appropriate for clients to want to know about the therapist's life." Rather, they ask themselves, can I as a unique person answer this question and still maintain a comfortable, open, and prizing relationship with this client?

ADAPTING THE APPROACH

Some clients experience one or more sorts of process that are difficult for them or for their therapists—most commonly, fragile process, dissociated process, or psychotic process (Warner, 1998, 2000; Prouty, 2001). And, some clients experience extremes of mistrust of personal experience or relationship (Warner 2001). Person-centered therapists have found that the same relational conditions that facilitate process in clients whose process flows more easily—empathy, congruence, and unconditional positive regard—are helpful to these clients whose experiences are more difficult (Warner, 2000; Prouty, 2001).

However, therapists need to take care that they are actually understanding the client's experiences rather than "normalizing" them to fit with experiences that are more familiar to the therapist. And clients in the midst of difficult process may have difficulty receiving complexly formulated expressions of empathy from others without becoming confused or disconnected from their own experiences.

In the case of difficult process, the therapist needs to be particularly sensitized to the extremely high levels of vulnerability or confusion that are involved for the client in attending to and expressing personal experiences. These high levels of vulnerability or confusion may make it harder for the therapist to follow clients as they express their most important personal experiences and such vulnerability or confusion may make clients particularly sensitive to the ways that therapists express empathy. Therapists may need to say very little or may need to stay very close to the client's exact words. They may need to cultivate an understanding of the client such that they can get the importance of brief and cryptic client comments that are embedded in long stories or thrown in as an afterthought as the client is leaving. Therapist sensitivity in connecting to difficult process can easily make the difference between the success and failure of the therapeutic relationship with these clients.

When clients feel extremely high levels of mistrust of personal experience and of human relationships, sessions that seem real and potentially productive to the therapist may feel actively dangerous to the client. The therapist may feel, "How wonderful that you have been able to touch the real anger you feel that your father abused you in this way." This client, on the other hand, may feel, "I should never have let myself feel this. I will be lost in this dangerous, destructive way of being from now on. And I should never have told my therapist this, I will never be respected or cared about again." Yet this mistrust of feelings and of relationships is typically balanced by an abiding human wish in clients to feel at one with themselves and connected to other human beings.

Therapists, then, need to be empathically attuned to this ambivalence. They need to understand the degree to which therapeutic relating that is rewarding for other clients may feel difficult and dangerous to this client, and recognize that clients have very good and personally grounded reasons for these fears. They also need to be empathic to smaller voices in the client that typically do not want to give up on connecting with experience or with human relationship. This sets up paradoxes in which the therapist needs to listen carefully to discern the clients' actual intentions and wishes. For example, clients who say that they will never trust a therapist are in that very statement trusting the therapist with a very personal aspect of their experience, and may feel disappointed if the therapist doesn't realize this. Clients who feel so poisonous that they believe that they will harm anyone who comes close to them may still feel abandoned if the therapist actually goes away completely.

Clients may also experience culturally based vulnerability in ways that parallel fragile process, and can easily get misdiagnosed as suffering from psychopathology as a result. When culturally based experiences are vulnerable, clients may need to be understood very explicitly to know that they have been heard and they may feel enraged or annihilated by small or large instances of therapist lack of understanding. The more therapists have in-depth familiarity with particular ethnic, racial, and lifestyle groups, the more likely they are to hear client issues with sensitivity and accuracy. And, the more therapists have reflected on their own cultural backgrounds, values, and biases, the more likely they are to be self-aware in relationship to issues that arise with clients.

Some clients have psychosomatic symptoms while feeling strongly disinclined to pay attention to their own emotions and experiences (Sachse, 1998). Under these circumstances, the whole project of therapy may not make sense to them and they are likely to ask their therapists how and why therapy will help them. Person-centered therapists may well want to explain their views as to how and why processing experience might be helpful to them in resolving their physiological symptoms.

FINDING YOUR NICHE

While all person-centered therapists believe in client self-direction, some therapists believe in a more pure form of "nondirective client-centered" therapy in which virtually all initiatives come from the client. Other experiential or process-experiential therapists are more likely to make suggestions to clients about things they could do to feel their experiences more vividly and immediately, to bring up ideas or suggestions from their own frames of reference, or to raise the possibility of various kinds of process-training. So, for example, an experiential therapist might suggest that clients pay attention to the feelings they are having in their body right at that moment, or a process-experiential therapist might suggest that some two-chair gestalt work might help clients feel into both sides of their feelings on a particular issue. If clients seem frustrated in relation to a particular aspect of their processing, many person-centered therapists will ask clients if they would like to undertake some more structured skills training or coaching in relation to that subject. For example, therapists might propose training in communication skills, progressive muscle relaxation, or experiential focusing.

Person-centered therapists often work with families as well as with individual clients. In family therapy, person-centered therapists try to develop empathy both for the individuals and for the group as a whole. They are likely to facilitate communication, hoping to engender empathy and genuineness within family relationships. When family members can be real about their own needs and wants and can empathically understand the needs and wants of other family members, they are likely to be able to find unique and creative solutions to family problems (Gaylin, 2001).

Person-centered therapists also have a long tradition of working with unstructured groups (Page, Weiss, and Lietaer, 2001). Groups that are facilitated by a leader who is genuine, empathic, and prizing tend to go through a process of gradually building trust with each other. While this process varies a great deal from group to group, members often come to a place in which they can express their true feelings in an understanding and caring environment while simultaneously remaining open to understanding and caring about the feelings of others. This sort of group experience is very moving, and for many group members it can be life-changing.

PROCESS AND CASE SUGGESTIONS

As I watch each of these client videos, I feel a lot of the same kind of excitement—mingled with a little bit of tension—that I usually feel in first client sessions. I wonder who *this* person will be, and will I be able to develop a helpful relationship with him or her?

1. *Elena.* Elena is instantly engaging to me. She seems quite depressed and upset about a variety of issues in her life. I sense that she is feeling this directly from the way she holds her body and the ways she speaks. A variety of themes emerge about the conflict between the values and expectations of her Mexican American family and her American friends. The broad issues seem very clear to her and I don't find it very hard to put myself in her shoes. I think, "Wow, if my family's culture was so

much the opposite of everything that my friends believed, I would probably find that hard to resolve, too." Still, as a European American, I feel the pull of the arguments that her friends make that she should be able to be independent and to get the best education that she can. I want to be careful here that I don't introduce a tilt in my responses. I want Elena to have the space to find the solutions that are really right for her. She needs to find her own personal mix of Mexican and American values.

2. *Jane.* The themes Jane talks about are easy for me to relate to empathically—I can readily imagine how difficult it is being a woman in a job where women aren't really accepted, or being judged on the basis of the "wild" behavior of an older sibling, living in a lukewarm marriage, and the like. But, as I listen to her, I am very aware that *she* doesn't feel these issues as connected to the things that are really bothering her—chest pains and shortness of breath. Jane may well feel that the fact that her doctor recommended therapy is something to be ashamed of, a sign that her symptoms aren't "real." If that issue emerges, I want to be open to discussing this with her honestly, letting her know the ways that I think therapy often helps, while really honoring her own right to decide what works for her.

3. *Theo.* I'm impressed by Theo as I listen to him. Here is a very intelligent and competent African American student, with a lot of awareness of the personal, racial, and family issues going on in his life. Yet he is saying that he has almost never talked about these issues at a deeply personal level, and that his angry feelings get very overwhelming when they do get triggered. A therapeutic relationship that Theo comes to trust could make a world of difference in his life, I think. Yet as a European American therapist, I am very aware of how vulnerable it often is for African American clients to talk about racial issues with white therapists. I'm hoping that I can respond in a way that is sensitive to Theo's issues and create a space that is open enough that we can discuss any relationship issues that do emerge between us.

SUMMARY AND SUGGESTED READINGS

Person-centered therapy has been undergoing a worldwide resurgence in the last two decades. For readers new to the approach, The *Carl Rogers Reader* (Kirschenbaum and Henderson, eds., 1989) offers a good introduction to Rogers' original thinking. Readers who would like to keep up with recent developments are referred to *Person-Centered & Experiential Psychotherapies,* the journal of the World Association for Person-Centered and Experiential Psychotherapy and Counseling. PCCS Books is also an excellent source for recent person-centered writings; listings of available books can be found at their website at www.pccs-books.co.uk. Readers who would like to get a feeling for person-centered therapies that offer more process suggestions to clients might look at E. T. Gendlin's *Focusing-Oriented Psychotherapy* (1996) or L. S. Greenberg, J. C. Watson, and G. Lietaer's *Handbook of Experiential Psychotherapy* (1998).

Person-centered conferences offer a great way to get a personal sense of the person-centered approach since they typically include considerable amounts of individual and group process as part of the conference formats. In any group session, participants may discuss interesting aspects of abstract therapeutic issues, while in the next moment raising very personal feelings that they are having in relation to their lives or to the group process of moment. You are likely to get a much more personal sense of connection to other conference participants than you do at more traditional conferences, and a feeling for the ways Rogers' core conditions play out in real relationships. You can find good listings of person-centered conferences all over the world at www.pca-online.net. The Focusing Institute website, at www.focusing.org, offers a good listing of experiential conferences and events.

REFERENCES

Bozarth, J. D., Zimring, F. M., & Tausch, R. (2001). Client-centered therapy: The evolution of a revolution. In D. J. Cain and J. Seeman (Eds.), *Humanistic psychotherapies: Handbook of research and practice* (pp. 147–88). Washington, DC: American Psychological Association.

Coffeng, T. (1996). Experiential and pre-experiential therapy for multiple trauma. In R. Hutterer, G. Pawlowsky, P. F. Schmid, & R. Stipsits (Eds.), *Client-centered and experiential psychotherapy: A paradigm in motion* (pp. 499–511). Frankfurt am Main: Peter Lang.

Cooper, M., Mearns, D., Stiles, W. B., Warner, M., & Elliott, R. (2004). Developing self-pluralistic perspectives within the person-centered and experiential approaches: A round-table dialogue. *Person-centered & Experiential Psychotherapies, 3* (3) 176–91.

Elliott, R., Greenberg, L. S., & Lietaer, G. (2004). "Research on experiential psychotherapies." In Michael J. Lambert, ed. *Bergin and Garfield's handbook of psychotherapy and change* (Fifth ed.) (pp. 493–539). New York: John Wiley.

Gaylin, N. L. (2001). *Family, self and psychotherapy: A person-centered perspective.* Ross-on-Wye: PCCS Books.

Gendlin, E. T. (1968). The experiential response. In E. Hammer (Ed.), *Use of interpretation in therapy* (pp. 208–227). New York: Grune & Stratton.

Gendlin, E. T. (1990). The small steps of the therapy process: How they come and how to help them come. In G. Lietaer, J. Rombauts, & R. Van Balen (Eds.), *Client-centered and experiential psychotherapy in the nineties.* Leuven, Belgium: Leuven University Press.

Gendlin, E. T. (1996). *Focusing-oriented psychotherapy: A manual of the experiential method.* New York: Guilford Press.

Gendlin, E. T., & J. I. Berlin. (1961). Galvanic skin response correlates of different modes of experiencing. *Journal of Clinical Psychology, 17* (1), 73–77.

Hendricks, M. H. (2001). Focusing-oriented/experiential psychotherapy. In D. Cain & J. Seeman (Eds.), *Humanistic psychotherapies: Handbook on research and practice.* Washington, DC: American Psychological Association.

Kirschenbaum, H., & Henderson, V. L. (Eds.). (1989). *The Carl Rogers reader.* New York: Houghton Mifflin Company.

Page, R. C., Weiss, J. F., & Lietaer, G. (2001). Humanistic group psychotherapy. In D. Cain & J. Seeman (Eds.), *Humanistic psychotherapies: Handbook on research and practice.* Washington, DC: American Psychological Association.

Prouty, G. (1994). *Theoretical evolutions in person-centered/experiential therapy.* Westport, CT: Praeger.

Prouty, G. (2001). Humanistic psychotherapy for people with schizophrenia. In D. Cain & J. Seeman (Eds.), *Humanistic psychotherapies: Handbook on research and practice.* American Psychological Association, Washington, DC.

Rogers, C. R. (1957). The necessary and sufficient conditions of therapeutic personality change. *Journal of Consulting Psychology, 21,* 2, 95–103.

Rogers, C. R. (1959). A theory of therapy, personality, and interpersonal relationships, as developed in the client-centered framework. In S. Koch (Ed.), *Psychology: A study of science,* Vol. 3 (pp. 184–256) New York: McGraw-Hill.

Rogers, C. R. (1980). Empathic: An unappreciated way of being. In C. R. Rogers, *A way of being* (pp. 137–163). New York: Houghton Mifflin.

Roy, B. (1991). A client-centered approach to multiple personality and dissociative process. In L. Fusek (Ed.), *New directions in client-centered therapy: Practice with difficult client populations (Monograph Series 1)* (pp. 18–40). Chicago: Chicago Counseling and Psychotherapy Center.

Sachse, R. (1990). The influence of therapist processing proposals on the explication process of the client. *Person Centered Review. 5,* 321–347.

Sachse, R. (1998). Goal-oriented client-centered therapy of psychosomatic disorders. In L. Greenberg, J. Watson, & G. Lietaer (Eds.), *Handbook of experiential psychotherapy.* New York: Guilford Press.

Warner, M. S. (1997). Does empathy cure? A theoretical consideration of empathy, processing, and personal narrative. In A. C. Bohart & L. S. Greenberg (Eds.), *Empathy reconsidered.* Washington, DC: American Psychological Association.

Warner, M. S. (1998). A client-centered approach to therapeutic work with dissociated and fragile process. In L. Greenberg, J. Watson, & G. Lietaer (Eds.), *Foundations of experiential theory and practice: Differential treatment approaches.* New York: Guilford Press.

Warner, M. S. (1999). The language of psychology as it affects women and other traditionally disempowered groups. In I. Fairhurst (Ed.), *Women writing in the person-centered approach.* Ross-on-Wye: PCCS Books.

Warner, M. S. (2000). Client-centered therapy at the difficult edge: Work with fragile and dissociated process. In Dave Mearns & Brian Thorne (Eds.), *Person-centered therapy today: New frontiers in theory and practice.* Thousand Oaks: Sage.

Warner, M. S. (2001). Empathy, relational depth, and difficult client process. In S. Haugh & T. Merry (Eds.), *Empathy.* Vol. 2 in the series *Rogers' therapeutic conditions: Evolution, theory, and practice.* Ross-on-Wye: PCCS Books.

Warner, M. S. (2002). Psychological contact, meaningful process, and human nature: A reformulation of person-centered theory. In G. Wyatt & P. Sanders (Eds.), *Contact and perception.* Vol. 3 in the series *Rogers' therapeutic conditions: Evolution, theory, and practice.* Ross-on-Wye: PCCS Books.

Chapter 7

Existential Psychotherapy

J. Michael Russell

Chapter Outline

Bridging the Theory-to-Practice Gap

Principles in Practice

Keys to Conceptualization

Interventions and Therapeutic Process

Short- and Long-Term Goals

Using the Relationship

Adapting the Approach

Finding Your Niche

Process and Case Suggestions

Summary and Suggested Readings

BRIDGING THE THEORY-TO-PRACTICE GAP

You don't have to be a student of counseling to encounter the impact of existentialism. Concerns about anxiety, intimacy, death, freedom, and meaning already figure into your life and the lives of everyone you know. That is why when we hear about what the existentialist philosophers have said, they seem to speak directly to us. This was certainly my experience when I had my first course in philosophy many years ago. I was amazed to stumble on a world of ideas that already seemed vaguely familiar to me even though I would not have been able to put them into words. So much of what I felt to be meaningful—or, in some cases, meaningless—is articulated by these thinkers. I hope you will come to feel, as I have, that becoming more attuned to the themes of existentialism profoundly enriches your capacity to be a helping professional. In this chapter I will try to lead you through some very compressed statements of existentialist theory to a real sense of how to draw from your own experience and put these ideas to work.

Existential counseling is more a way of thinking than any particular style of doing psychotherapy. It comes from existential philosophy, which emphasizes the idea that people are free. By our actions we give meaning to the circumstances in which we find ourselves, and we are responsible for how we choose to face—or run away from facing—these fundamental aspects of human experience. The main ideas have been developed by quite a number of philosophers, many of them notoriously hard to read. A typical philosophy course on existentialism would surely include Søren Kierkegaard, Fredrick Nietzsche, Martin Heidegger, Jean-Paul Sartre, and Simone de Beauvoir, along with a sampling from the somewhat more accessible contributions to literature from authors like Fyodor Dostoevsky, Leo Tolstoy, Franz Kafka, and Albert Camus. Theologians have contributed to the existentialist perspective, including Martin Buber, Gabriel Marcel, and Paul Tillich. Generally, these thinkers were not writing explicitly for therapists. Ideas from all these groups have trickled down into our culture generally, and they have influenced diverse therapists, some of whom identify themselves as particularly drawn to this or that thinker. We will get to some of the central contributors shortly. Your ability to approach counseling from an existentialist perspective will depend on your understanding of the philosophers' ideas in the background, and the degree to which you find that your own thinking takes a similar path. So, before we tackle the task of this chapter and our concern with existentialism in application to counseling, it will be useful to sample a few themes from the key philosophers. Here we are only trying to get a glimpse of extremely complex sets of ideas.

Since Kierkegaard usually gets credit for initiating much of existentialism (though this wasn't a term he used) we might start by noting that he advocated "subjectivity" in the task of examining one's life. A lot of people nowadays see going to a counselor as getting an objective expert to give you "the answers" to your problems. Providing answers certainly wasn't Kierkegaard's vision! Far from trying to remove the existential anxiety of having to make fundamental decisions about one's life, Kierkegaard would have wanted to heighten the difficulty—the "dread"—of pulling one's life together. What was needed, he thought, was not to be complacent and self-assured, but to risk a decisive kind of leap of faith. As a counselor, you will find that much of your work is more about people making decisions than discovering some objective truth.

Kierkegaard was a strong advocate of his religious beliefs; Fredrick Nietzsche was a harsh critic of the "other-worldly" dimension of most religions. Yet they have in common a readiness to have a really hard look at the way, as individuals, we arrive at our values. They push us toward taking responsibility for the values we embrace. Values are a choice. All too often, the values to which we give lip service really serve to rationalize the absence of feeling very creative or empowered in our own lives. Counseling can provide a creative reevaluation of what we find meaningful.

Kierkegaard and Nietzsche provide the nineteenth-century background for what in the twentieth century came to be called "phenomenology." Basically, this stands for a method and a commitment to taking very seriously our own individual and subjective ways of experiencing the world, in opposition to the general tradition of supposing that we get at truth by way of a detached objectivity. This idea has impacted all aspects of contemporary life, and it obviously runs through the many sorts of "talk-therapy." Of the philosophers who are described both as "existentialists" and "phenomenologists," the two twentieth-century giants are Heidegger and Sartre. Both of them are difficult to read. Heidegger made up his own vocabulary to try to capture the human being from an experiential or phenomenological perspective. He invented (in German) a word that refers to us as *Dasein* in order to highlight that our "being" (*sein*) is engaged in the world (*da* = "there"). Many of us do not face how we are engaged in the world in an *authentic* way. Being authentic is roughly a matter of being tuned into what we really care about as individuals. All too often we are inauthentic by being too ready to "fall in" with what others (*das mann*) want us to be, rather than really being the authors of our own lives and attending to what our moods can teach us about what we really care about. One of the ways we can better get in touch with what we care about, and our possibilities for being authentic, is to pay more attention to the reality of death. You have probably already found out the hard way that experiences of death and loss profoundly sharpen our sense for what is significant in our lives, much as we might prefer to avoid looking at this.

Heidegger and Sartre take significantly different directions. Heidegger's perspective was: I have my own way of "being in the world," and I may or may not deal with it. A basic feature of this being in the world is that I *care*. Whether I acknowledge it or not, I care. Care is basic to persons, to *Dasein*. My feelings and moods can tune me in to what I care about. I may or may not face these existential realities and how my moods alert me to them, but they are features of my very being. From this point of view, counseling is going to be about getting in touch with myself. In contrast, Sartre's view was: I don't really have any "being." I just am what I do. There isn't any "self" to be true to. At every moment, by my actions, I am making a choice about who I aim at being. Since what I *am* is always in the making it is never settled or fixed or finished. Every action is a fresh choice. So, when I try to pin down and label who or what I am, this is what Sartre calls bad faith or self-deception. It is running away from my freedom, at any moment, to choose differently. Even my emotions are choices: they don't just happen to me. Emotions are something I *do*. This difference between Heidegger and Sartre has implications for whether or not it is possible to get in touch with who or what I am. Even so, Sartre was of the opinion that what all the existentialists have in common is that they all "start from the subjective," and that they would all agree that people are running away from freedom when they pretend to have some "essence" or fixed nature that determines them. This is the meaning of the existentialist's slogan "existence precedes essence." It means that as long as we are alive we will be unable to honestly pin down a definitive account of what our lives are all about. Regardless of whether it may prove self-deceived, we will find people coming to counseling with all sorts of preconceived and static formulas about who or what they are.

This is not the place for reciting the many famous contributors to existentialist thinking in philosophy and literature. Much of what has influenced existential psychotherapy has come from literature rather than from the very technical philosophical works. Dostoevsky's *Notes From Underground,* Tolstoy's *The Death of Ivan Illych,* Kafka's *The Trial,* and Camus' *The Stranger* are classic works that illustrate the complex ideas that inform existential counseling. These have impacted our culture generally. Many contemporary films also raise existential issues when they challenge our sense of personal identity in an often absurdly violent and meaningless world. However, in order to set out the themes of this chapter it will help to mention Simone de Beauvoir. In her classic exploration of sex roles, she bridges existentialism and feminism by extending Sartre's ideas about the parts that other people play in our lives. The key idea is that in our impossible quest to know who or what we are, we try to get other people to define us. All too often our interpersonal relations rest on trying to impose an identity on *other persons* or to extract a (false) sense of identity from them. But just as who I am is never settled, so it is with who you are. From one moment to the next your possibilities are going to transcend my expectations and my efforts to impose an identity on you. For all that, we bear responsibility for what we invite (not cause) others to do. The way Sartre puts it, "When I choose, I choose for all mankind." This existentialist account of interpersonal relations will be important in application to the tasks of counseling. It can help us clarify how our clients may be orchestrating the reactions they get from others.

PRINCIPLES IN PRACTICE

According to Irvin Yalom, there are four central existential themes that are recurrent (and overlapping) concerns in psychotherapy. These are *death, freedom, isolation,* and *meaninglessness.* The following paragraphs will expand this list and provide a cluster of interrelated terms that round out an understanding of what existentialist philosophy is all about while also highlighting specific concepts and issues that routinely emerge in existential psychotherapy. When you try your hand at doing existential counseling, you will want to hold several of these concepts in mind and listen for their applicability.

1. *Freedom.* Remember, existentialism "starts from the subjective." It works from an experiential or phenomenological basis. This is not the place for an abstract debate about whether or not we really are "free." The point is that you and I—and the clients who consult us for counseling—will often struggle with how freedom shows up in our experience. This takes on two somewhat paradoxical forms. We are troubled when we think we aren't free and troubled when we think we are. Perhaps the most central of the existentialist concepts is that we run away from our freedom. At the same time, we long for freedom. It's not surprising that we would seek out counseling when we feel trapped in a relationship, a dead-end job, or by a lack of opportunities. Less obvious is why freedom should leave us with an aversive feeling. Evidently we have trouble

with not knowing just what to do or who to be. Of course this sense of being free might be viewed with a more positive term—like "excitement"—but people don't tend to come to therapy to talk about what thrilling and exciting lives they lead. When we *don't* like the experience, we call it anxiety. As counselors we learn to listen for areas of anxiety, and the existential therapist tends to think of this in terms of someone's being uncomfortable with some aspect of their freedom.

2. *Choice.* In existential counseling we hope that clients may come to see choices they had avoided seeing. Indeed much of the process of existential psychotherapy is about making a transition from "look what's been happening to me" to "look what I've been doing!" As with freedom, we often have a mixed attitude when it comes to choice. We resent it when we don't have choices, but we get anxious when we do! Existentialism is all about broadening the vision of our choices. From this perspective what we do "freely" covers a lot more ground than just what we choose with self-conscious deliberation. Many of our important choices don't even come into our explicitly conscious deliberations, and we are often in self-deception about those that do. As existential counselors we hope to narrow this gap between underlying choices and reflective awareness. This means that while we listen to our client's presentation of their subjective worlds we are also looking for the actual consequences of their actions. Outcome implies intention. The results of what clients do point to the possibility that these consequences are—at some level—what they sought. Obviously this guideline must be employed modestly, so that we are not blaming the victim for the realities of the world around, but we try to be alert to the possibility that clients are in some way getting what they want and might bear responsibility for the circumstances in which they find themselves. Enlarging the sense of freedom and responsibility (and meaning) are all different sides of the same thing. These central features of existential philosophy are also the central guidelines to existentialism in therapeutic practice. Your job as a counselor is to listen simultaneously to the way your clients represent their lived worlds, so that you can attend to the possible choices embedded in the worlds they actually seem to create, and work toward their seeing more clearly how they may have been telling themselves that they do not have alternatives.

3. *Responsibility.* Because existentialism takes a very broad view of freedom and choice, it also suggests a seemingly extreme perspective on conditions for which we bear responsibility. We routinely find people plainly evading responsibility in the real-life practice of therapy, but just as often we find people self-impose misplaced and exaggerated guilt. Ironically, excessive self-blaming can have the effect of becoming immobilizing—a martyr to guilt—and hence, in effect, be an evasion of responsibility. Part of the problem comes from confusing responsibility with blame. Describing your role in what has come about does not necessarily mean you should be blamed for not doing things differently. An effective counselor will have a good sense for when the language of responsibility is helpful and when it is not. While it often will clarify things to speculate that situations have come about because of actions that were in some way by choice, there are plenty of times when this perspective isn't helpful at all. In either case, there does not have to be an implication that what we did was wrong. As an existential therapist you

will want to be alert to a myriad of themes connected with the concept of responsibility and our talents for misusing it.

4. *Consciousness, meaning, and meaninglessness.* The technical philosophical works on existentialism are in-depth theories about the nature of consciousness. An inherent dimension of the counseling process is to broaden and articulate the consciousness of one's life. But we all know this can be overdone. Both the merits and liabilities of self-awareness arise as a common practical concern in counseling. Surely you have suspected at times that you think too much, analyze too much, and aren't too sure whether your introspective habits are entirely a good thing. Your clients will wonder about this too, and the struggle takes on very real consequences. Therapists can be too detached and can flounder in an excess of reflection. Finding the right blend is a fairly universal existential challenge that will often show up in the context of counseling. Your job as an existential counselor is to promote consciousness, but not to the point of becoming disengaged and all in your head.

   Certainly one of the most distinctive features of human existence comes from demanding that things be meaningful. Everything we do in life entails something about the meaning we have given to our circumstances. This doesn't happen in a vacuum; we share language, social and physical realities, cultural ties, and countless reminders and instructions about what we are expected to find meaningful. Even so, the inevitable subjective bottom line is that I give meaning to my situation. People come to counseling because there's something they want to make sense of. Maybe that search for meaning is about a job, a relationship, a tragedy, or some disturbing fear or feeling. From the perspective of existential therapy, this becomes an opportunity to clarify the implicit and explicit ways in which meaning figures into an individual's life.

   The flip side of the issue of meaning is the existential reality that sometimes there are features of life that seem meaningless, pointless, or absurd. Maybe when you were younger (or maybe still) you wondered, "What's the point of making my bed in the morning? It's just going to get messed up again tonight!" When this sort of discouraged rhetoric becomes global, it can represent a sort of potential spiritual crisis that is, arguably, pretty universal. It will almost certainly show up in the context of counseling and range all the way from, "There's no point to anything," to "My job is meaningless," to "There's no point in talking to you." Familiar triggers for the sense of meaninglessness include boredom and routine, perceived injustice, frustration, bureaucratic requirements, pointless regulations, failed projects, empty promises, betrayals, sudden losses, and the ending of relationships.

5. *Isolation.* One trigger for experiencing meaninglessness comes from having a sense of isolation. So often the clients who seek you out will feel isolated, different, and vulnerable in their interpersonal dealings. They will try hard to convince you that they are right about this, and it will be important to not rush to talking them out of it. Feeling understood will probably be more therapeutic. Paradoxically, loneliness is something we share. We do, in fact, share a world with other people. None of us live in a social or cultural vacuum, yet from a phenomenological point of view we all struggle with moments of loneliness, insecurity about our relationships with others, doubts about whether we are loved, maybe fears about whether we are able to love,

or whether anyone else can or would even care to truly understand us. These themes will come into the counseling setting, and existential therapists are typically alert to them as they connect with the quest for meaning.

6. *Death.* Perhaps the existential concern most often at the center of our concern for meaning is about death. My own death is practically inconceivable to me: how am I to understand the idea of the world going on without me, as seen from no particular point of view? Yet, how can I deny a platitude like, "We're all going to die sometime"? The death of others poses a different sort of threat to our subjectivity, but just as deep. We think nothing could tear us apart more than losing those we love, yet we behave as if we had all the time in the world to make improvements in these relationships, and often are the least kind to the people we say we love. The idea of death is a wake-up call, but it is also something we go to great lengths to avoid. Some people seem to think that nothing will have real meaning unless we and those we love live forever; others seem to think it is because no one lives forever that meaning and the limitations of time come into view. As a counselor, some of your clients will plainly be dealing with death. You will also come to see how plainly many of them—many of us—are not dealing with it at all.

7. *Authenticity.* Running through this rough list of existential concerns about meaning is the human quest for authenticity, honesty, integrity, and the contrary experiences of being ingenuous, not being authentic, lacking integrity with oneself and with others. One way to run away from the reality of death is to glibly reassure ourselves that we can expect "an average lifespan." Routinely we try to lower anxiety by establishing that something is supposedly "normal." One way to run from really challenging questions about what we value and how we most deeply would want to conduct our lives is to let other people define us with their expectations, their labels, or their rules. Like a supposed work of art that is not authentic, we are ready to "sign our names" on lives not much of our own making. Sometimes we hide from the future by living in the past; sometimes we try to pretend that our pasts shouldn't have any consequences. Often there is an alarming gap between what we do, what we tell others, and what we tell ourselves. When it comes to examining such things, the people motivated to come to counseling will oftentimes be unsure about how honest they want to be with you or even with themselves.

8. *Identity.* Central to the concerns that appear in existential therapy is the grand and global question, "Who am I?" People come to counseling with particular struggles and with the hope of getting some answers, but generally it will be understood that this takes place within a larger goal of getting to know ourselves and taking stock of our identity. This is somewhat misleading. Personal identity is more like something we are challenged to create than something we are going to "find" or discover. Much of the self-deception that may come to light within existential psychotherapy will be rooted in fictions about our identity that we are unwilling to give up. Yet if we cannot quite have an identity that is fixed and finished, neither are we likely to give up the quest. For both you and for your clients, existential counseling is going to pose the question, "Who do you think you are?" In countless ways our clients will be constantly telling us and telling themselves who they think they are, by allusions to social status, personality

traits, history, fears, age, physical characteristics—the possibilities for self-definition are endless. As existentialist counselors we are alert to these communications and interested in how they work for our client's.

KEYS TO CONCEPTUALIZATION

By now you should be getting some sense for what the existential therapist can do with all these philosophical notions and focal concepts. All the theories and principles presented so far translate into very specific ways of taking hold of the struggles our clients bring, and these provide the context for specific interventions. There are many different approaches to psychotherapy, and in ways, practitioners do many of the same things. An existential approach is likely to put a high premium on the creativity and unique individualities of the counselor and the client, and there are some aspects of this approach that are *especially* characteristic of an existentialist way of thinking when put into practice. Here we will sample some dimensions of the counseling encounter that any therapist might address, but which might especially engage the existentially oriented practitioner.

1. *Letting the client lead.* As a counselor of any persuasion, you presumably think you have something to offer, and that your clients have their reasons for seeking you out. If your clients come to you with pressing practical problems, you owe it to yourself and to them to be clear about the degree to which you feel prepared to address these. There are times when it is appropriate to be very directive. However, as an existentially oriented therapist, you presumably have a high respect for freedom—yours and your client's. You have the opportunity to be active and creative; this is part of what's involved in acknowledging your own freedom. That said, respect for the freedom of the other surely is central to the counseling encounter. If you think of yourself as in a sort of dance with the client, let them lead.

2. *Fleeing responsibility.* Often there will be something in your clients' presentation that suggests they will be using the counseling context to express a sense of victimization. While clients often come to counseling declaring that they want to change, they may prove to be more interested in validating how they see things presently. We may soon find that their whole emphasis is on complaining about misfortunes that have unfairly fallen upon them. Emphatically, existential counseling is not about scolding and lecturing clients into giving lip service to the idea that they are responsible for their circumstances. However, regardless of what you decide to do or say with them, you will be asking yourself to what extent they are trying to evade responsibility for their predicaments, and by what means.

3. *Small choices reveal big ones.* A practical implication of the idea that by our actions we are choosing to be what we "are" (or aim at) is that each little choice affirms a more global way of being. Sartre says that a gesture points to a whole view of the world. This means that anything and everything can prove worth exploring, on the reasoning that the larger organization of your client's life is probably compressed and captured in the details of how they are with you in the consulting room, and

reflected in most anything they elect to tell you about life outside your office. In principle, it's all of interest. Specifically, this means that your client's way of being with you can serve to communicate to you what things are like for them outside, now and in their life's history. Existential counseling is not just about the "official" topics of concern but the details of how clients present themselves, the small talk, speech mannerisms, the posture, and the surface features of appearance. The big picture is right there in the minutiae, if only we can learn to read it.

4. *Affects as choices.* Most likely your clients will present with some sort of feeling or mood they would rather not be feeling, such as anxiety or depression. From an existential perspective we are not so much aiming to rid ourselves from our feelings as to enhance our awareness of them. Even so, it will be important to wonder (and maybe ask your clients), what they are actually doing that looks like choosing to feel as they do? Minimally, we are responsible for how we contribute to the circumstances in which our emotions arise, whether a matter of getting enough sleep, drinking too much coffee, selecting maudlin music, or surrounding ourselves with downbeat friends. We are also responsible for how we deal with these feelings and for what we do that contributes to them, including how we express ourselves, what sorts of thoughts we dwell on, and how we represent ourselves to others. More controversially, as the philosopher Sartre held, emotions are something we just *do.* You may find that notion puzzling and counterintuitive, but just try thinking (inwardly) while you are listening to your client: "I'm aware of what you are feeling, and I'm wondering how you *do* that."

5. *In choosing for me, I choose for you—and vice versa.* Existentialism sees no contradiction in holding that we are free and yet also that each of us is responsible for how we influence others—how we invite the other person to be. When your clients are exploring issues with their important relationships, you will want to be alert for how others are affecting them, and equally, how they may be responsible for orchestrating the responses they get from others. You can also be sure that within the counseling room you each are having an impact on one another. As an existentially oriented therapist, you will be alert to ways in which each of you is making choices that impact the other. This concept can be immensely useful in counseling. In the early stages of our education as counselors we are taught that our reactions to others are rooted in traits and conflicts within ourselves. In the interest of being self-aware, nonjudgmental, and not blinded by labels and generalizations, we come to think we can't draw conclusions about the other person. This is all well and good, up to a point. But the other side of it is that our responses to the other person really may be because of something about them and not just about us. It should not surprise us that people get responses from us that they do; we have all had years to fine-tune our talents for eliciting from others just the responses we need, while being quite self-deceived about our doing so. Within the limits of reasonable modesty, the existential perspective suggests that our responses to our clients really are about them, even if also about ourselves.

6. *Whose life is it?* You may find it helpful to think of your client in terms of internal conflict, but another (complementary) perspective is to look for a collision between

their own path and the expectations of others. In many obvious respects this is a theme common to most perspectives on therapy, but you may find it has particular applicability in conjunction with the other central motifs of existentialism. Many of us evade our freedom and the responsibility that goes with choice by trying too hard to conform to the expectations of others, past and present. This much is guaranteed: no matter what issues your client brings to counseling, part of it will come from the influential ideas of others about how their life should go. When you look at the videos (i.e., Jane, Elena, Theo) that go with this book you will certainly find clients whose lives aren't quite their own in terms of the extent to which they feel they must conform to the values of other people. And as someone working toward a career in the helping professions there's a good chance that you carry plenty of inhibitions about whether it's alright for you have your own moments of fulfillment or relaxation, and sometimes wonder when, if ever, you get to "have a life."

7. *What's death got to do with it?* All therapists of all persuasions will eventually have clients who are explicitly faced with the death of another or the prospect of their own death. However, the existential perspective will allow us to be particularly alert as to how addressing death sharpens our awareness of meaning. It also helps us see such themes in less than obvious places like the death of a relationship or a dream, or in learning how we may have deadened ourselves so as to be impervious to disappointment or anxiety. Broadly conceived, we deal with deaths and losses all the time. Existential therapy provides an opportunity for acknowledging losses and, sometimes, finding a way to bury them.

8. *Is any identity better than none?* Recall Sartre's and de Beauvoir's idea that none of us has a fixed and "essential" nature. You can learn to look at the ways your clients may hide behind the labels and images with which they present themselves. In the counseling situation, your clients will often convey implicit or explicit messages about "who they are" such as: aged, unimportant, angry, guilty, unattractive, or depressed. Negative labels can work every bit as well as positive ones for giving people a role to play and a solution to the anxiety of freedom. One of the nagging questions of psychotherapy before and after Freud has been: why do people seem to repeat and stubbornly cling to awful features of their pasts? An existentialist answer is that a miserable identity is better than no identity at all. Look for this theme and you will find it.

INTERVENTIONS AND THERAPEUTIC PROCESS

Just as there is no single unified theory to existentialism, neither is there any universally agreed upon style or stockpile of techniques and interventions. Nonetheless, there are highly characteristic features of existentialist-based practice. As with those themes that catch a therapist's interest, you will see that many features of existential intervention are hallmarks of other therapy modalities, yet make their own kind of sense within the way existentialists tend to think.

1. *Caution: no soapboxes.* A very basic mistake for the beginning existential counselor would be to "intervene" by lecturing clients on how they really are free, have choices, and are responsible for the choices they make. If there is any deep truth to the existentialist way of thinking, the client has to come to this the hard way and not from misdirected, parental-sounding speeches. In existential counseling, we hope that clients will, in the long run, come to have a deeper understanding of their freedom, but that means that the client must *really see it* and not just say it. We want to promote the experience of possibilities and not mere lofty-sounding talk.

2. *Overall assessment.* Again, as with any approach to counseling, you will be evaluating whether a client is a good match for you and your way of thinking. Is this likely to be long-term counseling or brief? Is this someone you would like to see open up to feelings and broad insights, or someone with a very pressing practical issue calling for immediate and pragmatic action? Is this someone extremely raw with emotion, or confused, or traumatized, or so far from being "psychologically minded" that insight-oriented expression is obviously inappropriate? It is not uncommon for practitioners who identify themselves as existential to also be very critical of diagnostic language and labels generally. You may well believe that an existential philosophy and diagnosis are antithetical. Existential thinking is certainly opposed to losing sight of the individual with labels that are rigid and deterministic in their implications. However, language that facilitates understanding may enlarge the freedom of all. This is not the place for a lengthy debate on the seeming collision between an existentialist perspective and assessing client suitability. The reality is, you probably will have to deal with insurance companies, agencies, and bureaucracy. My position is that blindness to the applicability of diagnostic language is naive and irresponsible. You don't have to stuff your clients into boxes to know which ones more or less fit. For present purposes, suffice it to say that the selection of specific interventions requires a more global assessment, which, I hope, draws from good judgment. Over and above that, the existential perspective brings something new to the language of assessment since it addresses not an illness or condition suffered passively but—at a deep level—your client's choice of a way of being in the world.

3. *Providing the setting.* As with any approach to insight therapy, existential counseling provides a setting that encourages self-expression. The existential counselor does well to remember this when overly worrying about what to "do" with (for, or to) clients. You are inviting your clients to reflect on what they do, and how they might change, simply by providing an environment that is conducive. Beyond that, you might not need to do very much. However, the existential practitioner is often likely to take a fairly active stance. This certainly can include your advocating candid expression, and may include encouraging the client's expression of feelings of victimization, injustice, blaming, and other responsibility-deflecting sentiments. It could just as easily include being more confrontive and challenging from the outset. With plenty of latitude for the individual differences—in the client and in the counselor—the point is to advance the exploration of the issues the client brings to you. Existential themes and thinking provide you with some guideposts for considering how your clients construct their own meaning for the setting you provide.

4. *Here and now.* A general feature of an existentialist perspective is that choices are made in the present, from one moment to the next. Interventions may well call attention to the immediate reality of client and therapist encountering one another in the consulting room. Certainly we want to understand our pasts; it provides the context for what we do now. Certainly what we do now will make sense only by reference to a future that we seek to bring about. For all that, the present moment is critical. The meaning of the past and the prospects for the future are created in the here and now. In practice this means that the existential psychotherapist is likely to promote the client's looking at what it is like right now for the two of you to be in this room together. Together you can wonder how the struggles your client has elsewhere might come up for the two of you, right here in this room. The chances are that what your clients manage to bring about elsewhere will happen with you, too, in some subtle form. Opportunities for doing things differently tomorrow or the next day can begin right now, in this room, with new sorts of choices made here. Minimally, working in the "here and now" means addressing concerns that are emotionally present, and doing so in an engaged way with a kind of openness that feels "risky" and vulnerable. Beyond that, it can mean literally reflecting on the immediate encounter between therapist and client.

5. *Immediacy.* Existential philosophy may be abstract, but it is not likely to be so for an existentialist practitioner. There is no style or technique that is dictated by existentialist thinking and no unified school to regulate how therapists should work. Even so, if you can picture the stereotype of a psychoanalyst taking notes, with little to betray reactions, and if you can imagine a stereotype of the person-centered therapist, with body language that communicates warmth and acceptance, then picture the existential therapist whose physical demeanor conveys an energetic and alert engagement, and communicates the belief that what is really of the utmost importance is "right here, right now, between you and me." And whatever your demeanor, think of it as an invitation to your client to explore how they are with you.

6. *I and thou.* Martin Buber's words were meant to capture the immediacy, intensity, and ultimate importance of the relationship between believer and God. They have become a mainstay for the sort of counseling relationship to which the existentially inclined are drawn. You will have to find your own way to understanding what this means and what it means to you. Obviously, this will be far more than a matter of words. Even so, existential therapists will typically be drawn to expressing themselves in first-person, present-tense grammar. For example, as the author of a chapter on existential psychotherapy, I know I should make scholarly references to people like Buber and should document generalities about existential therapists and what is typical of them with a wealth of footnotes. Unfortunately, that sort of academic detachment is exactly what I would *not* want to model for my client as an existential practitioner. As a therapist, I would hope that how I express myself sets an example for you and that together, you and I—I and thou—may truly encounter one another in a deep and immediate way, in the here and now.

7. *Reframing the language.* Mindful of the importance of not preaching existentialism from a soapbox, you, the existentially oriented counselor, may find opportunities to

tactfully reframe language to better address existential issues. Suppose your client uses the expression "I couldn't help it." Regardless of when you might actually elect to substitute "you chose not to," you are aware of the difference. Your client says, "everybody gets lonely sometimes." You want to ask, "How about you? How about now?" When your client is complaining about "people" you are thinking, "Who, in particular?" If they complain about all the unjust things the world is doing to them, you are thinking, "What's your part in this?" When they say, "I've always been this way," you wonder, "Why do you hang onto it?" When they declare, "That's just how I am," you are thinking, "What do you do that makes that so?" If they say, "We are all going to die someday," you note how much detachment is achieved in the choice of words. The intervention of actually suggesting different wording must be used sparingly. Note that being given some latitude for self-expression as the suffering victim may set the stage, in the longer run, for assuming responsibility in a meaningful way. So promoting a vocabulary that emphasizes existential authenticity really must be saved for the right moment. Even your own modeling of speech can easily come across as contrived. Done with discretion and moderation, changing a way of talking can change a way of being in the world.

8. *Exaggeration.* Given the universal fears we have about such matters as freedom, responsibility, death, isolation, and meaninglessness, clients—all of us—routinely stifle our thoughts and feelings. From an existential perspective, when we are encouraged to be less guarded, we may be closer to being authentic. Ironically, by being a little less guarded about "The Truth" we come closer to truly addressing ultimate existential concerns. In practice, this sometimes (not always) means encouraging the expression of the client's point of view with room for some exaggeration. Techniques from Gestalt therapy often characterize an existentially based style.

9. *Paradoxical intention.* One particular intervention deserves special mention here. Victor Frankl developed a technique called "paradoxical intention" or "prescribing the symptom." (You will also find this in Adlerian therapy, Gestalt, and elsewhere.) Basically this amounts to recommending to clients that they make a point of doing what they are doing anyway. "You seem to be consumed with worry! How about making as long a list as you can of things to worry about?" This sort of remark can carry a touch of humor, irony, and if you aren't careful, might be very misplaced sarcasm. Be careful. There is, however, an existential truth implied in the technique: It provides an opportunity for clients to take control of their "symptoms," get clearer about how they bring these about, and get some insight into their possible payoffs.

10. *Planting seeds.* If the existential perspective is more or less right, no one (i.e., the counselor) is going to permanently "fix" or "cure" anyone. Even the word therapy is a bit misleading from an existentialist point of view. There is no cure for the human capacity for self-deception, and no guarantee that changes made today might not be undone tomorrow. What is realistic is that the client attains an expanded awareness of choices and possibilities. In that spirit, often as not, the techniques of existential intervention aim more at planting the seeds of an idea that may later develop into a more robust sort of awareness. All the techniques and interpretations and therapeutic encounters may contribute to that end.

SHORT- AND LONG-TERM GOALS

Obviously, the critical determinant of goals in counseling will be the stated or reasonably implicit goals of the client. At the same time, clients are turning to you with the expectation of some sort of expertise. Many of the short- and long-term goals common to most approaches to counseling take on certain nuances when approached from an existentialist's perspective. The simple opportunity to express concerns and feelings provides a space for clarifying the client's choices, options, and responsibility. What you can add may come from highlighting specific things you suspect clients do that contribute to their stated dilemmas. Short-term goals will often focus on questions of "How?" How does this person presently look at what is meaningful, or what choices are open to them for change? Short-term goals might be symptom specific. I will probably try to work with the client in addressing the specific problems for which they have sought assistance. My emphasis here is not so much on explicit insight as in discovering choice through practical action. This may or may not take place on a level of explicit awareness, though I might prefer there be experiential and memorable insights into practical options. I would like for my client to leave with some very specific and focused ideas about what it would be possible to do.

As for the long run, I would like to cultivate my client's capacity to be *interested* in their lived world, more accepting of the depth and ambiguities of existential concerns. There may be long-term goals, yet no opportunity for long-term counseling; often, it must suffice to plant the seeds now for forms of reflectivity they may develop later.

USING THE RELATIONSHIP

Debate continues about what makes for effective therapy, but there is general agreement that the genuineness of the relationship is especially important. Existentialists are likely to phrase this in terms of authenticity. Being authentic is hardly a technique, but if there is any single feature that stands out in what counseling is like from an existentialist point of view, it centers on the struggle to be authentic in addressing ultimate core concerns, trying to identify and unmask forms of self-deception, and trying to experience and even celebrate one's own freedom and the freedom of the other. Where does self-disclosure fit in? Self-disclosure is a technique, but also might be thought of as a feature of being authentic. Existential counselors are likely to be advocates of self-disclosure. This would follow from the belief that existential concerns are universal. None of us has the last word on how best to address the consequences of our freedom. Projecting the image that only one of the two people in the room struggles with how to address isolation or meaning or any of the core themes would be to contribute to an illusion. Candid expression of our experience often feels risky, and existential therapists will tend to advocate taking risks with what they say. Self-disclosure stands in contrast to the stereotype of classical psychoanalysis, where the anonymity of the therapist within a reliable and constant frame promotes an analyzable transference. You might want to follow Yalom in making a distinction between vertical and horizontal disclosure. In vertical self-disclosure therapists might share with clients their own experiences and struggles. Since existentialism does not stand for an organization or a rigid set of techniques, there is nothing to rule out this sort of expression. However, the consulting session is not usually thought of as a time for equal sharing of vulnerability regarding matters elsewhere. In contrast, horizontal disclosure centers on the therapist's here-and-now experience of the client. It makes your effort to remain authentic available while putting your experience at the service of your client. It involves your taking the risk of telling your clients your experience of being with them. The wisdom, nature, and timing of a therapist's self-disclosure presents one of the most fundamental topics about therapy technique. Disclosure is likely to be a feature of an existential approach.

As with techniques generally, some features of style in the existential approach might be more likely than others, but none are mandatory. In your course on approaches to counseling, you will be exposed to many memorable personalities, and see a world of difference between the styles of "giants" like Freud, Rogers, Perls, Glasser, or Ellis. Someone could think like an existentialist and yet come across like any of these vastly different human beings. What you can't do is avoid the bottom line: your style of relating is going to be critical to where your client will be able to go with you. From an existential perspective, all these famous therapists were using their style of relating in the service of respecting the ultimate freedom of the client, whether through being hidden or open, confrontive or supportive, directive or nondirective. From an existential perspective, clients have the inescapable responsibility for the use they make of the counselor, and counselors have inescapable responsibility for the invitation their style promotes. Being totally "nondirective" isn't an option: whatever I do or don't do, will imply in some way that I am seeking to have an influence on my client. Self-disclosure invites self-disclosure. Hiddenness invites the exploration of fantasy. Directiveness invites making changes. Nondirectiveness invites struggling with options. Supportiveness invites self-acceptance. Confrontation invites decisiveness.

Here I would like to indicate in a more personal—and controversial—way how I approach existential psychotherapy. Like most therapists, I share the view that the relationship between my client and me is fundamental to what makes a difference. Depending on the client, I do tend to be more self-disclosing than would be widely advocated by therapists (existential and otherwise). I was trained psychoanalytically, am well aware of the virtues of anonymity and maintaining a framework that promotes analysis of transference. Indeed, I rather like that methodology, and I think there's plenty of "relationship" that goes on within it. It just isn't who I typically choose to be. I would like to think of myself as someone who takes risks, particularly in terms of what I find it challenging to disclose. But more to the point, it fulfills *me* to be this way. If I am saying something partly because it is challenging to me, then I am doing it partly *for* me. The paradox here is that sometimes we do our best giving to others when we are (reasonably) willing to take for ourselves. Of course, I entirely agree with virtually all therapists that the bottom line is that I am putting myself at the service of my client. Even so, it is not really very self-disclosing to say something about myself when this involves no sense of vulnerability and is said only because I think it would be a good thing for the client to hear. In the absence of any willingness on the counselor's part to risk vulnerability and openness, that spirit of immediacy, I-and-thou, here-and-now authenticity, is likely to be absent as well. Prepackaged openness might be better left unsaid. It's phony. On the other hand, if it is about me, as a here-and-now disclosure within my relationship with you, even to the point that I am pushing my own comfort zone and to some extent, meeting my own needs in temporarily focusing on my own struggles, this may well be an appropriate part of an authentic relationship. This will be governed entirely by the individual client and situation. The rough guideline is this: If I say things difficult for me while mindful that I am with you, this just might be the sort of relationship I want for myself, which is also transformative for you.

ADAPTING THE APPROACH

Each of us must create our own style, attuned to the individuality of our clients. Different clients call for different styles. We will address this in light of some objections sometimes made to existential counseling.

The existential approach is sometimes portrayed as being overly intellectual and, hence, not suited to clients who are either not so intellectually inclined or simply are faced with more pressing and practical difficulties. This criticism rests on confusing how you think about your clients with how you actually talk to them. There are some clients who might do well with an explicitly philosophical discussion. More often, if a somewhat abstract discussion figures in at all, it will be about concepts like choice and responsibility without reference to academic sources. Even more often, you will join your client in looking at specific realities and looking for options, leaving the broader insights to take care of themselves. As an existential therapist, it is decidedly *not* your job to provide lofty-sounding lectures about freedom and responsibility. Your job is to join your clients at their level and to try to understand their world and their options.

Another common misconception is that because existentialism highlights individualism it won't be appropriate for populations where family and community receive priority over preoccupations with autonomy and personal fulfillment. In fact, communal values offer time-honored solutions to existential issues and are by no means incompatible. Your intervention might be to clarify what choices are embedded in your client's culture. What does follow from existentialism's philosophical insistence on freedom is that putting aside narrow self-interest is an available choice. Cultural sensitivity goes hand in hand with thinking of your client as having choices to make in what they treat as meaningful. Practically speaking, this means that you join with your clients in seeking to understand and appreciate their cultural world, rather than trying to win them over to yours.

A third common objection is that existentialism is naive in speaking of freedom in the real world of social, economic, and physical facts. No one denies this. Freedom and choice are always located within the reality of one's situation. As Sartre points out, prisoners may not be able to break out of their chains, but they define the meaning of those chains by struggling against them. Frankl argued that even when he was in a concentration camp his existence was meaningful. The point of the existential perspective is to focus on what you can do about your circumstances. The emphasis here is on action, not idle talk.

It is true that existential reflections have a natural home in circumstances where there really is time for reflection. For all that, the themes and the way of thinking that underlie existentialism have applicability to the whole range of human situations.

FINDING YOUR NICHE

In sum, there are all sorts of ways of bringing an existentialist way of thinking into your work as a counselor. Your own style may resemble that of practically any of the approaches to therapy that you will study in your classes, as long as it is in the interest of freedom and of cultivating your client's awareness of choices they have for addressing the range of existential themes. There's plenty of room for responding creatively to different populations while drawing from your own unique strengths and insights. There is no one right way to do therapy, and certainly no rigid doctrine for existentially rooted technique. What is crucial is that you create your own authentic way of being attuned to your clients. If you study some of the philosophers at the heart of existentialism, you may find that some of them speak to you more than others. You may find that there are certain existential themes that most help you focus the way you listen and relate. You will be more skilled at some kinds of interventions than others. Your idea of a meaningful relationship may differ from that of your colleague. You will choose what works for you. After all, the concern for *authenticity* is one of those core existential themes. Authenticity means being able to sign your own name on your work and your life. It means you will want to take responsibility for creating your own way of being a therapist.

PROCESS AND CASE SUGGESTIONS

When you have finished reading this chapter you will have an opportunity to respond to three cases on the website: Elena, Theo, and Jane, and then compare your responses with mine. There is no single right way to do existential counseling with these cases. You may or may not prefer to have advanced notice of the themes I will emphasize, drawn from this chapter. If you like, you can, for now, skip reading the next three paragraphs and come back to them after you have developed your own ideas about the cases. In my case reviews, I draw extensively from the particular sections of this chapter, including the snapshots of existentialist philosophers. While you may not feel confident about that abstract material, I urge you to look it over again and then try to anticipate case applications of the progressively more concrete ideas you have read to this point.

1. *Elena.* With Elena, I emphasize how conflicted she is over living up to the expectations of others and I mention all the listed philosophers in connection with this theme. Yalom's list of ultimate existential concerns fits Elena well, as do the specific principles in practice. In particular, I think she is too ready to hand over to others her own responsibility for her life.

2. *Jane.* I see Jane as disinclined to look for possible meaning in her physical symptoms. Again, I start with some ideas from the existentialist philosophers and then look at how specific concepts fit her case. Most of them do. I highlight meaning and meaninglessness, isolation and death. I borrow Jane's own phrases as tools with which to seek out further information.

3. *Theo.* With Theo, my focus is on how we might be responsible for our emotions and on how self-definitions of our identity can serve as a flight from freedom. I encourage you to review this chapter and then try your hand at putting the ideas into practice.

SUMMARY AND SUGGESTED READINGS

I hope you have found this chapter on existentialist psychotherapy both interesting and of practical use. There was no way to avoid bringing in a lot of seemingly abstract ideas, but I think what is most important is that you find your way of integrating these into your experience and practice. As Kierkegaard sees it, the art of becoming who you are—a human subject—consists in "interpenetrating existence with reflection." I hope you won't worry too much about whether what you do is truly and purely existentialist therapy. No one owns the word "existentialism." There are limits to what can reasonably be called existentialist, but within those rough constraints you can do what you choose with the ideas. Of course, that in itself is an existentialist declaration. The position taken in this chapter is that the ideas of certain philosophical innovators are at the heart of what the word means. Ideas and concerns which have trickled down into the culture have impacted psychotherapy. These existentialists' ideas took root with struggles and forms of awareness that have been with us all along. There is no single right way to proceed with existential awareness. I hope that as you grow professionally you will pay attention to how the language of freedom figures into who you are and how you work, and that you will give yourself permission to be creative in how you bring the consequences of freedom into practice.

Continued exposure to existentialist thinking can spread across a lifetime, as will your own development as a practitioner. If you are not already both philosophically inclined and exceptionally able to tackle obscure reading, I do not recommend that you try to take on the core philosophical works on your own. Ideally, a good college philosophy course that surveys existentialism might be best, and a well-selected literature course would complement this. You should be able to find a good anthology in the philosophy section of your campus book store and (especially with the help of an instructor) become grounded in the ideas of main contributors. My favorites include:

Luper, S. (2000). *Existing: An introduction to existential thought.* Mountain View, CA: Mayfield Publishing Company.
Kaufmann, W. (1975). *Existentialism from Dostoevsky to Sartre.* New American Library.

Existentialist literature, though generally more intelligible to the layperson than technical philosophical works, can also be pretty hard to understand. Still, if you want to try your hand, some classic works include:

Camus, A. (1942). *The stranger.* New York: Vintage Books.
Dostoevsky, F. (1972). *Notes from underground.* New York: Penguin Books.
Kafka, F. (1964). *The trial.* New York: Vintage Books.
Sartre, J-P. (1948). No Exit. In *No exit and three other plays.* New York: Vintage Books.
Sartre, J-P. (1959). *Nausea.* Norfolk, Connecticut: New Directions Press.
Tolstoy, L. (2004). *The death of Ivan Illych.* New York: Modern Library.

There are several well-known works written by existential psychotherapists; these may be your best starting place for something you find readable and comprehensible. Here are a few:

Deurzen, E. van. (2002). *Existential counselling and psychotherapy in practice* (2nd ed.). London: Sage.

Frankl, V. (1963). *Man's search for meaning*. Boston: Beacon.

Laing, R. D. (1965). *The divided self*. Baltimore: Pelican.

May, R, Angel, E., Ellenberger, H. F. (Eds.) (1958). *Existence: A new dimension in psychiatry and psychology*. New York: Basic Books.

May, R., & Yalom, I. (2005). Existential psychotherapy. In R. Corsini & D. Wedding (Eds.), *Current psychotherapies* (7th ed., pp. 269–298). Belmont, CA: Thomson Brooks/Cole.

Russell, J. M. (1978). Sartre, therapy, and expanding the concept of responsibility. *American Journal of Psychoanalysis, 38,* 259–269.

Yalom, I. D. (1980). *Existential psychotherapy*. New York: Basic Books.

Yalom, I. D. (1991). *When Nietzsche wept*. New York: Basic Books.

Presumably you are reading this book as part of a class that also has a main text on theories and techniques of counseling. There are plenty of good texts with good presentations on existential therapy. My own favorites include:

Corey, G. (2005) *Theory and practice of counseling and psychotherapy*. (7th ed.). Belmont, CA: Thomson Brooks/Cole.

Sharf, R. S. (2004). *Theories of psychotherapy and counseling: Concepts and cases* (3rd ed.). Belmont, CA: Thomson Brooks/Cole.

Chapter 8

Gestalt Therapy

Judith R. Brown

Chapter Outline

Bridging the Theory-to-Practice Gap

Principles in Practice

Keys to Conceptualization

Interventions and Therapeutic Process

Short- and Long-Term Goals

Using the Relationship

Adapting the Approach

Finding Your Niche

Process and Case Suggestions

Summary and Suggested Readings

BRIDGING THE THEORY-TO-PRACTICE GAP

The first thing people usually ask when they hear Gestalt therapy is what kind of word is *gestalt* and what does it mean? It is a German word and it means a whole or completion; a form or pattern that cannot be separated into parts without losing its essence. Three sticks form a triangle. Place the sticks randomly and there is no triangle. Return them to their original position and you complete the form—the gestalt. The final chord of a piece of music is another example of completing a gestalt; it brings completeness to what would otherwise be incomplete. Without the final chord we are left with an unsatisfactory musical experience.

Typically the second question is, "What does this have to do with psychotherapy?" Gestalt *psychology* is concerned with how and what we perceive and how we make meaning. Creating patterns and forming wholes is something the human brain does naturally. When you look at the starry night sky, from the black background with numerous points of light, constellations of stars—recognizable forms—emerge. They become *figural;* the form, or gestalt, is organized in the brain as we gaze at the heavens. A different type of whole, or gestalt, is created when we attend a meeting. It consists of a beginning (introductions), a middle (a discussion of some topic), and an end (wrapping up and goodbyes). If the meeting is interrupted before the goodbye, it will, like music without a final chord, be left unfinished: an incomplete gestalt. A flurry of emails will likely appear in an effort to bring some closure. When someone we know dies before we have a chance to say goodbye, we experience the pain of loss and the incomplete gestalt; emotions linger, interfering with our making good contact in new situations and blocking us in our efforts to get on with life.

This introductory paragraph is fundamental to basic assumptions that follow and the actual practice of Gestalt therapy. Our clients are like the night sky in that they reveal themselves and we therapists see (and hear) what is figural for them: their constellations, patterns, as well as their incompletions. Similar to the stars, our clients are always in motion, but unlike stars they help to set their own course, to create their own process. We notice what becomes figural for us in relation to them as they present themselves to us. Are they clear or hazy? Are they contactful or distant? Are they enthusiastic in life or resigned? There is excitement as you meet each person face-to-face. How do you feel in relation to her: Interested? Overwhelmed? Helpless? What are the unspoken messages he expresses through his voice, body posture and movements, facial expressions? Does he seem to flow in his process or interrupt himself? Awareness and process are central in Gestalt practice; they work as yeast works for bread. We help our clients become *aware* of their existence, what is going on moment by moment. Awareness leads to improved *contact*—being more in touch with their thoughts and feelings; and *integration* is what we are aiming for, discovering disowned fragments of their personality and creating a whole out of the parts. We guide our clients to consciousness and emotions where the layers of unfinished life situations lie. The sources of our information consist of how they talk to themselves, how they organize and make meaning of themselves in their environment, and how they interrupt their process with automatic behaviors that cause stuckness. What and how, here and now—the four pillars of gestalt.

Thus, in gestalt work our clients experience practical and effectual ways to become more aware of what is actual, to engage in their process of making conscious decisions; to hop off their merry-go-round of repetitive thoughts and focus on their senses. They respond to people and situations in new ways, improve their relationships, and foster their growth and sense of well-being. The task of helping our clients engage more fully sounds amazingly simple, but it is not necessarily easy, for awareness and conscious decisions can bring anxiety and uncertainty. Elena, young and at the onset of learning personal responsibility, says, "If I make the wrong decision I'll regret it forever." This thought is enough to scare anyone into nonawareness and nonaction. Despite our wanting relationships to be more satisfying, life to feel better, and to experience more peace within ourselves, we tend to hold desperately to habitual thoughts and behaviors that are so automatic that we are unaware of them. So we support our clients in discovering that there are countless ways to reorganize their "night sky," their world and relationships; to recognize novel figures and new formations that will serve them better. For my clients, this is extremely exciting and life affirming—as it also is for me.

You have only to hone your therapeutic skills of being present, paying attention, seeing and hearing your clients as they present themselves, and to respond to them human-to-human. As you are your instrument, your inner and outer awareness is key to the entire endeavor. The all-important relationship is the alliance you form with your client, engaging in the exciting process of exploration and discovery. Possibilities of growth are intrinsic within this relationship. The coming sections introduce the art and science of using creative experiments—gauged to your clients' readiness—to facilitate them in new experiences of contact, increased courage and resilience.

PRINCIPLES IN PRACTICE

In my work, I draw on years of practice using basic principles of Gestalt in my life and profession. They are the frames through which I view health and dysfunction, my clients, and my tasks as therapist. They influence how I organize and give meaning to what I see and hear during my sessions. Major considerations, such as theories of *self, holism, the field,* can be found elsewhere. In this chapter I aim to simplify the principles that are directly translatable to practice. To help you incorporate the gestalt approach into your *ground,* to inform your work, as well as your life, I emphasize the importance of staying in the moment, fostering awareness and contact, and bringing your clients from stuckness into process and integration.

First, consider that the *means* and the *ends* of the gestalt approach are in accord with one another. What I encourage during a session introduces and exemplifies fundamental goals of Gestalt therapy: first to *complete unfinished situations from the past that are obstacles to health, wholeness, and good contact with oneself and others;* and second, *to develop the capacity and skills to engage authentically, responsibly, and satisfactorily in the process of everyday living.* Therefore, Gestalt practice relates directly and immediately to improved health and more mature functioning, not only at some future time, but in the present.

1. *Here-and-now focus.* Now is the only time to be aware. Now you can be aware of what is *actual:* the existential moment: you reading the words on the page, feeling the temperature in the room, hearing sounds. *Now* is when you experience feelings

and make choices—you may make a decision to call your parent today, you *choose* to take the phone and call in some actual moment, or you don't. Now is the only time we have the power to influence an event, for events happen only in this moment. Last night I was thinking about what to write; now I participate in this event, as you also participate as you read this. The past is important for all the learning, the memories and emotions we have stemming from earlier times; we bring it into figure when it interferes with awareness, contact, and integration in the here and now. Perls advised therapists to make what is implicit explicit and state the obvious. This is the essence of *phenomenological inquiry,* paying attention to what is actual *now.* My clients and I attend to their moment-by-moment *process:* the flow of *now* moments. Emotions surface, feelings and thoughts are heightened: they become more totally engaged and the *dominant need*—what needs attention most—is revealed. An example might be of needing to cry, or of telling their mother they are angry. *Now* is the moment of possibility. There is no other place to go—only deeper into the experience of the moment, which opens up to the next moment. This is what I mean by *process.*

As Jane (from the website) talks of her situation in the present, I challenge her very gradually to increase her readiness to engage in new experiences, here and now, to increase her awareness and contact with her feelings and emotions. I might ask, "What do you experience now as you talk about your visit to your parents? I expect Jane would be exclusively with her thoughts, *talking about* rather than being in touch with any feelings. My intention is to help her take a step toward more contact with herself, the lump in her throat, what is happening in her chest area. I propose that she tell me *in the present tense,* as if she is actually walking down the corridor approaching their room, what she sees, hears, and smells. I wonder whether Jane is ready to awake to her senses, put aside for the moment all that she "knows" about herself and her parents and be more fully in her experience. Will she further her awareness and contact with what is happening, to realize more of her potential *here and now*? Each intervention is a possible step toward awareness, contact, and integration through exploration and discovery, using more power, becoming more authentic, contacting her feelings; in short, becoming more of herself.

2. *Content.* The *content* clients bring—their problems and issues—becomes the vehicle for *revealing, making explicit, and facilitating* the client's process.[1] My job is to watch and listen carefully, and to be aware of my responses. Thoughts, physical reactions, and emotions are all part of the same system: they stem from the inner being. I notice body movements, facial expression, tone of voice, level of engagement, and contact. Listen to how Theo speaks, see how Elena sits. Of what do you suppose they are aware as they speak? To what extent do they *express* their emotions? Do their facial expressions appear congruent with what is happening inside them? As Theo talks about losing control of his anger, I might ask him what he actually feels in his body, and direct him to his emotions. Each intervention is an experiment, a method for clients to discover—through experience—how they are and what they are doing and to express their anger, joy, or grief.

---

[1] "Process" is used to refer to the progression of the therapy as well as the sequences of experiences of the patient. It conveys movement rather than stuckness.

This is an introduction to the idea of *self-regulation*, attaining and losing homeostatic balance. Through early experiences when we are interrupted and frustrated in getting what we need we lose the ability to listen to our bodies, to know what we, as an organism, are lacking or have in too great abundance. Perhaps we need someone to hold close; or maybe we need to scream to express frustration; have a tantrum, for example. Thus we lose contact with ourselves and never come to trust that we know what we need. Such early experiences are the source of fragmentation, of being split between what we need and what others (society) demand of us. Mother tells us when we "must be" cold and to put on a sweater; or when we are hungry or have eaten enough. We learn to figure out what others think we need and wonder what they expect of us and will they love us, all of which exacerbate lack of awareness and faulty contact. We lose our here-and-now focus, become saturated with incomplete situations; we substitute figuring out, creating a merry-go-round of repetitive and automatic static in the brain. I refer to this pseudo-thinking as "going into your head."

3. *Awareness.* Awareness goes down the drain in conditions described above for it is possible only here and now. The primacy of awareness as a basic focus of gestalt therapy cannot be overemphasized. It is how we know what is going on, how we get in touch with our experiences and access the world through our senses. We feel tension, pain, or excitement. We tune in to what is happening in the environment. With awareness comes the possibility of options and making choices instead of plunging into unconscious, automatic (knee-jerk) reactions. You can easily help clients experience *now* and perceive what they need by asking questions that begin with the word *what.* You will direct their attention to the present moment. For example, what are you doing now? (Never asked as an accusation.) Or, what are you experiencing now? You help clients come out of their head to what is actual, the simplicity of the *now* experience. It can be a major discovery for clients as they "wake up" from anxiety and fantasy. They may experience relief in the moment as they quiet their habitually active minds. Awareness is a gateway to engagement and increased intensity, to contact with long-concealed feelings and stifled emotions, the remnants of unfinished situations that hinder movement toward growth and healing.

4. *The paradoxical nature of change.* You may be wondering how this emphasis on awareness and experience is facilitative. In any approach to psychotherapy interventions are based on a theory of how change comes about. How does a person change? From our own experience we know that wanting to change or thinking we ought to change usually doesn't work. And should someone else to tell us we should change, this does not alter our behavior. A major contribution of Gestalt is the paradoxical nature of change.[2] Change has little to do with logic or with what we think. Rather change *comes about* when structure is transformed to process. If you think of psychological structures—habits of thought and behavior—as frozen structure, then it is clear how structure is transformed to process by *living through* an experience. This is not you playing at, or pretending, or doing something as a task, but you totally experiencing an event: you in complete engagement.

---

[2]Explicated by A. Beisser, in *The Paradoxical Nature of Change,* 1970, based on Perls' work.

Gestalt therapists accept clients as they are; they are not oriented toward changing them. The paradox resides in this: we desire change but we don't know what this change will be. We can't know for it hasn't happened yet! We desire change for our clients yet when we suggest interventions we do *not* have a desired outcome. Our desire is for the experience itself. The motive for the intervention may not have a specific purpose, yet it is always intentional in its design: to *facilitate engagement in what the client is doing*. Growth and change are not forced to happen by design. The paradox is that when we stop trying, then change is likely. The following is an example of process and change.

Example: Carol, spends some time talking about how difficult her life is. She complains about husband, parents, and children. After hearing her out the therapist says, "It sounds like you have a lot to complain about." Carol agrees. The therapist suggests, "Now just focus on complaining to your heart's content." Carol begins quietly, then seems energized by this experiment and speaks louder and faster and begins to smile a bit. The therapist further suggests that she allow herself to enjoy her complaining. She thoroughly does this and laughs when she has finally finished. At the next meeting she tells the therapist it is as if something shifted inside her. Maybe her situation hasn't changed but everything seems easier. She adds, "Sometimes I still notice I want to be miserable, but then if I start complaining, it just sort of goes away." During the course of the therapy Carol referred back several times to "the day I stopped being miserable."

5. *Contact.* Contact is the *meeting* of yourself and what is different or other than yourself—other people and things in the environment. Contact can be as obvious and unmistakable as entering the cold ocean water, the smash of the waves against your body, or as ephemeral as what Martin Buber called the I-thou experience. Contact is experienced at the point of what is *I* and what is *other;* metaphorically "the boundary." It assumes an awareness and acknowledgment of the other's existence as a separate being. Through contact, people grow and change—something is exchanged. This is never a purely cognitive process, but rather involves the whole of your being when there is no "trying" but you surrender to the experience of the moment. Notice as you interact with your client/friend/parent whether there are times when you experience a special moment of sharing. It might include laughter or tears.

Contact can include your awareness and acknowledgment of your inner experience, such as being in contact with your anxiety through the feelings associated with it. Contact provides the possibility for relationship with others; it holds the potential for process, energy, dialog, and new meanings.

Example: Louise looks down as she says, "I'm having a very hard time in my life now."

Therapist: "I notice you are speaking into space. Say this directly to someone that you imagine sitting in this room; or to me. Notice whether it is the same experience or different." Louise does so with reluctance and reports, "It's very different; it makes me cry to say it to you." She knows implicitly that any human contact, any real "meetings," would intensify her experience. Through this experiment she discovers that she can tolerate this moment of uncertainty and anxiety. In the safety of the situation she experiences her vulnerability. She has acquired a habit, out of fear, that has become an obstacle to contact, both with others and with her emotions. She has for years automatically kept herself safely isolated with impermeable boundaries. Now she has a choice.

6. *Cycle of experience.* The concept of unfinished situations is central to Gestalt therapy and directly applicable to our interaction with clients in the clinical situation. A cycle consists briefly of sensation, action, contact, satisfaction, and withdrawal. Incomplete cycles make it difficult to be present now for we are partly in the past. Theo, Jane, and Elena are good examples of suffering in their present situations, in large part as a result of incomplete cycles of experience in the past.

KEYS TO CONCEPTUALIZATION

The presenting problems of our clients may seem like a tempting road to march right down; however, for the Gestalt practitioner it is not necessarily the way to go. The clients have assembled pieces of their puzzle into a figure, in the gestalt sense. Out of their ground, their perceptions, beliefs, and past nightmares have taken shape, coalesced, and become an obstacle and source of misery. Rather than being *here* and *now,* they are running around their brain on the same track over and over, stuck with *there* and *then.*

Perls was interested in promoting the growth process and developing the human potential.[3] He believed this could best be accomplished by *phenomenological inquiry,* which means dealing with what is actual in the moment. He defined dreaming, imagining, theorizing, and anticipating as *fantasy,* rather than *thinking.*[4] To focus on actual phenomena is the way to discovery, although we can't know for certain what we will discover. That is always true of a creative process. As a form of investigation of the client's present awareness, it is similar to pointing out stars in the night sky to someone who has never noticed them before. Observing my client I select and call attention to what I see and hear: movements, behaviors, and expressions; even the client's breathing. I listen not only to the words but also the quality of the voice and pay attention to how I respond to it.

This kind of phenomenological investigation is not a narrow path that leads to some predetermined place, but rather a broad embracing of client, therapist, surroundings, and stated problems; in a word, our present existence, here and now. I note the level of vitality and interest, the level of awareness, of contact with self and environment, evidence of incomplete situations, and lack of integration. An important function of this investigation is to dislodge clients' attention from the busyness in their head, their customary thoughts about problems and behaviors, with all the accompanying explanations, justifications, and rationalizations that they have repeated to themselves many times. Consider the cases of Elena, Jane, and Theo; by the way they tell their concerns to their interviewers, it is evident they have verbalized these experiences and ideas many times before, to themselves and

---

[3]Perls, F. (1988) *Gestalt Therapy Verbatim.*Highland, NY: The Gestalt Journal Press, p. 2. Originally published by Real People Press, 1969.
[4]P. 11. *The Gestalt Approach and Eyewitness to Therapy.*

possibly to others. From the frozen ground there is nothing new, no new formulations, feelings, or thoughts, only rigidity; but by staying here and now, comes a shift to awareness, contact, and the possibility of a new figure/ground relationship. To use the metaphor of the night sky, the *dominant need* emerges from the ground like a constellation: a *clear figure*. What had remained out of awareness, or covered by a heavy cloud layer, is now experienced. Without *going anywhere* the client discovers feelings and emotions connected to experiences from the past that demand completion. This is the golden moment of sensation—the first point that launches the client, who up until now has been blocked, along a cycle of experience. Succeeding moments, experienced as totally as possible, come about, taking a course that is unrehearsed, unexpected. Old figures destruct and new figures form. Some of the questions in my mind as I follow my clients' and my process are these: what are they/am I doing now? What is happening now? What are they/am I experiencing, or in contact with now? What are they/am I avoiding now? What do they want, what do I want now? Are they/am I fully engaged? Partly engaged? I listen for what Perls called "boundary disturbances," ways of being that interfere with contact, both with ourselves and others: introjection, projection, confluence, and retroflection. He wrote this brief explanation of each: "The *introjector does as others would like him to do, the projector does unto others what he accuses them of doing to him, the man (sic) in pathological confluence doesn't know who is doing what to whom, and the retroflector does to himself what he would like to do to others.*"[5] (Italics in original.)

I build on the presenting material by making explicit what is implicit through creative experiments. My client's behavior becomes the springboard of interventions.

INTERVENTIONS AND THERAPEUTIC PROCESS

Gestalt interventions serve as ongoing investigations, to make what is implicit, explicit, by engaging clients in *now* experiences. They are experiments, matched to the clients' level of risk revealed by their responses, and used to bring awareness and create meetings between conflicting thoughts and feelings. To help make blocked process and automatic behaviors conscious, I may ask clients to do more of what they are doing. If they speak very quietly I suggest we both whisper. We both stand and as we whisper we tiptoe around the room. Then we add words; for example, I won't make a wave, I won't upset you. We do the opposite and use loud voices and stamp our feet. We alternate, going back and forth from whisper to shouting. Always, we meta-process after.

A client, Jon, indirectly rejects a suggestion I make. This becomes the theme of an intervention: I ask Jon to experience just shaking his head, "no." Then to the words, "I won't do what you want." Notice this paradoxical instruction; by telling me what he won't do, he is doing it. Then I build on this. "Is there something else you want to say to me?" Jon replies, "I'll never do what you want." I ask: "Is there someone else to whom you could say this?"

---

[5]Perls, in *The Gestalt Approach and Eyewitness to Therapy.*

Jon says, "My girlfriend." He turns to face an empty chair. "I won't do what you want." I follow his process asking is there more he wants to say. Is there anyone else to whom he wants to say this? What is he in contact with as he says this? I give feedback on his voice (you sound like you're whining, or pleading), or his posture (I notice your hands in fists, or I see how you shake your finger at her) especially if they are inconsistent with his words. I ask what he is avoiding, if anything, or what he is wanting. In this simple example, you can see how I follow where the client is, to make more explicit what is going on, to encourage more engagement and expression of emotions. Depending on his experience moment-to-moment I may prompt him to more awareness and contact by asking *now questions*: what are you doing now? What do you experience (or feel) now? What is happening now? I always appreciate a client's courage to take even small steps toward becoming more of himself, however this is manifested. Jon reports later he pays more attention to saying yes, and meaning it, and to saying no directly to me and others.

To increase clients' awareness of self and others I suggest an *awareness continuum* to discover what is actual in the moment. Starting sentences with "Now I" they may literally "come to their senses." "Now I sit still. Now I see the brightness in the window. Now I don't breathe. Now I try to take a full breath. Now I feel a little anxiety here," putting their hand on their chest. "Now I want to stop doing this." This is difficult for some clients. Walking around rather than sitting in a chair may facilitate, or be creative; put a paperweight in a client's hand, hold a fragrant flower under their nose to stimulate the senses. If and when clients do "wake up" to their experience, suggest they intentionally resume the "figuring out" or thinking about, but now do this with intention. The basic idea is to make a conscious choice rather than slide into automatic behaviors.

Using two-chair work has many possibilities to meet blocks in process. In the above example Jon could sit in the empty chair and *become* his girlfriend or his mother and respond to Jon, whose chair is now empty. Through dialog I can hear and Jon can experience where he has power, how he uses it, what he projects onto the *other*, and how he maintains the adversarial relationship. I ask Jon to state his resentments, then demands (each resentment has an implicit demand), and appreciations to his mother. Resentments and demands, I remind Jon, don't have to be fair, or logical. We might even appreciate and resent the same thing. When resentments are totally expressed, clients tend to move, on their own, to appreciations and empathy. There are no hard-and-fast rules when Jon should change chairs and "become" his mother. Jon tells his mother, "I won't do anything you ask." Perhaps he stops there. I ask, "What's going on now?" Jon: "I'm thinking of what she would say to me." I tell him to move to the other chair, to sit like his mother, use her voice. If there is no energy, I check in, ask, follow Jon's process. Jon's facial expression changes as he speaks with his mother. I ask, "What just happened?" Jon: "I was thinking from her perspective." He moves to the other chair and speak as his mother. Thus what has been frozen interaction, with little or no self-disclosure of feelings or emotions, becomes something different. I remind Jon, when the dialog is finished, that mother was not really in the room. It was all him. I might talk about the power of the introjected negative parent to whom Jon gave so much power although she was never actually with us in the room.

This kind of process may help finish up grief over losing someone. It may sound strange yet there are often resentments toward the person who died, one being, "I resent you for dying and leaving me."

Clients are reminded to stay aware and pay attention when they avoid contact. The object of experiments is to heighten an experience, tease a clear figure from confused and inflexible ground, explore self-support in new situations. Clients enter the feeling that has been avoided—the stuck point—in a way they can tolerate. Imagine Elena having a dialog with her brother who was lucky enough to escape the family, or her sister whom she hates. We, as well as our clients, take risks when we/they enter the unknown. Emotions may be aroused, moved by our own unfinished situations; we can tear up, or feel anger with a woman who was raped. We share deep experiences and relationships are strengthened.

SHORT- AND LONG-TERM GOALS

The general goals for the short term and long term are to increase awareness of self and other, increase risk-taking, make conscious choices, enhance genuine self-expression, complete cycles of experience, and make explicit and integrate opposing aspects of the person to increase quality of life.

My short-term goal is to achieve a solid therapist/client relationship by building an alliance and establishing trust. This is an ongoing concern; in each session I include time for *meta-communication,* a time to check out how we are doing in our common pursuit. I also inform my clients that I always welcome their reactions to me and to the work we are engaged in.

The goals of increased awareness, contact, and integration are understood to lead directly to growth and change. They are neither long-term nor short-term but constant during sessions and throughout life. Inherent in the word "goal" is the idea of time. At some future time certain goals will be reached. If we do this, this, and that, *then* we will reach a desired state different from the one we are in now. This is an example of linear thought that is not in accord with the Gestalt approach. Whatever behaviors clients manifest when they appear at our door, there are possibilities of increased awareness, even when the awareness is of resisting awareness, or contact, and integration.

The idea of a goal is foreign to process as a method, for it takes us out of the existential *now*. Yet, this being said, is it possible *not* to have goals? It is so natural for clients to imagine how they'd like or think they ought to be different. Theoretically it makes sense to have goals for they give us direction. Operationally there *is* a direction in our selection of now moments to shine a light on. These include the therapist's and client's desires: to lessen pain, to achieve better relationships, to feel more whole. Yet as these do take us, momentarily, out of our experience of what is actual and into fantasy, these very fantasies can be useful in interventions.

USING THE RELATIONSHIP

Given the complexity of human interaction and the therapist/client interaction in particular, it is essential for me to know myself well. If I know my biases I may rise above them. If I have an unacknowledged desired outcome, I may unconsciously manipulate my client in an effort to reach that outcome. Above all I need to model awareness, good contact, and personal responsibility. This means I acknowledge and own my feelings, my emotions, and responses. *Self-awareness questions for therapists*: What is my bias in this situation? Am I threatened in any way by this client? Do I have a desired outcome for my client? Can I separate my material from my clients' material?

I must project nothing onto my clients. I must be clear in this regard. And I deal with my clients' projections on me at the time they happen. Elly comes in for her first visit, briefly discloses some recent behavior, and says to me, "You must think I'm awful." I get off my chair and ask her to sit there. "Now you be Judith, I tell her. How do you respond to Elly? She says you must think she's awful" Elly, as Judith, starts to berate herself at some length, stops, looks at me and says with surprise, "I sound just like my mother!" I am removed as a screen for her projection.

I listen carefully to clients and deal with their projections on me when they occur. Clients disown their power with comments such as, "You probably know what I should do," "You wouldn't put up with my situation," "Will I always be like this?" When they put themselves down like this, or complain about their behavior not being as it should, instead of asking questions I might ask them to teach me to be like them. In this way they become deeply aware of how and when they belittle themselves. With this awareness they now have a choice; at any moment can choose to do it (and enjoy it) or refrain from doing it. Surprisingly, this experiment seems to give them not only more awareness but appreciation for how expert they are in this particular behavior. It is also amusing for them to see me try to be as good as they are when I act out to their instructions, whether it is telling lies or being critical toward their spouse or verbalizing their internal monologue about their shortcomings: "Oh, I'm so bad, I'm so stupid."

My relationship with clients is based on genuine interpersonal connection and is a central part of the healing process. Clients know that I am present and available for contact and that I see and hear them. Together we cocreate the process, as in a dance. They experience my engagement when I join them in an experiment. For example, Ted complains he never seems to get anywhere in life. I suggest that he tell me how he might hinder *me* as he hinders himself. Ted walks toward me, his palms in "stop" position, and says, with some determination, "You're not going to get anywhere." I encourage him to elaborate on how he can keep me from getting anywhere. Then we change roles. Using the words he has said to me, I tell him he's not going to get anywhere and how I'll keep him just where he is. We meta-process; compare how we felt in each role. Ted recognizes each role and with whom in his life he has played these roles. He expresses anger and frustration in turn as he continues, using two chairs to dialog and facilitate his process.

I continually shuttle my attention from my clients to myself, aware of both, for I am my instrument to see, hear, and be in touch with their responses and my own. I serve as a model: authentic and spontaneous, experiencing, responding, and reporting in the present, when it may be facilitative to increase clients' awareness. Clients, in turn, respond to my life and humanness, encouraged to share more of themselves. We share exuberance, deadness, profound moments, and quiet times as well, during intervals when the grief is over, or the depression lifts and we stand together silent at the window.

Although I may enjoy using my creativity and learn from our sessions, they are, above all, for my clients. I am accepting of their total experience, willing to deal with the complexity of their existence while keeping my needs out. I support them in their goals by facilitating their self-actualization *in each moment*. When appropriate I kindle deeper levels of connection by *meta-processing*: I verbalize my experience, feelings, and thoughts, *always* in the service of clients' process, connection and growth. My self-disclosure further demonstrates my presence; I model *personal responsibility*; that is, acknowledge my feelings, thoughts, and behavior. I invite the same from my clients, who learn from my example. Like trust, an alliance is not created at once for all time; it is built, and may be challenged over the course of the therapy.

There is an *attitude* of Gestalt; to meet each client with respect and acceptance, focus on present-centeredness and process. I expect myself to set the example for presence, flexibility, spontaneity, and authenticity. The therapist/client interaction is extremely complex with the continual mutual influence of face-to-face encounters; human bonding is mysterious and powerful. As therapist *being there wholly* is the least and the most I can do for and with my clients.

ADAPTING THE APPROACH

In the Gestalt approach one is always adapting to the moment; the situation determines our actions and reactions. Each client is unique. How I meet them depends on what they say, how they look at me, and how I respond to them. Age,[6] gender, and ethnicity and culture may present different problems, vocabulary, and forms of interaction. Yet each person has emotions, interest, and contact and this is what we work with. I need only to hear what is true for clients in this moment, their story, their reactions to me and to being in this room; their pain and prejudices, beliefs and fears. I question often to make certain I avoid cultural misunderstandings. The qualities and behaviors of each client evoke something different from me, as I do from them; this is true for all times as we cocreate our interactions. I adapt primarily to the client's readiness to engage. Some clients are highly intellectual and want to know about my methods. I talk about process and emotions and my understanding of change. With others we jump right in, as in the following example. A call comes from an acquaintance that her friend, Shirley, is suicidal; may she bring her to me. Shirley arrives and whispers, "I don't know where to start." I see tears in her eyes and talk to her in a calm, strong voice: "Just experience what is happening right now," as I indicate the box of tissues on the table. She is trembling, unable to speak; she looks terrified. I wonder how she is terrifying herself. I take her hands and put them on my shoulders, saying, "Make *me* scared, Shirley, make *me* tremble. Do to me what you are doing to yourself." I speak with a strong voice, confident in her, in me, in the method. She shakes me vehemently and shouts out her anger that was meant, as soon became clear, for her grandmother who had once tried to kill her. Shirley gives up controlling her pent-up emotions, allows herself to *express,* and returns to homeostasis and self-regulation.

Eric talks about his father. "He was fierce; but you know being a farmer in Norway was hard work. He just did what he had to do. Once he threw a pitchfork at me from the hay wagon but it didn't hit me." Eric makes excuses for his father. "I was goofing off." He doesn't acknowledge anger or resentments. He maintains pride in his father and holds onto

---

[6]Violet Oaklander's *Windows To Our Children* is an excellent book on Gestalt therapy with children.

his way of interpreting that occasion. Yet he says he never grieved when his father died. I tread gently, hear his appreciations *and* his underlying fear and sadness; gradually he gets in touch with emotions and discovers he can allow his grief to surface.

FINDING YOUR NICHE

I believe there are no other theoretical orientations within the Gestalt approach to therapy. Some people combine Gestalt with other work, such as art or dance therapy, or bodywork such as the Rubenfeld Synergy Method. When we work with dreams we do not analyze or interpret, but facilitate integration of conflicting aspects of the personality as they appear in dreams. Gestalt work with children[7] and adults may include drawing and clay, music, and sand tables. However, the underlying theoretical implications of Gestalt theory demand a here-and-now focus—even when fantasy is included to expand a client's experience. Along with a here-and-now focus, cycles of experience, holism, and field theory are inherent in Gestalt. Analysis is antithetical to the holistic view where the whole is not taken apart for analysis, but rather is seen as more than the sum of the parts.

Gestalt requires a tolerance for process orientation in which the outcome cannot be known in advance. Those who want the security of being in control, who want to impart knowledge rather than highlight experience, will not be suitable for this approach. It requires flexibility of the therapist to move with the client as new figures emerge from the ground. It also asks that therapists be able to use their humanness to make contact with clients, profound connection that increases the possibility of change. The three aspects emphasized in this chapter—awareness, contact, and integration—all depend on staying with the experience in the moment and trusting the process.

PROCESS AND CASE SUGGESTIONS

1. *Elena.* It is my experience that a client's existential state can be contagious, and this is certainly true for me in relation to Elena. I could easily feel as overwhelmed and confused as she is in her situation. How to help this caring, intelligent, girl/woman at this extremely difficult juncture in her life? What, among all her contradictions, the pressures on her, her fears, is her most pressing need? Everything matters and nothing matters. Where to begin? Clear figures emerge for a fleeting moment, such as "I love my mother," and then we hear how resentful she is of her mother; she has lots of friends but they don't understand her and her situation, and so on. She needs an ally and I can be that for her. I am with her with no expectations, no "shoulds" for her. I am the outsider who can appreciate and support her, who can witness as she becomes more of herself, more mature, and moves in the direction of

---

[7]Ibid.

making some major life decisions. I need to remain clear and focused as I help her to complete small cycles of experience and become more clear and focused on what she needs, moment by moment.

2. *Jane.* I have many different responses to Jane. Although she mentions guilt and begins to cry at times during her interview, my sense is she has lived a life of controlled emotions and limited passion. Unlike her siblings who are "wild and crazy," she is extremely responsible, at her job and in her family. I appreciate her engagement during the interview, and want to cheer for her friend Barbara. Yet I would hope to introduce her to the Barbara in herself, facilitate her owning the qualities she has denied, and recognize the special person she is. I wonder whether she might become truly interested in herself and see that what we do together is not a waste of her time or irrelevant to her shortness of breath. I am left sad for her; she asks little for herself. I would love to see her accept that she is entitled to be more, feel more, and live fuller—to truly wake up and embrace life, as many post menopausal women do.

3. *Theo.* Theo seems extremely young socially, almost like a junior high kid who has latched onto his first girlfriend. His isolation and innocence touch the mother in me; he appears so lost. I wonder whether he might grow and develop more of an identity, become more self-confident and come to appreciate his positive qualities. I know I can't "grow him up," that he must do this himself, but I want to accompany him, support him, and even challenge him on his journey to manhood. As I work with him, I must forget any goals I might have for him and put aside the idea that I know what is best for him. For Theo, self-awareness may seem threatening, especially getting in touch with and expressing his anger. We go slowly and I trust him in his process of discovery: both how he limits himself and how he dares to take steps to own his power. I look forward to a trusting relationship in which he can share with me whatever he is struggling with.

SUMMARY AND SUGGESTED READINGS

Inherent in the paradoxical theory of change is the idea that growth and development are innate proclivities of the human organism. Our clients are often tethered to unfinished situations and established habits of thought and behavior with origins in early experiences. Using the experiential method of *now, focus and process* I can help bring the client to new possibilities in relationship and contact, closure of unfinished situations, and movement toward integration and maturity.

In this chapter, I have emphasized awareness, contact, and integration. Awareness is always in the *now*, contact is always in the *now*, and integration is wholeness, completion—a lifelong venture of reowning aspects of our being through awareness and contact. Gestalt sessions are an adventure in the sense that both the client and I take risks. We share heartfelt experiences that involve *process*, meaning our path is not well-worn but being co-created in the moment by me and my client. By surrendering to the forming moment, a new moment, and another moment, and yet another arrives.

Requirements for us as Gestalt therapists are consistent with this approach. Our relationship with clients is based on genuine interpersonal connection and is a central part of the healing process. We are engaged, responsive, and authentic; ready to move into the unknown with the client; willing to be self-disclosing when appropriate and facilitative to the client's process. We must have the courage that we ask of our clients to let go of desired outcomes and to discover and surrender to what emerges, moment by moment.

Brown, J. R. (1998). *Back to the beanstalk: Enchantment and reality for couples.* Cleveland, OH: Gestalt Institute of Cleveland Press.

Clarkson, P., & Mackewn, J. (1993). *Fritz Perls.* Newbury Park, CA: Sage.

Crocker, S. F. (1999). *A well-lived life: Essays in Gestalt therapy.* Cambridge, MA: Gestalt Institute of Cleveland Press.

Perls, F. S. (1969). *Gestalt therapy verbatim.* Lafayette, CA: Real People Press.

Perls, F. S. (1973). *The Gestalt approach and eyewitness to therapy.* Palo Alto, CA: Science and Behavior Books.

Woldt, A. L., and Toman, S. M. (Eds.). (2005). *Gestalt therapy: History, theory, and practice.* Thousand Oaks, CA: Sage.

Chapter 9

Behavioral Therapy

Christopher R. Martell

Chapter Outline

Bridging the Theory-to-Practice Gap

Principles in Practice

Keys to Conceptualization

Interventions and Therapeutic Process

Short- and Long-Term Goals

Using the Relationship

Adapting the Approach

Finding Your Niche

Process and Case Suggestions

Summary and Suggested Readings

References

BRIDGING THE THEORY-TO-PRACTICE GAP

Behavioral therapy is, perhaps, one of the most misunderstood of all the theoretical orientations and therapeutic practices. A Gary Larson cartoon spoofing a "radical treatment for fear of heights, snakes, claustrophobia, and the dark" shows a terrified man in a small, dark box hanging from a crane. Several snakes are poking their heads out of the tiny window through which you see the man's wide, frantic eyes. This cartoon humorously captures the stereotype of behavioral therapies. Call it "behavior modification" and the stereotype is even worse—a therapist saying "good job" and popping a raisin in the mouth of depressed clients who look the therapist in the eyes rather than staring at their shoes. Although behavior therapists do make use of such procedures as exposure (although the Larson cartoon would not be a good example of it), and reinforcement is central to the theory, the practice of behavior therapy consists of a natural interaction between human beings.

The origins of the therapy are in learning theory. Learning theory espouses the idea that much human activity is acquired from direct experiences with the developmental environment. A few basic principles of learning can account for a wide range of human behavior. The theory dates back to Ivan Pavlov's (Pavlov, 1927) classical conditioning experiments, and to B. F. Skinner's operant conditioning (Skinner, 1953). Psychologists Watson and Rayner (1920) demonstrated in their experiments with Little Albert how a small child could be conditioned to fear a white lab rat or a fuzzy rabbit by repeatedly pairing presentation of the animal with a loud noise that startled the child. It was therefore reasoned that, since fears could be learned, they could also be unlearned. Psychiatrist Joseph Wolpe (1958) was one of the first practitioners to call his treatment behavior therapy. By teaching people with specific phobias to eventually approach the object that they feared by gradually exposing them to it, Wolpe was one of the pioneers in behavior therapy.

Albert Bandura (1977) articulated a comprehensive social learning theory of human behavior. The significant contribution of this model was to focus attention on the possibility that people learn through observation of a model without direct reinforcement of the observed behavior. The social learning model represented the complexity of human functioning and learning in language that was accessible to the clinical community in a way that operant and classical conditioning models did not.

There are, generally, three variations of behavior therapy: applied analysis of behavior (dating back to Skinner), behavior therapy (similar to Wolpe), and cognitive-behavioral therapy (which adds the modification of thoughts to behavior therapy) following the social learning model of Bandura, and extensions of that model (for example, Lazarus, 1971; Meichenbaum, 1974). Some graduate psychology programs used to describe their theoretical orientation as "broad spectrum behavior therapy," indicating the breadth of the approaches. Most behavior therapists are pragmatists and use whatever works within the larger theoretical framework rather than rigidly adhering to one form of behaviorism or another. Behavioral techniques have been used to treat a variety of human problems including depression (Beck, Rush, Shaw, & Emery, 1979; Lewinsohn, 1974, Martell, Addis, & Jacobson, 2001), anxiety disorders, fears and phobias (Wolpe, 1958; 1982), obsessive-compulsive disorder (Foa & Goldstein, 1978); and even borderline personality disorder (Linehan, 1993).

PRINCIPLES IN PRACTICE

While there is a vast literature regarding behavior therapy in its various forms, the theory can be most easily explored by examining several basic principles. These principles have led to rich academic discussion about how conditioning and reinforcement works, what to do with covert (private) behaviors—thoughts and feelings that are not publicly observable—and what causes people to change. Thus, the practice of behavior therapy is also rich and exciting. The following explanation of these principles helps demonstrate the complexity of the issues and provides guidance for the therapist working with a client.

1. *Behavior, whether public or private, is strengthened or weakened by its consequences.* Every behavior results in consequences that either encourage or discourage that particular behavior. If we do something and are rewarded, we are likely to do the same thing again in similar circumstances. Rewards can be positive feelings such as a sense of accomplishment, or the sense of relief when negative feelings are dispelled, or they can be more tangible, such as money. For example, clients with a drinking problem, who feel good (the reward) when drinking with friends at a local pub, are likely to drink again, even if they want to stop, when at the pub with friends. Thus, the rewarded behavior—drinking—is maintained or increased. If the good feeling from drinking occurred when clients drank beer or wine, but hard liquor made them violently ill after even one drink, then they would be more likely to drink beer or wine (the rewarded behavior) and not drink hard liquor (the punished behavior). The principle of maintaining or increasing rewarded behaviors and decreasing punished behaviors applies to thoughts as well as actions. According to the behaviorist model, clients who persistently think, "I am a worthless piece of worthlessness," in a variety of situations will experience such a thought as punishing because it makes them feel awful, and thus the thought will decrease. This is only true if the client experiences the connection between the thought and the punishing consequence of feeling awful, or if the consequence of feeling awful is always punishment. Particular thoughts are often maintained because they feel right to the thinker. There may be a number of secondary reinforcers for a thought such as "I am a worthless piece of worthlessness" when it is spoken out loud, such as getting sympathy and attention from others. The client is not necessarily thinking or talking in a particular way in order to get sympathy, but rather may continue expressing thoughts that are also connected with negative feelings because those thoughts have in some way been rewarded some percentage of the time. Anger is a good example, particularly as it is experienced by Theo in the case study examples. Theo described many times when he was either accused of something that he did not do, such as his teacher accusing him of cheating, or when something he wanted was being denied him, such as sex with his girlfriend. His response was anger. Anger and aggression were both modeled by his parents, and reinforced in some fashion that increased the occurrence of outbursts.

2. *Behaviors that are rewarded are maintained or increased; those that are punished will decrease.* We know that behaviors do not need to be rewarded 100% of the time to

maintain or increase. Behaviors rewarded sometimes but not always not only increase, but may be more difficult to extinguish. People are not always aware of the rewards they receive. Jane, for example, has always been very accomplished in her work although she is not getting the recognition that she wants. There are intrinsic rewards that allow her to work hard, and she enjoys the intellectual stimulation she finds with her friend Barbara, thus spending more and more time with her. These rewards are natural, and are different from the crackers that Jane received as a child for reciting the commandments. Such a "reward" may actually have served as a punishment for keeping the commandments in mind as Jane separated from her parents rather than accomplishing what her mother desired, because earning crackers for her soup may have been paired with resentment, frustration, and other negative feelings that would, ultimately, decrease the behavior her mother was trying to instill. A behavior therapist cannot assume that any behavior is rewarded or punished based on the nature of the behavior itself, but rather by observing whether the behavior is increasing or decreasing. Under certain conditions crackers, or chocolate, may be rewarding and reinforce behavior; at other times, like in Jane's case, they are more likely to be aversive and ultimately decrease behavior.

3. *The approach is functional rather than structural.* By this I mean behavior is understood by the processes or functions that maintain it rather than by how it looks or according to some hypothesized structure in the brain. Behavior that was rewarded in the past may continue in the present with or without continued reward. Take memory as an example. We remember events because once they happen, we create a story about the events, pairing this story with the verbal and visual images associated with the event. There is a pleasant experience associated with the act of remembering a pleasant event, imagining the scene, and retelling the story. Thus, the act of remembering is rewarded at some time. Although the human brain is capable of making a seemingly infinite number of associations like this, we do not need to hypothesize that we have "a memory" as a thing, but rather that there is a process of remembering that allows people to recall historical events when provided with environmental cues.

4. *Neutral stimuli, paired with positive or negative environmental stimuli, can take on the properties of the environment in which they are presented and be conditioned to be positive or negative.* This has been demonstrated by classical conditioning experiments. If, for example, family holidays are happy, celebratory times, the particular foods served and music played from year to year may take on those properties, and when experienced in the present will make a person feel happy. Likewise, if a parent got abusively drunk repeatedly on a particular holiday, the adult child may continue to feel anxious and sad on that holiday, even when the drunken parent is no longer present. This is what occurred with Little Albert and the white rat. The neutral stimulus was paired with the loud noise (an aversive stimulus) and Albert was conditioned to experience fear in the presence of the rat and other furry creatures; hence the originally neutral stimulus had taken on aversive properties. These responses are conditioned emotional responses independent of remembering particulars of an event. Theo believed that people found him intimidating. This may have been the case given the negative images of African American males, frequently

portrayed in the media as being violent criminals. Neutral stimuli—skin color—has taken on many negative and positive properties for social groups as well as individuals.

5. *Behaviorism is antimentalist.* Behaviorists do not accept that there is a mind apart from the body. Human beings have sophisticated abilities to observe themselves and to describe what they experience in their bodies with words such as "afraid" or "discouraged." The behavior therapist does not consider human complexity as an indication that there are mental structures that make up a personality. Rather the complexity of associations, reinforcement contingencies, and the human environment better explain why people behave consistently in certain environments. Furthermore, language allows us to tell stories about ourselves and, in a sense, come to know ourselves with a consistent voice that we describe as "me," differentiating us from "you." While our behavior may change steadily over time, the "narrator" of our life story sounds the same because the recognition of self occurs in varied situations and across time.

6. *Behavior therapy is data-driven and empirically based.* Behavior therapists may follow a protocol that has been developed in randomized clinical trials, where techniques have been tested for a particular problem and client population, and have been shown to be efficacious, or they will rely on the progress in the individual case to determine whether techniques are effective for a particular client. Client self-report inventories are useful, but directly observed behavior is better. Such behaviors as work absenteeism, staying in bed, poor hygiene, and social isolation can all be symptoms of depression. They are also behaviors that can be quantified. Clients can keep track of the number of days they stayed home from work or were tardy, how many hours they stayed in bed, and the number of people that they telephoned or met in person during a week. Measuring whether therapy is effective requires that there be goals toward which the therapist and client are working.

   Therapeutic goals should be measurable and therefore problems must be identified in an objective, observable manner. In clinical practice, monitoring goals is usually a technologically unsophisticated process of discussion between therapist and client about how the client is doing between sessions. When your clients are trying to increase or decrease a certain behavior, such as smoking, keeping a running log of how many cigarettes they are smoking will be more accurate than relying on memory, so it would be helpful for you to assign written monitoring. Tape recorders, digital counting devices, pedometers, and the like have also been useful for measuring behaviors. Clients are not always certain what behaviors they want to change. In therapy, clients may talk about problems that the therapist thinks are vague and that don't readily provide concrete definitions. For example, Theo complained of being lonely. The behavior therapist needs to better define such a concept for Theo's specific situation. Knowing that he is "lonely" does not lead to particular behavior change, whereas knowing that he wants more close friendships or wants to have a frank discussion with his girlfriend regarding his feelings about sex does. Elena had felt "stuck," but in fact she lacked assertiveness skills to address family situations that were keeping her from fulfilling her goals. Also, there were cultural expectations that she should be responsible and take care of her mother that impacted her assertiveness. Specifying assertive behaviors that would be appropriate in the context of her cultural background would provide concrete goals for therapy rather than a vague goal that she be "unstuck."

7. *Changes clients make in therapy must generalize to their day-to-day lives.* Therapy is a collaborative process. In other words, the therapist and the client work together toward alleviating the client's suffering. Each session has a structure including setting an agenda for the particular session, working on the problems that are placed on the agenda, and assignment of homework or a real-life assignment. Clients in behavior therapy cannot expect to see a therapist once a week, talk about problems, and make progress. It is essential that the client continue the work begun in therapy throughout the week in their real life. Thus, another guiding principle is that behavioral changes that occur in the session will not endure outside of the session unless the therapist and the client set up situations that will increase the probability that new behavior will generalize to a variety of situations. This is the reason for assigning homework between sessions.

8. *Insight alone is not beneficial to a client.* The idea that insight alone is beneficial to a client is not consistent with behavioral theory. Certainly insight and understanding about your problems and the contingencies that exacerbate problems are important beginnings for motivation to change. However, knowing that you have a certain problem, and knowing how to change it are two different things. Even when clients work in therapy to understand what has caused their problems, change does not necessarily follow such insight. While behavior therapists may validate their clients' painful feelings about their life experiences the therapist's goal is to assist clients in making concrete changes in the present to improve their lives in the future.

KEYS TO CONCEPTUALIZATION

One of the greatest difficulties in conceptualization in behavior therapy is to understand how the client experiences the world and determine the behaviors that will be the targets for therapeutic change. This involves empathizing with the client's feelings and dilemmas while developing possible ways to resolve problems. With the many techniques available and decades of experimental literature at their disposal, behavior therapists have a rich pool of information from which to draw when conceptualizing a case. The literature is so vast, in fact, that it may be overwhelming to a novice wanting to know what to do with a particular client in a particular situation. As a way to begin, problems that are dealt with in behavior therapy can be broken down into four broad categories:

1. *Problems with regulation of emotion.* Clients presenting with anxiety, phobias, panic, depression, anger management problems, obsessive-compulsive symptoms, and emotional instability would fall into this category. Although it may sound trite, asking, "Is this client emotionally distressed?" is a meaningful question in case conceptualization. However, a behavior therapist will objectively define the distress. For

example: Is this client overreacting or having catastrophic emotional reactions to situations that most people would deal with without distress? Does this client experience emotions as out of control? Is this client engaging in escape or avoidance behaviors to try to neutralize the emotion? Is Jane overreacting to being away from home and is panic making her shortness of breath worse? Is Elena overreacting to her parents' desire for her to remain at home?

2. *Problems due to environmental contingencies.* This approach to behavior therapy places particular emphasis on reinforcement and punishment. It focuses on the contingencies that maintain behavior. It is possible to look at contingency management as a possible treatment for nearly all disorders. Depressed clients, for example, may be responding to environments where their proactive behaviors have been punished, or where their behavior is maintained through negative reinforcement—acting in order to escape or avoid a negative experience rather than meaningfully engaging with the environment (Ferster, 1973; Martell, Addis, & Jacobson, 2001). Elena, for example goes for walks to get away from everyone, and spends time alone in her room so as not to be around her family, whom she perceives as demanding and invalidating her wishes. The primary question the therapist needs to consider is "How is this person's environment maintaining problematic behavior or extinguishing desirable behavior?"

3. *Problems resulting from skill deficits.* Every person develops a repertoire of behavior as they grow up. Many factors come into play in this learning process. Everyone is born with different innate abilities, and social environments shape behavior. Clients presenting for therapy may lack certain behavioral repertoires that would improve their lives. This can be as obvious as clients who state that they do not know how to ask out someone to whom they are romantically attracted, or as subtle as a manager complaining of problems on the job that are caused by an inability to be assertive with coworkers. The question here is, "Are clients lacking particular skills that would enable them to improve their situation?" Some examples often encountered by behavior therapists are social skills deficits, lack of assertiveness, or poor problem-solving abilities. Or the client may be in a position academically or occupationally where a certain skill is lacking necessary for success in that environment. Theo may never have learned to properly assert his needs and concerns; thus he feels frustrated and is motivated to act only when he gets angry enough to act aggressively.

4. *Problems with perception of environmental cues.* Although behavior therapists may differ in the emphasis they place on cognition and perception, or may adhere to different theories about the nature of cognition and its significance in client problems, all behavior therapists understand that clients think. A person's "interior life" is an important part of experience. Specific techniques for dealing with cognitions have been considered elsewhere in this book and are not part of the scope of this chapter. However, it is important for therapists to ask whether the client may misperceive cues in the environment. For example, Theo perceives that other people find him intimidating. This may be true, but it may also be a misperception. Either actual experience with people shying away from him, or a misperception that they are

doing so, results in Theo avoiding close friendship with others at his predominantly white college. If he is misperceiving—whether or not it is a primary problem—the misperception is one link along a chain of responses that increase his unhappiness.

These four categories may not apply to all clients. Many clients will present with elements of more than one of these categories, and the treatments for a variety of these problems overlap, although some are more relevant than others for each group. For example, a socially phobic client—someone who fears social situations—may (1) be extremely fearful meeting new people—that is, have emotional or affect regulation problems, (2) avoid interactions that would reinforce approaching people—that is, have problems with environmental contingencies, (3) have never developed the ability to engage in small talk—that is, have a skill deficit, and (4) imagine that other people will be highly critical or rejecting—that is, have a problem with perception of environmental cues

INTERVENTIONS AND THERAPEUTIC PROCESS

Behavior therapists pride themselves on using empirically supported treatments (EST) or those techniques for which there is an empirical literature supporting their efficacy (Chambless & Hollon, 1998; DeRubeis & Crits-Christoph, 1998).

1. *Problems with regulation of emotion.* There are several different behavioral interventions for helping clients regulate emotion. First, skills can be taught to modulate emotion: for example, relaxation procedures, taking time-outs to manage anger, and systematic desensitization. Second, exposure techniques are particularly useful in panic disorder and obsessive-compulsive disorder. Treatment for each of these conditions should involve some method of exposure. Clients who experience panic usually do so in particular environments, although the panic may first be experienced as "coming out of nowhere." It is common for panic clients to begin to avoid the places where they had their first panic attack. Treatment includes exposure to the panic itself by inducing paniclike symptoms in the safety of the therapist's office. Clients with obsessive-compulsive disorder are treated with exposure and response prevention. Such a client who fears contamination and develops elaborate hand-washing rituals would be encouraged to handle common objects such as money, touch the floor, and eventually handle increasingly more "dirty" objects without being allowed to wash.

    These skills are often combined, as the following example shows. Imagine a person that has developed a fear of flying after having been frightened by excessive turbulence. Such a client would benefit from learning relaxation methods, and the therapist could use systematic desensitization procedures to help the client imagine the fearful situation while maintaining the relaxation response. Ultimately, the client would be exposed to the fear by taking an actual flight on an airplane. Most actual behavior therapy cases involve several target problems and multiple techniques for helping clients achieve therapeutic goals.

2. *Problems due to environmental contingencies.* In outpatient settings, therapists do not have control over all the contingencies that impact a client's behavior. Behavior

therapists in such settings work with clients to set up contingencies that will either decrease maladaptive behavior or increase adaptive behavior. In the first instance, techniques such as *stimulus control of behavior* are useful. A simple example of this technique would be the removal of all fatty and sugary foods from your home, and filling the refrigerator with vegetables and healthy snacks when trying to lose weight. Another example occurs frequently in the treatment of insomnia when therapists instruct clients to get up out of bed if they don't fall asleep within 10 or 15 minutes. The bed is paired only with sleep, and wakefulness occurs apart from the bed. Changing reinforcement contingencies is another technique that can be utilized. Although it is most effective that client behavior is reinforced naturally (for example, the positive reinforcement for completing an assigned paper is to get a good grade it), therapists can also make use of arbitrary reinforcement when trying to shape a behavior (for example, the procrastinating student can bake a batch of chocolate chip cookies and eat a cookie only after completing a certain amount of work on the paper).

3. *Problems resulting from skill deficits.* Many clients seek therapy because they lack ability or confidence in their abilities in certain situations. Social skills training, using role-playing and modeling of socially competent behaviors, and problem-solving therapy are skill building treatments. Theo is aggressive rather than asserting his needs, and Elena does not see a way out of the situation with her parents; which of these techniques would provide useful intervention strategies? Behavior therapists, being pragmatists, will also help clients to find educational and training resources that will aid in building skills necessary for work or academic endeavors.

4. *Problems with perception of environmental cues.* Although cognitive-behavior therapy techniques are often applied in these instances, there are recent trends in behavior therapy that hold promise. A treatment referred to as acceptance and commitment therapy (ACT) (Hayes, Strosahl, & Wilson, 1999) uses a strategy that helps clients recognize that beliefs are nothing more than words and should not be accepted and acted upon. For example, clients who tell themselves that they are "losers," and then do not pursue a desired job because they literally believe this to be true might be asked to say, "I'm a loser" repeatedly until the words sound like gibberish. The therapist explores this experience with them, suggesting that "I'm a loser" is just talk in their head. Clients then learns that they do not need to buy into the idea as if it is literally true. There is evidence also that changing behavior may be a useful way to change cognition (for example, a phobic client who approaches a feared object may no longer believe that the object is dangerous). Teaching clients to focus on the experience of their activities rather than to ruminate about problems has also been suggested as a behavioral way of dealing with problems in client's thinking (Martell, Addis, & Jacobson, 2001).

SHORT- AND LONG-TERM GOALS

Goals of therapy will depend on the presenting problem of the client. Because behavior therapists approach the long-term goals of clients, such as "not being depressed any longer," through concrete, measurable processes, the establishment of short-term goals is essential. Long-term goals will usually be determined early in therapy. Asking clients a question like "If I had a magic wand and could make things better for you, what would be different?" can indicate the types of changes that the client expects. Again, a client might say, "I'd just feel better." If this is the case, the therapist needs to ask questions that anchor the client in observable goals. Asking how the therapist would know if the client felt better might yield answers like, "I'd get out and see friends more," or "I'd be able to go on a walk without being afraid of every dog that I see." Both of these statements suggest long-term goals for therapy: the first is to increase social activity, and the second to no longer be afraid of dogs. Clients may have even longer-term goals such as "to meet the one I will love forever" that are not realistic therapy goals because there is no guarantee that such an event will occur in the course of therapy. However, a therapy goal like "asking people out on dates" will increase the likelihood of clients meeting someone with whom they can form a romantic attachment.

All long-term goals have logical short-term steps to achieve the desired outcome. Take the desire to meet a romantic partner as a goal. People do not meet potential mates by sitting by a telephone and waiting for it to ring. The first step is to go where other people are. Clients can attend a social gathering, go to a club, or join an on-line chat room. The second step is for the clients to introduce themselves to someone. Engaging in conversation is usually required as another step. Fourth, inviting an individual to coffee, dinner, or for a drink allows time to get to become better acquainted. Fifth, and most important, they must follow these steps repeatedly, tolerating occasional disappointments, and not giving up on the process. Although these steps certainly do not guarantee attainment of the client's long-term goal of meeting a life partner, they open opportunities that otherwise would not occur.

USING THE RELATIONSHIP

Because the theory does not include a notion of transference and countertransference, behavior therapists are sometimes depicted as being disinterested in the therapeutic relationship. Nothing could be farther from the truth, since no clients would be motivated to change behavior if they did not have a strong working alliance with a therapist. Furthermore, recent therapists (e.g., Kohlenberg & Tsai, 1991), have noted that the therapeutic relationship is an essential context in which to promote behavior change. The behavior therapist can best modify behaviors as they occur. Interpersonal behaviors are the most common during the therapy hour. If interpersonal deficits, thoughts about self or others, social anxieties, or hostilities occur during the clients' interaction with the therapist, the therapist can respond in a way that will help them better negotiate their interpersonal world outside of the therapy session.

Many problems that people present in therapy are interpersonal in nature. Depressed clients often feel isolated or rejected by others, or an interpersonal crisis like a breakup might have precipitated the depression. Likewise, people may worry about getting along with a boss or coworkers. Therapists have the perfect experimental environment in which to observe and modify client behavior through the therapeutic relationship. That relationship may also provide a context for healing with many troubled clients. Take, for example, a client that harbors a low self-opinion and never confronts others when offended. Imagine that, on an unusually hectic day, the therapist is five minutes late to start the session and the nonconfrontational client is annoyed. The client says, "I have so much to do today, I'm not sure if I'm going to have time for it all." The astute therapist will spot this as a possible clinically relevant behavior (Kohlenberg & Tsai, 1991), a disguised way for the client to complain about the therapist's tardiness. The therapist might say, "Are you upset that I was late today and my lateness will make your day even more crammed for time?" If the client says, "Well, yes, I guess it is really inconvenient, and I feel a little bit like you haven't taken my needs into account," the therapist has a perfect opportunity to reinforce an assertive response. This is particularly relevant within the context of the session because the natural reinforcement for a client's assertive comment is for the therapist to respond appropriately. The therapist might say, "I really am sorry that I was late, and it couldn't be helped. I was concerned that I was making you wait. Is there anything I can do that would make you feel better about this?" Should a client say, "I was so mad at you when you didn't return my call until an hour after I left a message yesterday!" therapists should validate the anger, while continuing to set their own limits or remind the client of any prior agreements.

ADAPTING THE APPROACH

Although there are many different techniques available to therapists, the approach is not technique-centered, but client-centered. Each individual client or couple is seen as unique, and is understood by the environment in which they have lived (including cultural factors), their particular means of adapting to that environment, and the consequences of their behaviors that get played out emotionally or practically. The principles by which we understand human behavior do not change, but cultural sensitivity is very important.

Take assertiveness skills training as an example. In western culture being properly assertive in getting needs met is considered appropriate for both men and women. In Elena's case there are cultural values about the importance of family that are vital to the situation and must be accounted for in the case conceptualization. Should a therapist be too eager to teach her to stand up to her family the therapist could do more harm than good. Frequently, the issue of culturally sensitivity and understanding diversity issues boils down to therapists not imposing their values on a client, and not using therapeutic techniques to manipulate clients to abide by those values.

FINDING YOUR NICHE

Behavior therapy is a rich and varied therapeutic field. There is no mystique here, however, and the understanding that behavior functions according to certain principles requires that the therapist be interested in looking for the conditions that control certain behaviors. You should not worry, however, that you would be required to ignore emotions or act like the doctors in Stanley Kubrick's *A Clockwork Orange*. Nevertheless, therapists who are more interested in helping people find insight into their lives or to determine reasons why certain things have happened to them are likely to be unhappy with a behavioral perspective. The behavioral approach is pragmatic, and people who enjoy solving problems in the here and now are likely to be attracted to this model. Therapists with an interest in empiricism will also find that they feel comfortable with behavior therapy because the approach emphasizes the need for ongoing evaluation of outcomes and efficacy of treatments.

Therapists working with clients in a behavior therapy framework are certainly bound by the same ethical standards that govern all therapy. There is a flexibility required in behavior therapy, however, that allows therapists to be very human with their clients. The therapeutic encounter is conversational. Because behavior therapists harbor no expectations that they should remain blank slates upon which their clients can project neurotic conflicts, they can make use of appropriate self-disclosure when necessary to provide feedback to clients about their behavior. Behavior therapy also may require therapists to leave their office with clients, to ride in a car with a client who has a fear of driving on freeways, for example. This is not an opportunity for socializing but rather to help the client face a fear and to monitor any interactions that could serve to maintain client avoidance, such as the client seeking reassurance that there are not many accidents on a particular highway. Therapists would not respond and would point out the function of such a question to try to alleviate fear. They would encourage clients to keep driving even though they may have this question in mind. In many cases, because the therapist is working collaboratively with a client to change a behavior or a situation that the client wishes to change, it is safe to say that practicing behavior therapy is fun.

PROCESS AND CASE SUGGESTIONS

Readers may wonder how behavior therapy can be applied in outpatient settings where client goals are not as specific as this therapeutic orientation requires. The three cases presented on the website are excellent examples of the challenges that behavior therapists face. Based on the information provided in the initial interview, it is challenging to determine the problems clients are encountering and to develop general ideas for the methods by which they can be helped. Therapists can ask themselves the following questions about each case to help in this process:

1. What are the problem behaviors that will need to be addressed in therapy? These may be identified by the client or the therapist, and may include a formal DSM-IV (American Psychiatric Association, 1994) diagnosis.
2. What are possible environmental factors that are maintaining these behaviors?
3. From the client's history, can you establish any behavioral patterns that may maintain the current behavior problems?
4. What functions do the client's behaviors serve that may maintain the problem?
5. How might the behaviors occur in session with the therapist?
6. What are the best methods for helping this client?

7. Are there special considerations that will influence the implementation of these techniques with this client?
8. How will you help the client to apply therapeutic gains to daily life?

The three practice case examples on the website are typical of clients seen by behavior therapists.

1. *Elena.* Elena presented with a very difficult, sad, and permanent life situation with her mother's illness. There were cultural variables involved also that have to be accounted for when developing a plan to help her. In daily practice, behavior therapists use standard diagnostic language, but emphasize the problem behaviors that will be treatment targets. It was easier to diagnose Elena than to suggest possible techniques for helping her. As her problem list was developed to include several targets for change, the techniques to achieve these changes became clear.

2. *Jane.* Jane is a typical client who believes she needs one thing, but it is likely that the therapist will believe she needs another. Jane could have several diagnoses. She feels generally unhappy. As I read her case and watched her interview, I hypothesized several reasons for her unhappiness having to do with guilt and fear. The latter problem is more easily dealt with in behavior therapy than the former, but I've made a few suggestions.

3. *Theo.* Theo, like Jane, could have several diagnoses, although it was less clear which would be appropriate. I wanted more information about Theo. Also, like Elena, there are cultural differences between Theo and me. Theo is a great example of how environment and an individual's behavioral repertoire interact in developing and maintaining problems. He also suggests a reason for his problems that at first can be taken as a misperception, but one needs to be culturally sensitive in this case, and consider the possibility that Theo may be onto something that the therapist will find challenging to help him overcome.

SUMMARY AND SUGGESTED READINGS

Behavioral theory is multifaceted with complex new ideas emerging frequently. Books on behavioral theory often use technical language due to behaviorists' penchant for specificity. There are a variety of techniques to learn. It is not as simple as Ivan Pavlov's dogs salivating at the sound of a bell. Nevertheless, one can begin to apply behavioral principles with nearly any client. The theory is intellectually stimulating and the practice fulfilling. Behavior therapy can also be incorporated into other approaches, but it is best to learn the theory and application well before indiscriminately adding techniques to other forms of therapy. Several good books that minimize technical language are the best place to start learning about the general practice of behavior therapy. Two excellent books on therapy are:

Goldfried, M. R., & Davison, G. C. (1994). *Clinical behavior therapy (Expanded ed.).* New York: Wiley Interscience.

Wolpe, J. (1982). *The practice of behavior therapy* (3rd ed.). Elmsford, NY: Pergamon.

One other work of a more theoretical nature is a good introduction to the variety of ideas in behaviorism:

Baum, W. M. (1994). *Understanding behaviorism: Science, behavior, and culture.* New York: HarperCollins.

REFERENCES

American Psychiatric Association (1994). *Diagnostic and statistical manual of mental disorders* (4th ed.). Washington, DC: Author.

Bandura, A. (1977). *Social learning theory.* Englewood Cliffs, NJ: Prentice-Hall.

Barlow, D. H. (2001). *Anxiety and its disorders: The nature and treatment of anxiety and panic* (2nd ed.). New York: Guilford.

Beck, A. T., Rush, A. J., Shaw, B. F., & Emery, G. (1979). *Cognitive therapy of depression.* New York: Guilford.

Chambless, D. L., & Hollon, S. D. (1998). Defining empirically supported treatments. *Journal of Consulting and Clinical Psychology, 66(1),* 7–18.

DeRubeis, R. J., & Crits-Christoph, P. (1998). Empirically supported individual and group psychological treatments for adult mental disorders. *Journal of Consulting and Clinical Psychology, 66(1),* 37–52.

Foa, E. B., & Goldstein, A. (1978). Continuous exposure and strict response prevention in the treatment of obsessive-compulsive neurosis. *Behavior Therapy, 9,* 821–829.

Hayes, S. C., Strosahl, K. D., & Wilson, K. G. (1999). *Acceptance and commitment therapy: An experiential approach to behavior change.* New York: Guilford.

Kohlenberg, R. J., & Tsai, M. (1991). *Functional analytic psychotherapy: Creating intense and curative therapeutic relationships.* New York: Plenum.

Lewinsohn, P. M. (1974). A behavioral approach to depression. In R. M. Friedman & M. M. Katz (Eds.). *The psychology of depression: Contemporary theory and research* (pp. 257–285). New York: Wiley.

Linehan, M. M. (1993). *Cognitive behavioral treatment of borderline personality disorder.* New York: Guilford.

Martell, C. R., Addis, M. E., & Jacobson, N. S. (2001). *Depression in context: Strategies for guided action.* New York: W. W. Norton.

Pavlov, I. P. (1927). *Conditioned reflexes.* Trans. by G. V. Anrep. London: Oxford University Press.

Skinner, B. F. (1938). *The behavior of organisms.* New York: Appleton.

Watson, J. B., & Rayner, R. (1920). Conditioned emotional reactions. *Journal of Experimental Psychology, 3,* 1–14.

Wolpe, J. (1958). *Psychotherapy by reciprocal inhibition.* Stanford: Stanford University Press.

Wolpe, J. (1982). *The practice of behavior therapy* (3rd ed.). Elmsford, NY: Pergamon.

Chapter 10

Cogntive Therapy

Rebecca J. Macy

Chapter Outline

Bridging the Theory-to-Practice Gap
Principles in Practice
Keys to Conceptualization
Interventions and Therapeutic Process
Short- and Long-Term Goals
Using the Relationship
Adapting the Approach
Finding Your Niche
Process and Case Suggestions
Summary and Suggested Readings
References

BRIDGING THE THEORY-TO-PRACTICE GAP

Although many of the students in my counseling courses are interested in cognitive therapy, they also initially think that cognitive therapy approaches are not exciting or appealing in comparison to other counseling theories. The beginning counselors with whom I work think, at first, that cognitive theory's conceptualizations of human beings and human problems are too rigid and structured. They often think that the theory is overly focused on what happens within a person's head and that it does not fully consider a person' environment and context. They are concerned that the therapeutic strategies are too highly formalized and inflexible, leaving little room for personal creativity and expression from a therapist. They also worry that the theory does not emphasize the importance of human relationships as a catalyst for change. I too had similar doubts and concerns about cognitive therapy during my training in graduate school. However, when I began my professional practice, I found myself again and again relying on cognitive therapy's perspectives, tools, and strategies, particularly when I was faced with challenging and complex client problems.

Cognitive therapy theory posits that difficulties in human thinking, feeling, behaving, and functioning stem from problems and inaccuracies in our thoughts and beliefs about ourselves, our relationships, the world, and the future. However, the theory also maintains that human beings have the capacity to direct thoughts, feelings, and behaviors toward beneficial outcomes and goals and to be active agents in our own lives (Dobson & Dozios, 2001). It is these capacities that form the basis for change in cognitive therapy. As I utilized this therapy in my work at an outpatient community mental health clinic with an array of clients of various developmental ages and socioeconomic and sociocultural backgrounds, I discovered how powerful its approaches could be. I found the theory's capacity to create change in my clients' lives. I learned how cognitive therapeutic approaches could facilitate the development of warm, collaborative relationships between me and my clients. I came to appreciate how the theory's conceptualization of human beings and human problems allowed me to address clients' difficulties, while also building on their assets and resources.

One of the reasons that I teach cognitive therapy theory to my students is that it can be used to address a range of mental health, physical health, and psychosocial problems. It can also be used in a variety of settings from private practice offices to inpatient hospitals to community outreach services. As the delivery of mental health and human services evolves and changes, it is important for therapists to have a set of tools that they can use with a variety of people, in various settings, with a range of presenting problems. Cognitive therapy provides these kinds of tools. Additionally, cognitive therapy has helped me maintain my therapeutic effectiveness even in the context of agencies and organizations that mandate time-limited, brief interventions. With its focus on the here and now, these techniques can be used with efficacy and can result in positive client outcomes even in a few meetings.

I am also an advocate of cognitive therapy because research and evidence shows that it has utility and therapeutic benefits. This therapy is shown to have a positive effect with a range of problems in human functioning and to help clients attain their goals when it is applied efficaciously and thoughtfully. We mental health professionals are now increasingly asked to use evidence-based practices and to show that our interventions make a difference. Cognitive therapy can become a foundational tool for our therapeutic practices because its effectiveness is well documented. Another appeal for me is that this therapy has a set of skills and techniques that can be learned, applied, and utilized by any practitioner who is willing to commit and learn the theoretical bases and necessary intervention skills (Leahy, 2002). Having these skills and techniques enables me to translate research knowledge about cognitive therapy practices to my own practice with fidelity and consistency. Having such clear therapeutic ideas and strategies is a tremendous resource for me when I am faced with a client's complex presenting problem.

Initially, cognitive therapy interventions may seem intuitive and straightforward. In actuality, the effective use of these therapeutic interventions requires extensive study, training, and practice because the theory's utility comes from its accurate and careful use. Effective implementation of these interventions requires that the practitioner be fully grounded in the therapy's theory and premises, and be able to use a range of associated techniques and interventions. All practitioners who want to become proficient in cognitive therapy will need to study its theoretical bases and practice its techniques in order to be able to adapt the theory to a variety of clients and their presenting problems. The first step in this study and practice is a solid understanding of the principles in practice.

PRINCIPLES IN PRACTICE

When beginning to work with clients using cognitive therapy, we should keep in mind the following theoretical principles to guide our interventions:

1. *Information processing.* Throughout our lifetimes and at any time in our waking lives, we human beings are bombarded with information from the environment. Consider your own experience reading this chapter. You are taking in information from the words on this page. But likely there are other things going on in your environment. Perhaps you are reading this while listening to music. Or perhaps you are reading this in a coffee shop, eavesdropping on the couple's conversation at the next table. Just like the words you are reading, this environmental noise is also information to which you may attend and respond or which you may screen and ignore. If you are able to focus on the words on this page, you may be able to screen out these other pieces of incoming information. In this way, you are using your thinking and feeling processes to direct your behavior towards a goal—finishing your assignment on time or learning this material before meeting with your new client. Some of this other incoming information may draw your attention away from this page. Perhaps a favorite song comes on the stereo. Perhaps in the couple's conversation you hear the name of a friend. These additional layers of information will be incorporated into your thinking and feeling processes. They will alter what information is important and salient to you, and may direct your behavior toward another goal or task. Perhaps you will decide to put the book down to enjoy the music or listen more closely to the conversation.

Importantly it is not only noise that is incoming information. The light, the temperature of the room, and your internal feelings (are you hungry? sleepy? content?) are also other examples of information about which you are thinking and feeling. At any one time human beings are receiving multiple amounts of complex information. As a result, we have developed elaborate thinking and feeling processes that enable us to screen out and ignore information that may not be useful, helpful, or important. As well, these same thinking and feeling processes enable us to attend to, incorporate, and make sense of information that is important, useful, and will enable us to behave and take actions toward meeting our needs (getting something to eat if we are hungry) and our goals (completing this reading so we can understand the material, complete the class, and get a good grade).

Thus, a principle of cognitive therapy theory is that human beings have thinking and feeling processes that enable us to manage multiple amounts of complex information and then use that information to direct our behaviors and actions, (Blankstein & Segal, 2001). This idea, which is key to cognitive therapy, is called information processing. Generally, we are not consciously aware of all these thinking, feeling, and behavioral processes; often they happen automatically (Mischel, 1999). The automatic nature of these processes is helpful and adaptive. What if every time you engaged in an activity or set of behaviors you had to think through every step of the activity? How cumbersome and challenging it would be to get anything accomplished. Likewise consider how long it takes to do a new activity until you learn the skill. However, with enough exposure to any new situation, activity, or information, human beings can learn how to manage the new information, situations, and activities in patterned and efficient ways that become automatic.

Human beings have patterned and stable cognitive-affective information processes for all aspects of our lives, not just skills, tasks, and activities. We have patterned and stable cognitive-affective information processes about self-concepts, relationships with others (friends, family members, intimate others), all aspects of the environment (neighborhood, communities), for all roles (work, student, parent), and for ideas about the future. Beck (1996) describes this as a complex interwoven, intrinsically connected system of cognitive-affective-behavioral networks. Moreover, each individual human being has patterned ways of thinking and feeling that are unique, individual, and particular to that person (Alford & Beck, 1997). Although processes of thinking and feeling are similar across human beings, the meanings of thoughts, feelings, and behaviors are unique and personal to the individual.

Although these patterned and stable thinking and feelings processes are usually helpful, cognitive therapy theory maintains that problems in human thinking, feeling, and functioning are caused by cognitive-affective processes that are problematic or are unhelpful (Beck, 1995). Sometimes these complex thinking and feeling processes contain information, beliefs, or ideas that are not helpful or not useful for a given situation, need, or goal. For example, perhaps you are working with a client who has a goal of wanting to find an intimate life partner. However, the client's self-concept includes these ideas and beliefs: "I am completely unattractive and unlovable, and no one will ever want to be with me." This stable, patterned way of thinking and feeling is likely to lead to problems in his cognitions and emotions, his relationships with others, and is likely to thwart his attempts to attain his goal of finding a life partner. Cognitive therapy posits that problems in thinking, feeling, and functioning develop from unhelpful, maladaptive, or erroneous beliefs and ideas about the self, the environment, the future, or all three of these areas (Beck, 1995; Alford & Beck, 1997). I want to emphasize now that although these thinking and feeling processes are likely to be patterned and stable, these processes are not immutable to change. In fact, cognitive therapy theories conceptualize human beings as active agents with the capacity to reflect on, monitor, and alter our thoughts and feelings. Cognitive therapy sees the therapeutic potential to analyze, understand, shape, and control thoughts and feelings because human beings have the capacity to think about thinking. With this capacity, we can consider the utility of our thoughts and feelings about ourselves, our relationships, the world around us, and our futures (Beck, 1996).

2. *Active agents.* Although cognitive therapy conceptualizes humans as being bombarded with environmental and internal information and stimuli, it also conceptualizes humans as active agents who are searching for meaning in their experience (Berlin, 2002; Dobson & Dozois, 2001). Cognitive therapy theories conceptualize human beings as having the capacity to purposefully seek out information that will help them to meet their needs and goals. Again, consider your experience in reading this chapter: you are seeking out information that will enable you to attain your professional and career goals. Moreover, cognitive therapy theories maintain that human beings actively use past experiences and understandings to make sense of and assign meaning to new information. The very act of information processing, the selection, choice, and use of information, assigns meaning to the information. As you read this chapter, you are likely using your past experiences and understandings (information from other courses or from your undergraduate work) to make sense of and assign meaning to this new information about cognitive therapy. Thus, human beings are not simply taking in information that the environment or their internal states may present to them. They actively seek out experiences that help them meet their needs and goals, and use past experiences and existing understandings to make sense of and assign meaning to this new information.

This capacity to monitor and adapt thoughts, emotions, and behaviors is the basis for cognitive therapy interventions. Although to a large extent, thinking and feelings processes are patterned, stable, and automatic, they are also accessible, adaptable, and can be altered. Humans have the capacity to track and monitor thoughts and emotions, as well as consider the utility of their thoughts and emotions in a therapeutic way. As cognitive therapists, we can help clients first to track and understand their ways of thinking and feeling and then help them to assess if these ways of thinking and feeling are helpful in meeting their needs and goals. In working with the client who believes that he is unattractive and unlovable, it would be helpful to use cognitive therapy techniques to highlight this belief and to help our client assess the validity and utility of this belief in relation to his goal of having a life partner. I will discuss the specifics of cognitive therapy techniques in greater detail later in the chapter. First, it is important to understand how thoughts and cognitions relate to emotions, and how both cognitions and emotions relate to behaviors.

3. *Relationship among cognitions, emotions, and behaviors.* One of the central guiding principles of cognitive therapy is the concept of the mediational model. The mediational model maintains that cognitions and cognitive processes shape and influence behaviors (Dobson & Dozois, 2001). As described earlier, cognitions and cognitive processes shape the meaning and understanding of incoming information and in turn determine behaviors and actions. Using the mediational model as a guiding principle means that when we help clients to modify and replace unhelpful cognitions, the desired behavioral change will inevitably result. Thus cognitions and cognitive processes are the primary targets for change.

   Although cognitive therapy interventions focus on and emphasize cognitions and cognitive processes, it is important for us to assess and attend to emotions as well. Emotions and cognitions have reciprocal relationships in that one tends to impact and influence the other (Dobson & Dozois, 2001). Emotions are a critical part of the mediational model because cognitions activate and heighten relevant emotions, which in turn impact and shape corresponding behaviors. Moreover, strong emotions can intensify thoughts or thought processes and make thoughts seem all the more pressing (Cormier & Nurius, 2003). Think about working with the client who is seeking the life partner one more time. The cognitions that the client holds that he is unattractive and unlovable, are likely to be associated with and help to activate emotions like sadness, hopelessness, and despair. These cognitions and strong emotions will likely reduce behaviors that may help the client reach the goal of finding a life partner. (The client may say, "Why should I go to the party? No will talk to me even if I am there." Or "Why ask anyone out on a date? No one would go out with me anyway.") Ultimately, there is an interdependent relationship among cognitions, emotions, and behaviors to the extent that a problem in one indicates a problem in the other two (Organista, 1995). As a result of the relationship of cognitions to emotions and behaviors, there is a therapeutic value in modifying cognitions because changes in cognitions will lead to the desired changes in emotions and behavior. Additionally, a change in behavior indicates a change in the corresponding cognition. Thus, as cognitive therapists, we will focus on identifying and altering problematic or unhelpful cognitions and cognitive processes in our clients that impact and shape feelings and behaviors in problematic or unhelpful ways.

4. *Core beliefs.* Cognitive therapy theory maintains that there are two primary types of cognitions: (1) automatic, surface thoughts and (2) core beliefs or schemas. It is possible to have unhelpful or problematic cognitions at both levels. In addition to working with the client's surface thoughts, which are associated with and in some cases inextricably tied to the client's presenting problem, we will also work with the client to identify the underlying, fundamental cognitive structures, the core beliefs that may be the foundation of the client's difficulties (Beck, 1995). Up to this point, I generally described automatic or surface thoughts. Unlike surface thoughts, which may be fleeting and transitory, core beliefs tend to be foundational, stable beliefs about the self, relationships, the world, and the future. For example, one person may tend to have a fairly optimistic view of life, relationships, the future, and the world, and may tend to endorse beliefs such as: the world is a beautiful place, things tend to work out for the best, and most people are good-hearted. Another person

may tend to have a pessimistic view, such as: the world is an unpredictable place, things never go my way, and you just cannot trust most people. All such ideas are reflections of core beliefs. Surface thoughts arise from core beliefs automatically. Core beliefs are the basic and foundational cognitive structures that help us to select, interpret, and make meaning from incoming information. As a result, core beliefs are well established, can be self-reinforcing, and are often resilient to change.

Core beliefs were likely formed in early life developmental stages because they tend to reflect such fundamental and foundational cognitions about the self, relationships, and reality (Beck, 2002). A specific core belief likely developed because it was helpful, useful, and adaptive to a person in a particular situation or time. For example, if a person grows up in a violent home with abusive caregivers, seeing the world as an unpredictable place where you do not readily trust others may be adaptive and allows the person to survive an otherwise untenable situation. However, once the person becomes an adult and leaves the violent home, such core beliefs may no longer be helpful and adaptive. Additionally, there may be ways in which core beliefs, though they sometimes cause problems, are still functional and helpful. We all likely carry with us and use core beliefs that are inaccurate, not helpful to us, and impede our capacities to reach our life goals (Alford & Beck, 1997). As we work with our clients using cognitive therapy, it is important for us to keep in mind that these core beliefs and patterned ways of thinking, feeling, and behaving are not problematic on their own. Instead, the problem comes from interactions between cognition and the context or situation. Just like any cognition, core beliefs, which are also described as schemas, can be challenging to modify but they are not impossible to change (Dowd, 2002). Many cognitive practitioners argue that lasting therapeutic change requires an alteration in problematic core beliefs (Beck, 1996). When using cognitive therapy, your aim will be both to help clients modify, adapt, and replace unhelpful surface thoughts that are directly connected to presenting problems, as well as to help them identify and change maladaptive core beliefs that may continue to cause difficulties if they are not addressed therapeutically.

5. *Person-in-environment.* Initially it may seem that cognitive therapy theory considers only what happens within clients, their thoughts, emotions, and behaviors. Although internal cognitive-affective processes are emphasized and are often the primary targets for change in cognitive therapy, person-in-environment interactions are also critical for our conceptualization of and interventions with a client's problems for two reasons (Berlin, 2002). First, clients' problems and difficulties are not simply due to internal processes. Patterned ways of thinking and feeling are generally activated by external events, situations, or external information (Persons & Davidson, 2001). Again, return to the example of our client who considers himself unattractive and unlovable but also yearns for an intimate life partner. External events, such as a friend's wedding or Valentine's Day, are likely to activate and make salient both the goal for an intimate relationship, as well as the belief that this goal is an impossibility. Relevant external events thus become triggers for the client's problematic and unhelpful thoughts and feelings.

Second, environmental, situational, and contextual realities can also shape the opportunities, experiences, and information to which a person has access. As a result, the environmental realities not only activate unhelpful thoughts and feelings but also reinforce these thoughts and feelings. Moreover, the actual opportunities to which human beings have access may limit their capacity to create alternative ways of thinking about themselves, relationships, the future, and the world. As Berlin (2002) states: "Problems result from an interplay between realistically difficult life circumstances and [core beliefs] that restrict one's ability to see a way out" (p. 16). Perhaps our client with the goal of finding an intimate life partner is a graduate student who is struggling to make ends meet financially. His limited budget makes it challenging for him to socialize and date. This financial reality may impede the client's ability to socialize and interact with others in ways that exposes him to new information and experiences that might challenge his core beliefs. For example, if the client is out with friends and an attractive person approaches him and asks him out, this would be an important experience and would present information that may modify or challenge his core belief. Thus, we must consider the environment in conceptualizing and intervening with our clients' problems in two ways. First, how does the environment activate salient, relevant yet problematic thoughts and feelings? And second, how does the environment structure a client's opportunities to have experiences and gather information in ways that may create barriers to change or that may facilitate adaptation?

In summary, when you are working with clients using cognitive therapy, keep in mind that human beings have complex thinking and feeling structures and processes that allow us to process and manage massive amounts of complex information. These structures and processes are adaptive because they are stable, patterned, and efficient. There are two main types of cognitions: core beliefs and surface thoughts. Core beliefs hold fundamental and foundational beliefs about the self, relationships, world, and future. Surface thoughts stem from core beliefs. Cognitive-affective structures and processes are frequently inaccurate and unhelpful, which leads to problems in thinking, feeling, and functioning. Thinking and feelings structures and processes are shaped by and influenced by the environment. However, human beings are active agents who have the capacity to seek out and make meaning from new information and experiences. We have the capacity to think about thinking and thus the capacity to change our thought processes to better meet our needs and goals.

KEYS TO CONCEPTUALIZATION

When using cognitive therapy, you become an investigator, scientist, or detective: "The practitioner helps the client to systematically gather data, evaluate evidence, draw conclusions, and generate alternatives" (Cormier & Nurius, 2003, p. 446). In order to conceptualize or understand a client's presenting problem from a cognitive therapy perspective, you must identify the cognitive content that relates to the client's situation and presenting problem. Specific techniques to identify the problematic and unhelpful cognitive content will be discussed later in the chapter. Here I first describe an overview of the process for how you will understand the client's presenting problem and generate a hypothesis about the problem in a way that leads to the selection of treatment goals and strategies.

The first step in conceptualizing the client's presenting problem is to identify and understand the relevant cognitions related to the presenting problem. For example, the client with the thoughts and beliefs about being unlovable and unattractive is unlikely to tell a therapist, "I am completely unattractive and unlovable, and no one will ever want to be with me" at the beginning of the first therapy meeting. Core beliefs like this are often automatic, implicit, and unscrutinized. Instead, the client will likely initially describe feeling "down, depressed, sad about my life." You should begin to explore with the client the underlying cognitive content (thoughts, ideas, beliefs) that is associated with the presenting problem. Additionally, you will also seek to determine what emotions go along with the cognitive content, as well as what situations or external information tend to activate the problematic thoughts and beliefs. These relevant emotions and situations can help highlight the cognitions that are creating the client's problems.

Once you have a global, as well as a detailed understanding of the relevant thoughts and feelings related to the presenting problem, you will next create a working hypothesis. In cognitive therapy, a working hypothesis describes how the client's patterned ways of thinking relate to the presenting problem, as well as what external events or situations activate the relevant thinking patterns (Persons & Davidson, 2001). Using all the gathered information, you should begin to specify what you think are the client's unhelpful thoughts and how they are the basis of the presenting problem. For example, with some therapeutic questioning, reflection, and time, the client who is seeking a life partner may begin to describe some of his unhelpful thoughts, such as, "I am so unattractive that no one would ever want to date me," or "I'm so lonely. But no one will ever love me, so why bother?" These unhelpful thoughts are the basis of the client's problem and are targets for intervention because they impede the client's ability to behave in ways that could help him find a life partner. Thus, a working hypothesis details the unhelpful thoughts and explains how they lead to the client's problems. Additionally, it also identifies how relevant situations and experiences activate the unhelpful thoughts and beliefs. For most clients, the unhelpful thoughts and the activating situation will be closely linked because of the overlapping content (think about the client with the unattractive/unlovable beliefs and Valentine's Day).

In addition to identifying automatic, surface thoughts as part of your hypothesis, your working hypothesis should also specify what core beliefs are causing and maintaining the client's problems in thinking, feeling, and behaving (Persons & Davidson, 2001). Is this core belief (or core beliefs) also causing problems in other aspects of the client's life? One technique that can help in conceptualizing the client's problems and difficulties in terms of core beliefs is to create an exhaustive list of all presenting problems (Persons & Davidson, 2001). The list will help you consider connections and relationships that underlie the problems. These may suggest a core belief (or set of core beliefs) causing problems for the client and needing modification or replacement. Thus, you will begin by working with a client's problematic surface thoughts, which are directly related to the presenting problem. Over time, you can then turn to the client's problematic core beliefs, which sustain the problematic surface thoughts, and may cause future difficulties if not addressed. Although core beliefs are sometime more challenging to identify and change than surface thoughts, the therapeutic tools I describe below work with both surface thoughts and with underlying core beliefs.

INTERVENTIONS AND THERAPEUTIC PROCESS

Consistent with cognitive therapy's key principles of the mediational model and considerations of human beings as active agents, cognitive therapy techniques are guided by three overarching ideas: cognitions shape and influence behaviors, cognitions can be accessed, examined, and adapted, and cognitive changes will lead to behavioral changes.

In using cognitive therapy, interventions and therapeutic techniques will thus be aimed at identifying problematic and unhelpful cognitions, as well as adapting and replacing these cognitions toward the desired behavior change. Additionally, you will use cognitive therapy interventions with the aim of building clients' knowledge, skills, and capacities so that clients are able to become, in a way, their own cognitive practitioners (Beck, 1995). In using cognitive therapy, you want clients to learn how to monitor, track, adapt, and replace unhelpful thoughts and beliefs in ways that will help clients not only with their current presenting problems but with managing multiple life problems in the future. A client will likely seek help with multiple and perhaps complex presenting problems. Rather than aiming to solve all presenting problems one at a time, you can endeavor to teach clients about the key principles of cognitive therapy theory and help them to develop skills to monitor, track, and alter their own cognitive processes.

You should start this cognitive skill building with clients by focusing on one presenting problem and the related set of unhelpful cognitions. By learning about cognitive processes and the skills to change unhelpful cognitions with one problem, clients will then be able to generalize their knowledge and skills to other problems in their life. As a result, cognitive therapy is largely a knowledge-building and skills-based activity (Beck, 1995), and focuses on psychoeducational activities (knowledge and skill building) throughout the therapeutic process (Cormier & Nurius, 2003). As with any knowledge acquisition and skill building, it is important that you strive to lead the client through this process one step at a time.

1. *Monitoring and tracking.* One of the first tasks of cognitive therapy is a "guided discovery process" in which you, in close collaboration with the client, seek information about the client's ways of thinking, feeling, and behaving (Padesky, 1996). For example, you can ask the client to think about a situation or problem and to describe associated thoughts and emotions. Alternatively, you may ask a client to think aloud ("Think back to when you started to feel anxious; now tell me everything you were thinking before, during, and after that anxiety attack.") or to role play the scenario ("Let's role-play the fight you had with your boyfriend; as we role-play, I'll have us stop periodically and then I'll ask you about your thinking and feeling in that moment.") (Blankstein & Segal, 2001). You can also have a client self-monitor thoughts, feelings, and behaviors outside of therapeutic meetings. You may ask the client to keep a record or log throughout the week of thoughts, feelings and/or behaviors. Alternatively you may ask the client to keep a log of thoughts, feelings and/or behaviors around situations that have been previously determined to be problematic. Having a client keep a detailed log like this for one week can provide important information that you and your clients can then use together to identify problems in thinking and problem situations that may point the way toward problematic core beliefs.

2. *Teaching cognitive theory to clients.* In conjunction with and after having clients track and monitor their thoughts, it is also important to teach clients about the mediational model: how thoughts impact and shape emotions and behaviors. The aim of this knowledge is to have clients understand the importance of monitoring, tracking, and examining their thoughts (Cormier & Nurius, 2003). In order to help them understand the utility of the tracking activity and thus to increase their participation in the activity, you will need to explain the concept of the mediational model. Additionally, you should also teach clients that human beings are prone to thinking in ways that do not help us to meet our needs and to reach our goals (DeRubis et al., 2001). These tendencies toward problematic thinking are called cognitive errors, and it can be helpful to provide clients with concrete examples of these. A few specific examples of cognitive errors are listed here (DeRubis, Tang, & Beck, 2001).

1. Overgeneralizations: the tendency to view one negative experience as the rule ("I am stupid and can do nothing right because I failed this one test.")
2. Discounting positives: the tendency to focus on negative information over positive information (Although a client's supervisor said many good things about in a performance review, your client can only focus on the one negative thing that was said.)
3. Mind reading: the tendency to think that we can know what is going on in others' minds without sufficient information ("My best friend did not call me back right away, so she must be angry with me.")

In teaching clients about these cognitive errors, it will be particularly effective and more meaningful to use relevant examples of the client's own cognitive errors that are associated with the presenting problem(s).

Once clients' less adaptive and unhelpful patterned ways of thinking are determined, you should encourage clients to view these thoughts as hypotheses instead of fact. You should ask clients to consider the specific belief or thought in this way: is this thought accurate? the truth? helpful to me? (DeRubis et al., 2001). Consider the client who in the above paragraph failed one test and has now decided that he is stupid and cannot do anything right. If you were working with this client using cognitive therapy, you would help the client to evaluate this belief. Is there evidence for this belief besides the one test? Is there contradictory information for or exceptions to the belief? To what extent is the client's belief based on cognitive errors? These questions can help the client determine the accuracy of the belief, as well as the usefulness of the belief for helping him behave in ways that enable him to meet his needs and goals.

Additionally, if a client holds an unhelpful belief that has some truth or validity to it, you may ask the client: what if this belief were true? What would that mean to you (Beck, 1995)? In the above paragraph, consider the example of the client who had negative information from a supervisor in the job performance review. It may be useful to ask the client, "So if your supervisor is right, what does this mean for you? Could you address or fix this one aspect of your job performance?" Having clients systematically and realistically examine their problematic and unhelpful cognitions is an important and critical step in cognitive therapy. This kind of assessment can lead to the clients' reevaluation of unhelpful thoughts, which in turn facilitates relevant helpful changes. But it is not sufficient to have clients only examine their unhelpful cognitions. An effective cognitive therapist will also help clients replace unhelpful cognitions with helpful ones.

3. *Replacing unhelpful thoughts.* An important part of cognitive therapy is giving clients alternative, helpful ways of viewing the self, relationships, the world, and the future. These alternative thoughts will facilitate cognitive change and build clients' capacities to cope with challenging situations and to direct behaviors toward goal attainment. These alternative cognitions should include both replacement thoughts, which clients can use as alternatives to unhelpful and problematic cognitions, and self-encouragement thoughts that help clients build their coping capacities and reinforce cognitive, emotional, and behavioral changes (Cormier & Nurius, 2003).

   In the above example of the client who believed that he could do nothing right after failing one test, it may be useful to coach the client to come up with his own replacement thoughts, such as: "I did do badly on one test; however, I have done well on many other tests and can do well on future tests," or "I messed up on the one test because I did not study hard enough. Studying more is something I can do, so I'll do better on the next test." Moreover, we can also help the client come up with encouraging thoughts—for example: "I have been studying every night this week for two hours. I am doing really well and am really taking steps to make certain I do better on the next test!" Although we, as cognitive therapists, can model replacement thoughts for clients, these thoughts are most powerful if they originate from the client. After giving clients a few examples of replacement thoughts, it will be most helpful to work with clients to help them come up with their own replacement and encouragement thoughts.

4. *Homework.* Cognitive therapies tend to use and emphasize the importance of homework and outside activities (Blagys & Hilsenroth, 2002). Therapeutic meetings are important for introducing and teaching clients about cognitive therapy concepts, as well as practicing cognitive change skills. However, clients will best be able to use their knowledge and skills if they practice them in their own lives outside of the therapy meetings. The earlier examples of having clients keep thinking, feeling, and behavioral logs are examples of homework. Likewise, you can have a client practice cognitive change skills outside of the therapy meetings. Cognitive therapy skill workbooks, which include techniques for therapists and homework forms for clients, can help clients practice cognitive change skills outside of therapy meetings (see, for example, Leahy, 2003). In therapeutic meetings, you should help clients identify problems and barriers that may arise in trying to practice new cognitive skills. Then when clients face challenges, they will be prepared to persevere in practicing their new thinking skills.

5. *Summary.* The interventions I presented here are not an exhaustive list, but these may help you begin to think about clients' problems from a cognitive therapy perspective. Keep in mind that when practicing cognitive therapy, you will be largely using psychoeducational techniques to enable clients to learn to monitor and to track cognitions, as well as recognize the relationships among thoughts, emotions, and behaviors. Next, you will work with clients to help them systematically examine their unhelpful and problematic cognitions, as well as replace unhelpful thoughts and beliefs with more helpful ones. You will start by working to change clients' automatic surface thoughts. Subsequently, as you and the client are able to identify unhelpful core beliefs that may cause problems in many areas of the client's life, you will also work together to modify these.

Again, these various interventions may seem pretty straightforward. However, as you being to use cognitive therapy, keep in mind how complex these tasks can be. In order to facilitate client success, you should break these large, complex intervention tasks down into small steps (DeRubis et al., 2001) and you should help clients practice cognitive skills and knowledge application during therapeutic meetings (Cormier & Nurius, 2003). Clients are more likely to be successful outside of their meetings with you if they have opportunities to practice their new knowledge and thinking with your guidance and support.

SHORT- AND LONG-TERM GOALS

The overall goals of cognitive therapy are to modify client's cognitions and cognitive processes to better help the client cope, manage life problems, and attain goals (Beck, 1995). However, the immediate focus and short-term goal of cognitive therapy is to address the presenting problem(s) that propelled the client to seek help. Cognitive therapy aims to create therapeutic change toward the client's presenting problems quickly (Beck, 1995), and often the practitioner and client will determine a set number of meetings or sessions (for instance, six to eight) (Dobson & Dozios, 2001). The goal(s) for focus and work should correspond to the client's presenting problem, as well as the client's problematic and unhelpful cognitions, particularly automatic surface thoughts. The treatment goals should be stated in terms of the desired thoughts, emotions, and behaviors that clients want to increase or enact in their lives. While identifying thoughts, feeling, and situations in your initial assessment with the client, you should strive to describe the client's problems concretely and in cognitive, emotional, and behavioral terms (Pearsons & Davidson, 2001). Concrete, specific descriptions of the presenting problem(s) will help you and help your clients to track changes, improvement, or increasing difficulty in the problem throughout the therapeutic work and will help you to create detailed treatment goals that correspond to the presenting problem(s). Within therapy meetings, you may want to use scales or tools to measure changes in client cognitions and emotions (for example, the Beck depression inventory, which measures depression-related cognitive content) so that you and the client can track progress and improvement.

In cognitive therapy, you will use concrete, specific, short-term goals to determine the utility of the interventions, as well as the validity of your working hypothesis of the client's problem. But what happens if the client is not improving and if goals are not met? If you and the client do not see improvements in the client's thinking, emotions, and behaviors, then your working hypothesis of the client's problem may be inaccurate. With a lack of progress, you may need to start again from the beginning of the cognitive therapy process. You should reevaluate your working hypothesis to determine what interventions or hypotheses will be most helpful for the client. However, in assessing lack of progress toward goal attainment, it is also important for you to keep in mind the importance of partializing goals. Clients may need time and repetition to successfully develop and implement cognitive changes in their life. If goals are large and complex, it may be useful to break them down into smaller steps. Successful attainment of even small goals can be reinforcing and provide encouragement for both the client and you!

Although the focus in the short term is on change in the client's presenting problems, the longer-term goal of cognitive therapy is to help the client generalize their new cognitive management skills from presenting problems to other life problems, as well as to future problems that the client will inevitably encounter (Beck, 1995; Dobson & Dozios, 2001). Once the client learns cognitive change skills and successfully applies them to one life problem, the client has new thinking and feeling management skills that can be applied to a variety of life problems (Cormier & Nurius, 2003). Another long-term goal is to help clients build capacities to be reflective about and evaluate core beliefs of the self, relationships, the environment, and the future. If the client has the capacity to evaluate and modify unhelpful core beliefs, then the client can use these cognitive management and restructuring skills towards meeting goals and needs, as well as heading off cognitive errors before they become stable and automatic. These longer-term cognitive therapy goals could be considered a type of relapse prevention or inoculation against future difficulties (Beck, 1995).

Clients may not learn cognitive change skills so well as to be able to use them across all life domains in one round of cognitive therapy. Two or more rounds of cognitive therapy may be necessary to help client's successfully attain and be able to utilize cognitive skills. Likewise, follow-up or "booster" meetings following a round of cognitive therapy may help clients to maintain and sustain their new cognitive skills. Regardless of the number of cognitive therapy sessions or rounds, the long-term goal of cognitive therapists is to provide clients with the skills and tools they need to effectively manage their thinking and emotions so they can develop the behaviors that will best help them meet their needs, goals, and cope with the challenges of life.

USING THE RELATIONSHIP

Cognitive therapy, like many other types of therapy, stresses the importance of a positive and warm relationship between the therapist and the client as important to goal attainment and therapeutic success (Beck, 1995; Burns & Auerbach, 1996). Some may think of cognitive therapists as cold and detached, with a steely focus on outcomes and goals, and only emphasizing cognitions, homework, and automatic-thought logs with their clients. However, effective cognitive therapists also emphasize empathy and genuineness in building rapport with clients and as key to successful therapeutic outcomes. Effective cognitive therapists are able to create trusting, collaborative relationships with their clients and often use humor and warmth to do so. When working from a cognitive therapy perspective, it is important for you to create cognitive hypotheses of presenting problems, to use psychoeducational and skill building techniques, to have concrete therapeutic goals, and to utilize homework activities. However, the best cognitive therapy techniques may fail to produce change, unless clients also feel positive about the therapeutic, working relationship.

Moreover, collaboration is essential to the success of cognitive therapy because both the client and the therapist bring useful knowledge and skills to the cooperative work (Alford & Beck, 1997). Although the therapist is the expert in creating change in thinking, feeling, and behaving, the client has important expertise, too. The client best knows his or her individual ways of thinking and feeling. This knowledge is crucial in cognitive therapy. Without information about the client's internal thoughts and feelings, the therapist cannot begin to create working hypotheses about the client's difficulties. Moreover, cognitive therapy requires that the client be an active agent in the change process, which is another reason why it emphasizes the importance of collaborative therapeutic relationships. Clients must actively work within and outside of therapy meetings to learn, practice, and enact the skills that will enable cognitive change and ultimately goal attainment. Thus, you should encourage clients to be active and interactive in the therapeutic meetings, to seek feedback, and to ask questions (Padesky, 1996). This kind of collaboration is impossible without a positive, warm, and trusting rapport.

As a beginning cognitive therapist, you should keep in mind that a cognitive therapy meeting tends to be fairly structured with set agendas, clearly defined goals, and specific outside homework tasks. Still, you should also adapt the therapeutic process and structure therapeutic interactions in a way that "maximizes collaboration and a positive therapeutic relationship" (Padesky, 1996, p. 271). Although effective techniques and interventions are critical to the success of cognitive therapy, you must also be attuned to the client's needs, feelings, and understandings. If, for example, a cognitive skill or homework task seems overwhelming or too complex for a client, you should adapt the skill or task in order to meet the client's capacities, functioning, and understanding. Thus, cognitive interventions and techniques are necessary for therapeutic success but not at the expense of the relationship with the client.

Although a positive client-therapist relationship is critical for success, an effective cognitive therapist believes that a good therapeutic relationship is insufficient for beneficial changes and goal attainment. Cognitive therapy theory maintains that the techniques, interventions, and therapeutic tools described earlier in the chapter are also critical for goal attainment. Having an excellent therapeutic relationship can help facilitate goal attainment; however, it is not an assurance of therapeutic success (Burns & Auerbach, 1996). A cognitive therapist strives to create a warm, empathetic relationship with clients while at the same time effectively using cognitive therapy techniques that will enable clients to create change in their thinking, feeling, and behaving.

ADAPTING THE APPROACH

Research shows that cognitive therapies can be efficacious with persons from many sociocultural, socioeconomic, and racial and ethnic backgrounds (Carter, Sbrocco, Gore, Marin, & Lewis, 2003; Organista, 1995). For example, African Americans may prefer cognitive therapies because they are short-term, problem-focused, and goal-oriented (Carter, et al., 2003). Although cognitive therapy has the potential to be effective with a wide range of clients, the practitioner will need to adapt the therapy so that it is consistent with and sensitive to the client's background and current sociocultural and socioeconomic context. Cognitive therapies should be tailored for diverse clients, including clients of various ages and physical abilities as well as clients who have faced discrimination, marginalization, and oppression. One way in which you can begin to adapt these therapies in your practice is to consider one of the key principles of cognitive therapy: environment and experiences shape thoughts, emotions, and behaviors, as well as patterned ways of information processing. When creating working hypotheses about clients' presenting problems, you should attend to how patterned ways of thinking, feeling, and behaving can be shaped, influenced, and maintained by the sociocultural, socioeconomic, and sociopolitical context (Cormier & Nurius, 2003).

Human beings who have faced discrimination, marginalization, and oppression likely have had some opportunities and experiences limited and restricted, which in turn shaped their core beliefs and information-processing systems in corresponding ways. Likewise, human beings who have faced discrimination, marginalization, and oppression may have developed unique opportunities and experiences. Keep in mind that humans are active agents who seek to create their own meaning and experiences, even in adverse and difficult circumstances. When working with a client who has faced discrimination, marginalization, or oppression, it is important for you to explore and account for how the client's sociocultural, socioeconomic, and sociopolitical context shaped core beliefs and information-processing systems.

Cognitive practitioners should also use the following recommendations for adapting cognitive therapy for all clients (Cormier & Nurius, 2003; Koh, Oden, Munoz, Robison, & Leavitt, 2002; Organista, 1995):

1. Use awareness in language to describe cognitions that may reinforce marginalization (e.g., some clients may find the term "irrational" derogatory when used to describe their thoughts and beliefs).
2. Adapt techniques to client's primary language, developmental age, education, hearing/seeing/reading abilities.
3. Avoid jargon.
4. Consult and collaborate with bilingual and ethnically similar therapists.
5. Consult with traditional healers and helpers.
6. Assess and consider psychosocial stress, discrimination, and marginalization.
7. Consider cultural and social forces that may exacerbate problems and create barriers to therapy.

Overall, cognitive therapy in itself is not likely to change societal discrimination and promote social justice. However, it can help clients to alter their ways of thinking, feeling, and behaving to increase awareness of injustice, reduce self-blame, and to promote coping skills that may help individual clients begin to enact social and structural change within their own communities and environments (Berlin, 2002; Brower & Nurius, 1993).

FINDING YOUR NICHE

In this chapter, I discussed cognitive therapy theory in a form that emphasizes the therapeutic utility of cognitions and cognitive processes. The cognitive therapy approach I presented here is most closely related to Aaron Beck's work. However, even within cognitive therapy there is a range of approaches to practice, as well as conceptualizations of human being and change.

For example, some cognitive therapists emphasize the behavioral aspects of the theory and thus also rely on behavioral techniques and therapeutic tools in their work with clients. (Dobson & Dozois, 2001). For cognitive therapists with this behavioral focus, changes in behavior can also lead to changes in cognitions, thinking, and feeling. The assumption is that human beings tend to think in ways that match their behaviors. So if a client can behave in helpful and adaptive ways, eventually their thoughts and beliefs will catch up with and match their behaviors. I have used this cognitive-behavioral approach with clients and found it successful. Using cognitive and behavioral therapies, I work on two fronts, emphasizing cognitive awareness and change along with focus on related behavioral changes. Specifically, I might ask a client struggling with depression to take a short walk every day in addition to working with the client to change the cognitions that sustain the depression. The walking in and of itself is not related to a specific cognitive change, though this mild exercise may help to elevate the client's mood. Improved mood, in turn, can help the client work toward cognitive change and therapeutic goals. This is one example of how I found the pairing of cognitive and behavioral therapies to work well and to help facilitate the therapy change process.

Cognitive practitioners also differ in their philosophical conceptualizations of reality. For most cognitive practitioners, the world is an external reality—a truth—that can be known and perceived. This knowing and perceiving of the external world may be flawed with cognitive errors, but the external world is there (Dobson & Dozois, 2001). Thus it is the practitioner's job to help the client evaluate the utility of cognitions and cognitive processes in relation to this external reality. Other cognitive practitioners (e.g., Guidano, 1991) maintain that human beings have unique and individual ways of constructing their realities. These practitioners, often considered constructivists, emphasize that what matters is the utility of cognitions and cognitive processes, not so much whether these cognitions and cognitive processes reflect the "truth" of the external world.

Cognitive therapists also differ in the extent to which the client's environment should be an area for focus in therapy and interventions. Many cognitive therapists do not see the client's environmental and social context as targets for change. However, others argue that cognitive therapists should consider advocating for and brokering on behalf of clients, particularly when a client is faced with marginalization, discrimination, and oppression, when issues of social justice are at stake, and when these activities are consistent with the client's goals and wishes. Environmental or social intervention changes can provide a client with new information and opportunities that enable or facilitate corresponding cognitive change and thus can help the client in attaining therapeutic goals. For example, I have conducted cognitive therapy with clients with few socioeconomic resources. I found that when I helped clients with concrete needs that improved their resources, I was then better able to use the techniques to address their other presenting problems of depression, anxiety, and substance abuse. Also, my advocacy on the client's behalf helped to create a positive, trusting working relationship, which in turn also helped the success of my cognitive therapy interventions.

These are just three ways in which cognitive therapy may vary. There are other ways in which cognitive therapists vary in their approaches to working with clients toward change.

If the view of cognitive therapy I presented here in this chapter does not fit with your view of human beings, change, and the helping process, I encourage you to explore and read about cognitive therapies further. There may be a form of the therapy that does fit well with your conceptualizations. Still, across many forms of this therapy, the key principles in practice will hold true.

PROCESS AND CASE SUGGESTIONS

Applying the information I discuss in this chapter to the three cases on the website are a useful way for you to begin to think about how you can use cognitive therapy. Additionally, your application of the therapeutic principles to these cases will help you begin to practice conceptualizing working hypotheses, forming goals, and intervening with a client's presenting problem from a cognitive therapy perspective. All three of the clients' intake interviews showed relevant beliefs, ideas, and ways of thinking that directly related to their presenting problems. For example, in the first case scenario, Elena appears to have two sets of conflicting cognitive core beliefs, which are shaping her view of herself, her relationships with others, and her future. In the second case, Jane's high expectations for herself suggest relevant cognitive content and possible targets for therapeutic interventions. In the last case, I was intrigued by thinking and hypothesizing about the cognitive content that underlies Theo's difficulty with anger, violence, and "losing control."

In my efforts to apply cognitive therapy to the case scenarios, I found that all three cases worked well with cognitive therapy theory and that this therapy could be an intervention with real utility in helping each of the three clients. Cognitive therapy theory gave me useful ways to conceptualize each case and to come up with possible intervention strategies. However, I found that I needed to adapt the cognitive therapy process to match the background, life experience, needs, and presenting problems. I also found elements in each case that were not easily addressed using cognitive therapy. These case elements challenged me to think about how I could apply it creatively, as well as how I might need to augment cognitive therapy with other counseling theories in order to best help each of these clients.

SUMMARY AND SUGGESTED READINGS

I hope this introduction to cognitive therapy will spark your interest in learning more about this therapeutic approach and its efficacy for helping clients with a range of presenting problems. I also hope that you will want to begin to consider how you might use cognitive therapy as you are beginning to work with clients. With a solid evidence base supporting its utility for a range of mental health problems, cognitive therapy is a useful tool for practitioners to have handy in their therapeutic tool boxes. This is a therapy, that when practiced correctly and thoughtfully, can be a staple of an effective therapeutic practice. However, the benefits do not come without effort. Cognitive therapy can be a complex practice that relies on you to have a solid understanding of the therapy's principles, the skills to effectively deliver cognitive interventions, and the capacity to adapt cognitive interventions to a range of clients with a variety of presenting problems. As with any new set of skills, it will take time, persistence, diligence, and repetition to develop the cognitive-affective-behavioral networks that allow you to practice this therapeutic approach in sophisticated ways that appear seamless and automatic. The utility of having this powerful therapeutic tool at your disposal will be well worth the effort.

Beck, J. S. (1995). *Cognitive therapy basics and beyond.* New York: Guilford Press.

Cormier, S., & Nurius, P. S. (2003). *Interviewing and change strategies for helpers: Fundamental skills and cognitive behavioral interventions* (5th ed.). Pacific Grove, CA: Brooks/Cole.

Dobson, K. S. (2001). *Handbook of cognitive-behavioral therapies* (2nd ed.). New York: Guilford Press.

Leahy, R. L. (2003). *Cognitive therapy techniques a practitioner's guide.* New York: Guilford Press.

Leahy, R. L., & E. T. Dowd (Eds.). (2002). *Clinical advances in cognitive psychotherapy theory and application.* New York: Springer.

REFERENCES

Alford, B. A., & Beck, A. T. (1997). *The integrative power of cognitive therapy.* New York: Guilford.

Beck, A. T. (1996). Beyond belief: A theory of modes, personality and psychopathology. In P. M. Salkovskis (Ed.) *Frontiers of cognitive therapy* (pp. 1–25). New York: Guilford.

Beck, A. T. (2002). Cognitive models of depression. In (R. L. Leahy & E. T. Dowd, Eds.) *Clinical advances in cognitive psychotherapy: Theory and application* (pp. 29–61). New York: Springer.

Beck, J. S. (1995). *Cognitive therapy: Basics and beyond.* New York: Guilford.

Berlin, S. B. (2002). *Clinical social work practice: A cognitive-integrative perspective.* New York: Oxford University Press.

Blagys, M. D., & Hilsenroth, M. J. (2002). Distinctive activities of cognitive-behavioral therapy: A review of the comparative psychotherapy process literature. *Clinical Psychology Review, 22,* 671–706.

Blankstein, K. R. & Segal, Z. V. (2001). Cognitive assessment. In K. S. Dobson (Ed.), *Handbook of cognitive-behavioral therapies* (2nd ed.) (pp. 40–85). New York: Guilford.

Brower, A. M., & Nurius, P. S. (1993). *Social cognition and individual change: Current theory and counseling guidelines.* Newbury Park, England: Sage.

Burns, D. D., & Auerbach, A. (1996). Therapeutic empathy in cognitive-behavioral therapy: Does it really make a difference? In P. M. Salkovskis (Ed.), *Frontiers of cognitive therapy* (pp. 135–164). New York: Guilford.

Carter, M. M., Sbrocco, T., Gore, K. L., Marin, N. W., Lewis, E. I. (2003). Cognitive-behavioral group therapy versus a wait-list control in the treatment of African American women with panic disorder. *Cognitive Therapy and Research, 27*(5), 508–518.

Cormier, S., & Nurius, P. S. (2003). *Interviewing and change strategies for helpers: Fundamental skills and cognitive behavior interventions* (5th ed.) Pacific Grove, CA: Brooks/Cole.

DeRubis, R. J., Tang, T. Z., & Beck, A. T. (2001). Cognitive therapy. In K. S. Dobson (Ed.) *Handbook of cognitive-behavioral therapies* (2nd ed.) (pp. 349–392). New York: Guilford.

Dobson, K. S., & Dozois, D. J. A. (2001). Historical and philosophical bases of the cognitive-behavioral therapies. In K. S. Dobson (Ed.), *Handbook of cognitive-behavioral therapies* (2nd ed.) (pp. 3–39). New York: Guilford.

Dowd, E. T. (2002). History and recent developments in cognitive psychotherapy. In R. L. Leahy & E. T. Dowd (Eds.), *Clinical advances in cognitive psychotherapy: Theory and application* (pp. 15–28). New York: Springer.

Guidano, V. F. (1991). The self in process. New York: Guilford Press.

Koh, L. P., Oden, T., Munoz, R. F., Robinson, A., Leavitt, D. (2002). Adapted cognitive behavioral group therapy for depressed low-income African American women. *Community Mental Health Journal, 38*(6), 497–504.

Leahy, R. L. (2002). Cognitive therapy: Current problems and future directions. In R. L. Leahy & E. T. Dowd (Eds.), *Clinical advances in cognitive psychotherapy: Theory and application* (pp. 418–434). New York: Springer.

Mischel, W. (1999). Personality coherence and dispositions in a cognitive-affective personality (CAPS) approach. In D. Cervone & Y. Shoda (Eds.), *The coherence of personality: Social cognitive bases of consistency, variability, and organization* (pp. 37–60). New York: Guilford.

Organista, K. C. (1995). Cognitive-behavioral treatment of depression and panic disorder in a Latina client: Culturally sensitive case formulation. *In Session: Psychotherapy in Practice 1*(2), 53–64.

Padesky, C. A. (1996). Developing cognitive therapist competency: Teaching and supervision models. In P. M. Salkovskis (Ed.), *Frontiers of cognitive therapy* (pp. 266–292). New York: Guilford.

Persons, J. B., & Davidson, J. (2001). Cognitive-behavioral case formulation. In K. S. Dobson (Ed.), *Handbook of cognitive-behavioral therapies* (2nd ed.) (pp. 86–110). New York: Guilford.

Chapter *11*

Rational Emotive Behavior Therapy (REBT)

Janet L. Wolfe

Chapter Outline

Bridging the Theory-to-Practice Gap
Principles in Practice
Keys to Conceptualization
Interventions and Therapeutic Process
Short- and Long-Term Goals
Using the Relationship
Adapting the Approach
Finding Your Niche
Process and Case Suggestions
Summary and Suggested Readings

BRIDGING THE THEORY-TO-PRACTICE GAP

I became interested in the REBT approach during my doctoral training. My Ph.D. program was highly psychodynamically oriented, and while I found the approach interesting, my clients made almost no progress in dealing with their everyday problems. So I enrolled for training and supervision in REBT at the Albert Ellis Institute and was swept off my feet. I found that REBT provided a great way—in a relatively short period of time—to move my clients from insight into making concrete changes in the here and now, with significant improvements in their relationships and life functioning. It also enabled me to have a more egalitarian, collaborative relationship with clients. Along with Arnold Lazarus, I came to see therapy as education rather than healing, growth rather than treatment; and that psychological change calls for problem-solving in the here and now rather than preoccupation with the hereafter or the heretofore. I remain passionately committed to this exciting, useful approach and over the past 30 years have seen wonderful growth in the clients with whom I have worked.

Rational emotive behavior therapy (REBT) is a humanistic, multimodal, psychoeducational approach that strives to empower clients by encouraging them to be active agents in setting and carrying out their own goals. Albert Ellis—the grandfather of cognitive behavior therapy—gave his first presentation of what is now called REBT to the American Psychological Association in 1956. His view that people are largely responsible for overcoming their own disturbances has its roots in the views of several early philosophers, including Buddha, Epictetus, and Marcus Aurelius. Some of its major assumptions include the following:

1. Most people have goals of remaining alive and reasonably happy. They then encounter events and adversities that block or thwart their desires for success, love, and comfort.
2. Dysfunctional thinking is a major determinant of emotional distress over the adversities that people confront. Simply stated, we usually *feel the way we think*. These self-defeating thought processes include self- and other-deprecation, catastrophizing, overgeneralization, and personalizing. The most fundamental disturbance-creating beliefs come from people's tendency to escalate their *preferences* (about how they would like themselves, others, or the world to be) to *shoulds* or *absolutistic demands*.
3. Although biological factors and familial and social treatment are important to people's initially acquiring their dysfunctional beliefs, people *maintain* their disturbance through a continued process of self-indoctrination with these beliefs. The emphasis in REBT is not on conducting an archaeological "dig" of people's early life experiences; rather, it's on identifying the *currently held* dysfunctional beliefs that underlie their disturbed feelings and self-defeating behaviors.
4. Since people have innate tendencies to think both rationally and irrationally, their dysfunctional beliefs can be changed—with a lot of hard work. This can be accomplished through clients' active and persistent efforts to recognize, dispute, and revise their core dysfunctional beliefs: this is REBT's conception of what constitutes "deep" change. Its "ABC" model provides clients with a clear step-by-step approach that they can learn to apply both to present and *future* disturbances.

5. Because cognitions, emotions, and behaviors all significantly interact, cognitive restructuring is done in conjunction with a wide variety of other emotive and behavioral methods, incorporated into regular "homeworks" designed to help people think, as well as act, against their disturbance.

A misconception that often arises with REBT—probably because of the word "rational" in its name—is that it promotes intellectualizing and discourages emotional expressiveness. Nothing could be further from the truth. It is *emotional disturbance*—being flooded with anger, guilt, depression, anxiety, and other feelings that suck the joy out of life—that is the main initial focus of this therapy. Once you help people free themselves from their disturbed belief systems and crippling emotions, they have a much greater ability to experience positive, life-enhancing emotions such as profound joy, love, and excitement. Moreover, when people manage to rid themselves of their self-defeating beliefs, they become freer to take risks and pursue those things that add pleasure and satisfaction to their lives.

Another misconception about REBT is that it is an overly structured, mechanical type of therapy. Although it has distinct organizing principles, there is no magical, one-size-fits-all formula. You need a great deal of caring, empathy, and ability to tailor it to the needs of your individual client in order to be an effective practitioner.

PRINCIPLES IN PRACTICE

The cornerstone of REBT practice is the ABC framework, which provides an exceptionally useful tool for you to organize a seemingly inextricable tangle of the client's feelings, thoughts, events, and behavior into a manageable structure. *A* in this framework stands for an *activating event,* which may be either external or internal to your client. When *A* refers to an external event, we can say that it actually occurred if descriptions of it can be confirmed as accurate by neutral observers. Activating events can also include *anticipated* or *imagined* events, emotions, or even thoughts. In other words, the activating event is the person, event, emotion, or thought that the client is upset about (Walen, DiGiuseppe, & Dryden, 1992).

B in the ABC framework stands for *beliefs.* These are evaluative cognitions or constructed views of the world that can be either rigid or flexible. When client's beliefs are flexible, they are called *rational beliefs.* Rational beliefs often take the form of *desires, wants, wishes,* and *preferences.* When clients adhere to such flexible premises, they will tend to draw rational conclusions from them. These conclusions take several forms:

- *Moderate evaluations of badness:* Your client concludes "it's bad" or "unfortunate" (rather than awful or terrible) when faced with a negative activating event.
- *Statements of toleration:* Your client has the view that "I don't like it, but I can bear it, even though it's uncomfortable or difficult."
- *Acceptance of fallibility:* Your clients accept themselves, others, and the world as being complex—composed of some good, some bad, and some neutral elements.
- *Flexible thinking about occurrences:* Rather than thinking something will *always* or *never* happen, your clients realize that things tend to occur along a continuum.

When people's beliefs are rigid, they are called *irrational beliefs* and take the form of *absolute shoulds, musts* or *have to's* (Ellis, 1994). When clients adhere to rigid premises, they will tend to draw irrational conclusions on the basis of them. These irrational conclusions, or *derivative* irrational beliefs, take the following forms:

- I-can't-stand-it-itis (low frustration tolerance)
- Damnation (of self, others, and/or life conditions)
- Absolute/never, dichotomous thinking (e.g., "I will *always* fail or *never* be approved of by significant others.")

C in the ABC framework stands for emotional and behavioral *consequences* of your clients' beliefs about the activating event (*A*). Emotional consequences are of two types. The consequences that follow from *absolute, rigid irrational beliefs* about negative activating events are disturbed and are termed *dysfunctional* negative consequences. The consequences that follow from *flexible, rational beliefs* about negative activating events tend to be nondisturbed and are termed *functional* negative consequences. REBT is unique in that no other therapy approach so clearly distinguishes between those negative emotions that are disturbed and those that are natural and appropriate in an aversive situation. It helps clients see that they have more than the two poles of being miserable about something or happy about it—neither of which is particularly helpful or appropriate when something bad happens.

Dysfunctional negative emotions include anxiety, guilt, depression, rage, low frustration tolerance, shame, hurt, and jealousy. They are dysfunctional for one or more of the following reasons:

- They lead to the experience of a great deal of psychic pain and discomfort.
- They motivate you to engage in self-defeating behavior.
- They prevent you from carrying out behavior necessary to reach your goals.

Functional negative emotions include disappointment, concern, annoyance, sadness, regret, and frustration. They are functional for one or more of the following reasons:

- They alert you that your goals are being blocked but do not immobilize you to cope with the frustration.
- They motivate you to engage in self-enhancing behavior.
- They encourage you to execute the behaviors necessary to reach your goals.

Although clients tend to express their irrational beliefs in their own individual ways, it is helpful to consider irrational beliefs to be variations on three basic *schemas* or *categories of musts*. These involve the following types of demands: *Demands about oneself:* These *musts* are frequently revealed in statements such as "I must do well and be approved of by significant others, and if I'm not, then it's awful—I can't stand it. It makes me an inadequate or lesser person when I am not loved, approved of, or don't do well." When you have these kinds of "musts," they often lead you to feel anxious, depressed, ashamed, or guilty. *Demands about others:* These *musts* are often expressed in statements like "You must treat me well and fairly, and it's awful and intolerable if you don't" or "You are damnable—a rotten person—when you don't treat me well, and deserve to be punished for doing what you should not have done." Beliefs based on this *must* are associated with the emotions of anger and rage and such behaviors as yelling or violence. *Demands about the world/life conditions:* These *musts* often take the form of beliefs such as "The conditions under which I live must absolutely be the way I want them to be, and if they aren't, it's terrible. Poor me—I can't *stand* it." Such beliefs tend to lead to feelings of self-pity and hurt, as well as problems of self-discipline, such as procrastination or addictive behavior.

This ABC conceptualization can serve as a superb organizing framework to help you, the counselor, thread through the tangled web of your clients' thoughts, feelings, and behaviors. When working with clients, it will be important to first identify situations that may be triggering relevant beliefs to be addressed. For example, with a client who has problems with substance abuse, relationships, anxiety, and depression, get him to choose a specific activating event, such as "I had a drink after my girlfriend flirted with another guy." By having him intensively reexperience the feelings, sensations and thoughts he had in this situation, you and your client will be better able to access some of his core beliefs and help replace them with more adaptive alternatives. This will help him deal not only with this specific event, but also with a variety of other present and future situations in his life. For example, if your client's girlfriend talked to another man at a party, and the client reacted by getting drunk and angry, he might have been thinking the following irrational beliefs: "My girlfriend *must* never show interest or spend time with any male but me; it's *awful and unbearable* if she does, and means she's a *rotten and untrustworthy person.* It also means that I'm not good enough—a *loser.*" By helping your client question his dysfunctional beliefs in this situation and replace them with more adaptive ones, you are also helping him reduce his anxiety and build self- and other-acceptance in *other* areas where people disappoint him, such as being "dissed" by a friend, family member, or teacher. Instead of getting angry, upset, and drunk, your client will learn to respond with more rational, flexible beliefs and behaviors.

Another very helpful concept emphasized in the REBT approach is the distinction between clients' *practical* problems and their *emotional* problems. Your client, for example, may be struggling with a problem of how to deal with her husband, who has invested a large sum of their joint finances without telling her. Her *practical* problem is expressing her feelings about this in an assertive, rather than an aggressive manner; her *emotional* problems are hurt, anxiety, and anger. As is often the case, the emotional upset gets in the way of practical problem-solving and effective communication. If she is depressed, she may just give up and say nothing. If she is unduly angry or anxious, she may not be able to effectively express herself nor to come up with good alternative solutions.

If instead you can help her to see herself (as well as her husband) as a fallible mistake-making persons instead of a hopeless, defective one, she will be in a better position to process the original problem of how to deal with her husband about his unilateral spending.

Perhaps the most important principle to get across to your clients is that while they may not have as much power as they would like over other people's (and the world's) behavior, they can exercise real power in stubbornly refusing to make themselves miserable about the adversities they encounter. It's important that your clients understand that their railing or depressing themselves over aversive situations and events, in a sense, "adds insult to injury": it increases their disturbance, depletes their energy, and reduces their problem-solving ability. On the other hand, if they can learn to acquire a more adaptive set of beliefs or life philosophy, they are likely to have more appropriate negative feelings (such as disappointment, concern, or apprehension), be less disturbed, and thereby be happier. The goal of REBT is not only to *feel* better, but to *get* better.

KEYS TO CONCEPTUALIZATION

In using REBT, try to use the following questions as your guide to helping you and your clients gain a deeper understanding of what is going on for them and thus be better able to translate insight into change.

1. What are my client's main *emotional problems*? What appears to generate these negative affects—certain cognitions, images, interpersonal conflicts? If your client is not particularly "in touch with" her feelings, she may need some preliminary training in accessing and labeling her feelings.
2. What *behaviors* is he engaging in (or not engaging in) that are getting in the way of his happiness or fulfillment (procrastination, aggression, social isolation, drinking)? What are the pros and cons of his maintaining these problem behaviors?
3. What is a *typical* (preferably recent) *situation* in my client's life in which she became especially upset and with which we can begin our therapeutic work? Be sure to get a recent specific example—the way a camera might record it.
4. Does my client have any *secondary disturbance*? For example, is he beating himself up for the way he has handled his life in general, as well as in specific situations?
5. What are my client's main attitudes and schemas, and how can I best help her access her irrational beliefs? What kinds of questions, imagery exercises, or other techniques will be most useful in drawing them out? Use a variety of questions to elicit the core beliefs. For example, "What was going through your mind when this happened?" "What kind of person do you think you were for stammering during your class presentation?" "What demands were you making in your head about the way your boyfriend should have responded to your request for more affection?"
6. What are some of the questions I can use to help the client *dispute* and change the beliefs that she devoutly believes are rational ("I'm unattractive and dull and will never have a successful love relationship. I am doomed to unhappiness.")?
7. How can I best teach the "B→C connection"—the fact that it is not the activating event (A) that causes his problem, but rather his "IB's"—irrational beliefs—about these events? Shall I use metaphors? A two-person example? Give him an article or cartoon related to his central problems that teaches this principle?
8. What *homework assignments* can I give my clients at the end of each session that are appropriate to their level of understanding and ability?
9. What are some of the things I can do to help *motivate* my clients to do the between-session work necessary to strengthen their rational thinking and help them take the risks necessary to get more of what they want out of life?

10. What are my client's likely resistances to our counseling work going to be, and how can I anticipate and most effectively deal with them?

11. How can I help my clients regularly *reinforce the new, adaptive self-messages* rather than revert to the irrational ones that have been practiced and reinforced thousands of times over the years?

It is very important for your client to learn the differences between *functional* and *dysfunctional* negative emotions early in therapy. Explain to her that if her boyfriend dumps her, the goal of counseling is not to be happy or neutral about it, but rather sad and disappointed (as opposed to depressed and self-downing). These "functional" emotions of sadness and disappointment will allow her to feel better and do better than if she is immobilized with misery or blocking out her feelings altogether.

In my own practice, I like to provide my clients with a preliminary conceptualization as to how I see them—both their strengths and main problems—and suggest some goals for our work together. For example, "I see you as someone who has had the strength and persistence to pursue your goals, even though you have had a lot of things working against you. Your main current problems, as I see them, are that you make yourself very anxious and depressed when it comes to performance situations, then become depressed and self-downing because you have made yourself so upset. This is understandable, as you were so often trashed as a child. You also seem to evaluate yourself as a terrible, abnormal person who is not really fit for human company. As a result, you isolate yourself, adding to your depression and "proving" to yourself that you can never succeed or be happy. What I'd like us to work together on in counseling is changing some of your negative and self-defeating views so that you can learn to define new goals and take risks to achieve them. As you begin to develop more social contacts, you will see you're not a 'freak'—just a normal human being struggling to overcome flaws and life stressors and become more self-accepting." I would also help her understand the process of therapy and develop the expectation of benefit by sharing with her that research has demonstrated the efficacy of REBT and cognitive behavior therapy (CBT) with problems such as hers.

INTERVENTIONS AND THERAPEUTIC PROCESS

Before beginning your actual REBT work, it is helpful first to get some basic demographic information, including whom your clients live with, their occupation, and a brief description of parents or parent-surrogates and siblings and the kind of relationship they had with them. Also ask about any previous counseling and whether or not it was helpful. To assess your clients' receptivity (or resistance) to counseling, begin the session by asking how they feel about being there and what they would like from you. Try to clear up any possible misconceptions they may have as quickly as possible.

If your client seems to be in a crisis and wants immediate practical help or emotional support, it is usually preferable to offer that rather than launch into an explanation of the ABC model and begin disputing irrational beliefs. For example, a rape victim may benefit more from your support and offer of resources than from disputing the "awfulness" of the situation. For a person with an important class presentation the next day, some tips and in-session practice on the presentation, with constructive feedback, may be a better bet than spending most of the session on teaching the ABC principles and how to dispute them. Both verbal and nonverbal behaviors can provide clues as to what would be the most appropriate intervention. For example, if your client seems very closed and guarded or panicked, counselor self-disclosure (to build a therapeutic alliance), clarification of misconceptions about what the counseling is about, or support and relaxation techniques to help reduce the crippling panic may be the best place to start.

In the first session, it is important to outline for your clients the process of therapy, along with their responsibilities: the importance of keeping regular logs of disturbing events, completing self-help forms to help dispute irrational beliefs, and regularly completing mutually agreed-upon cognitive, behavioral, and emotive homework assignments. It is helpful to give clients a brief handout summarizing what you've explained to them. You can enhance your client's motivation to do out-of-session work by sharing a brief article showing that those REBT clients who regularly complete homework tasks improved significantly more than those who do not. It is also extremely important to gear the assignment to the current level of ability of your client. For example, rather than requesting that an extremely shy client approach three people at a party, it would be preferable for you to assign him something less threatening, such as asking the person in front of him in the grocery line what kind of vegetable she has in her cart.

Clients who are not especially motivated to give up their self-defeating feelings, such as anger, may need to precede their cognitive restructuring work with another intervention. Encourage such clients to imagine how they would act and how the outcome might be different if they did experience the appropriate emotion in the context of the activating event (moderate frustration and annoyance rather than rage). Your clients will usually comprehend the advantages of the appropriate emotion and this understanding will increase their motivation to change the emotional consequence.

Generally, your session time is divided between cognitive restructuring work designed to reduce your clients' emotional disturbance and build emotional muscle, and role playing and problem-solving to help them deal with their practical problems in relationships, work, and family. Ultimately, the effective REBT counselor, while working clearly within the ABC framework, will balance science with artistry, and planned structure with creativity and flexibility.

SHORT- AND LONG-TERM GOALS

In REBT, the work that takes priority in most cases is helping your clients reduce their emotional disturbance. For example, a woman presenting with considerable guilt and anger at her teenage daughter for not living up to her expectations and who regularly becomes embroiled in shouting matches with the girl, might have as her emotional goal becoming less guilty, anxious, and angry. Her behavioral goal might be working on communicating with her daughter assertively rather than aggressively. To facilitate this process of building a better mother/daughter relationship, it would also be helpful to encourage her to implement such behavioral strategies as offering more positive feedback and rewards for good behavior and planning pleasurable mother-daughter activities together. Another helpful piece of behavioral work might be to have the parents join a parenting group. You would also work on helping her become less self-downing for the real and imagined mistakes she has made, past and present, in her behavior toward her daughter and in other aspects of her life.

The longer-term goal would be what we might call "self-actualization." You would lay the groundwork for this process in the first phase of counseling. It might include things like helping the client brainstorm long-range goals such as imagining what she would like her life to be like in six months, in a year, two years, five years, and up to age 95.

A tool that I have found especially helpful in setting and monitoring goals is a "3-Month Goal Sheet." Here's an example based on the client above:

Behaviors I wish to increase: (1) Giving my daughter more positive feedback. (2) Eating 3 well-balanced meals a day. (3) Completing at least two REBT self-help forms a week (Ellis, 1996) when upset and reading a minimum of one chapter a week of Albert Ellis's *A Guide to Rational Living* (Ellis & Harper, 1997).

Behaviors I wish to decrease: (1) Name-calling and shouting at daughter. (2) Drinking more than 2 glasses of wine 2 days a week. (3) Putting off writing reports until the day before they're due.

Emotions I wish to increase: (1) Self-acceptance. (2) Calmness. (3) Pleasure in my accomplishments.

Emotions I wish to decrease: (1) Anxiety over social events and work presentations. (2) Depression and self-downing when I "screw up." (3) Rage when others treat me badly or disappoint me.

Sensations I wish to increase: (1) Pleasure in my own body (independent of a partner's touching it). (2) My old pleasure in music, art, nature.

Sensations I wish to decrease: (1) Painful neck tension when anxious. (2) Feeling of emptiness in my chest when alone.

Thoughts I wish to increase: (1) I am a worthwhile human capable of happiness even if I never have a prestigious job. (2) Just because my body and personality are imperfect, doesn't mean I'm a worthless person. (3) It's a hassle, not a horror, when others treat me unfairly.

Thoughts I wish to decrease: (1) I must get my parents' approval and respect; and if not, it's awful and I must continue to convince them of the error of their ways. (2) I must not fail socially or academically; if I do, it means I'm a total failure. (3) People who treat me badly are rotten and deserved to be punished.

"Success" is viewed as continued progress in achieving some of the goals. Longer-term success often is a lifetime process involving the continued practice of a rational philosophy and the pursuit of eliminating bad habits and replacing them with more adaptive and growth-producing ones. Urge your clients to resist their ingrained habits of overfocusing on their real and imagined failures and beating themselves up for them. Instead, encourage them to regularly pat themselves on the back for their efforts, whether or not they are successful.

USING THE RELATIONSHIP

Your clients are giving you the gift of trust in sharing with you their pain, stuckness, and shameful secrets. I believe strongly that you, in turn, have the responsibility to regularly empathize with their pain and acknowledge their hard work and stick-to-it-ness. Being open, sensitive, and tuned in to clients' unique issues is a common practice among REBT therapists, although I have encountered (mainly among those who have viewed Albert Ellis's famous filmed demonstrations with "Gloria") the erroneous and stereotyped idea that the approach can be impersonal and confrontational. To enhance the therapeutic relationship, encourage your clients to give you regular feedback. This reinforces the idea that they are active participants in the goals and process of therapy and helps you monitor whether any of their typical out-of-session emotional reactions (such as viewing any feedback as rejection or proof of their worthlessness) might be triggered right in the session. Most importantly, try in every way to show clients *unconditional acceptance,* no matter what shameful things they think they have done. If clients are of a different gender, ethnic group, or social class, for example, you might have them share their feelings about working with you. You can also try to explore with your clients the context of some of their *shoulds* in terms of being part of a discriminated-against group, or the *shoulds* that may be gender-role-related.

Throughout, it is important to establish as much as possible an egalitarian relationship, as opposed to presenting yourself as a nondisclosing authority figure. I believe that a crucial aspect of therapy is to provide your clients with corrective emotional experiences, as opposed to the authoritarian one-up/one-down experience that has helped create many of their past or current problems. Where appropriate, you may want to self-disclose: for example, if clients believe I could never possibly understand their feelings of academic inadequacy because I have a Ph.D., I will share that I felt so inadequate as an undergrad that I dropped out of school three times, and took 10 years to get my bachelor's degree. Another example would be clients who become angry at you for not immediately understanding what they were attempting to convey. You can process this incident by having your clients voice aloud thoughts and feelings in response to your "blunder," then help them dispute any irrational beliefs that led to their getting so upset. Finally (without becoming defensive) you can role-play better ways of communicating their negative feelings to you assertively rather than aggressively.

In a situation where you may be experiencing "negative transference" toward a client, you can actually use the ABC format on yourself. For example, I found myself feeling irritable in response to a narcissistic, whining woman with few real-life stressors who spent her session time raging and obsessing about the fact that her liposuction left a nearly invisible dent in her abdomen. My *A* (activating event) would be the fact that this client is carrying on more than a single mother with four kids living below the poverty level, and my *C* (emotional and behavioral consequences) would be my low frustration tolerance, anger, and at times a somewhat irritated voice tone. My *IB's* (irrational beliefs) would be (1) She *should* not be such a whining baby—she should "get a life" and spend her money helping others, rather than devoting all her time to creating The Perfect Body; (2) it's awful and intolerable that I have to sit here listening to her when there are others so much more in need of help; (3) she's a narcissistic pain in the neck who doesn't deserve my time. By disputing these beliefs, possibly with the use of an REBT self-help form, I would arrive at the following self-statements to help me cope better with this situation:

"It would certainly be preferable if all my clients were motivated and compliant and only brought up substantive concerns, but, tough! Her problems are what they are, and I'd better not expect a disturbed person to act like a nondisturbed person. And although her problems may seem trivial to me, for her they're monumental. It's a hassle—not a horror—

that despite her many advantages, she still manages to disturb herself. But she's a fallible human being, who has a right to get herself disturbed. In fact, there's some research showing that women of the upper classes often have severe problems because of their very affluence and the extra-rigid social expectations held of them."

To sum it up: it's helpful in your therapeutic work to be a warm, accepting coach who regularly reinforces your clients' efforts to change and gently provides a "kick in the butt" if they seem not to be pushing themselves sufficiently to do their agreed-upon homework tasks. It's also important to try to model the kind of hard work that goes into personal change by going the extra mile to track down for your clients resources that might help them better understand their issues (information on serotonin reuptake problems or herpes management) and/or pursue their life goals (websites that provide statistics on careers with the greatest demand).

ADAPTING THE APPROACH

To establish rapport it is important for you as a counselor to tailor your language and interventions to the particular background (cultural, ethnic, or religious group) of your client. Although my personal style is one of directness, humor, and nurturance, there may be those who may misperceive the humor as somehow belittling them or not taking them seriously. If I am initially warm and nurturing, a person who feels profoundly unlovable may experience the "Groucho Marx" syndrome ("any club that wants me as a member must not be worth joining")! I and other REBT practitioners have found the approach to be well suited, however, to people from a wide range of cultural backgrounds. Many nonwestern clients and cultural minorities who come to see a counselor have the expectation that they will receive practical help and quick results. Their less than enthusiastic response to many of the more psychodynamic forms of therapies—while often construed as resistance—is more likely to be impatience or mistrust. They may believe that the counselor is not really listening to them and taking in their problem, since the overall process and goals in many other approaches have not been shared with them.

To be a cross-culturally competent REBT counselor, help your client to explore what the emotional and behavioral consequences would be for various choices (for example, people from other countries trying to be congruent with American culture at the risk of being considered deviant for their culture of origin). As an REBT counselor, your job is to help your clients anticipate potential negative reactions and figure out emotive and behavioral strategies for dealing with them. Because REBT helps people not to "awfulize" about rejection and unfairness, and learn to accept themselves despite societal rejection for having certain traits or group membership, it is an excellent therapy for clients of different cultures and religious groups.

REBT assumes no universal underlying reality, and therefore it doesn't try to force the client to fit the assumed underlying content. It assumes that people largely construct their reality via their behaviors and cognitions, and that it's the job of the counselor to help the client examine and challenge long-cherished cultural assumptions *only if those constructions lead to dysfunctional emotions or behaviors*. There is no attempt by counselors to force the client to think, feel, or behave like them in order to get better. Basically, we're trying to help clients to "think straight" about potential conflicts with the values of the dominant culture so they can work toward achieving their own personal goals within their own sociocultural context.

There are, of course, limitations. No matter how educated and sensitive you may be about your client's issues, there may come a point when the client may need to be referred (either temporarily or permanently) to a counselor with a similar religious or cultural background. This is especially true if your clients could use some good "coping models"— people in the same ethnic or religious group who have struggled with their issues and have successfully resolved them. Your client's needs at times may be better served (perhaps after or during an initial period of individual therapy) by joining a therapy group, a social skills group, or Parents and Friends of Lesbians and Gays, venues that can provide the kind of support, kinship with others with similar problems, and opportunities to practice new behaviors for which individual counseling may not be sufficient.

FINDING YOUR NICHE

Because REBT has been so strongly identified with its founder Albert Ellis, it is crucial that mental health professionals understand that they need not possess Ellis's particular style to effectively incorporate REBT into their own repertoire of interventions. Literally hundreds of thousands of students and professionals have heard his live or videotaped demonstrations, but contrary to popular belief, you definitely don't have to use an exhortative voice tone or four-letter words in order to be a good REBT practitioner. In my 30 years at the Albert Ellis Institute, my colleagues and I have supervised hundreds of fine practitioners whose style in no way resembles Ellis's, and yet who do excellent REBT. These include members of the clergy, soft-spoken nurses, working-class alcoholism counselors, and countless others who have embraced this useful and effective model and incorporated it into their own style. Those videotapes are listed in the publications section of the website www.albertellis.org.

A humanistic approach that helps people learn to empower themselves emotionally and behaviorally, REBT has enjoyed wide appeal among an extremely diverse group of mental health practitioners and laypersons. A large part of this appeal is that REBT promotes self- and other-responsibility and helps people learn a rational life philosophy that can endure well beyond therapy. It also has a clear structure (the ABC framework) that is teachable in a wide range of settings and populations, including elementary and secondary schools. One of the aspects many practitioners and clients find especially appealing about the approach is that it helps engender a better sense of humor and perspective about life, thus providing an antidote to what most emotional disturbance consists of: taking yourself and life too seriously.

PROCESS AND CASE SUGGESTIONS

I would enjoy the prospect of working with all three of these clients, each of whom seems motivated to work on therapy and seems to have the potential for considerable self-development and change.

1. *Elena.* I especially like working with late adolescents such as Elena, since they are so wide open to the world and eager to plunge into living life as fully as possible. (The downside of this, I've observed, is that clients in their late teens and early 20s, often more than any other age group, seem to believe that if they don't accomplish all their goals immediately they're washed up.) Elena has a good friendship network and is close (perhaps to a fault) to her family. She has ambitions to explore more of the world and to be a journalist. To do this, she will need to learn to overcome her guilt and break free from the rather constrictive life script her family and culture of origin have set up for her. With the support of a counselor and the additional help of exposure to other Latinas who have successfully struggled with these issues, I believe Elena can learn to balance family and career and have a happy and fulfilled life.

2. *Jane.* Jane's considerable emotional armor, rigid life rules, and guilt about deviating from the path of Right and Correct Behavior and Service to Others, will present a real challenge. She is not especially in touch with her feelings and is entering counseling mainly because of her physician's suggestion. There is a risk that she might flee from counseling if she feels things are getting too uncomfortable. She would probably be the most challenging of the three clients for me to work with—ironic, since she is closest to me in terms of being an upper-middle-class, middle-aged Caucasian female. Jane is bright and rational in many respects and I believe would ultimately respond well to the process of identifying and disputing her dysfunctional cognitions and embarking on horizon-expanding experiences. The fact that she is so excited about her new friendship and has continued it in the face of criticism from her parents and husband suggests that she is at a point when she is ready to give up her middle name of Should.

3. *Theo.* I find Theo's issues perhaps the most poignant of the lot. A large, imposing African American male whom others have so often rejected, misunderstood, or betrayed, he yearns to be loved, accepted, and connected. He is eager (unlike many others in his cohort) to engage in whatever work it takes to become less angry and isolated and more connected and loving. He has survived a tremendous number of stressful life circumstances that might have derailed a less tenacious person. REBT is an excellent modality to help him work on anger management and other relationship skills. I think Theo will take to it eagerly and work hard at his homework.

SUMMARY AND SUGGESTED READINGS

The most effective way for you to see how the REBT approach works in action is to try it out on the most important person in your life: you! In the three-day training practica given for professionals throughout the world by the Albert Ellis Institute and its affiliated training centers, three hours a day is spent on peer counseling, with one person presenting his or her own problems, and another person in the group serving as therapist. Following this, the trainer and other members of the group give feedback and suggestions.

You can begin your self-counseling by using the REBT self-help form shown in Figure 11.1. It provides a structure to help guide you through the process of formulating a specific problem, ferreting out your irrational beliefs, then disputing them and replacing them with more helpful alternatives. You can even give yourself a homework assignment! In addition, if you are able to enlist any friends or relatives who want to try out the approach on one

FIGURE 11.1

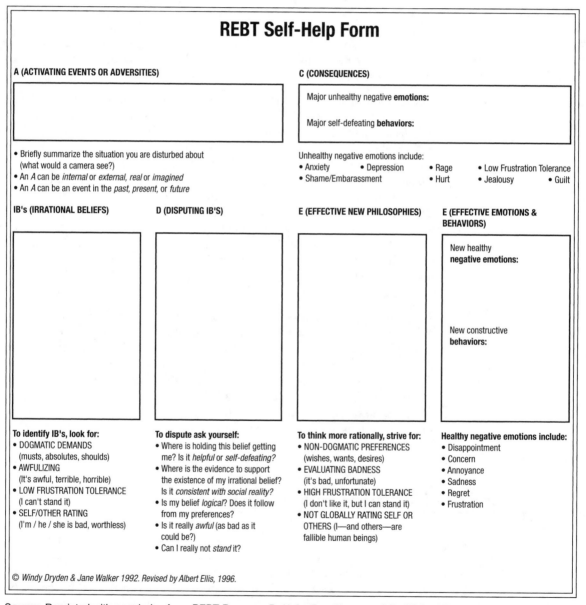

REBT Self-Help Form

A (ACTIVATING EVENTS OR ADVERSITIES)

- Briefly summarize the situation you are disturbed about (what would a camera see?)
- An *A* can be *internal* or *external*, *real* or *imagined*
- An *A* can be an event in the *past, present,* or *future*

C (CONSEQUENCES)

Major unhealthy negative **emotions:**

Major self-defeating **behaviors:**

Unhealthy negative emotions include:
- Anxiety • Depression • Rage • Low Frustration Tolerance
- Shame/Embarrassment • Hurt • Jealousy • Guilt

IB's (IRRATIONAL BELIEFS)

To identify IB's, look for:
- DOGMATIC DEMANDS
  (musts, absolutes, shoulds)
- AWFULIZING
  (It's awful, terrible, horrible)
- LOW FRUSTRATION TOLERANCE
  (I can't stand it)
- SELF/OTHER RATING
  (I'm / he / she is bad, worthless)

D (DISPUTING IB'S)

To dispute ask yourself:
- Where is holding this belief getting me? Is it *helpful* or *self-defeating?*
- Where is the evidence to support the existence of my irrational belief? Is it *consistent with social reality?*
- Is my belief *logical?* Does it follow from my preferences?
- Is it really *awful* (as bad as it could be?)
- Can I really not *stand* it?

E (EFFECTIVE NEW PHILOSOPHIES)

To think more rationally, strive for:
- NON-DOGMATIC PREFERENCES
  (wishes, wants, desires)
- EVALUATING BADNESS
  (it's bad, unfortunate)
- HIGH FRUSTRATION TOLERANCE
  (I don't like it, but I can stand it)
- NOT GLOBALLY RATING SELF OR OTHERS (I—and others—are fallible human beings)

E (EFFECTIVE EMOTIONS & BEHAVIORS)

New healthy **negative emotions:**

New constructive **behaviors:**

Healthy negative emotions include:
- Disappointment
- Concern
- Annoyance
- Sadness
- Regret
- Frustration

© *Windy Dryden & Jane Walker 1992. Revised by Albert Ellis, 1996.*

Source: Reprinted with permission from *REBT Resource Book for Practitioners*, ed. By Michael Bernard and Janet Wolfe. NY: Albert Ellis Institute, © 2000, pp. 111–113. www.albertellisinstitute.org

of their problems, you can do a mini-session with them. A study done several years ago at Cleveland State University in which one group of counseling students read *A Guide to Rational Living* and a second group read the book and practiced peer counseling, revealed that the second group had a significantly better grasp on the REBT process.

To learn more about the theory and practice of REBT, the following books and tapes are highly recommended:

Bernard, M., & Wolfe, J. (Eds.). (2000). *The REBT resource book for practitioners.* New York: Albert Ellis Institute.

Ellis, A. (1994). *Reason and emotion in psychotherapy* (Revised ed.). New York: Carol Publishing.

Ellis, A. (1996). *REBT self-help form.* New York: Albert Ellis Institute.

Ellis, A., & Harper, R. (1997). *A guide to rational living.* N. Hollywood, CA: Wilshire Book Co.

Lazarus, A., & Fay, A. (1975). *I can if I want to.* New York: William Morrow.

Vernon, A. (1989). *Thinking, feeling, behaving: An emotional education curriculum for children and adolescents.* Champaign, IL: Research Press.

Walen, S., DiGiuseppe, R., & Dryden, W. (1992). *A practitioner's guide to rational emotive therapy.* New York: Oxford University Press.

Young, H. (1974). *A rational counseling primer.* New York: Albert Ellis Institute.

Videotapes of Live Therapy Sessions

DiGiuseppe, R. (1997). *Coping with anger.* New York: Albert Ellis Institute.

Ellis, A. (1997). *Coping with the suicide of a loved one.* New York: Albert Ellis Institute.

Ellis, A. (1997). *Dealing with addictions.* New York: Albert Ellis Institute.

Wolfe, J. (1997). *Anger management with a recovering female addict.* New York: Albert Ellis Institute.

Wolfe, J. (1997). *Woman coping with depression and anger.* New York: Albert Ellis Institute.

Wolfe, J. (1997). *Overcoming low frustration tolerance.* New York: Albert Ellis Institute.

Chapter 12

Reality Therapy

Robert E. Wubbolding

Chapter Outline

Bridging the Theory-to-Practice Gap

Principles in Practice

Keys to Conceptualization

Interventions and Therapeutic Process

Short- and Long-Term Goals

Using the Relationship

Adapting the Approach

Finding Your Niche

Process and Case Suggestions

Summary and Suggested Readings

References

BRIDGING THE THEORY-TO-PRACTICE GAP

Practical, usable, efficient, orderly, workable, and functional have been characteristics of reality therapy since it was founded in the 1960s. Added to those descriptors within recent years are characteristics such as theory-based, empirically validated in a variety of settings, cross-culturally applied, and based on universal human principles. Uncharacteristic of reality therapy are qualities such as psychodynamic, abstract, limited to superficial problems, inapplicable to serious mental disturbance, encapsulated by "Euro-American cognitive processes," authoritarian, and unempathic.

When using genuine reality therapy, you can feel confident and excited that you are addressing real issues and root problems. While learning about clients' environments, cultures, experiences, and their perceptions of their place in the world, you can feel positive and secure in applying and adapting the universal principles embedded in the practice of reality therapy and in the underlying theory, choice theory.

Though reality therapy is usable and practical it should not be viewed as simplistic or shallow. On the contrary, it has been called "deceptively simple." It is easy to understand, and I encourage you to apply the skills and techniques learned in this chapter. But understanding the depth of the system and the ability to apply it spontaneously takes practice, study, and an inner belief in its foundational principles. For example, I urge you to view most human behaviors as choices. It might take time to come to this conviction and I hope you will reflect on this idea and see its hopeful implications when you implement reality therapy. Each time I see clients make more effective choices in their life, I come to a deeper appreciation of the efficacy of this principle.

Reality therapy is congruent with current emphasis on solution-focused therapy, brief therapy, and outcome-based and rapid-results counseling. And yet, it was originally used in a mental hospital with patients with long-term mental disorders and practiced in a correctional facility for girls with serious antisocial behaviors. Founder William Glasser, M.D., was originally trained in the psychoanalytic method of therapy. Working with his teacher, G. L. Harrington, M.D., he developed reality therapy based on his experience with mental patients. This work was summarized in the groundbreaking book *Reality Therapy* (published in 1965). In the beginning, Glasser's work was considered outside the mainstream. Guided by his vision and encouraged by the results achieved, he courageously proceeded to develop applications and extensions of the original reality therapy method. I have further applied the ideas to cross-cultural settings, gathered research studies, extended the system to group counseling, and extended the procedures, formulating them in teachable ways that you can remember and rely upon as you study reality therapy (Wubbolding, 2000; Wubbolding & Brickell, 1999). As I have studied reality therapy over the years, I have not abandoned previously learned skills but rather fortified them, and I believe you too will enhance your skills and enliven your career. You seek counseling credentials in order to help people. And when you ask appropriate reality therapy questions resulting in client improvement, something deep inside of you is satisfied.

Reality therapy has been applied to majority groups throughout North America and dozens of minority groups such as African Americans, Asians, First Nation, Hispanics,

Inuits, Native Americans, and many of their subgroups. Indigenous professional people from many cultures and nations have decided that reality therapy is practical, usable, congruent with and adaptable to their cultures.

PRINCIPLES IN PRACTICE

1. *Internal control psychology: Human beings are motivated by inner needs and wants.* Central to the practice of reality therapy is an understanding of human motivation, which guides counselors as they select specific interventions with clients. Very often clients seek help because they are frustrated with their circumstances. They believe that the world holds them back, creates barriers to their happiness, and even conspires against them. Counselors hear statements such as "I flunked because the teacher doesn't like me." "I hit him because he hit me first." "I'm depressed because nobody likes me." "I'm stressed because of my job and my boss." "He makes me mad when he. . ." "She upsets me when she says. . ." "I have trouble relating to people because I was abused as a child." These statements indicate a sense of *external* control. But when you practice reality therapy you operationalize a system of *internal* control psychology.

   Practicing reality therapy means that you gently but firmly lead clients to change not only their behavior but their perception that they are imprisoned by outside forces. Clients gradually learn that no matter what encroachments they've suffered from the outside world, no matter how they have been inconvenienced by external obstacles they need not remain in a state of victimhood. Seeing people move from a state of perceived victimhood to a sense of more effective control in their lives is one of the most exciting experiences for the practitioner of reality therapy.

2. *Human choice: Most behaviors, especially actions, are best treated as choices.* Reality therapists believe that clients are capable of choices that liberate them from their own internal and external impediments. Clients need not be confined to live in the past or be consumed by external roadblocks. As you discuss their current behaviors it will be evident to you that clients attempt to satisfy five needs: survival or self-preservation, love or belonging, power or achievement, fun or enjoyment, and freedom or independence. Through your skillful use of reality therapy clients learn that they have more control in their lives than previously thought. And when they realize that even in dire circumstances and in oppressive situations they have choices, they feel liberated and empowered. They feel connected with other people and they derive more enjoyment from life.

3. *Human relationships: Client unhappiness is most often rooted in dysfunctional relationships.* As you begin to use the principles of reality therapy, I suggest that you first assess the varying levels of need satisfaction, especially that of belonging. This serves as a kind of diagnosis, pointing the way toward more specific goals and wants. You can begin by helping clients define specific pictures or wants related to their human relationships—that is, the people important to them. When your client describes

feelings of hurt and rejection it is clear that the satisfaction of the need for belonging is deficient. Clearly this points the way toward a counseling goal. Similarly, when a client is faced with serious illness in the family, a sense of helplessness ensues. Addressing the clients' pain means assisting them to identify methods for satisfying ways to become closer to other people. Clients bored with life, disinterested in their work, or afflicted with workaholism seem to lack internal pictures or wants related to the need for fun. They seem to lack the capability of enjoying the company of others. People feeling trapped by poverty, prison, dysfunctional marriage, or a dead-end career need a discussion of realistically available choices connected to or even unconnected to the presenting problem. I urge you to commit to a relentless and tenacious search for alternative choices within the current purview of the client or even outside of it.

These principles in practice are best illustrated through the examination of a hypothetical case. Lou, 34 years old, a baggage handler, recently moved to a new city because his airline company has transferred its hub. He knows few people outside of work and is only casually known in the apartment building where he lives. As a 10-year employee he enjoys the benefits of seniority yet feels trapped because, "I have too much to lose if I quit but little to gain if I stay." His girlfriend dropped him when he moved, saying that their relationship was not a strong enough motivator for her to move, give up her family and friends, and start a new job. Lou has no hobbies, works as much overtime as possible, and spends his free time drinking beer and watching sports on TV.

Where to start with Lou: I would ask Lou about each of the needs, especially belonging (that is, his relationships), explaining that happiness and good feelings are primarily the result of satisfactory human relationships. Does he want better relationships with the people around him, maybe even a close relationship with a special person? Does he want more from his career than he is getting now? In what ways does his current job satisfy his inner need for achievement? How would his job be different if it were to be more pleasing to him, if it would be more challenging, and if he found delight is his work? How does he get along with his coworkers? Such questions implicitly teach him that there are degrees of fulfillment in his search for internal happiness.

Question: Which principle is illustrated by the above discussion?

Because behavior, especially action, is a choice and because the most controllable part of behavior is actions, Lou would describe his current actions related to each of the needs and what he would be doing if his actions were to be more effective in enhancing his sense of belonging, power, fun, and freedom. Because Lou feels trapped, detached, bored, and especially alone, I would encourage him to quickly choose some liberating, engaging, and interesting activities where he would meet people. The resulting plans would necessarily be geared to his personal interests or wants, his ability to reach out to people, and his willingness to follow through. Important as problem-solving is, the process of reality therapy is more than a piecemeal approach to each presenting issue. Through the conversation with me, Lou learns a more fundamental lesson: he has more control over his life than he first believed. And so while making plans to improve portions of his life he changes his self-talk and his view of how he fits into the world. Through his choices, he thereby fulfills the overall goals of reality therapy counseling: developing a range of effective action choices that satisfy his five genetic psychological needs (survival, belonging, achievement, fun, and freedom), as well as changes in thinking and his perception of his internal control.

Question: Which two principles are illustrated by the above discussion?

You are invited to consider how the above principles can be transferred to other specific cases and generalized to all counseling settings. Pay special note to what can be integrated into your already existing personal style and belief system. Is there anything that you find unacceptable or controversial?

You might be wondering what is unique about reality therapy. I prefer to think about what is most typical of reality therapy and why it is successful. When you implement the principles described above you communicate to clients hope for a better future and a specific method for attaining it. I believe that the emphasis on helping clients evaluate their own behavior and moving quickly to change it by learning that they have choices presents a unique contribution to the helping professions.

Practicing reality therapy means acknowledging the most obvious components of behavior: taking action, thinking, and feeling. Clients presenting with prominently emotional symptoms appreciate a counselor's skill in reflective listening and ability to demonstrate empathy, as well as the capacity for clarifying and distinguishing various levels of emotional intensity. However, as quickly as possible I urge you to assist clients in discussing feelings as part of a larger whole, technically called total behavior. Total behavior is made up of actions, thoughts, feelings, and even physiology. Because actions are intimately connected with the other components of total behavior and because they are more controllable, practitioners of reality therapy focus on a discussion of actions (i.e., choices), designed to change feelings and satisfy specific wants and general needs.

My counseling with Lou would emphasize helping him develop a meaningful relationship, satisfying his want and his need for belonging. Depending on Lou's willingness, part of the treatment plan could be engaging in an enjoyable activity such as an exercise program where Lou could strengthen parts of his body not used on his job.

Skill in assisting clients to self-evaluate occupies the keystone in the arch of reality therapy techniques and strategies. While other counseling approaches include such principles as "do more of what works and less of what doesn't work," reality therapy, from its origins, has enshrined the principle of self-evaluation as a necessary prerequisite for change in human behavior. If you meet Lou, ask him to conduct a searching self-assessment characterized by such questions as, "Lou, if you do nothing differently will anything change? Will you feel any better? Will your life improve or will it stay the same?"

Reality therapy constitutes an internal control psychology. Human beings are driven to generate current behaviors not because of society, oppressive forces outside of them, their early childhood experiences, or the cauldron of unconscious impulses. Whether behavior is chosen or driven by the unconscious as some contend, I urge you to help clients focus on the controllable aspects of their lives and see these aspects as choices.

KEYS TO CONCEPTUALIZATION

In conceptualizing cases, reality therapists view clients and their situations from a standpoint of hope for a better future. Such confidence springs from the undergirding principle of choice theory: people choose their behaviors and they have more control over them than they at first believe. When you ask clients, "Where do you go from here? What are your choices?" they learn something new: that they can improve their lives and that they have choices. Because of this new hope they feel a sense of liberation and at times a sense of uneasiness. On one hand, they realize that making better choices leads to a more satisfying life. They also gain the insight that blaming the outside world for their plight no longer serves any purpose and is but a temporary impediment to a hopeful and happy future. When you counsel in this way you are not "blaming the victim." I regard this slogan as useless and I encourage you to reject the implication that believing people have choices over their misery equates to blaming them for it. This is not to deny that some individuals *feel* oppressed, downtrodden, and rejected. It is your responsibility as a reality therapist to acknowledge their feelings, see their point of view, and help them move beyond a sense of powerlessness toward the conviction that no matter what their predicaments, some better options are available.

The hope for a better future is not a sentimental whim or wishful thinking. Immediate plans for alternative actions will help realize this hope and provide evidence for a better future even to reluctant or depressed clients. Consequently, a key to successful reality therapy is the mind-set expressed in the principle, "Let's make a plan, one you can do today or tomorrow that will help you even in a small way." The value of such plan-making extends beyond the plan itself. It communicates to clients there is hope, and success can be achieved by making action plans, determination, hard work, and consistent follow-through.

Reality therapy based on its justifying theory, choice theory, is a here-and-now process. The five needs are the sources of human behavior. These driving forces are current and always present as underlying engines of action, thought, and feelings (Glasser, 1998, 2003). As in Adlerian therapy (Milliren, Evans, and Newbauer, 2003), human relationships hold a central position. In fact, Glasser's personal position is that most long-term psychological problems are relationship-based. Dysfunctional relationships cause unhappiness, and unhappiness or misery causes people pain and therefore prompts them to seek help or prompt others to refer them for help. Whether or not you accept the centrality of damaged relationships as the primary cause of most problems, I suggest that regardless of the presenting issue, there is a relationship in need of repair. Consequently, whether the presenting issue is ADHD, antisocial behavior, or psychosis, you can discuss clients' interpersonal behaviors. When they improve their relationships, you can expect that clients will experience at least some amelioration of distress along their journey toward happiness. Consequently, their choices to improve human relationships accelerate need satisfaction, happiness, belonging, and fun. You can very quickly help them feel hope and empowerment. Keep in mind I am talking about helping clients improve their life situations but not cure all their emotional problems.

Helping clients unlock and articulate their unhappiness, distress, and injured relationships begins with an exploration of their quality worlds—that is, their collection of desires and wants related to their needs. Human beings fulfill their needs through the attainment of specific wants or yearnings. They become unhappy when they are unable to satisfy their longing for belonging, their quest for achievement, their thirst for freedom, or their eagerness for enjoyment or fun. Failing to fulfill wants is like a mental scale thrown out of balance. When clients experience intensely out-of-balance scales, they often resort to the only behaviors available: those characterized by harmful or destructive feelings, noxious self-talk, and ineffective, sometimes ruinous, actions.

Key to the effective use of reality therapy is also a nonjudgmental discussion of what others expect from clients: what their spouses expect of them, what their parents demand of them, what the courts require them to do, what their employers insist they do. Counselors then help clients decide whether they can accept the boundaries that encircle them and whether their wants conflict with the wants of other people.

Based on "deceptively simple" premises, reality therapy provides you with principles, theory, and a delivery system that you can integrate into other systems, and yet comprises a freestanding theory and method open to techniques and tactics developed in other systems.

INTERVENTIONS AND THERAPEUTIC PROCESS

As with most counseling approaches, interventions based on reality therapy are geared to each individual client. Selecting appropriate interventions results from trial and error, intuition formed by experience, and supervision/consultation. With this in mind it is possible to identify several categories of interventions for various types of clients.

A client demonstrating emotional upset or making toxic choices often needs an empathic listener, a counselor who expresses genuine concern by listening carefully and understanding the client's point of view. This client needs you! Be confident that you can be helpful! Reality therapy provides you with a structure for empathic listening and comprehensive counseling, the WDEP (Wants, Doing, Evaluate, Plan) system. Not only can you express accurate empathy by seeing the client's point of view, you can also use the WDEP system to help clients explore their *wants,* possible courses of action or things to *do,* opportunities for *self-evaluation,* and formulate *plans* for improvement. The WDEP system helps you understand the nature of your client's problem and determine the most productive interventions.

Exploring how clients see their situations—part of understanding the client's wants (W)—is a frequent starting point for reality therapy counselors. Clients are asked to describe their perception of the problem. Do they see themselves as victims? Do they see themselves as accountable for their plight? Do they perceive their own responsibility? Do they project blame on other people? Do they incorporate all the blame for themselves? Astute counselors also note the tone with which they describe their perceptions. Extending the exploration of their perceptions, clients are asked to assess the amount of control they currently have. They might even create two lists: factors over which they have control and elements beyond their control. In this way, counselors teach a basic choice theory/reality therapy principle: the only behavior clients can control is their own. Everything else is beyond direct control. Do you have a client who would benefit from the above process?

After acknowledging the client's perceived starting point in the counseling process, skillful reality therapists help them define what they want (W) from the counseling itself. Other W questions focus on what they want from the world around them—for example, parents, children, or employees. Clients with significant disparities between what they want and what they have need assurance that some of these out-of-balance scales can be put in balance or at least approach a position of near balance if they are willing to make some new and different choices. Ask yourself, "How could I use one of the ideas described so far?"

You could intervene by asking clients to describe their current, specific behaviors (D, or doing). These include actions, thoughts, and feelings. Useful questions include, "How did you spend your time yesterday? Tell me exactly what you did to fill the day on an hour-by-hour basis." "What thoughts went through your mind as you made your choices?" (Often clients' actions are accompanied by such thoughts as "I can't" or "They won't let me," and for acting-out clients, "No one is going to tell me what to do." Acknowledging but not dwelling on feelings is also a useful intervention when exploring current behavior.

Because most psychological problems have a significant relationship aspect, you can teach clients that improving interpersonal connections can improve their lives significantly. The predominant question for this intervention, "Is your current behavior bringing you closer to people important to you or is it driving you apart?" recurs like a haunting theme and is inserted throughout the counseling process. Self-evaluation (E) questions focus on many aspects of client behavior as well as their wants. The underlying rationale for these questions is rooted in the human tendency to disconnect specific wants from specific behaviors. Clients do not always see the link between a specific want and an action chosen to fulfill that want. If you were counseling Lou, he might well define and clarify his wants. He wants to feel less lonely and more involved with people. He wants a close relationship with a woman and he wants job satisfaction. His actions are incongruent with his wants. He avoids people and makes little effort to improve his job skills so as to achieve a higher level of achievement on the job. You might ask him, "Lou, if you remain disengaged from people in social settings and continue to coast on your job without demonstrating a higher level of energy or ambition, will you satisfy your inner need for belonging and self-esteem (power)?"

In the journey from loneliness to involvement, from powerlessness to empowerment, and from boredom to enjoyment, clients like Lou are led to align their wants, their expressed values, and their freely chosen actions. Aligning these components, a concept easy to understand, lies at the heart of effective reality therapy, yet client and counselor accomplish it through the skillful application of the WDEP system combined with the incorporation of AB—CDE (Wubbolding, 2004): "Always Be—Courteous, Determined, and Enthusiastic." As a reality therapist I always attempt to be courteous or respectful of clients' incongruities, false starts, backsliding, and resistance while remaining determined to help them proceed forward. For me, enthusiasm means looking for something to build on rather than merely attempting to help clients remediate their failures. I do not see enthusiasm as cheerleading; it is my willingness to relentlessly help clients identify their strengths and their opportunities. How can you incorporate any of the above ideas into your repertoire of skills?

SHORT- AND LONG-TERM GOALS

Choice theory, the basis of reality therapy, provides a structure for short-term and long-term goals. The fivefold need system serves to focus treatment planning and goal setting along specific pathways. All goals, short-term and long-term, spring from the human motivators: survival or self-preservation, belonging, power or achievement, freedom or independence, and fun or enjoyment. Working within socially acceptable and ethical boundaries, you will help clients set realistically achievable goals for improving health, enhancing human relationships, gaining a sense of inner control or power, becoming more autonomous, and enjoying life.

More specifically, your clients need to formulate specific wants related to their needs. When counseling Lou, I suggest you help him set the goal of better physical condition, involvement in an interactive group, initiating a hobby, or enrolling in an adult education program. His short-term goals would focus on taking initial steps along the above-mentioned pathways. Long-term goals center on maintaining effective need satisfaction. For example, because his unhappiness is largely due to unsatisfactory relationships, Lou might be willing to formulate the short-term goal of exploring a community activity where he would be able to meet people his own age. Do not force a long-term goal of establishing a relationship with a woman. Rather, encourage him to be open to this possibility. Similarly, you might help Lou investigate available adult education programs at a local vocational school. Discussing available educational opportunities with the counselor is likely to lead to self-evaluation (E). Consider asking Lou such questions as: "If you enroll in a course how might it help you?" "If you make no changes whatsoever in how you spend your free time do you think you will feel any differently than you do now?" Even in setting goals, you can intervene with self-evaluation questions.

Keep in mind, the overriding theme for goal setting is *improvement* rather than cure. Measurement for successful goal achievement is primarily the client's responsibility. Through self-evaluation and reflection, Lou will decide whether the counseling is successful. When he makes more efficacious choices and feels better, he will then decide that he has more control over his life than he at first believed. Do you have your own short- and long-term personal or professional goals? What's your plan?

USING THE RELATIONSHIP

As with many counseling theories and methods, reality therapy places the therapeutic alliance at the center of the counseling process. If clients feel connected to the therapist and if they feel that the therapist has demonstrated not only empathy and positive regard but skill and knowledge, they will feel hope for a better future and have confidence in their own potential.

Empathy, as seen from the point of view of reality therapy, means that you see the world from the perspective of the clients. But more importantly, you perceive clients as capable of choices and capable of living more effectively. In other words, try to view clients not merely as they are but as they can be. When you demonstrate this belief, you communicate a sense of hope and confidence that tomorrow will be better than today.

More specifically, the counseling relationship is made concrete when you help clients describe their wants and desires (W). Encourage them to express what they want from the world around them, including family, friends, and career. Skillful questioning about clients' level of commitment, how hard they want to work at bringing about change, communicates in a subtle and implicit way that clients have within them the power and ability to take better charge of their lives. Helping clients clarify their levels of commitment and their perceptions of themselves both present and future, deepens your therapeutic relationship and facilitates treatment planning.

Questions focusing on what clients are doing, current actions, cognition, and feelings (D), help counselors connect with clients by demonstrating a genuine interest in the specifics of how clients live. As the relationship develops, clients deepen their trust in you. A searching and fearless self-inventory focusing on the effectiveness of current choices, the attainability of wants, and the efficacy of clients' current level of commitment is built on this trust. Using direct but not harsh questions, you skillfully assist clients in their self-evaluation (E). Following this inner self-assessment or self-evaluation process is your encouragement to make specific plans for change (P).

When you use the WDEP system, you facilitate the client-counselor relationship. You also present to clients a detailed system for assisting them in examining their inner lives: wants, perceptions, level of commitment, current behaviors, self-evaluations, and willingness to make plans.

ADAPTING THE APPROACH

Implementation of the WDEP system of reality therapy includes adapting it to individual clients and cultures. While it applies to virtually every person and presenting issue, it needs to be adapted and harmonized with the many cultures represented in education, mental health, management, and supervision. At first reflecting the mindset of "Euro-Americans" and incorporating direct and assertive communicative styles, the system has been adapted by people whose communicative styles are vastly different from those described as Euro-American. Japanese, Korean, Chinese, and Middle-Eastern instructors have mastered the principles of choice theory and reality therapy and teach them according to their own style, language, and cultural values (Wubbolding, et al, 2004).

More controversial is how the current cult of victimhood connects with the inner control psychology contained in the principles of choice theory and reality therapy. Seeing clients, especially minorities, as victims disempowers them, demeans them, and condemns them to a mental state characterized by self-talk such as "I can't because they won't let me." Reality therapists believe that no matter what people have suffered they need not remain in the position of victim. Even people seriously abused as children and into adulthood have choices. While they deserve empathy and understanding, the effective use of reality therapy emphasizes the controllable parts of their lives and their current abundant choices.

When it is applied to individuals who communicate less directly than majority cultures in North America, reality therapy is adjusted to indirect communication. To ask *some* Japanese clients about their wants might sound harsh and intrusive to them. The question "What do you want?" is often translated as "What are you looking for?" To the western ear these questions might sound identical but to the Japanese client the second question is more acceptable (Wubbolding, 2000).

Reality therapy is based on universal principles: all people have a system of inner needs, all people make choices, all people seek to impact the world around them and to communicate with it. Putting these principles into action requires creativity, sensitivity to cultures and individuals, as well as flexibility in implementing the WDEP system.

I suggest that you begin using reality therapy with people who feel powerless and disconnected from others. I believe that you will see improvements within a few sessions.

Keep in mind that reality therapy started in a mental hospital and a correctional institution and has been shown to be effective with clients who see themselves as broken and discarded by society. Regardless of their presenting problems, if you can establish a relationship with your clients they are likely to improve their lives no matter how desperate they feel at first. It is quite effective with adolescents, and I cannot think of a single type of client to whom reality therapy does not apply.

FINDING YOUR NICHE

The WDEP system of reality therapy provides a structure for dealing with clients from the point of view of internal control psychology. The underlying theoretical justification for reality therapy, formerly known as control system theory and now more appropriately known as choice theory, is an internal control psychology. This means that human motivation and behavior spring from within the human person. If you, as a counselor, believe that people need not be victims of external circumstances and if you believe that democratic societies provide an atmosphere for self-fulfillment, then you are more likely to accept that your clients not only have choices about how they perceive the world but they also have opportunities to satisfy their needs.

The system of reality therapy, summarized in the acronym WDEP, should be seen not as a step-by-step cookbook approach. Nor should it be worn as a tight wetsuit. Rather, it is a loose fitting overcoat. It provides a flexible, adaptable, and open system to be used with clients who present with many personal growth issues, major or minor problems, and even with apparently hopeless conditions.

At times the reality therapist emphasizes a safe and understanding atmosphere in counseling sessions. A person who is reluctant to disclose embarrassing behaviors needs an understanding and less assertive climate for self-disclosure. On the other hand, some bipolar clients need a more direct-action-centered set of guidelines. In collaboration with clients, the reality therapist establishes rules and boundaries. A specific client might need simple and direct rules such as, "always drive within the speed limit, shop only for what is absolutely necessary, rise every day at a regular hour, not too early and not too late, do not make decisions about medication without first consulting your physician."

I encourage you to examine a wide range of counseling approaches: cognitive, humanistic, behaviorist, psychodynamic, and others. Then decide which approach or which combination of approaches matches your core beliefs. In order to make such decisions, I urge you to first examine what you believe about human nature. Then decide how you will identify and formulate your core beliefs and how you will develop them into a system that you can articulate and that influences the way you live your life as well as the way you counsel others.

In my opinion, practicing reality therapy and accepting its philosophical foundations means accepting a core belief that people are motivated in the here and now from an internal source, and that their behavior is a result of contemporary wants, hopes, and desires. Human beings need not be victims of society, of their past, of real or imagined oppression. Regardless of past experiences human beings have a wide range of current choices. It is your responsibility, as a reality therapist, to discourage a victim identity and an oppressed self-image. On the contrary, it is vital for you to accept your clients, not only for what they are and where they are, but also for what they can be and where they will be if they take charge of their lives through the power of making effective and appropriate choices on a consistent basis.

PROCESS AND CASE SUGGESTIONS

1. *Elena.* Feeling alienated, alone, misunderstood, and pulled in opposite directions by her own hopes and dreams on one hand and parental expectations on the other, Elena can find no immediate relief from her conflicts. She tries an illusory solution and realizes that it provides only momentary relief resulting in more pain. I would help her focus on what she can change, accept what she cannot change, and gain the wisdom to know the difference. I would also help her cope with the frustration of her journey from adolescence to independence compounded by the cultural clash of values between her and her parents. I would help her embrace the conflict and accept the fact that it cannot be resolved easily or quickly.

2. *Jane.* With multiple presenting issues Jane offers the counselor a cafeteria of starting points. Reality therapy helps the counselor find a way to assist Jane in a most efficient manner. A therapist applying the WDEP system would ask Jane what she wants to work on while suggesting that relationships seem to be a theme. Jane might choose to select the most difficult issue to begin with or the easiest. I would ask her about the many aspects of her relationships, help her to define what she wants, describe what she has done to fulfill her wants, examine the effectiveness of her choices, and formulate doable plans.

3. *Theo.* A starting point with Theo could be an explanation that anger is a behavior and that the actions accompanying it are choices. The discrepancy between what a person wants and what a person has can be intense and painful, thereby prompting equally intense behaviors such as anger. I would ask Theo what he wants that he does not have and how intensely he desires to fulfill his wants. I would further explore what his life would be like if his rage would evaporate. I would help Theo examine his patterns of communication, evaluate them, and make plans to relate to people in ways that win them over rather than turn them away.

SUMMARY AND SUGGESTED READINGS

As stated earlier, effective, practical, usable, theory-based, cross-cultural, and founded on universal human principles describe the WDEP system of reality therapy. When counselors and therapists implement the principles by identifying wants, describing current behavior, and helping clients self-evaluate and make plans, they become enthusiastic and interested in using these principles more skillfully and efficiently. The concepts apply to virtually any presenting issue regardless of clients' diagnoses, cultural backgrounds, or strife experienced in family or in society at large.

FIGURE 12.1 Summary Chart

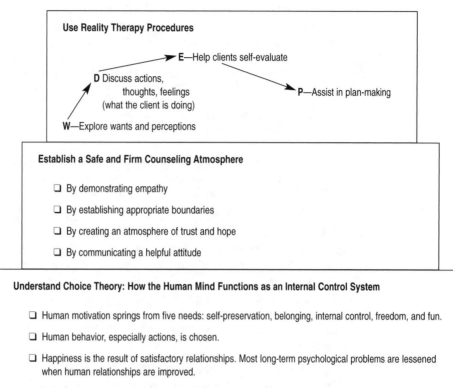

Use Reality Therapy Procedures

E—Help clients self-evaluate

D Discuss actions,
　　thoughts, feelings
　　(what the client is doing)

P—Assist in plan-making

W—Explore wants and perceptions

Establish a Safe and Firm Counseling Atmosphere

❑ By demonstrating empathy

❑ By establishing appropriate boundaries

❑ By creating an atmosphere of trust and hope

❑ By communicating a helpful attitude

Understand Choice Theory: How the Human Mind Functions as an Internal Control System

❑ Human motivation springs from five needs: self-preservation, belonging, internal control, freedom, and fun.

❑ Human behavior, especially actions, is chosen.

❑ Happiness is the result of satisfactory relationships. Most long-term psychological problems are lessened when human relationships are improved.

Based on choice theory, an internal control system, reality therapy must be interpreted and applied to each individual with the counselor acknowledging that clients are, in fact, unique individuals, not merely representatives of a group. Through supervision, training, and practice you can learn to trust the process of reality therapy and to rely on your instincts while adhering to the principles summarized in the WDEP formulation shown in Figure 12.1.

Choice theory constitutes an explanation of human motivation. People choose their behaviors in an attempt to impact the world around them and to communicate a message. If you view the world through the lens of choice theory, an internal control psychological theory, you will see human beings as capable of making need-satisfying choices, which lead them to more productive and positive living. This is not to say that clients are *cured*. It is to assert, however, that you can help clients *improve* their lives.

Following are some suggested readings.

Wubbolding, R. (2000). *Reality therapy for the 21st century.* Philadelphia: Brunner Routledge.

The most comprehensive and detailed treatment of reality therapy. A seven-year project, this book contains an overview of choice theory along with several extensions of the theory. Chapter 9 contains major amplifications of the procedures summarized in the WDEP formulation, a practical and teachable tool.

A major contribution of this book is the application to cross-cultural counseling: Japanese, Koreans, African Americans, Hispanics, Chinese, and others. Reality therapy empowers clients and provides an alternative to the victimology often presented in multicultural literature and the oppression worldview espoused by some multicultural writers.

Answering the criticism that reality therapy lacks a research base, Chapter 12 presents a summary of many studies demonstrating the effectiveness of reality therapy applied to addictions, education, delinquency, residential programs, and others.

Wubbolding, R., & Brickell, J. (2001). *Counselling with reality therapy*. Bicester, Oxon, UK: Speechmark Publishing, Ltd.

Written for international use, this book emphasizes relationship counseling, reality therapy applied to addictions, and stages of group development. Along with the use of metaphors, listening for themes, and the use of silence, paradoxical techniques are applied to difficult client behaviors such as resistance. The authors also explain additional topics such as creating client anticipation, communicating hope to them, and how to use reality therapy in schools.

Wubbolding, R., & Brickell J. (2001). *A set of directions for putting and keeping yourself together*. Minneapolis, MN: Educational Media Corporation.

Practical, usable, hands-on source for self-help use with individual clients, students, and groups. Specific planning activities designed for each need: belonging, achievement, fun, freedom, and health, are presented in an easily manageable format. Ways to combat negative actions, thoughts, and feelings provide the reader with tools for self-help and for use with families.

Glasser, W. (1998). *Choice theory*. New York: HarperCollins.

Provides a detailed exposition of choice theory as an internal control psychology. It is an extension of a previous book, *Control Theory,* and marks the change in the name of the theory underlying reality therapy. It also contains applications to marriage and family, education, the workplace, and the "quality community." It is a foundational book for students of reality therapy who desire an extended treatment of choice theory.

Glasser, W. (2003). *Warning: Psychiatry can be hazardous to your mental health*. New York: HarperCollins.

A controversial discussion of the use of psychiatric drugs. Because of the alleged hazard to mental health, Glasser suggests that every effort should be made to help people live without their use. He proposes the study of choice theory and its incorporation into daily living as an alternative. In this way the two interlocking characteristics of mental health, a sense of well-being or happiness and better human relationships, are brought to fruition.

REFERENCES

Glasser, W. (1965). *Reality therapy.* New York: HarperCollins.

Glasser, W. (1998). *Choice theory.* New York: HarperCollins.

Glasser, W. (2003). *Warning: Psychiatry can be hazardous to your mental health.* New York: Harper Collins.

Milliren, A., Evans, T., and Newbauer, J. (2003). Adlerian counseling and psychotherapy. In D. Capuzzi and D. Gross (Eds.), *Counseling and psychotherapy theories and interventions.* Upper Saddle River, NJ: Merrill/Prentice Hall.

Wubbolding, R. (2000). *Reality therapy for the 21st century.* Philadelphia: Brunner Routledge.

Wubbolding, R. (2004). *Reality therapy training manual* (13th edition). Cincinnati, OH: Center for Reality Therapy.

Wubbolding, R., & Brickell, J. *Counselling with reality therapy.* (1999). Bicester, Oxon, UK: Speechmark Publishing Ltd.

Wubbolding, R., Brickell, J., Imhof, L., Kim, R., Lojk, L., and Al-Rashidi, B. (2004). Reality therapy: A global perspective. *International Journal for the Advancement of Counselling,* 26(3), 219–228.

Chapter 13

Family Systems Theory

Nancy L. Murdock

Chapter Outline

Bridging the Theory-to-Practice Gap

Principles in Practice

Keys to Conceptualization

Interventions and Therapeutic Process

Short- and Long-Term Goals

Using the Relationship

Adapting the Approach

Finding Your Niche

Process and Case Suggestions

Summary and Suggested Readings

References

BRIDGING THE THEORY-TO-PRACTICE GAP

Imagine a young man raised in a complex and somewhat unusual family situation during the 1800s. He was the first child of his mother, who was his father's second or third wife (there is some controversy surrounding this). His father had two sons from his first marriage who were about the same age as the young man's mother, who was 20 years younger than the father. The other half brother was married and had a son, so the young man had an older nephew, with whom he was very close. Six younger siblings were eventually born to the mother and father. The family's favorite child, the young man was closer to his dominant mother and had ambivalent feelings towards his father.

The young man became a physician, and was fascinated by the way the mind works. He set out to discover explanations for these phenomena and in doing so, created a knowledge system still with us today.

Do you recognize the young man in the above story as Sigmund Freud? Although it may seem a strange exercise, think for a minute about Freud's early family life. What did he learn about relationships and about being a man in relation to women and to other men? Take a minute and think about what you know about psychoanalysis. Can you make any links between Freud's early upbringing and what eventually appears in his theories?

I (as have others) would argue that you in fact can make these connections and that further, understanding an individual's family environment, both current and past, is essential in understanding the person and to helping them achieve the life goals they set. Think about your own family of origin (the term used for the family in which you grew up). What was the structure of this family? What were the expectations of you as a child? What was the role of the adults? Did you have older or younger siblings and were they sisters or brothers? In what ways did your early experience shape who you are now?

To me, these kinds of questions are fascinating, and I'd go further to say that such self-exploration is critical to becoming a competent therapist. That is why I am a family systems therapist. Family systems theory is a general term used to describe a set of theories that share the perspective that the best way to understand individuals is by seeing them as members of a broadly defined family system. We family system theorists believe that individuals simply do not exist in a vacuum; our happiness, sadness, pain, and glory are significantly influenced by those around us, and most critically, by those important others who were around as we grew up and became individuals.

There are several major approaches to family systems theory, which you can explore by reading a basic family therapy textbook. In this chapter, I will focus on one approach: Bowen's family systems theory (BFST), also known as Bowen theory or multigenerational family therapy. Developed beginning in the 1950s by Murray Bowen, this approach has the benefits of having rich, elaborate, elegant theory (sort of a fusion of psychoanalytic theory with evolutionary theory) and is currently used by many family systems therapists. A benefit of this approach is that it can be used with individuals, couples, or whole family groups. Guerin and Guerin (2002) maintain that a distinction can be made between Bowen theory and Bowenian therapy. Bowen theory, in this view, is the "orthodox" or "by the book" version of BFST that follows closely to the original work of Bowen (Bowen, 1978; Kerr & Bowen, 1988). Bowenian therapy is based in Bowen's theory but is a broadened and modified version of BFST. This chapter will touch on both the orthodox and the Bowenian therapy approaches.

BFST emphasizes the importance of personal identity and relationships. It is therefore considered to be universally applicable if the counselor is sensitive to differences in how these constructs manifest across diverse cultures and individuals. However, feminists and others have offered criticisms of the approach on the basis of ethnic/cultural issues. These commentaries are briefly discussed in a subsequent section on adapting the theory.

The big headache in learning to use family systems theory is to learn to think in *systems* rather than in individual mode. Here's an example. Picture a mobile with little stars, moons, asteroids, and assorted other celestial bodies of your choice on it. What's important is that all of these objects are connected by an overarching structure, so that if you bother one aspect of the system, such as a moon, the others will respond, too. Families, according to systems theorists, are like this: all connected. However, it is sometimes difficult for beginning (and even more advanced) therapists to understand this perspective—they want to see the moons as following the stars, or the sun as bullying the asteroids. Suppose you witness a fight between your friends Suzie and Tom—Suzie starts throwing things at Tom. You might be tempted to see Suzie's behavior as the result of Tom's criticism, but ask yourself what was going on before and after the criticism, and in the interpersonal situations of Tom and Suzie about the same time? Another way of explaining a systemic view is to consider the notion of *circular causality*, which basically says that where you look in a given chain of events determines your perception of the "cause" of an event. However, events preceding and following any given event also are related to the way the sequence plays out.

Before going on to BFST in particular, it may be helpful to very briefly review some other systems constructs. First, as illustrated above, systems theorists emphasize the connections between family members. Events in systems do not happen in isolation: what affects one element in the system can affect all the others, too. For this reason, when families present with a member who is *the problem*, family systems therapists call that person the *identified patient*. If you accept the notion of family as system, then the existence of problems purely within an individual is not possible. Everyone else is involved in some way and so the "patient," if one chooses to use that word (and most systems therapists would not), is the family, not the person the family offers as the problem. If you think about the other counseling theories you have studied, you will find in most of these, the client *has* a problem, rather than being a part of the problem.

In the early history of family systems theory, the notion of homeostasis, or the tendency of family systems to preserve themselves in their current forms, was emphasized. This stance generated the often-useful observation that if a member changes her behavior in isolation and then goes back into the system, the system will demand that she return to the "old" behavior. However, if you overemphasize homeostasis, you risk overlooking the natural flexibility and potential for growth that families bring to therapy. A rigid belief in family resistance is probably outdated at this point, but a healthy respect for the power of the system is not.

PRINCIPLES IN PRACTICE

Bowen theory begins with the notion that humans are pulled by two conflicting, biologically rooted forces: togetherness and individuality. The way in which individuals manage these two forces is termed *differentiation of self*. This term is most often used to describe a quality of individuals (as in an individual's level of differentiation of self from the family of origin), but it can also describe a family (as in well-differentiated family system). Bowen theory also emphasizes the importance of the *triangle*, a construct that is widely recognized by family therapists as important in family functioning. Basically, a triangle is when two people in a relationship pull in a third to manage conflict or anxiety. The third person either becomes the special confidant of one of the original dyad (is "in" and the other person is on the "outs"), or can get caught in the middle. In either form of the triangle, the original duo is not managing their affairs and the new person is likely to feel stressed. BFST takes a *multigenerational* perspective on family processes—levels of differentiation and patterns of interaction are thought to be transmitted through early learning within the family unit. These three constructs, differentiation, triangles, and multigenerational transmission, are the ones that are most important for you to understand if you are going to be a family systems therapist.

1. *Differentiation.* Probably the key construct in BFST is *differentiation*. From this perspective, we are studying the individual's presentation to determine how well they balance the pulls of relationships and the need for individuality. People fall on a range of differentiation of self, from low to high, and you can observe differentiation in the balance of energy devoted to relationships with that devoted to individualistic concerns. Another way of conceptualizing differentiation is the person's ability to separate emotional and intellectual functioning (Papero, 1990).

   In discussing differentiation, Bowenians like to talk about the person's sense of self in relation to others; people with little sense of self tend to be swayed easily by others and seem to have few opinions or thoughts of their own. In contrast, someone with a solid sense of self is able to be herself in relation to others and is comfortable allowing others to be themselves, too. In interaction with the all-important family of origin, the individual must stay emotionally connected, yet maintain a sense of self in these interactions such that her behaviors are self-determined rather than emotionally based reactions to the family's pulls. Each family has its own emotional system (that is more or less differentiated) that dictates how members are to relate to one another and what happens if individuals don't follow the prescribed rules. This system is passed on across generations through lessons taught early in life. The individual's level of differentiation is thought to be set early in life and is relatively difficult to change (Papero, 1990).

   A key to understanding differentiation is *anxiety*. From its early origins in the mother-child relationship, anxiety is a significant influence on how we negotiate relationships. We don't like anxiety in ourselves or in important others. Individuals who are low in differentiation are most reactive to anxiety. They have difficulty sorting out emotions and thinking in situations in which there is a lot of anxiety either in an important other or in an important relationship. They tend to either lose themselves in the relationship by fusing with the other and appearing to have no sense of self, or they cut off emotionally to avoid the unpleasant experience. As a Bowenian therapist, you should be alert for either of these two patterns in deciding what is going on with your clients. For example, consider the anxious 10-year-old boy who wants to do everything his mother does, including shopping for clothes, going to lunch, drinking diet soda, and going to the health club. On the other end of the continuum, you might observe that the family you are seeing fails to bring one member to the session ("she just refused to come and she doesn't have much to do with us").

Individuals high in differentiation of self are able to maintain a solid sense of who they are as they relate with others even in situations with fairly high levels of stress and anxiety. They are able to be objective in their relationships with others, making decisions based upon intellect or reason rather than on the basis of emotional reactions. Relating objectively to others, however, does not mean that feelings are not a part of important relationships—indeed, a well-differentiated person has a strong enough sense of self to be emotionally involved with important others while maintaining a sense of who they are in the relationships. Another important part of differentiation is allowing others to be who they are; insisting on conformity from others is a sure sign of a shaky self.

Individuals lower in differentiation seem to be less securely based in their interactions—pushed and pulled by the forces of the family's emotional system. The term *fusion* is used to describe the process of being "stuck to" other family members and is virtually synonymous with low differentiation. In fusing with the family or a particular family member, an individual is giving up autonomy because he fears that establishing a separate self will result in the loss of love or approval. Alternatively, an individual can deal with the stress of relationship pulls through psychologically or physically distancing from the relationships, a process called *emotional cutoff* or *reactive distancing*. Although emotional distancing is a natural response and can be temporarily helpful if the individual chooses deliberately and objectively to do so, the emotionally reactive (automatic pilot) form can be dysfunctional. Think about the person you know who refuses to engage in arguments or even discussions of differences with his father—that person is likely to be in emotional cutoff. Cutting off, according to BFST, does not solve the person's problems, because the dynamics of the relationships from which one distances seep into other relationships in the person's life. Cutting off becomes a habitual way of dealing with relationship strife. Or, these newer relationships can become almost too important to the individual. She then focuses heavily upon them, increasing her risk and the pressure on the other individuals. The person fuses with her new "family" and these relationships can then become emotionally tense and problematic.

2. *Multigenerational transmission.* Bowen believed that families had a characteristic level of differentiation of self that is inherited from the parents' families, a process he called *multigenerational transmission*. Further, people are thought to be attracted to others who are of similar level of differentiation of self. They marry and have children. The average level of differentiation of the children is probably about the same as the parents', although they will vary somewhat. One child may be higher in differentiation and will seek a partner with approximately the same level of differentiation. Similarly, the child with a lower level of differentiation will seek a similar partner. This mate-matching process is thought to explain how families can change somewhat in differentiation over generations. However, it is important to note that Bowen thought

that the individual's level of differentiation was established very early in life and was relatively resistant to change. Although not technically considered multigenerational transmission, BFST theorists also emphasize that relationship themes and dynamics can be passed down from generation to generation. In working with families, then, you might look for patterns such as idealizing men, encouraging independence in young women, or dealing with relationship issues by fusing or triangling.

3. *Triangle.* In Bowen's view, the *triangle* is the most stable basic unit of interaction. Life is full of triangles. A triangle typically involves two people who are "in" and a third who is "out" or caught in the middle. A common triangle can be seen when a child gets caught between her two parents, or is a special confidant of one. Triangles become most visible when moderate anxiety is present in a system. Two person relationships (dyads) are usually functional when times are calm, but inevitably, anxiety intrudes upon them and a third person is pulled into the relationship to redistribute the anxiety. Triangles are thought to contain or bind anxiety by redistributing it through the extra relationship bonds established with the third person. In this way, triangling decreases the disruption in the original dyad, but the problem is that they generally keep the difficulties in the original two-person relationship from being resolved. Also, the third person who is pulled into the triangle can suffer as a result of the emotional stress resulting from either taking sides or feeling caught in the middle. You should remember, however, that triangles, according to Bowen theory, are natural occurrences but are usually dysfunctional when they last over time (i.e., are chronic ways of relating). Individuals or families with lower levels of differentiation are thought to triangulate more often and more easily in comparison to those with higher levels of differentiation. Also, keep in mind that any family may have multiple triangles operating at any one time because there are multiple possibilities for combinations of members. Also, don't forget that triangles can involve members from other generations (grandparents, aunts, uncles) or individuals who are technically not members of the family system (for instance, when a spouse has an extramarital affair).

KEYS TO CONCEPTUALIZATION

To use BFST, we look mostly for *how* individuals in a family (or couple, or other significant group) interact with one another, especially when times are tough. Like most systems theorists/therapists, BFST counselors are more interested in describing the *ways* in which a family relates, or the family interpersonal process, than they are in the *whys* of an event within the system. As you begin to work with your clients, some questions you might ask yourself are the following:

1. Do individuals seem to react to one another without thinking?
2. Who confides in whom? Who doesn't talk to whom? Who fights with whom?
3. What happens when disagreement surfaces in the family (if it does at all)?
4. Is there a lot of emotion in the family? If so, in which relationships does it show the most? In which the least?

On another level, looking for two basic things helps in understanding a client's presentation: levels of differentiation and triangling. Individuals' levels of differentiation are observed in two ways: (1) how they interact with others in their significant relationships and (2) when an individual client is seen, through his descriptions of their relationships and verbal and nonverbal cues present as they describe these. The most obvious evidence is found in emotion displayed (anxiety, anger) in these relationships. However, a noted absence of emotion can suggest emotional cutoff. Patterns of communication, again, are very important. For example, a recent client of mine reported not talking much to his sister, except upon a superficial level. In contrast, his mother knew all about his love life and he never spoke of these things with his father. I hypothesized that he was cut off from his sister and triangled with his mother and father. Although this client displayed a relatively high differentiation of self, some of this behavior was reactive, rather than objective ("my sister and I have nothing in common—she is dull and stuck in her routine" and "I am so different from my father").

Psychological dysfunction develops when stress increases in or around the family. Whether individuals become symptomatic depends primarily upon their levels of differentiation of self. Individuals with relatively higher levels of differentiation are more adaptive in the face of stress, have better coping strategies, and are able to confront and work on problems in productive ways. In contrast, those with lower levels of differentiation are more likely to develop dysfunction because they are less able to cope with the stress and the resulting increases in family/relationship tension. If you see a really calm family come to therapy, you could consider at least these hypotheses: (1) the family is under little stress at present; (2) everyone is emotionally cut off; (3) the family is relatively differentiated and therefore functional. However, how often do we see really calm families in therapy? Not often.

As a Bowenian therapist, you should be looking for four basic patterns of dysfunction (Bowen Center for the Study of the Family, 2000–2004). These are *marital conflict, dysfunction in one spouse, impairment in one or more children, and emotional distance.* It is important to remember that triangles form under stressful conditions and that the problems listed (for example, dysfunction in children) can be the result of triangulation. In fact, some Bowenians suggest that all presenting problems should be conceptualized in terms of triangulation (Carter & McGoldrick, 2005). When a therapist observes an active triangle, it is usually doing one of three things: "stabilizing an unstable dyad, displacing dyadic conflict, or avoiding intimacy in a dyad" (Guerin, Fogarty, Fay, & Kautto, 1996, p. 57).

The most common triangles are between parents and a child (whether married or divorced) or between a parent, a member of another generation (such as the parent's parent or in-laws), and a child. When working with an adult client, Kerr (1984) contended that the most important triangle is the one with her parents or any triangle involving the mother. I recall a client who was the primary caretaker for her mother and had a terrible relationship with her husband. I saw a triangle immediately.

Another commonly identified triangle is the parents who are overfocused on a child (as a way of avoiding their own conflicts) who then displays symptoms as a result of the pressure. From the BFST perspective, triangles can also involve nonhuman entities, such as work or money (Carter & McGoldrick, 2005). For example, a typical (and stereotypic) triangle is seen in the conflicted couple. Often, one member of the couple is immersed in work to the detriment of the relationship with the partner. One very hot triangle is seen in extramarital affairs. Even if the affair has physically ended, the paramour can still be very present in the couple's relationship.

INTERVENTIONS AND THERAPEUTIC PROCESS

Traditional or orthodox BFST therapy is a long-term approach, for it requires clients to study, understand, and change their patterns of behavior in the family of origin. Once change is initiated, clients then are tested—they must deal with the reaction of the family, whose typical message is "change back." Although BFST is a family systems theory, therapists in this approach often work with only one member of the system, the one with the highest level of functioning. The reasoning here is that the most well-differentiated person is the one most likely to be able to change his or her behavior and withstand the system's reaction to the change.

The classic intervention in BFST is the *family journey*. Bowen thought that it was critically important for the client to immerse herself in the original family system (and extended family system where appropriate). When members are living, the client can actually visit, write letters to (or these days, email), or telephone family members. Clients can "connect" with members who are deceased through genealogical research and consulting with individuals who knew the target individual. The idea is for the client to understand the workings of his family system through the years, so that the patterns passed along and likely replicated in his current situation are recognized, understood, and therefore amenable to change.

Interventions in classic BFST are more general than those found in many other theoretical systems. Bowen himself identified few specific techniques or interventions; he emphasized theory over strategy. The second- and third-generation Bowenians are a little more technique-focused, so the discussion below draws from both sources (major resources for these are listed at the end of the chapter).

Contemporary BFST therapists may stick to the classic version, or modify it somewhat by combining interventions that seem more immediate to clients. A tension in BFST can arise between attending to the presenting problem and focus on the extended family system. In many cases, it is important to devote significant time to the presenting problem because the client is in crisis and unable to focus on family of origin work. In this case, the therapist would encourage calm, objective problem-solving around the presenting problem. Another issue is that it is sometimes difficult for clients to see the relevance of family of origin work when there is a big, fat problem staring them in the face in the immediate family. You probably should be prepared for your clients to ask "What is the relevance of all of this family history stuff?" When this happens, the wise therapist will pay attention to these feelings and have a ready answer (or be willing to shift gears rather rapidly).

One of the most important interventions in BFST is also a method of assessment, the *genogram*. The genogram is something like a family tree drawing that helps clients get a larger perspective on themselves and their families. All family members are represented on the genogram and it is typical for three generations to be included. Important nonfamily members are often included, too. A sample genogram is shown in Figure 13.1.

FIGURE 13.1 Sample genogram of Derril and three generations of his family

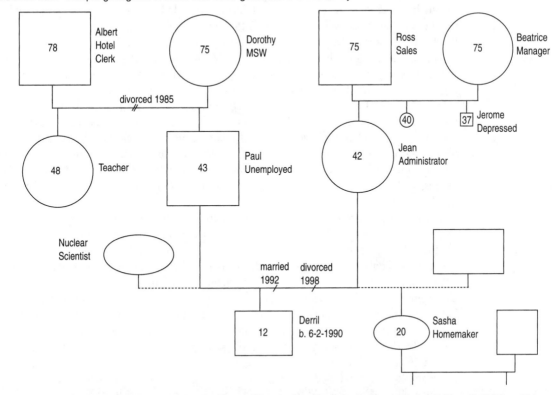

Source: Murdock, Nancy L., *Theories of Counseling and Psychotherapy: A Case Approach,* 1st Edition, © 2004, p. 394. Reprinted by permission of Pearson Education, Inc., Upper Saddle River, NJ.

Genograms contain more than just a who's who of the family. To fully understand a client from the BFST perspective, the genogram should include important events in the family history, family themes, myths, rules, and roles. Relationships among members can be depicted through the use of specialized notation, as can be seen in Figure 13.1. A comprehensive and interesting guide to constructing genograms can be found in McGoldrick, Gerson, & Shellenberger (1999).

The process of BFST typically begins with an exploration of the presenting problem, but very quickly, the BFST therapist moves into constructing a genogram. Generally, you begin the construction of the genogram in the first session. I often warn my clients that I will be scribbling while they talk to me and that essentially, I am drawing a family tree so that I can keep up with all the players in their drama. Therapists often draw genograms on large flip-charts or white boards so that the genogram can be easily seen by the client(s). A copy of the genogram is saved; it is used in subsequent sessions and updated as necessary.

BFST therapists, as noted earlier, are interested in understanding the *how* of a family's communication. *Process questioning* is the primary way in which this information is brought out in a therapy session. These questions focus on the process of communication in the family—how the family talks to each other. Above I identified a few examples of these and here are some more: When you get upset, who do you talk to? Who is your closest ally in the family? Suzie, how do you know when dad is upset? What do you do when you notice that he is? What happens in the family when dad gets upset? Who responds first? Who is more difficult to talk to, your brother or your sister? Why?

Learn to observe family interactions and to control emotional reactions. The therapist in BFST helps the client to sift through the process of interaction in her family, identifying signs of triangulation. One of the surest signs of triangulation is talking to one person about a third person. For instance, mom talks to her mother about her problems with her husband. Gradually, clients will learn how to objectively observe the relationships in their families and instead of responding in the ways of the past (probably in an emotionally reactive way), they learn to put emotional reactions on hold and respond more thoughtfully. In this process, the client learns to take an "I-position"— expressing her feelings and thoughts about an issue but also respecting those of other family members.

Detriangling is another very basic technique in BFST. In fact, Bowen calls it "an absolute necessity" (1978, p. 542). One way in which detriangling is accomplished is seen in traditional BFST. The therapist teaches clients about triangles and their operation and then encourages clients to put this knowledge to use in their own families of origin. To detriangle, the client first needs to identify a moderately hot emotional issue within the family. The client's job is to then be in consistent and neutral contact with two other family members about the issue. Taking sides with either family member is not allowed, nor is defending one's position. Objectivity is key. Silence is not an option, either, because it is likely to be seen by the others as something, and the something can't be predicted or controlled.

Guerin et al. (1996) discuss many ways of working with triangles in families; their work is a example of an expanded approach to BFST. I'll give one example here—that of the classic "overinvolved" with child mother and "distant" father. Basically, the goal is to encourage the mother to distance and to get the father more engaged with the child. Although at first relieved of the need to focus on the child, the mother begins to feel abandoned or depressed. The father is at a loss about how to deal with the child and turns to the mother for support or approval. The mother becomes impatient at the father's lack of progress. You can just feel the emotionality arising at this juncture—this unbalancing has the effect of allowing the conflict between the parents to emerge. Another interesting discussion in Guerin et al.'s work is determining when a three-person system is a triangle and when it is not (pp. 46–50).

Bowen noted that the therapist's job in therapy was to learn how to remain calm in the face of triangles presented in families. Basically, the therapist is to stay in contact with both members of the triangle, remain neutral, and help the members see the emotional process in their relationship. For this reason, Bowen insisted that therapists needed to complete their own family journeys in order to increase their ability to work calmly and objectively in the charged environment of psychotherapy.

Once patterns of interaction have been defined through process questioning, *relationship experiments* can be devised that offer the opportunity to try out new ways of relating (Guerin & Guerin, 2002). Often these tasks involve detriangling or disrupting pursuit-distancing patterns. For example, the therapist might instruct a couple to spend time together without discussing any "hot" issues. Because the pursuing pattern often involves one partner's insistence on talking about the couple's difficulties, the assignment would interrupt this pattern.

SHORT- AND LONG-TERM GOALS

BFST counseling has one major goal—increasing the differentiation of self in the family of origin. To accomplish this objective, clients need to establish one-on-one (or person-to-person) relationships with the members of their immediate and extended families. With the help of the therapist, clients are to identify the triangles in which they participate and change how they behave in these situations. Patterns of interaction or values passed down through generations are important to study and understand. Note that the key here is changing how one interacts with the family of origin. It is not good enough to have insight into behaviors and patterns; the client must understand how they influence his current behavior and then change how he reacts. Therapeutic tasks include observing typical patterns of interaction, understanding one's participation in triangles, and monitoring emotional reactions, but not acting on the these feelings. Behavior is to be based on objective appraisal of the situation and the client's own thoughts about it. The client works to stay in contact with the family in a meaningful way but her behavior is not dictated by the family's emotional system. Learning to take an I-position in relation to others is a very important sign of client improvement.

A short-term goal in BFST may take the form of working to reduce chaos in the family by intervening around the presenting problem. In doing so, the therapist may help reduce stress on the system from outside or anxiety within the system. For example, a distressed couple with an acting-out eight-year-old could be given the task of having one partner observe while the other intervenes with the child. Afterward, each member of the couple writes an evaluation of the intervention using *I,* not *you* language. The partner intervening probably becomes more aware of how she is intervening (and perhaps less emotional while doing so), the partner observing becomes appreciative of the struggles of his partner, and who knows? The child might change a little, too.

USING THE RELATIONSHIP

The relationship in BFST is conceptualized a little differently than in many other theoretical systems. Primarily, the BFST therapist is a *coach*. Think about great coaches—they are astute observers of the game, are geniuses at strategy, and work to get the best performance out of their players. The players do all the work and sometimes the coach is even up in the press box looking at the overall picture of the game rather than on the field. If you are a Bowenian therapist, you must not be afraid to emotionally support your clients, and even to give advice.

Using this approach, the therapist attempts to establish a warm and respectful relationship with the client while at the same time avoiding being snared into the client's relationship dynamics. Remember, the therapist-coach must remain objective and nonreactive in the face of clients' emotional displays. The therapist directs the client's attention to how she relates to her own family and tries to keep the relationship in therapy reality-based and objective. When working with family units, the therapist must deal objectively with all members of the family in a calm, considered way. All family members are encouraged to give their opinions and the use of I language is the rule.

In classic BFST, the therapist does not deal with in-session dynamics at all, instead focusing on what happens in the family system of the client. The worst thing a BFST therapist can do is get triangled into the family in some way. As I noted above, staying out of triangles requires objectivity. However, do not equate objectivity with total neutrality (Guerin et al., 1996). When counselors do take a position on issues (as they should, at times), the intervention (regardless with whom in the client's system it might agree) must be determined based upon the therapist's knowledge about what works in families. Sometimes a therapist must side with one person in a triangle, temporarily, to get clients to change their behaviors. For example, when one client is overfunctioning (that is, taking care of everything for a couple or family), the therapist will likely tell that client to selectively stop doing so much for the unit and to think of some ways to do something for himself. The clients may then be asked to discuss what will happen when the overfunctioner changes his behavior and what the other partner will do in response to this new situation.

ADAPTING THE APPROACH

Experts on ethnic/cultural diversity have maintained that BFST can be of disservice to individuals from cultures other than the white, European American varieties. In this view, the notion of differentiating from the family of origin (and extended family) is counter to the norms of many cultures. For example, encouraging a client from a Latino family to differentiate might be seen as creating difficulties because it is contrary to the tradition of connection among members found in Hispanic/Latino cultures.

Some have argued that differentiation is a biased construct in that high differentiation appears to embody characteristics stereotypically associated with masculinity. Low differentiation, associated with emotionality, seems to match stereotypes about women. The goal of BFST is differentiation of self, so therefore, in this view, the theory risks valuing male behavior over female. Bowenians reply that differentiation is always construed in relation to others and that the theory emphasizes the ability to have meaningful intimate relationships with important others, which cannot be achieved if one is fused or distanced from them (McGoldrick, Anderson, & Walsh, 1989). Balancing separateness and connectedness is achieved in the individual's context. These same arguments would probably apply to concerns of culture/ethnicity as well.

Bowen did not write a lot about cultural norms, so a potential problem with BFST is the lack of attention to social processes that dictate that women and minorities relate in passive or submissive ways. The active, self-determined assertive behavior associated with differentiation is discouraged by societal norms for the behavior of women and other diverse individuals. Girls and women are trained to put the need of others first and their own second. Deferring to whites is the ordained role for people of color, and individuals who are gay, lesbian, bisexual, or transsexual are told to hide who they are (Carter & McGoldrick, 2005). The wise BFST therapist recognizes these oppressions and tries to help the client recognize them as well. In fact, becoming aware of these societal forces and reacting objectively is a part of the process of increasing differentiation.

FINDING YOUR NICHE

If you are considering an approach based in BFST, you should first note the two general approaches to the orientation described in the beginning of this chapter, the classic Bowen approach or the Bowenian one. The Bowen approach is based more heavily on family of origin work as the ultimate solution to presenting issues. The Bowenian approach is a bit broader in perspective, but it also can include the classic work as well.

Individuals considering a BFST orientation should be aware that it is considered very important to do extensive work on your own family of origin to be a good therapist. Indeed, one of the most powerful references in this approach is Bowen's description of his own work, first presented anonymously and then printed with authorship (Bowen, 1978). You should be willing to explore the operation of emotionality and triangling in your own family, and to work toward relating to others in an objective I-position way.

This approach can be quite structured, requiring a lot of directive behavior from the therapist, including asking a lot of questions of the client. In fact, most family systems approaches require the counselor to "take charge" in ways that some more individually focused approaches do not. I am fond of telling my students that being a family systems counselor is like being a ringmaster in a circus at times; families come to you knowing each other and their rules, and sometimes to the outsider-therapist, things look more than a little chaotic in sessions. Being able to objectively pull yourself out of the ring when necessary is very helpful and if you can get the bird's-eye view from the trapeze you will do even better because then you can more easily see the system in operation.

PROCESS AND CASE SUGGESTIONS

1. *Elena.* Elena presents an interesting and complicated picture that involves cultural and gender issues. Her family has experienced the trauma of her mother's illness just as Elena is on the brink of becoming more independent. An extreme BFST position might be that mother's illness is a way of keeping Elena at home (and involved in the primary triangle). Understanding Elena's presentation from the perspective of BFST was fascinating because it involved explaining several interlocking triangles that I see as critical to the formation of her present symptoms. Using the construct of differentiation of self from the family of origin in this traditional Mexican family was a challenge.

2. *Jane.* Jane presents the challenge of explaining, using a theoretical lens, what seem to be physiological symptoms with no physical basis. Bowen's ideas about physical symptoms are fascinating—he saw physical illness as arising from the same dynamics as the psychological, namely the translation of relationship anxiety as a method of binding it. In Jane's case we see hints of multiple forms of maladaptive coping from the BFST perspective—emotional distancing, impairment in a child, and dysfunction in a spouse. However, Jane is calm, smiling, and reports that her life is good.

3. *Theo.* One of the most difficult client issues to work with, in my opinion, is anger that the client believes to be uncontrollable. That Theo is African American adds to the complexity of the case and spiritual issues appear to be involved as well.

SUMMARY AND SUGGESTED READINGS

The central assumption of BFST is that our family experience is critical to our psychological and physical functioning. Individuals inherit a level of differentiation of self from their families, and this level determines how adaptive they are in the face of stress, how much relationship anxiety they can tolerate, and mechanisms they will typically use to cope with stress. Differentiation is described as the degree to which the individual can balance the pulls of individuality and togetherness that are inherent in the human condition. Differentiation can also be seen in the individual's ability to respond to adversity using the cognitive rather than the emotional system.

BFST counseling involves helping clients to understand their relationship systems and the operation of triangles within them. Genograms are used to illustrate the client's system—the simple act of putting relationships on paper can help clients become more objective about their relationship worlds. Therapists rely heavily on process intervention to help clients describe their relationship systems and personal stances in objective ways. Although objectivity is important in BFST, it does not involve the sacrifice of emotion or intimate relationships with others. In fact, the goal is to help the clients differentiate so that they can participate in important relationships in meaningful, satisfying ways.

Becoming a BFST therapist involves examining your own family of origin dynamics. The process of learning about your family helps one to learn how to use BFST theory in practice. Working with more experienced BFST therapists in supervision/consultation is also important in solidifying your understanding of this approach and how your particular relationship style plays into the relationships with your clients.

Some important readings in BFST are the following:

Bowen, M. (1978). *Family therapy in clinical practice*. New York: Jason Aronson.
Guerin, K., Fogarty, T., Fay, L., & Kautto, J. G. (1996). *Working with relationship triangles: The one-two-three of psychotherapy*. New York: Guilford Press.
Kerr, M. E., & Bowen, M. (1988). *Family evaluation: An approach based on Bowen theory*. New York: Norton.
McGoldrick, M., Gerson, R., & Schellenberger, S. (1999). *Genograms: Assessment and intervention,* 2nd ed., New York: Norton.

REFERENCES

Bowen Center for the Study of the Family (2000–2004). Nuclear family emotional system. Retrieved March 8, 2005, from www.thebowencenter.org
Bowen, M. (1978). Family therapy in clinical practice. New York: Jason Aronson.

Carter, B., & McGoldrick, M. (2005). Coaching at various stages of the life cycle. In B. Carter & M. McGoldrick (Eds.) *The expanded family life cycle* (3rd ed.; pp. 436–454). New York: Allyn & Bacon.

Guerin, K., Fogarty, T., Fay, L., & Kautto, J. G. (1996). *Working with relationship triangles: The one-two-three of psychotherapy.* New York: Guilford Press.

Guerin, K. & Guerin, P. (2002). Bowenian family therapy. In J. Carlson & D. Kjos (Eds.) *Theories and strategies of family therapy* (pp. 126–157). Boston, MA: Allyn & Bacon.

Kerr, M. E. (1984). Theoretical base for differentiation of self in one's family of origin. *The Clinical Supervisor, 2(2),* 3–36.

Kerr, M. E. & Bowen, M. (1988). *Family evaluation: an approach based on Bowen theory.* New York: Norton.

Lerner, H. G. (1988). Is family systems theory really systemic? A feminist communication. In L. Braverman (Ed.) *A guide to feminist family therapy* (pp. 47–63). New York: Harrington Park Press.

McGoldrick, M., Anderson, C., & Walsh, F. (1989). Women in families and family therapy. In M. McGoldrick, C. Anderson, & F. Walsh (Eds.), *Women in families: A framework for family therapy* (pp. 3–15). New York: Norton.

McGoldrick, M., Gerson, R., & Shellenberger, S. (1999). *Genograms in family assessment* (2nd ed.). New York: Norton.

Papero, D. V. (1990). *Bowen family systems theory.* Boston, MA: Allyn & Bacon.

Chapter 14

Feminist Counseling

Lucia A. Gilbert and Jill Rader

Chapter Outline

Bridging the Theory-to-Practice Gap

Principles in Practice

Keys to Conceptualization

Interventions and Therapeutic Process

Short- and Long-Term Goals

Using the Relationship

Adapting the Approach

Finding Your Niche

Process and Case Suggestions

Summary and Suggested Readings

BRIDGING THE THEORY-TO-PRACTICE GAP

Feminist theories are relatively new to counseling practice and grew out of critiques of women's treatment within the mental health system. Such critiques coincided with the 1970s' feminist movement in the United States. Advocates for women's health raised objections to sexism in theories regarding diagnosis and treatment. Early feminist counseling efforts focused on valuing women's experiences, attention to their political realities, and advocacy for their unique issues within a patriarchal system that typically ignored or pathologized issues that women brought to counseling. For example, early feminist theories guiding counseling stressed the importance of creating safe therapeutic spaces in which women could productively discuss issues of sexism, discrimination, rape, and domestic violence. Current approaches and thinking have built upon these efforts, while also focusing on the harmful effects of societal power abuses on *all* (not just women) clients, abuses that range from racism to homophobia to the cultural shaming of men who do not adhere to masculine stereotypes.

Feminist theories thus provide an important, overarching theoretical framework for all approaches to counseling. The crucial link between feminist theory and counseling practice is the consideration of social context. Carolyn Sherif was among the first of prominent psychologists who questioned the validity of a psychological science that overlooks the reality that individuals develop in a social and cultural context. This science has stripped individuals of their cultural backgrounds, personal histories, and gender, factors that have a profound impact on how they develop, how they are viewed and treated by others, and how they respond to particular situations.

Feminist counselors shift the focus of the therapy away from the client's intrapsychic life to the context of the client's life. That is, we focus on the actual problems and difficulties experienced by clients and how societal realities, such as women's social inequality, may contribute to their problems. This change in focus has challenged the medicalization of women's problems, particularly the treatment of women's depression. As Phyllis Chesler (1972) documented in her groundbreaking book, *Women and Madness,* increasing numbers of women in the 1950s and 1960s were medicated for depression and anxiety because it was assumed that there could be no "external" reason for their conditions. The origin of their difficulties was presumed to be biological or physiological in nature and not societal. The goals of treatment at that time included neither helping women recognize the real-world reasons for their distress (for example, many women were denied educational, athletic, and career opportunities solely on the basis of their biological sex and regardless of their interests, talents, and abilities), nor questioning the oppression they felt in their lives.

Feminist theorists have also reframed the nature and goals of the counseling relationship. Rather than viewing the counselor as an expert on the needs of the client, we emphasize the importance of a relationship based on mutuality; we therefore grant the client autonomy and authority to the greatest extent possible. Clients are encouraged to ask questions of counselors before entering into treatment and to trust their *own* assessment of the usefulness of treatment. Rather than assuming that any counselor is going to be helpful and/or an appropriate match, clients are encouraged to gather information about the depth of a counselor's experience with particular populations and issues pertinent to the client. For example, a client might want to ask questions about a counselor's experience working with dual-earner families, lesbian and gay couples, or adolescents. Or a client might be seeking specific help with such issues as sexual abuse, grief, or marital difficulties, and might inquire about a counselor's training in these areas.

If feminist counseling just sounds like "good therapy," as theorist Laura Brown has pointed out, then you have some indication of how much feminist theory has changed the way that counseling is practiced in the United States. Feminist counselors have been nothing less than revolutionary in their innovations of counseling theory and practice. Particularly important among these innovations are power-sharing with clients, cultural critiques of counseling practice including what constitutes good assessment, and the validation of women and their normative experiences. We have challenged long-held patriarchal views that "good" clients are those who defer to professional experts and who maintain a passive role in their own treatment. We also have challenged theories that marginalized or pathologized women, and research paradigms that omitted women's experiences.

Feminist critiques of traditional theories and practices have therefore brought about significant theoretical and professional advances in counseling practice. In addition, the focus on context, and understanding context, has broadened and shifted notions of gender, race, ethnicity, and sexuality from static, biologically located and determined concepts to gender, race, ethnicity, and sexuality as fluid and socially located and constructed concepts. In the case of gender, specifically, theorists have recognized that women and men are not "born" with gender (the static, categorical perspective); rather, they *become* women and men within the context of their culture (the fluid, socially located perspective). Similarly, research has increasingly made clear that race and ethnicity are dimensions, not static categories, of human experience, and that their psychological meanings come from an individual's social and cultural locations. Feminist counseling is grounded in this body of research, and we, as feminist counselors, stay abreast of evolving views around gender, race, and ethnicity.

To summarize, the goals and objectives of feminist counseling frame client concerns within their larger sociocultural context and include considerations of gender, race and ethnicity, and sexuality. Instead of "blaming the victim" for those aspects of the culture that contribute to a client's distress, we consider the client within this larger social framework.

PRINCIPLES IN PRACTICE

Feminist counselors combine the principles of feminist therapy with their other theoretical approaches to counseling. A feminist framework integrates well with most other theories of counseling. As feminist counselors, we might use, for example, a cognitive behavioral (CBT) approach to counseling or a gestalt approach. The feminist framework informs these other theories of practice by emphasizing a client's agency and control. For example, a client seeking treatment for a phobia might work with a feminist counselor who employs standard CBT interventions for this problem, such as systematic desensitization; however, the feminist counselor will work collaboratively with the client in establishing treatment goals and in determining the timing and intensity of this treatment.

It is important to recognize that being a feminist does not *necessarily* make one a feminist counselor. Our approach to counseling is specifically informed by a feminist political philosophy, an understanding of gender processes and their reproduction, and a commitment to social change in the world, with the aim of promoting equity and well-being among all peoples. As feminist counselors, we are therefore not just *committed* to feminist ideals, but *educated* with a body of knowledge regarding women's therapeutic issues, societal power dynamics, gender socialization, sex similarities and differences, counseling ethics, and the therapeutic alliance. In particular, feminist counselors are familiar with the theoretical writings and empirical research on the practice of feminist counseling and psychotherapy. Research on feminist counseling has been actively pursued for the past 25 years, and this research has led to some agreement regarding the central principles of feminist counseling and how they are applied in practice.

1. *The personal is political (the importance of sociocultural context).* Sociologist Jessie Bernard has clarified what is meant by this phrase, "The personal is political." She pointed out that changes at the individual level do little if the structures of a society remain unchanged: "So long as the institutional structure of our society favors men, the question arises as to (whether) women, no matter how well prepared psychologically and intellectually, (can) expect to be dealt with on the basis of their merits rather than on the basis of their sex" (Bernard, 1975, pp. 17–18). Sexism is still institutionalized within our culture and thus remains central to the context of women's and men's normative personal development and experience. Feminist approaches consider individuals (the personal) within their social context (the political) and acknowledge societal contributions to women's and men's individual problems.

   An example of "the personal is political" comes from the case of a young single woman who sought counseling to deal with the depression that ensued when she was expected to resign her teaching position because she was pregnant. She was viewed as a negative role model for students because she was pregnant and not legally married. Her status as an unwed mother would have therefore challenged patriarchal, heterosexual rules for parenthood and legitimacy. She lost her job not for personal reasons (she was still an excellent and well-regarded teacher and she loved her work), but for political and societal reasons (pregnant women without husbands do not belong in the classroom).

   Several well-established counseling practices and goals are associated with the principle that the personal is political. These include separating the internal from the external, reframing pathology, and emphasizing societal change rather than "client adjustment."

   Separating the internal from the external refers to counselors working with clients to differentiate between what they have been taught and accepted as socially appropriate behavior (the external) from what they personally consider to be appropriate for themselves (the internal). Thus, counselors encourage clients to evaluate the influence of social roles and norms on their personal experiences and to recognize the relationship between societal factors and psychological factors. Separating out what has been taught and accepted, and becoming clear about one's own sense of self, is central to the process of client empowerment. However, because we, as feminist counselors, value an ethic of relatedness as well as an ethic of empowerment, a client's journey towards self-actualization always occurs within a context of social supports, personal commitments, and ties to others, rather than being seen as a blind and unchecked pursuit of individualism.

A specific counseling example might include the process of working with a new parent struggling with the decision to take a six-month unpaid leave from employment. The issues for a new mother might be guilt related to wanting to continue her work or hesitation at asking a spouse to be more involved in the care-taking; issues for a new father might be fear of what peers and supervisors might think should he choose to be the primary caregiver, along with concern that it would negatively impact his career opportunities, or anxiety about being competent to provide adequate care for a newborn. A feminist counselor avoids making assumptions or predictions about how parents might behave based on their biological sex.

Reframing pathology refers to counselors not blaming clients for thinking, acting, and feeling in ways that are consistent with living in a sexist society but, rather, understanding that they are adapting to those unwritten codes for female and male behavior. The counseling process helps clients come to understand the role of society in shaping all individuals, including themselves. Clients may begin to see certain past and present behaviors as understandable efforts to respond adaptively to oppressive, sexist conditions, including those they may have shame about. Thus, for women, their anger at being psychologically battered in a marriage or abused sexually is framed as an adaptive response to an oppressive situation in which they had little power. For male clients, feelings of failure associated with being physically overpowered by male peers or abused sexually is similarly framed as a realistic response in a situation in which they had little power.

Emphasizing societal change rather than individual adjustment refers to the feminist theoretical belief that healthy functioning cannot be achieved solely through individual changes. As Bernard's earlier quote indicates, societal changes are necessary to bring about social, economic, and political equality for women and men and for other groups within our culture. This need for social change in order to create less gender-biased conditions perhaps most directly pertains to the relationship between the personal and the political. It may take the form of clients suggesting family leave policies to employers, giving teachers feedback about sexist practices in the classroom, or helping sons and daughters to recognize sexist messages in the media. In the process of therapy, clients therefore learn not only to advocate for themselves but also for the empowerment of others. Learning how to advocate for one's needs and well-being is a central feature of most counseling practices, and a feminist approach enriches this personal advocacy by attending to sociopolitical realities. For example, working with a victim of sexual assault is enhanced if clients understand that sexism within the legal/judicial system is neither their fault, nor something they need to internalize. Specifically, understanding our culture's tendency to "blame the victim" would help lessen feelings of shame that may arise following an attack. Minimization of victim shame would further enable survivors of violence to better advocate for themselves within the system, to stand up for their rights, and to demand dignity and respect. In doing so, they alter others' perceptions of them, command greater authority, prompt better treatment, and act as change agents within the system.

2. *Striving to create an egalitarian relationship with clients.* As feminist counselors, we strive toward an egalitarian and nonauthoritarian counselor-client relationship that is based on mutual respect. Moreover, the goals, direction, and pace of feminist counseling are determined in a collaborative process. These processes directly counter aspects of traditional socialization in which women are viewed as the "lesser" sex, are expected to listen to authorities, and to look to others, especially men, to set their life goals. Feminist counseling processes also counter socialization in which men are expected to act independently, to not need help, and to use their power to control, rather than to negotiate, in relationships.

Two therapeutic practices are particularly associated with viewing the counseling relationship as egalitarian. The first is *establishing a therapeutic relationship that the client experiences as empowering and affirming.* The second is the counselors' *continual monitoring of their own biases, distortions, and limitations,* particularly with respect to gender processes.

Power and male privilege are central to situations that perpetuate conventional gender relations. As described earlier, in patriarchy, it was assumed that men had authority and control over women, and that this situation was as it had to be, given the essential "opposite sex" natures of women and men. Both women and men often internalize and act out of these beliefs in their interactions with both sexes, including therapists who have unique power and privilege in relation to their clients.

A crucial issue addressed in feminist approaches to counseling is how we, as counselors, can inadvertently use our authority and position to recreate gender dynamics characteristic of heterosexual identity development, such as empowering men's sexual expression more than women's, working in ways that reinforce male authority over women, pathologizing women's sexuality and sexual concerns, and engaging in erotic relations with clients. Male therapists' sexual exploitation of female clients, for example, remains a serious concern; a substantial portion of sexual misconduct violations continues to involve male psychologists with adult female clients (Gilbert & Rader, 2001).

Counselors recognize their power to facilitate transformation, and accordingly convey their own valuing of the change process to their clients. They are ever-mindful of their influence on clients and the potential power of their privileged position in relation to individuals who seek their help. Finally, clients are not only encouraged to find a therapist with whom they are comfortable, but also to question counselors' assumptions and interpretations.

3. *Valuing women's experiences and perspectives.* As feminist counselors, whether we are working with female or male clients, we work with clients in ways that value women's contributions to society and their emerging characteristics and roles. Historically, women have been less valued than men in our society and were primarily considered in relation to men. Rarely was it asked, "What are women for themselves?" Rather, the healthy, well-adjusted woman was expected to live for others, to accommodate her needs to others, and to devote her life to the care of others. Traditionally, women were expected to act in ways that empowered others but not themselves.

This principle of feminist counseling addresses the importance of countering pervasive traditional images that devalue women and limit their life roles, and the effects of these images on both women and men. For example, women are bombarded with messages that connect their value to their attractiveness and ability to please others, yet they are also devalued if they are perceived as being too appearance-focused or compliant. This principle also has important implications for counseling with men. Many men have learned to devalue women's contributions in the home and the work-place. Through counseling, men can come to recognize how they might have been raised to devalue women, including the women they care dearly about—their spouses, daughters, and/or female colleagues and employees. As feminist counselors, we might help a male client to explore his own unconscious ideology about gender, his tendency to make gender-based assumptions about career planning, child-rearing, housecleaning, and so on. Our goal is not to vilify the male experience but to open up the realm of possibilities for living as a man in this culture—for example, to recognize that being male does not necessarily make one more suited to a corporate career over child-rearing, stoicism over vulnerability, or silence over the open expression of emotions.

Feminist counseling practices and goals associated with this principle further include appreciating female-related values such as cooperation and affiliation, valuing women and relationships with women, accepting and liking one's body as a woman, trusting women's perceptions, and giving voice to women's experiences. Particularly crucial in this regard is giving voice to women's experiences of their own sexuality, given societal practices that present women as sexual objects and also given the alarming prevalence of sexual abuse and sexual assault. In short, girls and women in Western culture are consistently and painfully reminded that their bodies are not entirely their own.

In summary, the central aspects of feminist approaches to counseling as reflected in the three main principles just described are as follows:

1. The recognition of female and male oppression based on gender, race, and class
2. The centrality of sociocultural context in understanding individual behavior and reframing pathology
3. The separation of a client's needs and goals (the internal) from the societal constraints and expectations (the external)
4. The emphasis on change both in therapy and in society
5. The view of the counselor-client relationship as egalitarian
6. The ongoing self-examination of values on the part of the therapists
7. Valuing the female perspective and women's empowerment

KEYS TO CONCEPTUALIZATION

Client conceptualization from a feminist theoretical perspective always considers possible links between the concerns individual women and men bring to therapy and the particular features of their lives. A feminist perspective requires that counselors have knowledge of gender and gender processes affecting both women and men and familiarity with the scholarly literature on the psychology of women and gender. A male client's concerns about his unsatisfactory dating relationships, for example, may be associated with his looking to women to provide him with emotional care, a common problematic gender dynamic in heterosexual relationships. A female client's presenting problem such as poor work performance evaluations or low self-confidence may be associated with an employment context in which women's contributions are differentially valued from men's. Counselors need to use knowledge about gender processes to explore with their clients possible connections between their symptoms and the larger context of their lives. They also need to use this knowledge to avoid reproducing gender dynamics in their own counseling. Knowledge about gender processes must include an understanding of the differences between *sex* and *gender*.

Sex (being a woman or a man biologically) distinguishes human individuals. Gender is not simply biological sex, however. A woman or man is not "born" with gender. One *learns* how to become a woman or a man, and that highly complex social psychological process varies across cultures and historical periods. Contrary to conventionally held views, women and men are more similar than they are different; the sexes clearly are not opposites. An important concept to introduce here is the "iron rule." The iron rule says that for any psychological or cognitive variable studied by psychologists, the differences *within* each sex are always greater than the differences *between* the two sexes. That is, there is more difference, say, in engaging in assertive behavior within a group of men and within a group of women, than between the men and women.

Men's and women's cognitive abilities such as math and verbal ability and prosocial skills such as helping behavior and leadership skills are more similar than they are different. Meta-analyses have shown with very conclusive evidence that the gender difference in tested verbal abilities is now negligible, as are the differences in mathematics performance, with the exception, beginning in high school, of problem-solving (Gilbert & Scher, 1999; Hyde, 2005).

Gender pertains to what we assume is true, or will be true, of someone who is born biologically female or male. Thus, gender concerns personal and societal beliefs, stereotypes, and ingrained views about the fundamental nature of women and men. Such views are created and maintained through interpersonal interactions, formal and informal institutional practices, and other complex processes within a societal and cultural environment that considers such practices just and appropriate. That women provide care in relationships, and that love is what women do best and most need from men, is at the heart of patriarchal views of womanhood, as are assumptions of men's entitlement to women's care and to women's bodies.

Central to an understanding of gender is an understanding of power in relationships. Patriarchal power rests on the social meanings given to biological sex differences and to their reproduction as societal discourses and norms regarding what it means to be a woman or a man. This is a crucial point, and one that we believe must be understood by counselors. Common societal discourses include the "male sexual drive discourse," which views men as not responsible for their sexual behavior, and the "female nurturing imperative," which assumes caring for others is primary in all women's lives. These discourses derive from power relations and take many forms that directly influence behavior and outcomes in work settings and personal relations. Such discourses can have a very real and frightening impact when, for example, a woman is sexually assaulted by a man who subscribes to rape myths ("no means yes") or when a man is denied workplace support when he needs to take time off to care for an aging parent or sick child.

As mentioned previously, an understanding of power dynamics also extends to the therapeutic relationship. As feminist counselors, we recognize that we have unique power and privilege in relation to our clients and do not use our authority and position to recreate conventional gender dynamics based on traditional gender roles. Historically, women were positioned differently than men in terms of the power they held in defining their own lives. Conventional socialization practices encouraged women to look to others, especially those considered experts, to make decisions about what was best for them. Examples of how counselors reinforce traditional views of gender in their work with clients might include inappropriately using power and influence in their role as counselor (for example, determining the goals of counseling unilaterally or acting in ways that shame a client) and conceptualizing client's concerns within gender-role constraints and dominant-discourse themes (for example, assuming a female client in a dual-earner family should be the partner who changes work schedules or positions to attend to family and child-rearing needs).

Research findings from studies on the psychology of women and gender are central to counseling practice from a feminist perspective. Counseling practice from this perspective must be guided by the ongoing nonbiased research that illuminates the lives of women and girls. Examples include reframing the human importance of female-related values such as altruism, cooperation, and affiliation, clarifying the meaning of consent to sex, making visible the prevalence and consequences of childhood sexual abuse and domestic violence, and broadening the study of women to include areas such as career development and work-family issues. Scholarship on the psychology of women and gender has been instrumental in making visible a previously hidden form of rape now known as "acquaintance rape" or "date rape" as well as in the reframing of rape from blaming women for what happened to them to viewing men as perpetrators of violence and as responsible for their actions. Similarly, understanding women's occupational work and its relation to their family life has been central to the emerging scholarship on women and gender. Women and men both combining occupational work and family life is quite common and the dual-earner family is the normative family form in the United States. A large body of research indicates that engaging in family and work roles is beneficial for women and men, as reflected in indices of physical health, mental health, and relational health. Research on gender has also helped illuminate important aspects of men's lives such as their experience of trauma and their normal dependency needs and relational qualities.

INTERVENTIONS AND THERAPEUTIC PROCESS

Key to feminist approaches to counseling are the establishment of collaborative working alliances and a vigilance for not reproducing conventional gender dynamics.

We strive to develop a collaborative and nonauthoritarian therapeutic relationship based on mutual respect and on knowledge about the psychology of women and gender processes. The counselor's ability to assist a particular client is dependent upon knowledge and expertise in the areas of the client's concern, knowledge of what brings about lasting therapeutic change, and the ability to practice in accordance with the ethical and legal codes of the profession. We typically provide clients with a rationale for the treatment they receive and a plan for termination. Moreover, we take into account the concepts and background clients bring to therapy.

A key part of the counselor's role is to provide accurate, empathic understanding—to sense the world as seen and experienced by the client. Also central is the counselor's ability to communicate that understanding to the client in a nonjudgmental way, with genuineness and respect for the client's experience. Thus, the counselor is a real person who is collaboratively involved in the helping relationship. This mutual involvement extends to ways the counselor and the client work together in establishing agreed-upon therapeutic expectations and goals.

Essential to effective feminist counseling is the development of an emotionally safe relationship with a counselor who clients believe can provide help and engender their trust. The goals, direction, and pace of the therapy are developed within a collaborative process in which clients are viewed as the experts on their own lives and experiences. The counselor provides new learning experiences, engages clients emotionally, works with clients to enhance self-efficacy, and provides opportunities to practice new learning within a safe relationship.

SHORT- AND LONG-TERM GOALS

Short-term goals include the development of a collaborative relationship, establishing mutually agreed-upon goals, and affirmation of the client's experiences. Feminist counselors offer clients a relationship that emphasizes autonomy and equality. It is critical that a collaborative relationship be established with clients from the beginning of the process, so that clients feel that they have been the architect of their own counseling agenda. By taking an active role in establishing their own short-term goals, clients develop confidence in themselves and in their ability to effectively orchestrate change. Collaboration also facilitates the therapeutic alliance and trust between client and therapist.

As feminist counselors, we accept responsibility for providing clients with information that allows them to make informed decisions about their therapy and we supply them with a contract that outlines our expectations (for example, fees, length of sessions, and relationship boundaries). In addition, we accept responsibility for informing clients of their rights with regard to challenging counselors who practice outside their areas of competence or violate the boundaries of the therapeutic relationship, and informing them as to where the client can file ethical complaints.

Empowering the client is at the heart of counseling from this perspective and is the overarching long-term goal. We work with clients to make knowledgeable decisions in areas of concern and participate in this process by providing them with a broader and more informed contextual lens for framing and making sense of their experiences. The ongoing counseling process of recognizing unhealthy situations, building on strengths, and affirming self-knowledge assists clients in identifying, confronting, and effectively dealing with current issues and future difficulties.

USING THE RELATIONSHIP

As with person-centered therapy (Rogers, 1961), through the process of counseling, clients learn to be the experts on themselves. The process of empowering and affirming clients and seeking to understand the clients' concerns from their perspective begins at the onset of counseling. Within a safe therapeutic environment, clients explore their own self-definitions and needs, with the assistance of the counselor, and set mutually agreed-upon treatment goals. It is our role as counselors to support clients' developing confidence in their own perceptions and judgments. Because the psychotherapeutic relationship is so personal and private, and clients enter the relationship seeking assistance, the counselor takes the responsibility of informing clients about the nature and boundaries of the counseling relationship. The effectiveness of counseling resides in the relationship totally focusing on the needs and growth of the client. Counselors cannot be the personal friend, sexual partner, employer, supervisor, or business partner of their clients. Sexual intimacies with a counselor and other forms of dual relationships are unethical and violate the principles of an effective therapeutic relationship.

ADAPTING THE APPROACH

Most counselors currently practicing in the United States ascribe to an eclectic orientation in which they integrate aspects of various theoretical viewpoints into their practice. And most counselors work with women and men. Those identified with a feminist orientation are no different, often embracing a range of theoretical viewpoints, including cognitive, behavioral, psychodynamic, and humanistic approaches. They work with a wide range of female and male clients. Moreover, both women and men identify themselves as feminist counselors.

Understanding issues with regard to gender, race, and sexuality, however, are central to feminist practice, regardless of the use of other paradigms and whether a counselor is female or male. As feminist counselors, we are sensitive to how such issues affect individuals in their day-to-day living and also how these issues are perpetuated by cultural discourses and by dynamics played out in the therapeutic setting. Particularly crucial is understanding that ethnicity, gender, and sexuality are contextual and socially constructed. Their meanings vary not only across historical time periods but also across nations and regions during the same time period. For example, an out gay male client working in the Bay Area is likely to encounter different issues in the workplace than a closeted gay male client working in a small, midwestern town, and first-generation and third-generation Mexican-American women may experience role strain (for instance, in work and home lives) differently, depending on issues of acculturation, familial obligations, level of education, socioeconomic status, and level of community racism.

Karen Wyche (2001) describes the cultural competence needed for counseling with women of color. One core competence is understanding that the worldviews of women of color are based on multiple identities involving gender, culture, and ethnicity. Culturally skilled psychotherapists are also aware of their own cultural assumptions, biases, stereo-types, and the limitations of their backgrounds in understanding clients' concerns. They monitor their biases so as to not impose their values on their clients, value their clients' definition of their problems, and use culturally relevant solutions that build on their clients' existing strengths. Ruth Fassinger and Beth Richie (1997) describe the competencies important for counseling with lesbian, bisexual, and transgender women and report that: effective counselors have examined their own heterosexist attitudes and their possible homophobia; they understand the social oppression, invisibility, and isolation clients may experience; and they are knowledgeable about the social, political, and legal realities of their clients' lives, including knowledge of community resources that might be available to provide additional support and assistance.

FINDING YOUR NICHE

In thinking about whether to consider this approach for counseling, we suggest you reflect on what would draw you to a feminist counseling approach. Is it your agreement with the basic principles of feminist counseling? Is it your comfort with letting clients be the expert on their lives? Do you envision yourself working to empower clients and involve them more actively in the therapeutic process? Personal explorations of these questions may provide you with important insights about how you view yourself as a counselor and what motivates you to use this perspective in your work with clients.

There are a number of ways to learn more about feminist counseling. As a first step, we recommend that you enroll in courses on women, men, and gender and/or the psychology of women and gender; they would be of critical importance for those wanting to find their niche in feminist counseling. Feminist mentorship and counseling supervision would also be very important. In addition, there are a number of valuable resources for those counselors in training who are interested in integrating a feminist framework: The Society for the Psychology of Women (Division 35) within the American Psychological Association, the Association of Women in Psychology, and the Feminist Therapy Institute are good places to connect with others who are interested in feminist counseling.

PROCESS AND CASE SUGGESTIONS

The cases on the website accurately capture the complexity of individuals who seek counseling and highlight the importance of the counselor's knowledge base. The case of Elena requires an understanding of ethnicity, culture, and female adolescent development within that context; the case of Jane requires knowledge of dual-career family life, women's work experiences, and women's midlife development; and the case of Theo requires knowledge of race and male adolescent development within the context of a racist society and a difficult family situation. Two of the cases also require an understanding of sexuality and gender.

Questions to Ask Yourself as You Conceptualize the Cases

1. What assumptions about women and men might guide your counseling with the client?
2. What assumptions about race and ethnicity might guide your counseling with the client?
3. What body of knowledge would you want to have in working with the client?
4. How might you reproduce gender in the counseling with each client?
5. What contextual factors do you see as more salient in each case?
6. What might interfere with the establishment of a collaborative counseling relationship with each of the clients?
7. How would you know if you were working effectively with the client?
8. Think about the theoretical orientations that currently guide your perceptions of counseling. How might a feminist approach be incorporated?

SUMMARY AND SUGGESTED READINGS

In this chapter, we described feminist approaches to counseling that incorporate contemporary thinking about gender processes within patriarchy and other contextual variables such as race and sexuality. Principles presented in the chapter are *essential* to an understanding of feminist counseling. These principles include an understanding that the personal is political, an attempt to build collaborative relationships with our clients, and a valuing of women's experiences.

Barnett, B. C., & Hyde, J. S. (2001). Women, men, work, and family: An expansionist theory. *American Psychologist, 56,* 781–796.

Bernard, J. (1975). *Women, wives, and mothers.* Chicago, IL: Aldine.

Brooks, G. R., & Good, G. E. (2001). *The new handbook of psychotherapy and counseling with men.* Vol. 1 & 2. San Francisco, CA: Jossey Bass.

Brown, L. (1994). *Subversive dialogues: Theory and feminist therapy.* New York: Basic Books.

Chesler, P. (1972). *Women and madness.* Garden City, NY: Doubleday.

Crawford, M., & Unger, R. (2004). *Women and gender* (Rev. ed.). New York: McGraw-Hill.

Fassinger, R. E., & Richie, B. S. (1997). Sex matters: Gender and sexual orientation in training for multicultural competency. In D. B. Pope-Davis & H. L. K. Coleman (Eds.), *Multicultural counseling competencies: Assessment, education and training, and supervision* (pp. 83–110). Thousand Oaks, CA: Sage.

Gilbert, L. A., & Rader, J. (2001). Counseling and psychotherapy: Gender, race/ethnicity, and sexuality issues. In J. Worell (Ed.), *Encyclopedia of women and gender, volume one.* (pp. 265–277). San Diego, CA: Academic Press.

Gilbert, L. A., & Scher, M. (1999). *Gender and sex in counseling and psychotherapy.* Boston: Allyn & Bacon.

Greene, B. (Ed.). (1997). *Ethnic and cultural diversity among lesbians and gay men.* Thousand Oaks, CA: Sage.

Hare-Mustin, R. T. (1994). Discourses in the mirrored room: A postmodern analysis of therapy. *Family Process, 33,* 19–35.

Hare-Mustin, R.T., & Marecek, J. (1990). *Making a difference: Psychology and the construction of gender.* New Haven, CT: Yale University Press.

Hyde, J. S. (2005). The gender similarities hypotheses. *American Psychologist, 60,* 581–592.

Levant, R. F., & Pollack, W. S. (1995). *A new psychology of men.* New York: Basic Books.

Rogers, C. R. (1961). *On becoming a person.* Boston: Houghton Mifflin.

Westkott, M. (1986). *The feminist legacy of Karen Horney.* New Haven, CT: Yale University Press.

Worell, J., & Remer, P. (2003). *Feminist perspectives in therapy: Empowering diverse women* (2nd ed.). New York: John Wiley.

Wyche, K. F. (2001). Sociocultural issues in counseling women of color. In R. K. Unger (Ed.), *Handbook of the psychology of women and gender* (pp. 330–342). New York: John Wiley.

Chapter 15

Constructivist Counseling

Alissa Sherry

Chapter Outline

Bridging the Theory-to-Practice Gap

Principles in Practice

Keys to Conceptualization

Interventions and Therapeutic Process

Short- and Long-Term Goals

Using the Relationship

Adapting the Approach

Finding Your Niche

Process and Case Suggestions

Summary and Suggested Readings

References

BRIDGING THE THEORY-TO-PRACTICE GAP

A client recently came to counseling saying that she had found a greeting card that expressed what she wanted to accomplish in counseling. It read, "Life isn't about finding yourself. Life is about *creating* yourself." If the constructivist approach could be simplified into two sentences, these would well represent the approach. These sentences gave this client new hope that she could rewrite her personal story and recovery in any way she needed. The role of the counselor is to provide her the space to do it. As freeing and open as this approach can be for both counselors and their clients, it is rarely covered in theory textbooks. This is partly because relative to some of the other theoretical approaches like psychodynamic and behavior therapy, its application to the practice of counseling is fairly new, with much of its mainstream growth occurring in the last 20 years or so. A second reason is that constructivist language and perspective is deeply rooted in philosophy and sometimes difficult to understand. The purpose of this chapter is to help bridge that difficulty and introduce constructivist counseling in more simplified terms. I hope that you will feel about the approach as many constructivists feel: that at its core, it profoundly highlights many of the reasons people decide to become counselors in the first place. It has a humbling respect for individual experience and the power of the human change and growth process.

The history and origin of constructivist theory are complex and stem from many more disciplines besides counseling. As such, it may be more important for you to understand only a few of the more critical aspects of the theory before moving forward. The constructivist approach to counseling is an epistemological position, or in other words, a particular theory about the way people "know" or understand things. It is considered a postmodern cognitive theory and as such emphasizes the personal and collective process of knowing. This is contrasted with what is referred to as a "rationalist" assumption of knowing that is common in modern cognitive approaches. This distinction between modern and postmodern cognitive approaches is essential. The modern view, corresponding roughly to the first part of the 20th century, asserts that reality is stable, singular, and objectively knowable. The postmodern view, corresponding roughly to the second part of the 20th century, asserts that reality is subject to shifting, competing, individual constructions, none of which can be authorized as true or justified to the exclusion of others. This approach pays special attention to the ways in which clients make meaning and organize their world through language, schemas, and other cognitive means. It is a process-oriented approach in that all information contributes to a dynamic system of knowing where knowledge is always changing and evolving.

Because of its basis in philosophical thought and the notion that a rational, objective truth is not possible, constructivism can be difficult for beginning counselors to embrace. Many novice counselors actively seek structure and often think of counseling interventions in terms of "right" and "wrong." To assert that there are virtually no wrong answers and no wrong interventions can be confusing and anxiety provoking. However, it can also be freeing. Remember that constructivism at its core is a process of knowing, and interventions that might prove to be less therapeutic still provide a window into that knowing process. From that perspective, an "ineffective" therapeutic outcome is not "wrong," but informative. For example, suppose a letter-writing intervention used to help a woman grieve for her lost child was instead making her grief more intense. Is there something about the intervention that is reminding her of other things? Should this change in intensity be viewed as a breakthrough rather than a breakdown? While the therapist's initial intention of the letter-writing intervention was to lessen the woman's grief, her reaction clearly indicated that more needed to be understood and gathered. As therapists and clients create a shared knowing together, these missteps can be just as powerful in the understanding of a client as being right on target. In the same vein, to assert that the client has virtually no wrong beliefs or no irrational fears is in opposition to much of what beginning counselors learn. Suppose the client's response to her intensified grief reaction was, "I just can't get over this. I will never feel better about my child's death," even though her reason for coming to counseling was to do just that. What would it be like for the counselor to allow the client to explore this deep sadness and realization? Might the counselor learn new things about the client if he or she was allowed this freedom? Within this shared knowing process, the counselor is also investigating with the client what is and is not working from the client's perspective and meaning structure, rather than from the counselor's view of health or truth.

PRINCIPLES IN PRACTICE

Constructivism draws from a long history of philosophical positions as well as from a number of currently existing counseling theories. Therefore, it is difficult to highlight those principles considered purely constructivist and not mention some of the principles that constructivists value that are also shared by other counseling theorists. In general, most constructivists value the research that has been done in the area of "common factors." This line of research supports the notion that common factors like the therapeutic relationship, hope, or the expectation of change are more powerful than any specific counseling technique. These highlight the humanistic properties of counseling that constructivists believe are at the heart of the effectiveness of the constructivist perspective.

Many counseling approaches often focus on symptom control, rational belief systems, and the elimination of negative emotions. After all, clients come to us because they want to feel better, right? But a constructivist approach asserts that symptoms and negative emotions are naturally occurring, powerful knowing processes to be understood and valued. All beliefs are viable and serve a function in organizing one's experience. They contribute to how people make meaning out of their world, and constructivists believe that this meaning-making process truly helps people to feel better about the issues that bring them to counseling. For example, resistance on the part of the client is seen as contextual, reflecting a natural attempt to protect the self rather than something to work "against" or somehow abolish. Similarly, relapse and regression are not seen as failure. They are regarded as important opportunities for learning that also occur in an important context. In these ways, constructivist approaches validate clients in more holistic ways, approaching all information from the perspective of providing knowledge and valuing the phenomenological realm of the complex human experience.

From this fundamental paradigm shift come several basic principles of constructivist counseling practice. These are (1) meaning making, (2) relinquishing the expert role, (3) the limitations of diagnostic classifications, (4) realizing the complexity of change, (5) honoring the social context, (6) the importance of language, and (7) recognizing multiple realities.

1. *Meaning making.* Meaning making refers to the development of viable and workable constructions of people, things, and events. Multiple meanings can be created for the events in people's lives and each meaning helps people to understand and respond creatively to their own personal experiences. Remember the greeting card. "Life is about *creating* yourself." This creation can shift and take on new or even multiple meanings based on the client's context and personal goals. People have an incredibly individualized meaning-making process. No two Native Americans make meaning out of the historical genocide of their people in the same way. No two gay men experience the AIDS crisis in the same way. In a sense, regardless of background, people have their own psychological fingerprint that guides their future constructions and helps them make meaning of past events. In many ways, this is where the term constructivist originates—to construct meaning.

2. *Relinquish the "expert" role.* Constructivist approaches view the client-counselor relationship in egalitarian terms. The client is on a quest for guided discovery with the counselor facilitating the journey. The client is thus free to develop alternative, more flexible perspectives on issues brought into counseling. Allowing clients' control over their own process allows them to be more creative, more active, and ultimately more empowered. The core assumption is that the *client* is the expert in his/her life. This is contrasted with the traditional cognitive notion of the counselor as the "expert." The counselor's expertise is in guiding the process and helping the client explore what is no longer working while at the same time honoring the client's expert view of their own life. This is a client-centered perspective that is nonjudgmental, requires unconditional positive regard for the client, and allows the client to set the pace for their own process. What's more, it challenges the traditional social power structure of the counseling relationship where the counselor is the holder of what is considered to be "good mental health." Instead, the process of determining what is no longer working for the client becomes collaborative and mutual.

3. *The limitations of diagnostic classifications.* The concept of the limitations of diagnostic classifications is related to the importance of breaking down the traditional social power structure of counseling. There are three primary limitations to diagnostic classifications according to constructivist perspectives. The first limitation has to do with the fundamental inability of diagnostic categories to capture the richness of individual experience. For many diagnoses, there can be thousands of possible combinations of symptoms that might warrant giving someone a diagnosis. However, the diagnosis itself conveys no real or specific information about the ways in which people's current meaning-making process is no longer working for them. The second limitation is related to principle 2 in that these classifications reinstate the counselor's role as the expert. Often diagnoses are "given" to clients with very little input or collaboration. In addition, the process of diagnostic labeling often undermines the empowerment clients can feel in more collaborative counseling relationships. Keep

in mind that the two primary goals of diagnosis are to guide treatment and to convey information to other professionals. When a counselor gives a client a diagnosis of major depressive disorder, the diagnosis gives no information about what treatment approach might work best for this client or anything specific about how this client experiences depression, as diagnostic categories are devoid of context. Finally, diagnostic categories are unable to address the function of any one particular symptom. A diagnosis reveals nothing about the client's thoughts, feelings, or behaviors that generated the symptoms that led to the diagnosis. If a particular symptom is really in place to protect the client from something feared, for example, the diagnosis can be useless in conveying this information. Consider a child who complains of horrible headaches every Monday morning as an attempt to stay home from school. While this child may be given a diagnosis of hypochondriasis, that diagnosis has no utility in discovering that the real function of that symptom is to avoid a bully at school.

4. *The complexity of change.* Constructivists contend that the goal of therapy is to elicit long-term, core change that in many ways may transcend the initial symptoms that nudged someone into therapy. Lyddon (1990) refers to this as second-order change and Ecker and Hulley (1996) refer to the therapeutic channel towards second-order change as "depth-oriented." The goal of many brief therapies is to simply reduce symptoms in order to make clients more functional in their day-to-day living. The goal of constructivist approaches, however, is to help clients make fundamental shifts in how they experience their world that lead to lifelong improvements in the quality of life. This is an individual, unique knowing process for each client. The assumption is that there is a discrepancy for clients between the realities they have always known and some disconfirming piece of information they are having trouble assimilating into their existing view of reality. The goal of the counseling process is to help clients identify contextual aspects of their life (cultural, biological, social, developmental, historical) that are contributing to feelings of concern. Once these aspects are identified, clients can reorganize their worldview around new meaningful perspectives. Consider, for example, a client who is beginning to question his sexual orientation. Contextually, this client may come from a religious background that prohibits homosexual expression. He may have received homonegative messages from his parents but he may believe that biologically he is gay. Other contextual layers could include being from a small southern town with virtually no gay-friendly organizations and no out-gay culture. Coming to terms with this disconfirming information (the notion that he might be gay) would require the reorganization of much of his prior contextual reality. It is the counselor's role to help the client identify the sources of discrepancy and to support and encourage this reorganization and any aspects of this new reality the client chooses to embrace.

With each client, the therapist must develop a new expectation for change that is individual to that client. Each client has a unique yardstick for measuring change and success in therapy. It is important not to hold one client to the change standards of another, even if on the surface their concerns are similar in nature. Some traditional counseling approaches posit that it is the counselor's responsibility to show clients both how and why they need to make changes. These approaches leave little room for the client to decide that change might be premature, too costly, or just simply no longer desired. One of the hardest things for a new constructivist counselor to realize is that change for some people may be the realization that they no longer desire change, and that this in no way represents failure in the therapeutic process.

5. *Honoring the social context.* The value placed on the importance of recognizing that a client's realities are largely influenced by social contexts makes constructivist approaches ideal for counselors who desire a feminist or multicultural-friendly approach to counseling. Constructivist approaches have a pluralistic emphasis. For example, a client is not merely just a client. She is, for example, an African American, Baptist, elderly woman who was raised in the inner city. Because of this, her race, sex, age/generation, religion, and socioeconomic status, among a multitude of other things, impact her worldview and her concept of reality. Each social context contributes to the way this client constructs and organizes her reality. Because constructivists believe that individuals cannot be separated from their social context, problems brought to counseling are often better understood within this context than by viewing them as deficits lying solely within the client. For example, if this woman is more suspicious of people than other clients might be, it likely has more to do with living in the inner city than it does with any pathological conceptualizations of paranoia. In a sense, reality is replaced by relativism because belief or understanding is more dependent on social context than on objective empiricism.

6. *The importance of language.* The use of language in constructivist approaches is related to the value placed on socially contextual realities. If knowledge is socially constructed, what are the scaffolds of that construction? From a constructivist perspective, what people understand about the world is limited to the words we have to define and categorize it. These words, categories, and constructs are coconstructed through social interchanges throughout history. The extent to which words or categories continue to exist through time is largely dependent on social processes. Words and categories often have multiple meanings and to the extent that a word means one thing over another often depends on who is saying it, the context in which they mean it, and the historical relevance of the term. Consider the word "consumption." In the early part of the nineteenth century, it was most often associated with having tuberculosis. However, since the industrial revolution and the shift towards consumerism in American culture, "consumption" is now typically defined as wanting and using economic goods. Other examples highlight the ways in which language can be used to disparage groups of disenfranchised people. Often these pejorative words can be "reclaimed" and the meaning of the word, now used by the minority group, completely changes.

The importance of this illustration is to highlight the joint meaning-making process that occurs between counselor and client using language. It is important for the counselor never to assume to know what the client means based solely on the counselor's understanding of the language used. Meaning is thus clarified in the counseling process using metaphor, client narratives and stories, or inquiry techniques from the counselor. If a client uses the word "sad" instead of "depressed," what does the client mean exactly? What about the word "depressed" doesn't fit for the client and what about the word "sad" does? What does it mean for clients when they describe themselves as "sad"? It could mean anything from crying once in the last six months, to crying daily and unable to get out of bed. Constructivists believe that how the client defines "sad" has a lot to do with his social, family, cultural, and community contexts. It is the counselor's responsibility to recognize and clarify the meaning of language, its social antecedents, and its cultural and historical contexts.

7. *Recognizing multiple realities.* The notion that multiple possibilities can emerge once one has recognized there is no one stable empirical truth is central to the paradigm shift from traditional cognitive counseling to postmodern constructivist counseling. Recognizing multiple realities in therapy can be as simple as changing "or" to "and" when telling a client about possibilities. For example, there is a subtle but important difference between "Are you feeling sad or happy?" and "Are you feeling sad *and* happy?" Acknowledging that even competing realities can coexist for clients can also give them permission to attend to each of them more fully. One example is in the concept of the "self" in counseling. Traditional cognitive counseling viewed the self as singular, self-contained, and fully integrated. However, metaphors about the self in constructivist approaches highlight the coexistence of multiple views of the self. In particular, the notion of clients having multiple selves when describing their experience can create a new environment of self-acceptance for them. Similarly, the idea of possible selves can provide hope for a client who might have been previously hopeless. Recognizing multiple realities is also important in doing couples and family counseling, where more than one reality needs to be validated and considered in order for counseling to progress with all parties invested. Constructivist theorists have proposed almost limitless multiple selves such as the future self, the narrative self, and the sociopolitical self that all emphasize the idea that the self is a multidimensional, multicontextual, evolving entity.

KEYS TO CONCEPTUALIZATION

One of the more difficult aspects of becoming a constructivist is grappling with the notion that essentially all points of view are viable. After being trained as a traditional cognitive therapist, this was a difficult assumption to negotiate. As a student, I tried to think of an example of a potential client that might have a point of view that according to my worldview simply could not be validated under any circumstances. I said, "What about someone who is a self-proclaimed racist?" My professor's response was to ask this person, "How has that been working for you?" Chances are, if this person were in counseling, the answer on some level would be: "Not so good." At this moment, the key to constructivist conceptualization became clear. It is not the counselor's job to assess and diagnose the client's problem, but to help the client figure out what may not be working for the client anymore. In this process, the counselor asks many of the traditional counseling questions like what brings someone to counseling, how long have the symptoms existed, or has anything helped in relieving the pain? Once the counselor has a sense of what brings the client in, it is important to examine the areas where clients feel the most blocked or restricted in their life. These may be things that prevent them from realizing their full potential, or relatively minor aggravations. In the midst of this exploration process, the counselor is exploring meaning through the language used in the session. What does it mean to feel blocked or in pain? What does it mean to feel aggravated? How is that working for you? What would it mean to you to be different? Always using the client's language, this joint meaning-making process helps the counselor gain a deeper understanding of the client's presenting problems and what is hoped to be gained from counseling.

At the core of conceptualization is the notion that people seek change when a current concern no longer fits with their current worldview. When something does not fit, helping a client draw those distinctions can become a fundamental level of knowing for that person. Some other questions that might assist a counselor in helping a client draw distinctions might be: Can you remember a time when you felt similarly? What was similar about that time? What was different? Many of these questions may also encompass contextual aspects of the client's concern like: How has your religion been a comfort to you? In what ways has it not been a comfort lately? Once the counselor has helped the client recognize what distinctions represent a departure from the client's existing worldview, the client can then decide on what level change can occur. This decision will be based largely on exploration in counseling around alternative worldviews, multiple solutions, and the client's desire to make changes at that point in time.

Questions counselors might want to ask themselves are (1) Have I considered all the contextual influences for the client's presenting concerns? (2) Do I understand the language clients have used to explain their presenting concerns? (3) Are there any points that need further clarification either for myself or for the client? (4) Do I have a sense of how this presenting concern represents a departure for clients from their existing worldview or reality? (5) Is there anything about my worldview that is preventing me from understanding the client more fully? (6) Have I made any assumptions that may not represent the clients' view of their concerns? (7) Have I created an environment where clients feel safe to explore alternative realities and solutions to their concerns?

INTERVENTIONS AND THERAPEUTIC PROCESS

For the most part, constructivist approaches do not endorse a bag of tricks to be used as techniques in counseling. Because each client is different and the counseling session is a co-constructed and co-created endeavor between counselor and client, interventions tend to be creative and spontaneous and as such require a great deal of practice and skill in their timing and implementation. It has been said, "To make shorter the therapy, make longer the training" (Ecker & Hulley, 1996). This speaks to the notion that effective counseling requires skills that take time to develop. Because problems have a historical context, interventions need to be process-oriented and developmentally focused with the understanding that this process and development are ongoing, providing new opportunities for exploration (Mahoney & Lyddon, 1988).

In their book, Ecker and Hulley (1996) do an excellent job of outlining many constructivist interventions within the therapeutic process. Central to these interventions is the acknowledgement by the counselor that the concerns brought to counseling have deep personal meanings for clients. As such, symptoms should not be simply disallowed, but instead viewed as functional and adaptive. Anxiety is a perfect example of a symptom that often has functional and adaptive qualities. Trying to simply eradicate or disallow the symptom of anxiety can result in the loss of important contextual and functional information. Once the client and counselor have some clarity around these concerns and their importance to the person, the goal is not to talk *about* the problem, but process the problem within an experiential context.

Consider a client who talks about a lump in his throat from which he never feels free. In order to get the client to process these symptoms experientially, a counselor might ask: What does the lump look like? What color is it? What is its shape? If you could talk to it, what would you say? How might it respond? What would it be like if you woke up tomorrow without the lump? With these questions, the concern stays in the room and is processed at a deep, emotional level, rather than intellectually. Intellectual process can keep clients from truly connecting with the personal meaning the concern provides for them. In addition, the counselor is acknowledging that the concern is very real and present instead of reinforcing the position they have likely held for some time that the lump needs to just "go away"—when they haven't understood its function.

One of the core questions counselors should ask themselves about a client's symptom is, What belief exists that makes having the symptom more important than not having it? This is where contextual factors often come into play. The counselor should investigate the various contexts that make the symptom or concern a viable position for the client. The counselor should also investigate the ways in which the symptom, given this context, may be to the client's benefit rather than detriment. The counselor should also explore what might be the consequences if the symptom was no longer present for the client. Counselors can explore answers to these questions using techniques that elicit the experience of bringing these contextual factors into awareness. Using the example above with the client who had a lump in his throat, the following questions could represent this process: What would it feel like to not have the lump in your throat anymore? What part of you might miss the lump after it is gone? When the lump is gone, what other things do you think might also be gone? Client's responses to such questions vary widely according to the context. For example, a client might express that no longer having the lump would mean that he would be able to play his flute again, a hobby that displeases his father because he wants him to be involved in more sport-like activities. For another client, the lump might mean he doesn't have to speak out loud at work, and life without the lump would mean there would be no other impediments to his speaking. This might have implications reaching back to messages about achievement in his family background or pressures he places on himself.

The overarching goal of constructivist techniques is to help the client experience the symptom, illuminate its meaning or purpose, and draw from that the contextual issues that might be in place to perpetuate the symptom. Illuminating the meaning or purpose of symptoms can be accomplished in many ways besides the questioning highlighted above. Constructivists value techniques like the use of metaphor as a way to highlight relatedness, connection, and meaning making in the therapeutic relationship. For example, a client might say, "It felt like I was standing at the edge of a swimming pool, but I just couldn't jump in." The therapist might follow with questions designed to join with the client in a meaning-making process such as, "How deep was the water? What was the temperature? What would it be like to put your toe in?" and these questions could lead to further clarification about the metaphor and its meaning and importance in the client's life. The use of metaphor is an example of how constructivists use language in counseling and highlights an overarching theme of constructivist counseling, which is client's ability to reauthor, reconstruct, or even multiply construct their life narrative or story.

Thus, the therapeutic process as described by Neimeyer and Stewart (2000) is one that can be defined as the subtle interchange and negotiation of meaning that serves to articulate, elaborate, and even revise the constructions that clients use to organize their experience. The techniques and approaches used towards this end reflect a basic human need for connectedness and relatedness grounded in a common language and a desire to bridge common experience.

SHORT- AND LONG-TERM GOALS

Just as interventions tend to be idiographic, so do short- and long-term goals. From a constructivist perspective, short- and long-term goals are considered to be working goals and are subject to shifts and changes as the client shifts and changes. What's more, the client, not the counselor, identifies these goals. This can sometimes be a difficult adjustment for people trained in other approaches because often counselors in training are anxious to help the client "see" or realize areas of improvement from the counselor's so-called objective perspective. For example, consider an adult woman with an overly enmeshed relationship with a frequently verbally abusive parent with whom she lives. From a counselor's perspective, modern techniques and theories might support the idea that the woman should detach from this parent, become more autonomous or more self-sufficient, and live alone. However, this completely ignores the client's context. The woman may come from a culture or background that values taking care of parents, regardless of the quality of the relationship. This culture may also have collectivist values rather than individualistic values. Finally, she just may not want to move out of her mother's home. Allowing clients to make their own decisions regarding the goals for therapy is an important part of empowering the client in the therapy process. For the client in this example, just this sense of empowerment could prove to be a shifting force. Experiencing control and empowerment in the counseling session may help her discover other ways of becoming empowered in other areas of her life.

Goals will shift in the therapy as clients change. As meanings become illuminated and clearer, goals will reorganize to reflect this new level of understanding. Therefore, it isn't necessary to set hard and fast short- or long-term goals. There is some expectation that clients will come to therapy with at least one goal in mind, but it may not be well formulated or a client may have a hard time articulating it. It could be that all clients are able to convey is that they want something to be different—they want change. At the same time, given this desire, the process of therapy could prove otherwise for the client. For example, in the case of the man with a lump in his throat, it is possible his initial desire in therapy was to get rid of the lump. However, upon further exploration into the meaning and purpose of the lump for him, he discovers that it may serve an important function and abandoning this may not be an option for him. The point is that not being able to achieve a goal or find a solution to the initial presenting problem does not mean that counseling was not successful. Success is not determined by the extent to which goals are set and then achieved. Success is determined by the ability of clients to experience a shift that was necessitated by a deeper level of understanding and the creation of new meanings about their own existence and process.

USING THE RELATIONSHIP

One key to understanding the counseling relationship using constructivist approaches lies in the ability of counselors to shift their own assumptions about what a counselor-client relationship is "supposed" to look like. The relationship will look different with every client but it is almost always founded on the notion that people seek relatedness and connection. People seek to be understood. It is from this notion that the therapeutic relationship is formed in constructivist practice. Often, to practice from this stance, it is important to shift away from notions that the therapeutic relationship is about technical instruction or guidance. Instead, the relationship is about a humanistic, safe, caring, and often intense context from which people are able to explore their world in relation to themselves (Mahoney & Lyddon, 1988).

Always striving to understand clients as one way to facilitate the counseling relationship often means resisting temptations to diagnose or view dysfunction in a pathological light. Such views tend to increase the interpersonal gap between counselor and client because it is not a collaborative process of understanding but rather an "expert" role process of labeling. The collaborative process of understanding also sets the groundwork for an egalitarian relationship between counselor and client in which the client feels a sense of empowerment and control in the counseling process. Clients are the expert on their own experience, and the counselor is the expert in the facilitation of the process. Both of these perspectives are integral in the counseling experience—one cannot exist with the other.

Patience is another aspect inherent in the process of understanding that helps facilitate the counseling relationship. A great deal of patience is needed whenever two people decide to converge on a meaning or meanings they can both understand. While this is a value shared by many orientations, the concept of patience goes beyond just giving clients time to consider their options and make sense of new discoveries. It also involves counselors having patience with themselves as well, resisting temptations to intervene prematurely or in a way that might leave the client feeling less understood. Patience is a particularly important concept for clients who have long-term issues and may not have been as responsive to treatment in the past. For these clients, patience is an even greater therapeutic factor because it often represents a shift from how much of the rest of the world reacts to their concerns.

In general, counseling is something that counselors do "with" a client, not "to" a client, and this can be an important distinction. The counseling relationship is predicated on mutual understanding. As mentioned earlier, resistance is viewed as a natural self-protective process rather than a lack of motivation or avoidance. As such, resistance in the counseling relationship is worked "with" rather than "against" (Mahoney & Lyddon, 1988). Similarly, transference and countertransference are important opportunities for meaning making and learning that could potentially transform relationships and personal meanings.

ADAPTING THE APPROACH

Constructivist approaches work well with a variety of clients because of the emphasis on the idiosyncratic ways people make meaning and the emphasis on context. Because of this, these approaches dovetail nicely with cultural and feminist perspectives, as social constructs of gender, race, and ethnicity can be explored. It is important to keep in mind that individuals cannot be separated from their social context. Social contexts also exceed gender, race, and ethnicity and include other socially constructed categories of socioeconomic status, sexual orientation/identity, religious affiliation, and regional, national, and international differences. Remember, though, constructivist perspectives are about joint meaning making and relational processes, not about being able to understand every social context before interacting with your clients. Cultural competence is certainly important, but cultural competence is not always sufficient. The counselor needs to be open to the education clients can provide about their personal experience.

Counselors often find that there are less common but equally important social contexts for them to consider and for which they cannot always prepare. For example: What is the social context of a client who has been on psychiatric disability, is visually or hearing impaired, cares for a parent with Alzheimer's disease, is raising four children alone, or is a famous basketball star? That is not to say that these descriptions define the clients, but they contribute to the many socially constructed pieces of who they are. Each piece is open to a deeper understanding of how it has shaped who they are. Each piece is also open to a different place in the ordering of what clients believe identifies them. The important part to consider when adapting constructivist perspectives to different clients is that each piece can be a source of valuable information and filled with meaning that can be explored if the client desires it to be.

Overall, it is important to resist making assumptions based on your own worldview and social context. Just because both counselor and client happen to be from the same race, ethnic background, sex, sexual orientation, religion, and socioeconomic status does not mean they have experienced those constructs in the same ways or made meaning out of them similarly. But constructivist perspectives are easily adapted to a variety of counseling clients and contexts.

FINDING YOUR NICHE

Finding your niche in constructivist practice can be an exciting endeavor because there are so many aspects to this approach. First, it should be noted that constructivist approaches draw heavily from a variety of counseling approaches. From a humanistic perspective comes the emphasis on unconditional positive regard as well as the emphasis on personal choice and agency. From interpersonal psychology comes the importance of the relationship providing valuable information that can be used in the counseling setting. From George Kelly's personal construct theory comes the idea that people have complex meaning systems organized around a core construct of the self. Adlerian psychology emphasizes the idea that individuals actively reconstruct their past and anticipate their futures. Developmental theory places emphasis on a historically situated context, and of course cognitive theory emphasizes the importance of cognitive schemas and the organization of cognitive material.

Several subtypes of constructivist counseling have emerged from the many perspectives that inform this approach. Neimeyer and Stewart (2000) present a list, although not an exhaustive one, of some subtypes of constructivist counseling such as contemporary personal construct theory, psychoanalytic constructivism, Ecker and Hulley's (1996) Depth-Oriented Brief Therapy, humanistic constructivism, and systemic constructivism. While this list of subcategories of constructivist orientations is not exhaustive or detailed, I hope it will provide enough information to lead interested individuals in the right direction.

PROCESS AND CASE SUGGESTIONS

Because constructivist approaches can seem fairly theoretical and abstract, sometimes it is difficult to understand how to apply them to clients. The cases of Elena, Jane, and Theo provide an excellent opportunity to see how constructivist theory can be applied to three very different people. Each case presents many of the core struggles we have as human beings as they each try to organize their lives around salient aspects of their self-identities and interpersonal relationships while trying to make meaning from their personal histories and current issues.

1. *Elena.* It can be very difficult for clients to grapple with two decisions that are equally important to them. This is the case with Elena, a 17-year-old high school student who describes herself as being "stuck in the middle" between her desire to go to college and her family value of caring for her dying mother. From a counselor's point of view, it is especially difficult because any of us who might work with Elena have had the privilege of going to college and possibly graduate school. We have seen firsthand what an education can provide. However, this is only our perspective. How do you think you will be able to bridge that gap for Elena and help her with this decision? Here are some questions to consider if you decided to take a constructivist perspective:

   • What costs might Elena believe she would have to endure if she chose to go to college or chose to care for her mother?
   • Can Elena describe the many "selves" she uses to identify who she is?
   • Which "self" does she feel is being silenced the most?
   • Which "self" has the most to gain?
   • What contrasts does she see between herself and her family members?
   • What similarities does she see?

2. *Jane.* As noted in her intake, Jane is not particularly psychologically minded. However, this isn't to be confused with an inability to experience her emotions. Jane appears to be experiencing her current emotions through physical means. How do you think you might help Jane become aware of the function her chest pains serve? Here are some questions to consider if you take a constructivist perspective:

   • How can you help Jane experience her chest pains in a way that puts her in touch with some of the emotions that might be behind them?
   • What do you think Jane would say if you asked her what it would mean to her life if the chest pains were to suddenly disappear?
   • How would things be different for Jane if she no longer had to think about her chest pains?
   • How can you help Jane make some important distinctions between her relationship with her husband and previous friendships and her current relationship with Barbara?
   • What about this new relationship is different for Jane that adds more meaning to her life?

3. *Theo.* Theo's case has three elements that make constructivist work fun and interesting. He clearly has a strong relationship with his girlfriend that means a lot to him, yet his angry behaviors are getting in the way of bringing her closer to him. He indicates that he desires intimacy and also fears it. He is clear his anger is no longer working for him in his current relationship, but what might be the developmental functionality of it? At what point in time did his anger work to his advantage and how is it working differently now? He wants to distance himself from his parents, he wants to connect more with his brothers, and he is actively involved in campus organizations with which he strongly identifies. He also brings to the table a sense of what it means to be a black man and the responsibilities entailed in that. How might you help him explore his identity or multiple identities? Here are some questions to consider from a constructivist perspective:

   • What function does Theo's anger serve currently and how can you as a counselor get him to acknowledge the ways in which this has been functional in the past?
   • What impact does the context of his race have on his feelings of anger and feeling misunderstood by others?
   • In what ways can you help Theo explore the multiple identities he experiences within himself?

SUMMARY AND SUGGESTED READINGS

Constructivist perspectives are as much a philosophy as a counseling approach. As such, the best way to learn these perspectives is to immerse yourself in constructivist readings and if possible, align yourself with a constructivist supervisor who can coach you through the process. This is particularly important because constructivist perspectives do not rely heavily on techniques, tend to focus on in-the-moment interventions, and tend to be more dynamic and less linear, making it a bit harder to grasp initially. However, the approach often becomes a life perspective for the counselors who align with the central principles. For that reason it can be just as life-changing for you as a counselor as it can be for your clients. Following is a list of readings that will be helpful in the pursuit of this new knowledge. In addition, as you search for readings on your own, some suggested authors in the field are Michael Mahoney, William J. Lyddon, Greg J. Neimeyer, Robert A. Neimeyer, Leslie Greenberg, and Allen Ivey.

Anderson, H., & Goolishian, H. (1992). The client is the expert: A not-knowing approach to therapy. In S. McNamee & K. J. Gergen (Eds.), *Therapy as social construction: Inquiries in social construction* (pp. 25–29). London, England: Sage Publications.

Barton, S. (1994). Chaos, self-organization, and psychology. *American Psychologist, 49,* 5–14.

Clarke, K., M. (1991). A performance model of the creation of meaning event. *Psychotherapy, 28,* 395–401.

Bugental, J. F. T., & Bugental, E. K. (1984). A fate worse than death: The fear of changing. *Psychotherapy, 21,* 543–549.

Cox, L. M., & Lyddon, W. J. (1997). Constructivist conceptions of self: A discussion of emerging identity constructs. *Journal of Constructivist Psychology, 10,* 201–219.

Ecker, B., & Hulley, L. (1996). *Depth-oriented brief therapy: How to be brief when you were trained to be deep—and vice versa.* San Francisco: Jossey-Bass.

Fiexas, G. (1992). A constructivist approach to supervision: Some preliminary thoughts. *International Journal of Personal Construct Psychology, 5,* 183–200.

Hoskins, M., & Leseho, J. (1996). Changing metaphors of the self: Implications for counseling. *Journal of Counseling and Development, 74,* 243–252.

Lyddon, W. J. (1990). First- and second-order change: Implications for rationalist and constructivist cognitive therapies. *Journal of Counseling and Development, 67,* 442–448.

Lyddon, W. J. (1993). Contrast, contradiction, and change in psychotherapy. *Psychotherapy, 30,* 383–390.

Mahoney, M. J. (1990). Representations of self in cognitive psychotherapies. *Cognitive Therapy and Research, 14,* 229–240.

Mahoney, M. J. (2003). *Constructive psychotherapy: A practical guide.* New York: Guilford Press.

Mahoney, M. J., & Lyddon, W. J. (1988). Recent developments in cognitive approaches to counseling and psychotherapy. *The Counseling Psychologist, 16,* 190–234.

Markus, H., & Nurius, P. (1986). Possible selves. *American Psychologist, 41,* 954–969.

Neimeyer, R. A., & Mahoney, M. J. (Eds.). (1995). *Constructivism in psychotherapy.* Washington, DC: American Psychological Association.

Neimeyer, R. A., & Stewart, A. E. (2000). Constructivist and narrative psychotherapies. In R. E. Ingram & C. R. Snyder (Eds.), *Handbook of psychological change: Psychotherapy processes and practices for the 21st century.* New York: John Wiley.

Steenbarger, B. N. (1991). All the world is not a stage: Emerging contextualist themes in counseling and development. *Journal of Counseling and Development, 70,* 288–296.

REFERENCES

Ecker, B., & Hulley, L. (1996). *Depth-oriented brief therapy: How to be brief when you were trained to be deep—and vice versa.* San Francisco: Jossey-Bass.

Mahoney, M. J., & Lyddon, W. J. (1988). Recent developments in cognitive approaches to counseling and psychotherapy. *The Counseling Psychologist, 16,* 190–234.

Chapter 16

Solution-Focused Brief Therapy

Thorana S. Nelson

Chapter Outline

Bridging the Theory-to-Practice Gap

Principles in Practice

Keys to Conceptualization

Interventions and Therapeutic Process

Short- and Long-Term Goals

Using the Relationship

Adapting the Approach

Finding Your Niche

Process and Case Suggestions

Summary and Suggested Readings

References

BRIDGING THE THEORY-TO-PRACTICE GAP

Counselors and therapists are often very curious about the differences between Solution-focused Brief Therapy (SFBT) and other models or approaches to counseling and therapy. In psychology classes and graduate school, we are taught to focus on problems and their causes as necessary for helping people meet the goals that bring them to a counselor. This way of thinking arises from the analogies that are made between mental health and medical models of disease. In these models, it is necessary to diagnose a problem and to understand its cause in order to find a way of resolving it. In many instances, medical problems are best conceptualized this way. That is, it is important to diagnose certain pains or infections in order to know what medicines or procedures to administer or prescribe.

In mental health, knowing diagnoses and causes isn't always helpful to us as counselors. For example, knowing that client was abused as a child may help explain her current behaviors or symptoms, but says very little about how I can help change them. As an analogy, think of discovering that your car has a flat tire. Knowing the cause (a nail) and even how the cause came to be (traveling on a road near a construction site) may be useful to preventing more flat tires. However, this knowledge does nothing to help you fix the tire so that you can drive the car. The solution—plugging the hole and putting air back into the tire—is not *necessarily* related to the problem. You could go the rest of your life, never knowing what caused the flat tire, and still fix it and drive on it until it was bald. This way of thinking—solutions are not necessarily related to problems—is a basic tenet of SFBT and one of the most difficult ideas for those new to the approach to understand. It also is one of the most powerful and freeing ideas I have ever encountered as a therapist. Once you grasp this idea and stop trying to find causes, all sorts of solutions become apparent.

Think, for example, of a person who states that she has a problem with alcohol and may even "be" an "alcoholic."[1] In traditional mental health, it is important for the therapist to determine whether the person truly is an alcoholic and to identify what may be causing the alcoholism or, at least, what leads to problematic drinking. Solutions, then, follow a prescribed pattern of intervention that includes "breaking denial" and "confronting the disease." In SFBT, however, we look for ways to help clients reach their goals whether they seem related to drinking or not.

When asked how her life would be different when she no longer abused alcohol, another client responded with a list of goals that included improved relationships, more discretionary money, keeping a well-paying job, and having better health. Using SFBT, I asked Carrie how she knew she could reach those goals, not what led to her drinking too much. Carrie responded that she knew she could reach her goals because she already was doing some of them. By exploring how Carrie had known she could do this and what steps she was taking toward her goals, I helped her design a plan that continued this progress in small and realistic steps. Of course, as you might imagine, one of those steps included

---

[1]Quotation marks are used because ideas about fixed traits and the ways to work with them, such as "alcoholic," are not part of constructivist thinking, the philosophy that underlies SFBT. Constructivism suggests that meanings of words are constructed and exist only in context. Such ideas may be seen as part of the problem and therefore not useful in constructing solutions.

finding ways to replace drinking with behaviors that moved her toward rather than away from her goals. She began walking on a daily basis and whenever she had the urge to drink. I did not need to educate Carrie on alcoholism as a disease, identify triggers (because she knew these quite well), or analyze why she drank. Carrie was more interested in moving on with her life. Knowing why was not necessary for a process of building solutions toward desired goals, such as improved relationships.

In this chapter, I hope that you will learn the concepts that are important and helpful to you for understanding how focusing on solutions rather than problems is a useful way to be a counselor.

PRINCIPLES IN PRACTICE

SFBT was developed by Steve de Shazer, his wife Insoo Kim Berg, and others as an approach for helping clients with their problems. de Shazer and Berg developed their ideas after studying the Mental Research Institute (MRI) approach of brief therapy. Rather than looking for the underlying causes of emotional and behavioral problems, the MRI folks developed a *problem-focused* approach, one that focused on the problems themselves rather than their underlying causes (Watzlawick, Weakland, & Fisch, 1974). By understanding problems and the solutions that had been attempted to resolve them, MRI therapists could learn more about what had not helped resolve the problem and then design interventions that were different and thus more likely to be effective. de Shazer and Berg began looking not at problems and solutions that had not worked, but at solutions that had worked in the past, even a little bit, and at times when the problem was not present or was not as severe. They discovered that clients could be helped even more quickly and efficiently than with the MRI brief approach. They also discovered that therapy moved more quickly when clients were moving toward clear goals (the presence of something) rather than away from problems (the absence of something).

Theories of counseling or therapy often begin with philosophical ideas about people, so-called normal development, the development of problems, and explanations for problems. As you might imagine, these ideas are not necessary in SFBT. Thus, SFBT is not a theory of how people come to be the way they are. Nor is it a theory of how problems develop or how therapy works. de Shazer and Berg were much more interested in *what* works for clients and descriptions than *why* something might work and explanations. This section describes some of the assumptions and basic concepts that are most useful in the practice of SFBT.

1. *Each person is unique and so are their symptoms, problems, and solutions.* In SFBT, it is important for us to understand that even if a client has been diagnosed with a problem that is similar to another person's, those two people *experience* the difficulty differently and therefore attach different meanings (constructivism). Because they do not have exactly the same symptoms, behaviors, and meanings associated with the problem, they likely will find different solutions. Because SFBT therapists take a constructivist perspective, there is no such "thing" as "depression"; it cannot be put into a wheelbarrow or taken from one person and transferred to

another. It is a word in language that has come to mean the same thing as a long paragraph of descriptions of certain behaviors and feelings that most people find distressing. Of course, there are similarities across clients who have been described as depressed; however, the solution-focused therapist focuses on the uniqueness of the client's experiences and descriptions rather than similarities with others.

As an SFBT therapist, I know that I can never really know what a particular client's experience is and therefore cannot make assumptions about it and how it might be problematic, or how to resolve it. Sadness or depression was a problem for Ken because he was not able to concentrate on his work; it was a problem for Sharon because she felt awful, was not eating or sleeping, and her family was worried about her. The solution-focused therapist would focus on ways that Ken is able to concentrate at work even a little, and helping Sharon think about her life when her family is not worrying about her. These are clear, unique solutions based on the clients' descriptions of their experiences rather than assumptions about what "depression" *really* is. Focusing on these particular goals might or might not be sufficient to resolve the difficulty. However, it is a start and it points the therapy in the direction of solutions and the future rather than problems and the past, and it is more likely to be fruitful in terms of helping clients move on in their lives.

2. *Clients are experts on their own lives.* A concept related to the uniqueness of each person is that just as clients experience problems with similar labels differently, so will they develop and experience solutions uniquely. Some clients may develop a more positive or happy outlook by taking care of themselves better; others may do better by taking care of someone else. Only clients are capable of determining the best solutions to their problems. If, as a therapist, I insist on helping my clients understand and change their distorted thoughts as causing their depression, I may be completely offtrack for some of them. When asked what had helped him recover from depression, Jim said that exercising and listening to music were helpful. He also said that focusing on his thoughts had not seemed helpful because he then began to feel guilty, ashamed, and despairing that he could ever live a normal life— he became depressed about being depressed! The solution-focused therapist pays close attention to what clients say works *in their own lives* rather than assuming that what has worked with anyone else will work for a particular person. *Listening to what clients say* is much more important in this approach than knowing theory, technique, or clinical problems.

   At the same time, however, therapists should not assume that the clients are experts on everything about therapy. This sort of thinking easily leads to frustrating conversations, frustrated clients, and frustrated therapists. Rather, the therapist also is an expert but, in this case, an expert on solution-building conversations: ways of noticing things and helping clients develop and make progress toward their goals.

3. *There is no such thing as resistance.* In 1994, Steve de Shazer declared the "death of resistance." He believed that it is not useful to think of clients as resisting therapists and therapy. This way of thinking puts the therapist in a position of "fighting back" and attempting to "break through" the resistance. Even thinking of benign reasons for what appears as resistance, such as fearing change, was problematic for de Shazer because it pitted therapists and clients against each other. Rather, de Shazer

believed that clients cooperate and communicate with therapists, although sometimes in ways therapists do not understand. If clients do not do what a therapist suggests or change suggestions, they are providing information to the therapist about what will help them work toward their goals. This message often is that the suggestion was the therapist's idea about what would be helpful, not the client's, or that the therapist was moving too quickly. One client came to a second session of therapy not having made a list of goals as requested. It would be easy to see this client as resistant to therapy because she refused to cooperate. A solution-focused therapist, however, might ask questions about the suggestion, what was helpful, and what was not helpful. The therapist might discover that Karen was simply unable to think about goals other than to "stop being depressed." This step was too large and the client needed help thinking about goals and the skills she had to help her reach those goals.

Similarly, other clients might come to a second session of therapy with lists of goals that require other people to change. Although such descriptions were not the intent of the therapist's suggestion, their responses would be clue about their perspectives on change. The responses would indicate that therapy would need to help the clients develop perspectives about their *own* changes in order for things to be different because it is not possible to change other people.

Sometimes, people might visit with several therapists, looking for one with whom they feel comfortable. Such shopping is not necessarily a sign of resistance but may be one of agency and independence. Other so-called clients might be ordered to therapy by the courts or brought by other people. These people cannot usefully be called clients unless and until they are able to identify for themselves some goals for therapy and some steps that they might take toward those goals. These visiting people might begin to be clients if they can identify what would need to happen for the other people to stop hassling them.

According to the SFBT view, people are not resistant to therapy; they may be taking care of themselves or they may not have heard anything that convinces them that hope for change is possible in their circumstances. These three stances or therapeutic relationships—visiting, complaining, and customer for change—are important to understand in the context of both readiness for change and the therapist's role: hosting, listening, and facilitating change. Confusing the different relationships leads to frustration on the parts of both the therapist and the client and to the labeling of clients as resistant.

4. *Everyone has strengths and resources required to resolve difficulties.* At face value, the concept that everyone has the strengths and resources required to resolve difficulties makes no sense. If clients already possessed the requisite strengths, skills, and resources for changing their circumstances, they would not come to therapy. How often have any of us experienced a time when a problem was solved and, looking back on it, the solution seemed both obvious and within sight? One of the tenets of SFBT is that the therapist's job is to help clients become aware of those things *that may already be happening* that may help them resolve their problems. We often forget or don't think about what has happened in the past that might give us ideas about a current problem. Now, this doesn't mean that we just sit back and fish for

some mysterious thing inside clients that will resolve all difficulties. Rather, the therapist's job is to help clients notice what is already happening that can serve in the solution-building conversation—not necessarily a cure-all, but something that can help build solutions to the current problem. Also, this doesn't mean that clients don't sometimes need information. Solution-focused therapists, however, are reluctant to simply advise clients; they know that what is good information or solutions for one client may not work well for another.

5. *Change happens; nothing is the same all the time.* Nothing remains constant. This is true in terms of the kinds of problems that people bring to counseling. Even when a problem seems constant, it doesn't retain the same characteristics or intensity at all times—sometimes it's worse and sometimes it's better. The solution-focused therapist capitalizes on this observation by helping clients to notice what is going on in their lives that suggests that change already is happening or that the problem is not constant.

6. *Small changes lead to big changes.* The notion that the only constant is change leads to an important corollary: Often, a counselor can help the client get the ball rolling in such a way that very little therapy is needed. Solution-focused therapists look for the smallest change that will help clients get on a track toward their goals. Sometimes, simply identifying concrete or observable goals is sufficient to help clients get unstuck and moving forward in their lives. Ripple effects are powerful and it is not necessary for therapists to engage clients in therapy until all goals are reached. Sometimes, it is enough to know the goal and the process, and to experience some small success where previously there only was a sense of failure. We sometimes get the process started and then get out of the way.

   Thinking in terms of big changes is often discouraging for clients and may actually forestall therapy. When attempts are made to go too quickly or accomplish too much in one step, it is easy for clients to fail and become discouraged. Rather, small, intermediate changes can foster hopefulness and optimism, and keep clients focused on solutions and goals rather than problems.

7. *Solutions may not seem related to problems.* As mentioned previously, this may be one of the most confusing concepts in SFBT. However, it also is one of the most freeing and allows counselors and therapists to work quickly and efficiently toward the clients' goals. One client, Anna, came to therapy quite anxious and stressed about her job. When the counselor asked her what would be different when the problem was solved (miracle question or presuppositional question), both were surprised when she clearly stated that she would be getting along better with her daughter. Another therapist might have pressed for details about the job situation and given advice about either changing things on the job or about coping with stress. However, by realizing that her sense of job stress was related in some ways to concerns about her relationship with her daughter, Anna and the counselor were able to identify steps she could take with her daughter that improved both that relationship and her ability to cope with her job stress.

   This is not to say that some problems are not complicated. One of the most frequent criticisms I hear about SFBT is that it is a quick fix, a bandage, and not suited for "real" problems. One of the videos available to help counselors and therapists learn about SFBT is a series of actual sessions that Steve de Shazer had with a client who was convinced that her upstairs neighbor was sending beams through the ceiling that disturbed her sleep (de Shazer, n.d.). Other therapists could easily have diagnosed this woman as delusional, psychotic, and paranoid. de Shazer, however, took her at her word, learning more and more about her abilities to observe and notice strengths and resources. The problem was redefined as a sleep problem (this was the area that was most distressing to the client because lack of sleep was affecting her ability to perform effectively on her job). The client and de Shazer together explored ways that the woman could obtain the sleep she desired. de Shazer suggested moving the bed so as to confuse the neighbor. This was not possible for the client, but she began to think that she could sleep on the floor, avoiding the signals, and getting the sleep she desired. Although the client did not say that the beams went away, they were no longer a problem for her and thus not a problem for therapy.

Now, it's probable that some of you are thinking, "Uh-oh. This was a bad move on the part of the therapist. The client is psychotic and needs to have medication to bring her delusions and hallucinations under control." However, let me point out that except for her sleep problems, this woman had no difficulties functioning. She may have benefited from medication, in which case a solution-focused therapist would talk with her about how the medication helps and how she helps the medication work. On the other hand, not everyone responds well to antipsychotic medication, and helping them to function as well as they can is a noble objective.

KEYS TO CONCEPTUALIZATION

In other chapters of this book, authors provided you with ideas on how different models conceptualize presenting concerns. In the solution-focused approach, it is very important to understand that we are not trying to understand people's problems, provide explanations for problems, or solve problems. Rather, the SFBT conceptualization is organized around solutions and movement toward goals. Although this usually takes people away from their problems, it might be easier to think of this in terms of finding ways to reach goals *in spite* of some of those things that are called problems. Anna, a client discussed earlier in this chapter, experienced no less frustration on her job. However, by realizing that her goal was positive family relationships and that the job stress was interfering with that goal, she was able to focus on the times when things were going well at home, which helped her cope with the difficulties at work and to think of different solutions for them. Her subjective experience of the job softened and she labeled it less and less as stressful.

The key ideas of SFBT help us as we think about how to conceptualize clients and their problems, particularly in the first session of therapy. As solution-focused counselors or therapists, we look for things about our clients that are different and unique; we try to understand their lives from *their* experiences, not *ours*. We ask questions that help us and them to realize and understand these experiences from *their* perspectives, not ours as experts on mental health issues. We strive to perceive clients as doing the best they can, not as resisting our efforts to help them when their behaviors or answers to our questions (the ubiquitous "I don't know") seem contrary. We consciously look for their inherent strengths and their unique resources. We look for times that the problem is not happening or is experienced differently. We recognize that change happens in small steps, not all at once, and that small changes lead to bigger changes. Finally, we attempt to push out of our minds the possible causes and explanations for problems and attempt, instead, to help clients identify changes that will be meaningful to them, not to us, and will indicate that the problem is gone or is no longer distressing. With these ideas in mind, we enter into a conversation *with* the client rather than an interview *of* the client; we develop this conversation so that, together, we can build solutions that are satisfying to the client.

INTERVENTIONS AND THERAPEUTIC PROCESS

In this section, I will discuss the four chief techniques or practices of SFBT. These include noticing exceptions, the miracle question, presuppositional questions, and scaling.

Exceptions

Recall that one of the basic tenets of SFBT is that nothing is happening all the time. There are times when the problem is not present, when it is less severe, or when it is not occurring, although it would be expected to occur. As solution-focused therapists, we help clients to move away from the tendency to overfocus on the problem and to see what else is going on. These exceptions provide clues to things clients might do to help the situation or to change their focus from it to something that is the achievement of a desired goal. Examples of questions we might ask clients include what changes they noticed between the time of making the appointment and the first session (presession change; de Shazer, 1985, 1988) that they would like to keep in their lives (Formula First Session Task; de Shazer & Molnar, 1984), and what is different when the problem is not present or less severe. Often, when clients are asked to notice before the next session what's going on that they'd like to keep, they identify changes for the better, even though the therapist didn't ask them to notice changes. Such requests help people notice the positive things that are happening that may have not been noticed because the problem seemed so prevalent.

Miracle Question

One day in therapy (De Jong & Berg, 2002), a client responded to a question from Insoo with, "Well, that would take a miracle." Insoo immediately responded, "If the miracle happened, what would be different?" This spontaneous exchange has shaped the use of solution-oriented questions ever since. The therapists says, "Suppose tonight, while you are asleep, a miracle happened and all these things that brought you to therapy are gone. What's the first thing you would notice that would tell you that a miracle happened?" Of course, clients often respond with unrealistic things: "I'd win the lottery." So, the next question is, "If you won the lottery, how would that make a difference for you, what would others see that would tell them that something had happened? What would be different about you? When is that happening now, even a little?" or, "When was the last time something like that happened?"

The miracle question helps clients to define goals when the problem seems vague and broad. Often, the problem seems so big that all that clients can think about is having it gone; they don't think about what life will be like, in detail, when the situation is no longer problematic. An example is the way a client named Fred responded, who had said his problem was that he was depressed. When I asked what would be different, Fred said that he would notice that he fixed breakfast and then called a friend to go out to dinner with him. I might follow up with questions about the last time that such a thing happened and how Fred made that happen, what he might need to do to prepare for such actions, or what others would notice about him when he was fixing breakfast and asking friends out. Fred began to actually see himself doing these things, which made it much easier to actually do them. This might not fix all the problems, but it is a part of a conversation about how clients can help themselves and how they already are doing some of those things, perhaps without even being aware.

I have noticed that people become quite isolated in the midst of problems that seem overwhelming and forget about others who care about them. Follow-up questions to the miracle question help to increase the client's vision of what is going on in important relationships that the client cares about. For example, asking Fred about what others would notice about him that would tell them that the miracle had happened puts him in a position of looking at himself from their perspectives, reconnecting him with positive relationships, and disconnecting him from isolation.

Presuppositional Questions

Good counselors know that open questions are often more effective at helping enlarge clients' sense of options than closed ones. So, too, we can say that presuppositional questions put clients in positions of opening up possibilities. These questions assume that changes take place and that these changes might as well be positive. For example, a solution-focused therapist might ask about *when* something happens rather than *if* it happens. Notice the different perspective you develop with the following questions: "If you were able to control your drinking, what would be different?" and, "When you are able to control your drinking, what is (or will be) different?" In the first question, clients are likely to focus on "if" and, perhaps, get stuck there because they cannot envision such a circumstance. On the other hand, "when" assumes that it can and does happen and the client is more likely to be able to think about making it happen more often. If the client responds as though the question were "if," the counselor can always respond with, "Oh, sure, I know it might be difficult to think about this, but let's just suppose..." Another presuppositional question asks clients about positive changes that have occurred since the time of making the appointment. Again, clients often respond with a multitude of descriptions of things that were already different, providing clues about goals and desired changes.

Scaling

One of the most useful practices in SFBT is the use of scaling questions. These questions assume that sweeping changes are unlikely and that progress toward goals is incremental, often taken in small steps. The general form of the question suggests that ten is the desired goal and that zero is the opposite. The counselor then asks where the client is toward the goal at this time and what one point up on the scale might look like. When clients focus on the small steps, they are more likely to continue moving toward the goal and less likely to become discouraged. Scaling questions can be very specific ("What's the next small step you might make in order to go from a four to a five on your scale of controlling your temper?" "You're at a four. What would a five look like?"). Questions can also be rather ambiguous ("Let's suppose that ten is the happiest you've ever been and that zero is the opposite. Where are you now? Three? OK, what would a three and a half look like?"). The form of this question has changed for some solution-focused therapists (Y. Dolan, personal communication, September, 2005). Formerly, zero stood for the worst and ten the best. However, asking clients to picture the worst focuses their attention on the problem and its severity rather than on what they would like things to be. "The opposite" is sufficiently vague and ambiguous that the client may more easily disengage from the problem and focus on the more concrete "best."

It is important to notice anything other than zero as progress toward goals. We may respond to a response of "two" with, "Wow! How is two better than one?" or "How do you cope?" Ways of coping often give clues to ways for making progress.

Scaling questions can be followed up with relational questions, just as with the Miracle Question. In this way, the client's relational world is enlarged by asking what others would notice and what they might see in those others that would tell them (the clients) that the others had noticed. Enlarging clients' subjective world increases possibilities and options.

Therapeutic Process

Solution-focused brief therapy is considered brief because it typically takes fewer sessions than other kinds of counseling. It requires not one more nor one less session than necessary (S. de Shazer, personal communication, November, 2004) to get the client on track toward their goals *to their satisfaction*. That is, clients do not need to actually reach their goals to be finished with therapy; they may be satisfied with changing direction and understanding what they need to do, even without therapy. This approach does not pathologize people and therefore does not require that therapists be the ones who decide when therapy is finished.

The first session focuses on listening to the client's concerns; determining goals that are small, behaviorally defined (perhaps with a scale), realistic, and framed as hard work; and developing a relationship that can be seen as building solutions rather than processing problems. The session ends after the therapist takes a short break to think about what has been said, compliments clients based on what they have said, and offers suggestions such as the Formula First Session Task ("Notice this week, so that you can tell me next time we meet, what's going on in your life [often related to the presenting concern] that you want to keep" or, "Notice the signs that might tell you that change is possible.")

The second session begins with the question, "What's better?" and then might look like a first session. Progress is noted with compliments and "cheerleading." Small changes are complimented and clients are asked in detail how they made those things happen. When clients report no changes, they might be asked how they kept things from being worse or coped with the situation. Therapy is over when clients decide that they have made sufficient progress toward their goals.

SHORT- AND LONG-TERM GOALS

Long-term goals are determined by the client through conversation with the therapist in as much detail as possible. Although goals may change during therapy, we describe them in detail so that progress can be noted. Short-term goals are the steps that clients take toward the long-term goals. These are noted as progress and commented on frequently. Some therapies define goals in terms of growth, differentiation, ego strength, self-efficacy, or healed wounds. SFBT is very behavioral and focuses not on grand changes, but the smallest changes necessary to make a difference so that clients can get on with their lives. Coming to therapy ought not to be an invitation to a counselor to take over the whole of a person's life. When examined carefully and in great detail, many aspects of our clients' lives are working quite well and can serve as tools for helping them toward their goals.

USING THE RELATIONSHIP

Lambert (1992) suggested that the single most important factor in therapy for helping people change is the therapeutic relationship. This includes empathy, positive regard, and all the other things that we learn about building good relationships with clients. The key, however, is not what we *do,* but what clients *perceive.* If the client does not perceive a positive relationship, none of the other things we do will be helpful. Although little is written on the therapeutic relationship in SFBT, it is clear that clients do well and reach their goals. Therefore, we can infer that they feel cared for even if the approach does not explicitly address this area. It is probable that clients who feel listened to and who are helped to think of positive and concrete steps toward goals perceive a positive relationship with us. de Shazer (personal communication, June, 2001) suggested that we can assume that we start with a good relationship and then, "All you can do is mess it up."

It is very important, as solution-focused counselors, that we remember that the relationship is made up of both clients and counselors. That is, we, the counselors, have great responsibility for the relationship; we cannot easily blame stuck therapy or failure solely on the clients. When we perceive that a person is visiting, not sure of therapy goals, etc., we must act as hosts, being very sympathetic and, perhaps asking questions around what others see as problems that they have sent the client to a counselor to resolve. We might then *tentatively* ask what the visitor thinks needs to be different to help the referring person believe that counseling is not necessary. When we perceive that our relationship is one of complainant/listener, we must be sympathetic and, perhaps, ask questions about how the person copes with such difficult situations. In this way, the counselor may help move the conversation toward one of customer/therapist. Only when the relationship is one with a client who wants change, is able to perceive some agency of their own for working toward that change, and is able to identify some concrete goals should the therapist ask questions around changes the client could make. To do this too soon is almost a guarantee for a dropout client and a frustrated counselor.

ADAPTING THE APPROACH

It may seem arrogant to suggest that SFBT can be helpful in nearly all client situations and that little must be done to adapt the approach to different concerns. Because the approach is flexible and is tailored to each client's unique situation, we can use it with as many kinds of concerns as we are comfortable treating. Some ask about cultural differences in the approach. Because the approach is fitted to each client, cultural requirements are automatically accommodated. When in doubt, we need to ask clients about what might be appropriate or not appropriate, possible or not possible within their culture. Remember that solutions are devised by the clients from their own expertise and this includes their experiences within their own cultures. We must adapt the approach in every session in order to move with clients toward their goals. At the same time, we must be sensitive to constraints and possibilities within different cultures and clients' unique experiences of those cultures.

FINDING YOUR NICHE

The Solution-Focused Brief Therapy approach to therapy is often described as a way of thinking more than simply as a set of techniques or practices. de Shazer was fond of adamantly asserting that SFBT is not a theory but a description of what occurs in therapy that clients report as being helpful. As a way of thinking, the solution-focused approach eschews diagnosis and labels, emphasizes strengths and problem exceptions, and thoroughly believes that clients are not inherently flawed just because they come to therapy. Importantly, through focusing on discovering and developing solutions rather than focusing on causes and patterns of problems, the ideas and practices can easily be integrated with other models simply. For example, a cognitive behavioral therapist can point out times that clients are able to resist temptations to generalize and distort thinking; Bowenian therapists can use genograms to help clients notice family patterns that were/are more helpful to ameliorating problems, and interpersonal therapists can focus on patterns of communication and interaction that are helpful. Given the desire to not pathologize clients, SFBT is particularly helpful when the therapist feels caught up in the totalizing nature of some diagnoses (e.g., "borderline personality disorder" or "narcissistic") and wants to look beyond these labels to other aspects of clients that can be used to their benefit. In my own life, I'm a bit of a pessimist and cynic, so using SFBT helps me be a more positive person and to see possibilities for my clients (and myself!) rather than just problems. Optimists also like integrating SFBT ideas into their practices for its naturally inherent focus on what works rather than the downward-spiraling effects of problem talk.

PROCESS AND CASE SUGGESTIONS

In this section, I will try to help lay a foundation of thinking as appropriate for each case. In SFBT, the information that is most useful to us is what is presented by the client. Although there is a basic template for us to use in sessions, each question that we ask follows from the information given by the client in response to the previous question. We do not ask questions about all the information presented. Rather, we focus on solution-building conversations that will help clients move toward their goals. Clients often present us with a lot of information that could easily entice us into discussing problems and contextual issues around the problem.

1. *Elena.* Elena, for example, in addition to dealing with her confusion and difficulty making a decision about college, also was coping with a very ill mother and her family's expectations that she help take care of her mother. She easily could have named as a goal a relationship with her mother that would allow her to leave home without feeling guilty. In such a scenario, a solution-focused therapist would, perhaps, help her focus on nonproblematic aspects of her relationship with her mother, what would be different for her if she had a different relationship with her mother, and exceptions to her sense of guilt vis-à-vis her family role. By framing Elena's situation as one of decision-making, the solution-focused therapist can help her to move away from the paralyzing contextual issues and into solution-building. She clearly has been able to make decisions for herself in the past and one of the things that might be different for her should she be able to make this decision is a sense of freedom in her relationship with her mother.

2. *Jane.* Jane presents as a visitor to therapy. She is cooperative with the counselor in responding to his questions, but she is not sure how aspects related to work and so forth might be related to her physical problems. My first job as a solution-focused therapist would be to try to move the conversation from one between a visitor and host to one of an engaged client and therapist. If I were able to do this, I might discover goals for Jane that are not clearly associated with freedom from pain and anxiety. For example, I might focus on Jane's relationships with her family or coworkers, which might then free her to interact differently with her doctors.

3. *Theo.* Theo clearly is a customer for change, even though he came to therapy at the insistence of his girlfriend. I would want to help Theo define clear goals for therapy and identify steps for reaching those goals, including ways that his girlfriend would notice after he makes the changes. Some therapists might have concerns about Theo's ability to learn to behave better, but I would notice his strong motivation and believe that he has the resources to reach his goals. My job would be to help him

clearly identify those goals, what would be different when he reached them, how much of that already is happening, and what steps he needs to take to come closer to his goals.

It may seem that in all three cases, a solution-focused therapist ignores a myriad of contextual concerns. In these interviews, much more information is solicited than the solution-focused therapist might need. The therapist *might* use the information, but only as it is brought up by the client. In all cases, the therapy is built around the client's concerns and goals. What might seem complex easily becomes clearer when the therapist focuses on the present and future, goals and exceptions, rather than the past, problems, and pathology.

You may have found other things to focus on for Elena, Jane, and Theo. *Wonderful!* Although I chose certain things to focus on for this exercise, you or the clients could very well determine other areas for noticing goals, exceptions, miracles, and scales.

 ## SUMMARY AND SUGGESTED READINGS

These few words that I have written about solution-focused brief therapy can capture only a glimpse of the richness and utility of the approach. Although many therapists find the approach simplistic, there is a difference between simplistic, simple, and easy. SFBT is simple but not necessarily easy. I have found that therapy is both more enjoyable and more effective when I use this approach. I am always on the lookout for opportunities to notice things that clients are doing well that may be helpful toward resolving their difficulties, I notice times when the problem is not present or not so awful, I wonder what the client did to help make that happen and how that has affected or been noticed by others. I help clients identify small but measurable and possible steps toward their goals, redefining the intermediate steps along the way.

American Psychiatric Association. (1994). *Diagnostic and statistical manual of mental disorders* (4th ed.). Washington, DC: Author.

Berg, I. K. (1994). *Family-based services: A solution-focused approach.* New York: Norton.

Butler, W. R., & Powers, K. V. (1996). Solution-focused grief therapy. In S. D. Miller, M. A. Hubble, & B. L. Duncan (Eds.), *Handbook of solution-focused brief therapy* (pp. 228–50). San Francisco: Jossey-Bass.

Cade, B., & O'Hanlon, W. H. (1993). *A brief guide to brief therapy.* New York: Norton.

de Shazer, S. (1982). *Patterns of brief family therapy: An ecosystemic approach.* New York: Guilford Press.

de Shazer, S. (1984). The death of resistance. *Family Process, 23,* 79–93.

de Shazer, S. (1991). *Putting difference to work.* New York: Norton.

de Shazer, S. (n.d.). *Coming through the ceiling: A solution-focused approach to a difficult case* [Video]. Milwaukee, WI: Brief Family Therapy Center.

Dolan, Y. (1992). *Resolving sexual abuse.* New York: Norton.

Durrant, M. (1993). *Residential treatment: A cooperative, competency-based approach to therapy and program design.* New York: Norton.

Durrant, M. (1995). *Creative strategies for school problems.* New York: Norton.

Furman, B., & Ahola, T. (1992). *Solution talk: Hosting therapeutic conversations.* New York: Norton.

Gingerich, W. J., & Eisengart, S. (2000). Solution-focused brief therapy: A review of the outcome research. *Family Psychology, 39,* 477–98.

Hudson, P. (1996). *The solution-oriented woman.* New York: Norton.

Lambert, M. J. (1992). Psychotherapy outcome research. In J. C. Norcross & M. R. Goldfried (Eds.), *Handbook of psychotherapy integration* (pp. 94–129). New York: Basic.

Lipchik, E. (2002). *Beyond technique in solution focused therapy.* New York: Guilford Press.

Miller, S. D., & Berg, I. K. (1995). *The miracle method: A radically new approach to problem drinking.* New York: Norton.

Miller, S. D., Hubble, M. A., & Duncan, B. L. (Eds.). (1996). *Handbook of solution-focused brief therapy.* San Francisco: Jossey-Bass.

Selekman, M. D. (1991). The solution-oriented parenting group: A treatment alternative that works. *Journal of Strategic and Systemic Therapies, 14,* 55–63.

Sharry, J., Madden, B., & Darmody, M. (2003). *Becoming a solution detective: Identifying your clients' strengths in practical brief therapy.* New York: Haworth.

Tohn, S. L., & Oshlag, J. A. (1996). Solution-focused therapy with mandated clients: Cooperating with the uncooperative. In S. D. Miller, M. A. Hubble, & B. L. Duncan (Eds.), *Handbook of solution-focused brief therapy* (pp. 152–83). San Francisco: Jossey-Bass.

Walter, J. L., & Peller, J. E. (1992). *Becoming solution-focused in brief therapy.* New York: Brunner/Mazel.

REFERENCES

De Jong, P., & Berg, I. K. (2002). *Interviewing for solutions* (2nd ed.). Pacific Grove, CA: Brooks/Cole.

de Shazer, S. (1985). *Keys to solution in brief therapy.* New York: Norton.

de Shazer, S. (1988). *Clues: Investigating solutions in brief therapy.* New York: Norton.

de Shazer, S., & Molnar, A. (1984). Four useful interventions in brief family therapy. *Journal of Marital and Family Therapy, 10*(3), 297–304.

Watzlawick, P., Weakland, J., & Fisch, R. (1974). *Change: Principles of problem formation and problem resolution.* New York: Norton.

INDEX

A

AB–CDE (Always Be–Courteous, Determined, and Enthusiastic), 200
ABC framework, and rational emotive behavior therapy, 179–181, 182, 183–184, 185, 188
Absolutistic demands, and rational emotive behavior therapy, 178, 180
Acceptance and commitment therapy (ACT), 151
Acceptance of fallibility, and rational emotive behavior therapy, 179
Acquaintance rape, 233
Action-oriented interventions
    Adlerian psychology and, 44, 45
    reality therapy and, 196, 197, 198, 200, 201
Activating events, and rational emotive behavior therapy, 179, 180
Active agents, and cognitive therapy, 161, 172
Acts of other toward self, 80, 81
Acts of self, 80, 81
Acts of self toward self (introject), 80–81
Actuality, and Gestalt therapy, 128, 129–130
Adapting approaches
    Adlerian psychology and, 47–48
    analytical psychology and, 32–33
    behavioral therapy and, 153
    cognitive therapy and, 171–172
    constructivist counseling and, 250
    existential psychotherapy and, 122
    family systems theory and, 220
    feminist counseling and, 235–236
    Gestalt therapy and, 138–139
    person-centered case conceptualization and, 101–102
    psychoanalytic psychotherapy and, 17
    rational emotive behavior therapy and, 187–188
    reality therapy and, 202–203
    self psychology and, 69–70
    Solution-focused Brief Therapy and, 266
    time-limited dynamic psychotherapy and, 86–88
Adler, Alfred, 38, 39, 47
Adlerian psychology
    adapting approach of, 47–48
    conceptualization of, 42–44
    constructivist counseling and, 251
    finding niche and, 48
    interventions and therapeutic process, 38–39, 40, 41–42, 44–45, 47
    introduction to, 38–39
    principles in practice, 39–42
    process and case suggestions, 49
    short- and long-term goals of, 45–46
    therapeutic relationship and, 39, 40, 41, 42, 43, 44, 45, 46, 47
Adler School of Professional Psychology, 48
Adversarial interactions, and self psychology, 60
Affect. See Emotions

B

Aggression
    Adlerian psychology and, 39
    behavioral therapy and, 145
    self psychology and, 64, 69–70
Albert Ellis Institute, 178, 188
Alter-ego selfobject experiences, 59, 60, 63
Analytical (Jungian) psychology
    adapting approach of, 32–33
    conceptualization of, 28–29
    finding niche and, 33–34
    interventions and therapeutic process, 23, 29–30
    introduction to, 22–24
    principles in practice, 24–28
    process and case suggestions, 24, 29, 34–35
    short- and long-term goals of, 31
    therapeutic relationship and, 22–23, 27–29, 30, 31–32
Antimentalism, and behavioral therapy, 147
Anxiety
    constructivist counseling and, 247
    family systems theory and, 212–213, 214
Applied analysis of behavior, 144
Archetypes, and analytical psychology, 22, 25, 34
Articulation of client's subjective experience, and self psychology, 56, 61, 69
Art therapy
    Adlerian psychology and, 44, 47
    Gestalt therapy and, 139
Assessment
    existential psychotherapy and, 117
    feminist counseling and, 226, 227
    lifestyle assessment, 43–44
    psychoanalytic psychotherapy and, 15, 17
Assets, and Adlerian psychology, 44
Association of Women in Psychology, 236
Attachment theory
    self psychology and, 71
    time-limited dynamic psychotherapy and, 77
Authenticity
    existential psychotherapy and, 109, 113, 120, 121–122, 123
    Gestalt therapy and, 129, 137, 138
Awareness, and Gestalt therapy, 128, 129, 130, 131, 134, 135, 136, 137, 139, 140
Awareness continuum, 135

B

Bandura, Albert, 144
Beck, A. T., 160, 172
Behavioral therapy
    adapting approach of, 153
    conceptualization of, 148–150
    finding niche and, 153–154
    interventions and therapeutic process, 150–151
    introduction to, 144
    principles in practice, 145–148

C

process and case suggestions, 145, 146–150, 151, 153, 154–155
short- and long-term goals of, 151–152
therapeutic relationship and, 147, 148, 152–153, 154
Beliefs
    cognitive beliefs, 42, 43
    constructivist counseling and, 247
    core beliefs, 162–163, 164, 165, 166, 168, 170, 172, 203
    derivative irrational beliefs, 180
    irrational beliefs, 180, 182, 183, 184, 185
    lifestyle beliefs, 39, 40, 45
    rational beliefs, 179
    rational emotive behavior therapy and, 179–181, 185
Berg, Insoo Kim, 257, 262
Berlin, S. B., 164
Bernard, Jessie, 228, 229
BFST. See Family systems theory
Binder, Jeffrey, 76, 87
Birth order, and Adlerian psychology, 39, 40
Blaming the victim
    feminist counseling and, 227, 229
    reality therapy and, 198
Blank screen, and psychoanalytic psychotherapy, 12–13, 15
Blocks, and analytical psychology, 24
Boundary disturbances, and Gestalt therapy, 134
Bowen, Murray, 210, 211, 213–214, 216, 218
Bowenian therapy, 210–211, 216, 221
Bowen's family systems theory (BFST). See Family systems theory
Brown, Laura, 227
Buber, Martin, 108, 118, 132
Buddha, 178

C

Camus, Albert, 108, 110
Catastrophizing, and rational emotive behavior therapy, 178
Categories of musts, and rational emotive behavior therapy, 180–181
Change
    behavioral therapy and, 145, 147, 148, 152, 154
    cognitive therapy and, 158, 162, 166, 168, 170–171, 172, 173–174
    constructivist counseling and, 243–244, 246, 248
    family systems theory and, 216, 219, 220
    feminist counseling and, 229, 234
    Gestalt therapy and, 131–132, 136, 138, 139
    person-centered case conceptualization and, 93, 96, 97, 99–100, 101, 102, 103
    rational emotive behavior therapy and, 178
    reality therapy and, 195, 201
    Solution-focused Brief Therapy and, 259, 260, 262, 263, 264–265

Chesler, Phyllis, 226
Child development. *See also* Developmental
    perspective
    Adlerian psychology and, 40, 44
    psychoanalytic psychotherapy and, 6, 8
    self psychology and, 59, 64
Choice
    constructivist counseling and, 251
    existential psychotherapy and, 108, 111,
        114–115, 118, 120, 122, 123
    Gestalt therapy and, 130, 135, 137
    reality therapy and, 194, 195, 196,
        197–198, 199, 201, 202
Choice theory, 194, 197–198, 201,
    202, 203, 205
Circular causality
    family systems theory and, 211
    time-limited dynamic psychotherapy
        and, 78
Classical conditioning, 144, 146
Clear figure, and Gestalt therapy, 134
Client-led therapy
    constructivist counseling and, 242,
        243–246, 248
    existential psychotherapy and, 114, 117,
        120, 121
Client's agency
    feminist counseling and, 227
    Solution-focused Brief Therapy and,
        266, 267
Clients as experts, 258, 266
Client's inner guidance, and analytical
    psychology, 23, 25
Clockwork Orange, A, 154
CMP. *See* Cyclical maladaptive pattern (CMP)
Cognitions
    cognitive therapy and, 162, 165, 166, 172
    rational emotive behavior therapy
        and, 179
Cognitive-behavioral therapy, 144, 151,
    173, 178, 183, 227
Cognitive beliefs, and Adlerian psychology,
    42, 43
Cognitive development, and psychoanalytic
    psychotherapy, 6
Cognitive errors, and cognitive therapy,
    167, 173
Cognitive processes, and cognitive therapy,
    162, 172
Cognitive restructuring, and rational emotive
    behavior therapy, 179, 184
Cognitive therapy
    adapting approach of, 171–172
    conceptualization of, 164–165
    finding niche and, 172–174
    interventions and therapeutic process, 158,
        159, 165, 166–169
    introduction to, 158–159
    principles in practice, 159–164
    process and case suggestions, 174
    short- and long-term goals of, 169–170
    therapeutic relationship and, 158, 169,
        170–171
Collective unconscious, and analytical
    psychology, 22, 25, 34

Common factors, and constructivist
    counseling, 241
Communal values, and existential
    psychotherapy, 122
Compensation, and Adlerian
    psychology, 39
Complexes
    analytical psychology and, 22, 23–35
    as autonomous, 25
    case studies and, 34–35
    client's dealing with, 31
    client's presentation and, 28–29
    countertransference and, 32
    discussion with client on nature of, 34
    feeling-toned nature of, 24–25
    healing of, 26–27
    inferiority complex, 39
    long-term work on, 33
    mother and father complexes, 25–26
    size of, 26–27
    stages of working with, 29–30
Compulsion, and psychoanalytic
    psychotherapy, 13
Conceptualization
    of Adlerian psychology, 42–44
    of analytical psychology, 28–29
    of behavioral therapy, 148–150
    of cognitive therapy, 164–165
    of existential psychotherapy, 114–116
    of family systems theory, 214–216
    of feminist counseling, 231–233
    of Gestalt therapy, 133–134
    of person-centered case conceptualization,
        95–97
    of psychoanalytic psychotherapy,
        6, 10–11, 18
    of reality therapy, 197–199
    of self psychology, 62–65
    of Solution-focused Brief Therapy,
        261–262
    of time-limited dynamic psychotherapy,
        79–82
Conditioning, and behavioral therapy,
    144, 145, 146
Conscious decisions, and Gestalt therapy,
    128, 129, 135, 136
Consciousness, and existential
    psychotherapy, 112
Consequences
    behavioral therapy and, 145
    rational emotive behavior therapy
        and, 180, 183
Constructivism
    cognitive therapy and, 173
    common factors and, 241
    humanistic constructivism, 251
    origin of theory, 240
    Solution-focused Brief Therapy and,
        256n, 257–258
    systemic constructivism, 251
Constructivist counseling
    adapting approach of, 250
    finding niche and, 250–251
    interventions and therapeutic process,
        240–241, 246–248

    introduction to, 240–241
    principles in practice, 241–245
    process and case suggestions, 251–253
    short- and long-term goals of, 243,
        248–249
    therapeutic relationship and, 240, 241,
        242, 245–246, 247, 248, 249–250
Consultation, and psychoanalytic
    psychotherapy, 17
Contact, and Gestalt therapy, 128, 129, 130,
    131, 132–133, 136, 137, 139
Containment practice, and Adlerian
    psychology, 45, 49
Content, and Gestalt therapy, 130–131
Continuum of client clearness, and person-
    centered case conceptualization, 98
Core beliefs
    cognitive therapy and, 162–163, 164, 165,
        166, 168, 170, 172
    reality therapy and, 203
Countertransference
    analytical psychology and, 31–32
    behavioral therapy and, 152
    constructivist counseling and, 250
    psychoanalytic psychotherapy and,
        15, 16–17, 18, 19
    time-limited dynamic psychotherapy and,
        78, 81, 85, 88
Creative experiments, and Gestalt therapy,
    129, 134, 137
Creativity of individual
    Adlerian psychology and, 38, 41, 42, 46
    cognitive therapy and, 158
    constructivist counseling and,
        240, 242, 246
    existential psychotherapy and, 114
Crisis intervention
    family systems theory and, 216
    psychoanalytic psychotherapy and, 14, 17
    rational emotive behavior therapy and, 183
Cultural issues
    Adlerian psychology and, 40, 44, 47, 48
    behavioral therapy and, 153, 155
    cognitive therapy and, 158, 171, 172
    constructivist counseling and, 243, 244,
        248, 250
    existential psychotherapy and, 122
    family systems theory and, 211, 220, 221
    feminist counseling and, 226, 227,
        235–236
    Gestalt therapy and, 138
    person-centered case conceptualization
        and, 94–95, 96, 97, 102, 103–104
    rational emotive behavior therapy and, 185,
        187, 188
    reality therapy and, 194–195, 202, 204
    self psychology and, 69, 70
    Solution-focused Brief Therapy and, 266
    time-limited dynamic psychotherapy and,
        87, 88
Cycles of experience, and Gestalt therapy,
    133, 134, 136, 139, 140
Cyclical maladaptive pattern (CMP), and
    time-limited dynamic psychotherapy,
        79–82, 83, 84, 87, 88

D

Dance therapy
  Adlerian psychology and, 44
  Gestalt therapy and, 139
Date rape, 233
Death, and existential psychotherapy, 109,
  110, 113, 116
Death of Ivan Illych (Tolstoy), 110
De Beauvoir, Simone, 108, 110, 116
Defenses
  psychoanalytic psychotherapy and, 7–8,
    12, 15, 17, 18
  self psychology and, 55
Defensiveness
  person-centered case conceptualization
    and, 93, 99
  self psychology and, 55, 56, 59, 64
  time-limited dynamic psychotherapy
    and, 83
Demands about oneself, and rational emotive
  behavior therapy, 180
Demands about others, and rational emotive
  behavior therapy, 180–181
Demands about world/life conditions, and
  rational emotive behavior therapy, 181
Denial
  Adlerian psychology and, 40
  psychoanalytic psychotherapy and, 6, 8
Depleted self, and self psychology, 58
Depth-Oriented Brief Therapy, 251
Derivative irrational beliefs, 180
De Shazer, Steve, 257, 258–259, 261, 265
Desires, 179, 198
Detriangling, 218
Developmental perspective
  constructivist counseling and, 251
  psychoanalytic psychotherapy and,
    6, 8–9, 18
  self psychology and, 64–65
Diagnostic classifications, and constructivist
  counseling, 242–243, 249
Differentiation
  family systems theory and, 212–214, 215,
    216, 219, 220, 221
  person-centered case conceptualization
    and, 94, 95
Difficult process, and person-centered case
  conceptualization, 96–97, 101–102
Discounting positives, and cognitive
  therapy, 167
Discrimination, and feminist counseling, 226
Disruption-repair sequence, and self
  psychology, 62, 65–66
Dissociated process, and person-centered case
  conceptualization, 96–97, 101
Domestic violence, and feminist counseling,
  226, 233
Dominant need, and Gestalt therapy, 130, 134
Dostoevsky, Fyodor, 108, 110
Dreams
  Adlerian psychology and, 44–45
  analytical psychology and, 22, 23, 24, 25,
    27, 32, 34
  Gestalt therapy and, 139

psychoanalytic psychotherapy and, 10
  self psychology and, 65, 66, 71, 73
Dynamic unconscious, and psychoanalytic
  psychotherapy, 7, 9, 16, 17, 18
Dysfunctional negative consequences, and
  rational emotive behavior therapy,
  180, 183
Dysfunctional thinking, and rational emotive
  behavior therapy, 178
Dysfunction patterns, and family systems
  theory, 215

E

Early recollections (ERs), and Adlerian
  psychology, 41, 44
Ecker, B., 243, 246, 251
Ego
  Adlerian psychology and, 38
  analytical psychology and, 25, 27
Ellis, Albert, 178, 184, 188
Emotional cutoff, and family systems theory,
  213, 215
Emotional disturbance, and rational emotive
  behavior therapy, 179, 184, 186
Emotions
  behavioral therapy and, 148–149, 150,
    153–154
  cognitive therapy and, 161, 162, 165, 168
  constructivist counseling and, 241, 252
  existential psychotherapy and, 115
  family systems theory and, 212, 213, 214,
    215, 218, 219, 221
  rational emotive behavior therapy and, 178,
    179, 180–181, 182, 184, 185, 187
  reality therapy and, 197, 199
Empathic failures, and self psychology, 55
Empathic listening perspective
  reality therapy and, 199
  self psychology and, 56–58, 61, 68, 69, 70
Empathic understanding
  feminist counseling and, 234
  person-centered case conceptualization
    and, 94, 98
  self psychology and, 54, 55, 56, 62,
    63, 65, 66, 68
Empathy
  behavioral therapy and, 148
  cognitive therapy and, 170, 171
  person-centered case conceptualization and,
    92, 93, 96, 97, 100, 101, 102, 103
  rational emotive behavior therapy and,
    179, 184
  reality therapy and, 197, 200–201, 202
  Solution-focused Brief Therapy and, 265
Empirically supported treatments (EST), and
  behavioral therapy, 150
Empiricism
  behavioral therapy and, 147–148, 154
  reality therapy and, 194
Empowerment
  constructivist counseling and, 242, 248
  feminist counseling and, 227, 228–229,
    230, 233, 234, 235

person-centered case conceptualization
  and, 95
  reality therapy and, 200, 202
Enactments
  psychoanalytic psychotherapy and, 13
  self psychology and, 69
Environment, and cognitive therapy, 160, 161,
  163–164, 172, 173
Environmental contingencies, and behavioral
  therapy, 149, 150–151
Epictetus, 178
ERs. *See* Early recollections (ERs)
Essence, and existential psychotherapy,
  109–110, 116
EST. *See* Empirically supported treatments
  (EST)
Ethical convictions, and Adlerian
  psychology, 39, 40, 44
Exaggeration, and existential
  psychotherapy, 119
Exceptions, and Solution-focused Brief
  Therapy, 262
Existentialism, 108–110
Existential psychotherapy
  adapting approach of, 122
  conceptualization of, 114–116
  finding niche and, 123
  interventions and therapeutic process,
    116–119
  introduction to, 108–110
  principles in practice, 110–114
  process and case suggestions,
    123–124
  short- and long-term goals of, 120
  therapeutic relationship and, 114, 118,
    120–122
Expectations
  behavioral therapy and, 154
  existential psychotherapy and,
    115–116, 123
  reality therapy and, 198–199
  time-limited dynamic psychotherapy
    and, 78, 80
Expert language, and person-centered case
  conceptualization, 95
External control, and reality therapy, 195

F

Family constellation, and Adlerian
  psychology, 38, 40, 41, 43, 44
Family journey, 216
Family systems theory
  adapting approach of, 220
  conceptualization of, 214–216
  finding niche and, 221
  interventions and therapeutic process,
    216–218
  introduction to, 210–211
  principles in practice, 212–214
  process and case suggestions, 221–222
  short- and long-term goals of, 216, 219
  therapeutic relationship and, 218,
    219–220, 221

Family therapy
  Adlerian psychology and, 47
  constructivist counseling and, 245
  person-centered case conceptualization
    and, 103
Fantasy
  Gestalt therapy and, 133, 139
  self psychology and, 66
Fassinger, Ruth, 236
Felt minus, and Adlerian psychology, 41
Felt plus, and Adlerian psychology, 42
Feminism
  constructivist counseling and, 244, 250
  family systems theory and, 211
  feminist counseling and, 228
Feminist counseling
  adapting approach of, 235–236
  conceptualization of, 231–233
  finding niche and, 236
  introduction to, 226–227
  principles in practice, 227–231
  process and case suggestions, 236–237
  short- and long-term goals of, 234–235
  therapeutic relationship and, 226–227,
    228, 230, 233, 234, 235
Feminist Therapy Institute, 236
Field, the, and Gestalt therapy, 129, 139
Figural, and Gestalt therapy, 128
Figure/ground relationship, and Gestalt
  therapy, 134, 139
Finding niche
  Adlerian psychology and, 48
  analytical psychology and, 33–34
  behavioral therapy and, 153–154
  cognitive therapy and, 172–174
  constructivist counseling and, 250–251
  existential psychotherapy and, 123
  family systems theory and, 221
  feminist counseling and, 236
  Gestalt therapy and, 139
  person-centered case conceptualization
    and, 103
  psychoanalytic psychotherapy and, 18
  rational emotive behavior therapy and, 188
  reality therapy and, 203–204
  self psychology and, 70–71
  Solution-focused Brief Therapy and, 266
  time-limited dynamic psychotherapy
    and, 88–89
Flexible thinking, and rational emotive
  behavior therapy, 179, 180, 181
Formula First Session Task, and Solution-
  focused Brief Therapy, 264
Fragile process, and person-centered case
  conceptualization, 96, 101
Fragmented self, and self psychology, 58
Frame-related issues, and psychoanalytic
  psychotherapy, 11–12
Frankl, Victor, 119, 122
Free association, and psychoanalytic
  psychotherapy, 13
Freedom
  existential psychotherapy and, 108, 109,
    110–111, 114, 115, 116, 117, 120,
    121, 122, 123, 124

  person-centered case conceptualization
    and, 92
Freud, Sigmund
  Adler and, 38, 47
  early family life of, 210
  existential psychotherapy and, 116
  Jung and, 22
  psychoanalytic psychotherapy and, 6, 9,
    10, 14, 15, 16, 17
Fromm-Reichmann, Frieda, 86
Functional approach, and behavioral
  therapy, 146
Functional negative consequences, rational
  emotive behavior therapy and,
    180, 183
Fusion, and family systems theory, 213
Future
  cognitive therapy and, 160, 161, 164
  reality therapy and, 197–198

G

Gender
  Adlerian psychology and, 39, 47–48, 49
  constructivist counseling and, 250
  family systems theory and, 220, 221
  feminist counseling and, 226, 227, 228,
    229, 230–232, 233, 235, 236
  Gestalt therapy and, 138
  rational emotive behavior therapy
    and, 185
  self psychology and, 68–69
  time-limited dynamic psychotherapy
    and, 88
Gendlin, E. T., 98
Genograms, 216–218
Genuineness
  cognitive therapy and, 170
  existential psychotherapy and, 120
  feminist counseling and, 234
  person-centered case conceptualization
    and, 92, 93, 95, 96, 97, 100,
    101, 103
Gerson, R., 217
Gestalt, meaning of, 128
Gestalt therapy
  adapting approach of, 138–139
  conceptualization of, 133–134
  existential psychotherapy and, 119
  feminist counseling and, 227
  finding niche and, 139
  interventions and therapeutic process,
    130, 131, 132, 134–136
  introduction to, 128–129
  principles in practice, 129–133
  process and case suggestions, 129, 130,
    133, 136, 139–140
  short- and long-term goals of, 136
  therapeutic relationship and, 129, 133,
    135, 136–138
Glasser, William, 194, 198
Goal-oriented perspective, and Adlerian
  psychology, 38, 39, 41, 42, 43
Goals. *See* Long-term goals; Short-term goals

Ground, and Gestalt therapy, 129, 133
Group work
  Adlerian psychology and, 39, 46, 47
  person-centered case conceptualization
    and, 103
  psychoanalytic psychotherapy and, 17
  rational emotive behavior therapy
    and, 188
  reality therapy and, 194
Guerin, K., 210
Guerin, P., 210, 218
Guided discovery process, and cognitive
  therapy, 166
Guilt, and existential psychotherapy, 111

H

Happiness
  rational emotive behavior therapy and, 178
  reality therapy and, 195–196, 198, 201
Harrington, G. L., 194
Heidegger, Martin, 108, 109
Here-and-now focus
  cognitive therapy and, 158
  existential psychotherapy and, 118
  Gestalt therapy and, 129–130, 131, 133,
    136, 137, 138, 139
  rational emotive behavior therapy
    and, 178
  reality therapy and, 198
  time-limited dynamic psychotherapy and,
    79, 86
Heterosexism, 236
Holism
  constructivist counseling and, 241
  Gestalt therapy and, 129, 139
Homeostasis, and family systems theory, 211
Homeostatic balance, and Gestalt therapy,
  131, 138
Homework
  behavioral therapy and, 148
  cognitive therapy and, 168, 171
  rational emotive behavior therapy and, 179,
    182, 184, 186
Homophobia, 226, 236
Horizontal self-disclosure, 120, 121
Hulley, L., 243, 246, 251
Humanistic constructivism, 251

I

Idealizing selfobject experiences, 59, 60, 63
Identified patient, and family systems
  theory, 211
Identity
  constructivist counseling and, 251, 252
  existential psychotherapy and, 110,
    113–114, 116, 124
  family systems theory and, 211
Immediacy, and existential
  psychotherapy, 118
Improvisational techniques, and Adlerian
  psychology, 44

Incongruence, and person-centered case conceptualization, 93
Individualism, and existential psychotherapy, 122
Individuation, analytical psychology and, 22–23, 29
Inferiority complex, and Adlerian psychology, 39
Inferiority feelings, and Adlerian psychology, 38, 40, 41, 43, 45
Information processing, and cognitive therapy, 159–161, 172
Insight
  Adlerian psychology and, 39, 41, 44, 45, 46
  analytical psychology and, 23, 25, 32
  behavioral therapy and, 148, 154
  existential psychotherapy and, 117, 122
  family systems theory and, 219
  psychoanalytic psychotherapy and, 13–14
  reality therapy and, 198
Integration, and Gestalt therapy, 128, 129, 136, 139
Interactive countertransference, and time-limited dynamic psychotherapy, 81
Interfering convictions, and Adlerian psychology, 44
Internal control psychology, and reality therapy, 195, 197, 202, 203
Internalized experiences, and psychoanalytic psychotherapy, 9, 15–16
International Congress of Adlerian Summer Schools and Institutes (ICASSI), 48
Interpersonal relations. *See also* Therapeutic relationship
  Adlerian psychology and, 38, 39, 41, 43, 44
  behavioral therapy and, 152–153
  cognitive therapy and, 158, 160, 163, 164
  constructivist counseling and, 250, 251
  existential psychotherapy and, 110, 115
  family systems theory and, 211, 212–213, 214, 219
  feminist counseling and, 232, 234
  Gestalt therapy and, 129, 132, 135, 136
  person-centered case conceptualization and, 93, 97
  rational emotive behavior therapy and, 186
  reality therapy and, 195–197, 198, 200, 201, 202, 204
  self psychology and, 57–58, 63–64, 65, 67, 68, 73
  Solution-focused Brief Therapy and, 260, 263, 267
  time-limited dynamic psychotherapy and, 76–85, 86, 87–88, 89
Interpersonal schemas, and time-limited dynamic psychotherapy, 77, 84
Interpretation, and self psychology, 61
Interpretation of Dreams, The (Freud), 10
Intersubjective approach, 71
Interventions and therapeutic process
  Adlerian psychology and, 38–39, 40, 41–42, 44–45, 47
  analytical psychology and, 23, 29–30
  behavioral therapy and, 150–151

cognitive therapy and, 158, 159, 165, 166–169
constructivist counseling and, 240–241, 246–248
existential psychotherapy and, 116–119
family systems theory and, 216–218
Gestalt therapy and, 130, 131, 132, 134–136
person-centered case conceptualization and, 92, 97–99
psychoanalytic psychotherapy and, 6, 8, 9, 10, 11–14, 18
rational emotive behavior therapy and, 183–184
reality therapy and, 195, 199–200
self psychology and, 65–67
Solution-focused Brief Therapy and, 262–265
time-limited dynamic psychotherapy and, 82–85
I-position, 219, 221
Irrational beliefs, and rational emotive behavior therapy, 180, 182, 183, 184, 185
Isolation, and existential psychotherapy, 110, 112–113

J

Jacobi, Jolanda, 26–27
Journaling, and Adlerian psychology, 42, 44
Journal of Individual Psychology, 48
Jung, C. G., 22, 23, 30
Jungian psychology. *See* Analytical (Jungian) psychology

K

Kafka, Franz, 108, 110
Kelly, George, 251
Kerr, M. E., 215
Kierkegaard, Sören, 108–109
Knowing process, and constructivist counseling, 240–241, 243
Kohut, Heinz, 54, 59, 65
Kubrick, Stanley, 154

L

Lambert, M. J., 265
Language
  constructivist counseling and, 240, 244–245, 246, 248
  existential psychotherapy and, 118–119
  person-centered case conceptualization and, 95
LaRoche, M. J., 87
Larson, Gary, 144
Lazarus, Arnold, 178
Leading edge of personal development, and self psychology, 59

Learning process, and Adlerian psychology, 46
Learning theory, 144
Lifestyle assessment, and Adlerian psychology, 43–44
Lifestyle beliefs, and Adlerian psychology, 39, 40, 45
Lifestyle inventory (LSI), and Adlerian psychology, 40–41, 44
Lifestyle (LS), and Adlerian psychology, 38, 39
Lifestyle patterns, and Adlerian psychology, 38, 39, 40, 41, 42, 46
Life task challenges, and Adlerian psychology, 38–39, 40, 42, 43, 45
Line of movement, and Adlerian psychology, 43–44
Long-term goals. *See also* Short-term goals
  Adlerian psychology and, 45–46
  analytical psychology and, 31
  behavioral therapy and, 151–152
  cognitive therapy and, 170
  constructivist counseling and, 243, 248–249
  existential psychotherapy and, 120
  family systems theory and, 216, 219
  feminist counseling and, 235
  Gestalt therapy and, 136
  person-centered case conceptualization and, 99–100
  psychoanalytic psychotherapy and, 14–15
  rational emotive behavior therapy and, 186–187
  reality therapy and, 201–202
  self psychology and, 67–68
  Solution-focused Brief Therapy and, 265
  time-limited dynamic psychotherapy and, 86
LS. *See* Lifestyle (LS)
LSI. *See* Lifestyle inventory (LSI)
Lyddon, W. J., 243

M

Maladaptive relationship patterns, time-limited dynamic psychotherapy and, 77–79, 85
Marcel, Gabriel, 108
Marcus Aurelius, 178
Masculine protest, and Adlerian psychology, 39, 47–48
McGoldrick, M., 217
Meaning
  Adlerian psychology and, 38
  cognitive therapy and, 160, 161, 172
  existential psychotherapy and, 112, 116
  Solution-focused Brief Therapy and, 262
Meaningful experiences, and psychoanalytic psychotherapy, 9
Meaninglessness, and existential psychotherapy, 110, 112
Meaning making, and constructivist counseling, 241, 242, 244–245, 246, 247, 248, 249, 250
Mediational model, and cognitive therapy, 162, 167

Memory
  behavioral therapy and, 146
  self psychology and, 66
Mental health
  Adlerian psychology and, 38
  Solution-focused Brief Therapy and, 256
Mental Research Institute (MRI), 257
Metacommunication
  Gestalt therapy and, 136
  time-limited dynamic psychotherapy and,
    79, 84, 86
Mind reading, and cognitive therapy, 167
Miracle questions, and Solution-focused Brief
    Therapy, 262–263, 264
Mirroring selfobject experiences, 59–60, 62,
    63–64, 68, 73
Models
  behavioral therapy and, 144, 145
  cognitive therapy and, 168
  rational emotive behavior therapy and, 186
Model scene construction, and self
    psychology, 64–65, 66, 67
Moderation in evaluation, and rational
    emotive behavior therapy, 179
Monitoring and tracking, and cognitive
    therapy, 166, 167, 168
Motivation
  rational emotive behavior therapy and,
    182, 184
  reality therapy and, 195, 201, 203
Motivational systems theory, 70
MRI (Mental Research Institute), 257
Multigenerational family therapy. *See* Family
    systems theory
Multigenerational transmission, and family
    systems theory, 212, 213–214

N

Narrative
  Adlerian psychology and, 40, 41,
    42–43, 44
  behavioral therapy and, 146, 147
  constructivist counseling and, 240, 248
  psychoanalytic psychotherapy and,
    9–10, 18
  self psychology and, 58, 63
  time-limited dynamic psychotherapy
    and, 80, 81
Needs
  and Gestalt therapy, 130, 134
  and reality therapy, 195, 196, 197, 198,
    201, 202
  and self psychology, 58–59, 70, 73
Neimeyer, R. A., 248, 251
Neurosis, and Adlerian psychology, 43
Neutral stimuli, and behavioral therapy,
    146–147
Nietzsche, Fredrick, 108, 109
Nonlinear dynamic systems theory, 71
North American Society of Adlerian
    Psychology (NASAP), 48
Notes From Underground (Dostoevsky), 110
Now questions, and Gestalt therapy, 135

O

Openness to correction, and self
    psychology, 57
Operant conditioning, 144
Other-centered listening perspective, and self
    psychology, 57–58
Other-deprecation, and rational emotive
    behavior therapy, 178
Outcome-based counseling, 194
Overcompensation, and Adlerian
    psychology, 39
Overgeneralization
  Adlerian psychology and, 41
  cognitive therapy and, 167
  rational emotive behavior therapy and, 178
Overstimulated self, and self psychology, 58

P

Paradoxical intention, and existential
    psychotherapy, 119
Participant observer, and time-limited
    dynamic psychotherapy, 76, 78, 89
Past experiences, and cognitive therapy, 161
Patriarchy, 227, 230, 232
Pavlov, Ivan, 144
Peer support communities, and Adlerian
    psychology, 46
Perception of environmental cues, and
    behavioral therapy, 149–150, 151
Perceptions
  reality therapy and, 199
  Solution-focused Brief Therapy and, 265
Perls, Fritz, 130, 133, 134
Personal construct theory, 251
Personal is political, and feminist counseling,
    228–229
Personality style, and time-limited dynamic
    psychotherapy, 76
Personality theory, and psychoanalytic
    psychotherapy, 6, 8, 9, 18
Personalizing, and rational emotive behavior
    therapy, 178
Personal unconscious, and analytical
    psychology, 22
Person-centered case conceptualization
  adapting approach of, 101–102
  conceptualization of, 95–97
  feminist counseling and, 234
  finding niche and, 103
  interventions and therapeutic process,
    92, 97–99
  introduction to, 92–93
  principles in practice, 93–95
  process and case suggestions, 103–104
  short- and long-term goals of, 99–100
  therapeutic relationship and, 92, 93,
    94–95, 96, 97–98, 99, 100–101, 102
Person-in-environment, and cognitive therapy,
    163–164
Phenomenological inquiry, 130, 133
Phenomenology, 109, 241
Phobias, and behavioral therapy, 144

Play therapy, 70
Postmodern cognitive theory, 240
Power relations
  constructivist counseling and, 242
  feminist counseling and, 226, 232–233
Precipitating events, and psychoanalytic
    psychotherapy, 11
Preference questions, and Adlerian
    psychology, 40
Preferences, and rational emotive behavior
    therapy, 178, 179
Present, emphasis on
  cognitive therapy and, 158
  existential psychotherapy and, 118
  Gestalt therapy and, 129–130, 131, 133,
    136, 137, 138, 139
  rational emotive behavior therapy and, 178
  reality therapy and, 198
  time-limited dynamic psychotherapy
    and, 79, 86
Presuppositional questions, and Solution-
    focused Brief Therapy, 263
Principles in practice
  Adlerian psychology and, 39–42
  analytical psychology and, 24–28
  behavioral therapy and, 145–148
  cognitive therapy and, 159–164
  constructivist counseling and, 241–245
  existential psychotherapy and, 110–114
  family systems theory and, 212–214
  feminist counseling and, 227–231
  Gestalt therapy and, 129–133
  person-centered case conceptualization
    and, 93–95
  psychoanalytic psychotherapy and, 7–10
  rational emotive behavior therapy and,
    179–182
  reality therapy and, 195–197
  self psychology and, 56–62
  Solution-focused Brief Therapy and,
    257–261
  time-limited dynamic psychotherapy
    and, 77–79
Private behaviors, and behavioral therapy, 145
Private logic, and Adlerian psychology, 39, 41
Prizing, and person-centered case
    conceptualization, 92, 93, 96, 97,
    100, 101, 103
Problem-solving
  Adlerian psychology and, 43
  behavioral therapy and, 154
  family systems theory and, 216
  person-centered case conceptualization
    and, 99
  rational emotive behavior therapy and,
    178, 182, 184
  Solution-focused Brief Therapy and, 256,
    257, 266
Process, and Gestalt therapy, 128, 129, 130,
    134–135, 136, 137, 138, 139
Process and case suggestions
  Adlerian psychology and, 49
  analytical psychology and, 24, 29, 34–35
  behavioral therapy and, 145, 146–150,
    151, 153, 154–155

cognitive therapy and, 174
constructivist counseling and, 251–253
existential psychotherapy and, 123–124
family systems theory and, 221–222
feminist counseling and, 236–237
Gestalt therapy and, 129, 130, 133, 136, 139–140
person-centered case conceptualization and, 103–104
psychoanalytic psychotherapy and, 18–19
rational emotive behavior therapy and, 188–189
reality therapy and, 204
self psychology and, 55, 58, 63, 65, 71–73
Solution-focused Brief Therapy and, 266–267
time-limited dynamic psychotherapy and, 88, 89–90
Process questioning, and family systems theory, 217–218
Progress assessment, and psychoanalytic psychotherapy, 15
Projections, and Gestalt therapy, 137
Prouty, G., 96–97
Psychic structures, and psychoanalytic psychotherapy, 9, 15–16
Psychoanalytic psychotherapy
adapting approach of, 17
conceptualization of, 6, 10–11, 18
finding niche and, 18
interventions and therapeutic process, 6, 8, 9, 10, 11–14, 18
introduction to, 6–7
principles in practice, 7–10
process and case suggestions, 18–19
short- and long-term goals of, 14–15
therapeutic relationship and, 6, 7, 8–10, 11, 12–13, 14, 15–17
Psychoeducational approach
cognitive therapy and, 166, 168, 170
rational emotive behavior therapy and, 178
Psychopathology, and psychoanalytic psychotherapy, 6, 8
Psychosomatic symptoms, and person-centered case conceptualization, 102
Psychotic process, and person-centered case conceptualization, 101
Punishment, and behavioral therapy, 145–146, 149

R

Race
Adlerian psychology and, 39
cognitive therapy and, 171
constructivist counseling and, 244, 250
feminist counseling and, 226, 227, 235, 236
person-centered case conceptualization and, 104
psychoanalytic psychotherapy and, 17
time-limited dynamic psychotherapy and, 88

Rape, and feminist counseling, 226, 229, 232–233
Rapid-results counseling, 194
Rational beliefs, and rational emotive behavior therapy, 179
Rational emotive behavior therapy (REBT)
adapting approach of, 187–188
finding niche and, 188
interventions and therapeutic process, 183–184
introduction to, 178–179
principles in practice, 179–182
process and case suggestions, 188–189
short- and long-term goals of, 186–187
therapeutic relationship and, 181, 184–186, 187
Raynor, R., 144
Reactive distancing, and family systems theory, 213, 215
Reactive patterns, and Adlerian psychology, 41
Reality
constructivist counseling and, 240, 243, 244, 245, 246
rational emotive behavior therapy and, 187
Reality therapy
adapting approach of, 202–203
conceptualization of, 197–199
finding niche and, 203–204
interventions and therapeutic process, 195, 199–200
introduction to, 194–195
principles in practice, 195–197
process and case suggestions, 204
short- and long-term goals of, 201–202
therapeutic relationship and, 200–201
Reality Therapy (Glasser), 194
REBT. *See* Rational emotive behavior therapy (REBT)
Reframing language, and existential psychotherapy, 118–119
Reframing methods, and Adlerian psychology, 44
Reframing pathology, and feminist counseling, 228, 229, 233
Regression
constructivist counseling and, 241
psychoanalytic psychotherapy and, 10–11
Reinforcement
behavioral therapy and, 144, 145, 149, 151
rational emotive behavior therapy and, 183
Relationship experiments, 218
Relationships. *See* Interpersonal relations; Therapeutic relationship
Religious/spiritual issues
Adlerian psychology and, 40, 44, 47, 48
constructivist counseling and, 244, 250
existential psychotherapy and, 109
rational emotive behavior therapy and, 187, 188
self psychology and, 60, 69
Reorientation, and Adlerian psychology, 42
Repetition
Gestalt therapy and, 129, 131
psychoanalytic psychotherapy and, 13

self psychology and, 56, 59
time-limited dynamic psychotherapy and, 79, 86
Replacing unhelpful thoughts, and cognitive therapy, 168
Repression, and analytical psychology, 23
Resistance
constructivist counseling and, 241, 249–250
family systems theory and, 211, 214
rational emotive behavior therapy and, 183, 187
reality therapy and, 200
Solution-focused Brief Therapy and, 258–259, 262
time-limited dynamic psychotherapy and, 84
Responsibility
existential psychotherapy and, 111–112, 114, 115, 116, 119, 120, 121, 122, 123
Gestalt therapy and, 129, 137, 138
rational emotive behavior therapy and, 188
Rewards, and behavioral therapy, 145–146
Richie, Beth, 236
Ridley, C. R., 88
Rogers, Carl, 92, 93, 94, 99
Role playing
Adlerian psychology and, 44
rational emotive behavior therapy and, 184
Rubenfeld Synergy Method, 139

S

Safety
Adlerian psychology and, 45
constructivist counseling and, 249
feminist counseling and, 226, 234
Gestalt therapy and, 132–133
person-centered case conceptualization and, 97, 98, 102
reality therapy and, 203
self psychology and, 67, 68
Sartre, Jean-Paul, 108, 109, 110, 114, 115, 116, 122
Scaling questions, and Solution-focused Brief Therapy, 264
Schemas
cognitive therapy and, 162–163
constructivist counseling and, 240
rational emotive behavior therapy and, 180, 182
Secondary disturbances, and rational emotive behavior therapy, 182
Self
cognitive therapy and, 163, 164
constructivist counseling and, 245, 252
family systems theory and, 212
Gestalt therapy and, 129
person-centered case conceptualization and, 93
self psychology and, 54, 55, 56, 58–59, 72
time-limited dynamic psychotherapy and, 80–81, 84, 85, 86

Self-actualization
  feminist counseling and, 229
  Gestalt therapy and, 137
  rational emotive behavior therapy and, 186
Self-coaching, and Adlerian psychology, 42, 46
Self-concept
  Adlerian psychology and, 39, 40, 44
  cognitive therapy and, 160, 161
Self-deprecation, and rational emotive behavior therapy, 178
Self-directed change, person-centered case conceptualization and, 93, 96, 97, 99–100, 101, 102, 103
Self-disclosure
  behavioral therapy and, 154
  existential psychotherapy and, 120–122
  Gestalt therapy and, 138
  rational emotive behavior therapy and, 184, 185
  reality therapy and, 203
Self-enhancing strategies, and self psychology, 64
Self-evaluation, and reality therapy, 197, 199, 200, 201, 202
Self-expression
  existential psychotherapy and, 117, 119
  Gestalt therapy and, 130, 136
Self-ideals, and Adlerian psychology, 39, 40, 44
Self-indoctrination, and rational emotive behavior therapy, 178
Self-monitoring, and cognitive therapy, 166
Selfobject experiences, and self psychology, 54, 55, 56, 59–61, 62, 63–64, 65, 73
Selfobject failure, and self psychology, 66, 67
Selfobject needs, and self psychology, 58–59, 70, 73
Selfobject transferences, and self psychology, 65–66
Self-protective strategies, and self psychology, 64, 67
Self psychology
  adapting approach of, 69–70
  conceptualization of, 62–65
  finding niche and, 70–71
  interventions and therapeutic process, 65–67
  introduction to, 54–56
  principles in practice, 56–62
  process and case suggestions, 55, 58, 63, 65, 71–73
  short- and long-term goals of, 67–68
  therapeutic relationship and, 54–58, 59, 60, 61, 62, 66, 67, 68–69, 70
Self-reflection
  Adlerian psychology and, 42, 44, 46
  self psychology and, 71
Self-regulation, and Gestalt therapy, 131, 138
Self-soothing competence, and self psychology, 60
Self states and patterns, and self psychology, 62–63
Self-understanding, and psychoanalytic psychotherapy, 6, 8
Separating internal from external, 228–229

Sexism, and feminist counseling, 226, 228, 229
Sexuality
  Adlerian psychology and, 38, 44
  feminist counseling and, 227, 232, 235, 236
  Freud and, 22
Sexual orientation, 69, 226, 235, 236, 242, 243, 250
SFBT. See Solution-focused Brief Therapy (SFBT)
Shellenberger, S., 217
Sherif, Carolyn, 226
Short-term goals. See also Long-term goals
  Adlerian psychology and, 45
  analytical psychology and, 31
  behavioral therapy and, 151–152
  cognitive therapy and, 169–170
  constructivist counseling and, 248
  existential psychotherapy and, 120
  family systems theory and, 219
  feminist counseling and, 234–235
  Gestalt therapy and, 136
  person-centered case conceptualization and, 99–100
  psychoanalytic psychotherapy and, 15
  rational emotive behavior therapy and, 186
  reality therapy and, 201
  self psychology and, 67
  Solution-focused Brief Therapy and, 265
  time-limited dynamic psychotherapy and, 85, 86
Short-term therapeutic interventions. See also Solution-focused Brief Therapy (SFBT); Time-limited dynamic psychotherapy
  and psychoanalytic psychotherapy, 17
Shoulds, and rational emotive behavior therapy, 178, 180, 185
Skill deficits, and behavioral therapy, 149, 151
Skinner, B. F., 144
Social context
  constructivist counseling and, 243, 244, 250, 253
  feminist counseling and, 226, 227, 228–229, 235
Social expectations, and time-limited dynamic psychotherapy, 78
Social interest, and Adlerian psychology, 38, 39, 43, 45, 46
Socialistic humanism, and Adlerian psychology, 39
Socialization
  Adlerian psychology and, 42, 43
  feminist counseling and, 228, 230, 233
Social learning theory, 144
Social roles
  Adlerian psychology and, 39, 43
  cognitive therapy and, 160
Societal change, emphasis on, and feminist counseling, 229
Society for the Psychology of Women, 236
Socioeconomic levels
  Adlerian psychology and, 39, 40, 47
  cognitive therapy and, 158, 171, 172, 173
  constructivist counseling and, 244, 250

psychoanalytic psychotherapy and, 17
rational emotive behavior therapy and, 185
Solution-focused Brief Therapy (SFBT)
  adapting approach of, 266
  conceptualization of, 261–262
  finding niche and, 266
  interventions and therapeutic process, 262–265
  introduction to, 256–257
  principles in practice, 257–261
  process and case suggestions, 266–267
  reality therapy and, 194
  short- and long-term goals of, 265
  therapeutic relationship and, 258–260, 265–266
Statements of toleration, and rational emotive behavior therapy, 179
Stewart, A. E., 248, 251
Stimulus control of behavior, and behavioral therapy, 151
Stranger, The (Camus), 110
Stressors
  family systems theory and, 214, 215, 219
  psychoanalytic psychotherapy and, 9, 10
  Solution-focused Brief Therapy and, 260
Structural perspective, and psychoanalytic psychotherapy, 9–10, 17
Strupp, Hans, 76, 87
Subjective world of client, and self psychology, 54, 55–56, 57, 58, 61, 62, 65, 66, 67, 68
Subjectivity, and existential psychotherapy, 108, 109, 110, 113
Surface thoughts, and cognitive therapy, 162, 163, 164, 165, 168
Synchronicity, and analytical psychology, 22
Systemic constructivism, 251
Systems theory, 211

T

Talking cure, and psychoanalytic psychotherapy, 9
Talk-therapy, 109
Telephone hotlines, 17
Theory-to-practice gap
  Adlerian psychology and, 38–39
  analytical psychology and, 22
  behavioral therapy and, 144
  cognitive therapy and, 158–159
  constructivist counseling and, 240–241
  existential psychotherapy and, 108–110
  family systems theory and, 210–211
  feminist counseling and, 226–227
  Gestalt therapy and, 128–129
  person-centered case conceptualization and, 92–93
  psychoanalytic psychotherapy and, 6–7
  rational emotive behavior therapy and, 178–179
  reality therapy and, 194–195
  self psychology and, 54–56
  Solution-focused Brief Therapy and, 256–257

time-limited dynamic psychotherapy
and, 76–77
Therapeutic process. *See* Interventions and
therapeutic process
Therapeutic relationship
Adlerian psychology and, 39, 40, 41, 42,
43, 44, 45, 46, 47
analytical psychology and, 22–23, 27–29,
30, 31–32
behavioral therapy and, 147, 148,
152–153, 154
cognitive therapy and, 158, 169, 170–171
constructivist counseling and, 240, 241,
242, 245–246, 247, 248, 249–250
existential psychotherapy and, 114, 118,
120–122
family systems theory and, 218,
219–220, 221
feminist counseling and, 226–227, 228,
230, 233, 234, 235
Gestalt therapy and, 129, 133, 135,
136–138
person-centered case conceptualization
and, 92, 93, 94–95, 96, 97–98, 99,
100–101, 102
psychoanalytic psychotherapy and, 6, 7,
8–10, 11, 12–13, 14, 15–17
rational emotive behavior therapy and, 181,
184–186, 187
reality therapy and, 200–201
self psychology and, 54–58, 59, 60, 61, 62,
66, 67, 68–69, 70
Solution-focused Brief Therapy and,
258–260, 265–266
time-limited dynamic psychotherapy and,
76–79, 80, 81, 82–83, 84, 85, 86,
87, 88, 89–90
Thinking and feeling processes, and cognitive
therapy, 159–161, 164
Tillich, Paul, 108
Time-limited dynamic psychotherapy
adapting approach of, 86–88
conceptualization of, 79–82
finding niche and, 88–89
interventions and therapeutic process,
82–85
introduction to, 76–77
principles in practice and, 77–79
process and case suggestions, 88, 89–90
short- and long-term goals of, 85–86
therapeutic relationship and, 76–79, 80,
81, 82–83, 84, 85, 86, 87, 88, 89–90

Tolstoy, Leo, 108, 110
Trailing edge of personal development, and
self psychology, 59
Transcendent function, and analytical
psychology, 30, 31
Transference
analytical psychology and, 31, 32
behavioral therapy and, 152
constructivist counseling and, 250
existential psychotherapy and, 121
psychoanalytic psychotherapy and,
15, 16, 17, 18
rational emotive behavior therapy and, 185
time-limited dynamic psychotherapy and,
78, 81, 88
Transformation
analytical psychology and, 23, 30, 31, 34
feminist counseling and, 230
Trial, The (Kafka), 110
Triangles, and family systems theory, 212,
214, 215–216, 218, 219, 220, 221
Triggering events
cognitive therapy and, 163
existential psychotherapy and, 112
self psychology and, 59, 61, 62, 72
Twinship selfobject experiences, 59, 60, 63
Two-chair work, and Gestalt therapy, 135
Typology, and Adlerian psychology, 41, 46

U

Unconditional acceptance, and rational
emotive behavior therapy, 185
Unconditional positive regard
constructivist counseling and, 242, 251
person-centered case conceptualization
and, 101
Unconscious
Adlerian psychology and, 38
analytical psychology and, 23–24,
25, 26, 30
collective unconscious, 22, 25, 34
dynamic unconscious, 7, 9, 16, 17, 18
personal unconscious, 22
Unconscious conflicts, and psychoanalytic
psychotherapy, 7, 10, 11, 13, 18
Unfinished situations, and Gestalt therapy,
129, 131, 133, 134
Uniqueness
analytical psychology and, 22–23, 32, 33
behavioral therapy and, 153

constructivist counseling and, 243
existential psychotherapy and, 114
Gestalt therapy and, 138
person-centered case conceptualization
and, 92
rational emotive behavior therapy
and, 184
Solution-focused Brief Therapy and,
257–258, 262

V

Values
Adlerian psychology and, 40, 41, 44
behavioral therapy and, 153
constructivist counseling and, 248
existential psychotherapy and, 109
feminist counseling and, 230–231
Vanderbilt Therapeutic Strategies Scale, 82
Vertical self-disclosure, 120–121
Victimization
existential psychotherapy and, 114
feminist counseling and, 227, 229
reality therapy and, 195, 198, 202, 203

W

Wants, 179, 198, 199, 201, 203
Warner, M. S., 93
Watson, J. B., 144
WDEP (Wants, Doing, Evaluate, Plan) system,
199, 200, 201, 202, 203, 204, 205
Wishes, 179
Wolpe, Joseph, 144
Women and Madness (Chesler), 226
Women's experiences/perspectives, and
feminist counseling, 226, 230–231
Working alliance, and psychoanalytic
psychotherapy, 10, 14, 15
Worldview
Adlerian psychology and, 39, 40
constructivist counseling and, 243, 244,
246, 250
Wyche, Karen, 235

Y

Yalom, Irvin, 110, 120, 123

Website Access Code for
Applying Counseling Theories: An Online, Case-Based Approach
Aaron B. Rochlen
With Contributions to the Website by Alicia Cho

This interactive website is designed to help you understand what the sixteen counseling theories covered in the book look and feel like in practice. Once you have logged onto the website, you will:

Read a completed intake form for each client.

View three video cases that capture the intake interviews of three diverse clients and their unique presenting problems and concerns.

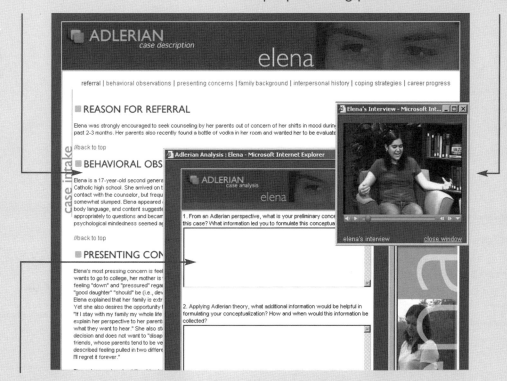

Analyze and conceptualize the cases from each theoretical perspective using the foundational concepts discussed by the authors in the book. Read the case conceptualizations of expert practitioners in each of the sixteen counseling theories.

READ BEFORE USING ACCESS CODE!
This access code card cannot be returned for a refund. By scratching and revealing this access code, you are agreeing to all terms and conditions as detailed on our website at http://www.prenhall.com/mischtm/legal_fr.html

Scratch here to reveal your non-reusable
ACCESS CODE TO ONLINE CONTENT
at http://www.prenhall.com/rochlen

For registration and technical support, please visit http://247.prenhall.com

To register for the online tutorial, type the following address into your Internet browser: http://www.prenhall.com/rochlen.

You will be prompted to log in. Before you can log in, you must register using this access code. To do so:

- Click the "REGISTER" link
- Create your User ID and password
- Provide the required registration information
- Enter the access code provided on this card. Please remember that this code is usable only once, so it is imperative that you write down your User ID and password.

Once you have registered, each time you come back to the site you can use the user ID and password created during registration to gain access to the online tutorial.